# CHARACTER-ANALYSIS

# Works in English by Wilhelm Reich

THE DISCOVERY OF THE ORGONE: Vol. 1, THE FUNCTION OF THE ORGASM
   Orgone Institute Press, 1942. First Edition

CHARACTER-ANALYSIS
   Orgone Institute Press, 1945. Second Edition

THE SEXUAL REVOLUTION
   Orgone Institute Press, 1945

THE MASS PSYCHOLOGY OF FASCISM
   Orgone Institute Press, 1946

THE DISCOVERY OF THE ORGONE: Vol. 1, THE FUNCTION OF THE ORGASM
   Orgone Institute Press, 1948. Second Edition

THE DISCOVERY OF THE ORGONE: Vol. 2, THE CANCER BIOPATHY
   Orgone Institute Press, 1948

LISTEN, LITTLE MAN!
   Orgone Institute Press, 1948

ETHER, GOD AND DEVIL
   Orgone Institute Press, 1951

COSMIC SUPERIMPOSITION
   Orgone Institute Press, 1951

THE ORGONE ENERGY ACCUMULATOR
   Orgone Institute Press, 1951

THE ORANUR EXPERIMENT, First Report (1947-1951)
   Orgone Institute Press, 1951

THE EMOTIONAL PLAGUE OF MANKIND: Vol. 1, THE MURDER OF CHRIST
   Orgone Institute Press, 1953

THE EMOTIONAL PLAGUE OF MANKIND: Vol. 2, PEOPLE IN TROUBLE
   Orgone Institute Press, 1953

CONTACT WITH SPACE, Oranur Second Report (1951-1956)
   Core Pilot Press, 1957

WILHELM REICH: SELECTED WRITINGS
   Farrar, Straus & Cudahy, 1960

# WILHELM REICH

## CHARACTER-ANALYSIS

*Third, enlarged Edition*

*translated by*
THEODORE P. WOLFE, M.D.

THE NOONDAY PRESS
a division of
**FARRAR, STRAUS & GIROUX**
*NEW YORK*

# CONTENTS

## PART I

## TECHNIQUE

# PART II

## THEORY OF CHARACTER FORMATION

## PART III

## FROM PSYCHOANALYSIS TO ORGONE BIOPHYSICS

# PREFACE TO THIRD EDITION

The second edition of this book (1945) was soon sold out, and the great demand for it could not be satisfied for more than two years. Our Press was busy with publications devoted to the newer field of orgone biophysics (THE DISCOVERY OF THE ORGONE, vol. II: THE CANCER BIOPATHY, 1948, etc.). Furthermore, I hesitated to issue a new edition of CHARACTER-ANALYSIS. This book still uses psychoanalytic terminology and a *psychological* description of the neuroses. In the fifteen years since the publication of the first edition, I had to redesign and rewrite our picture of emotional disease. During this time, many important developments took place: "character" became a term signifying typical *biophysical* behavior. The "emotions," more and more, came to mean manifestations of a tangible BIO-ENERGY, of the organismic orgone energy. Slowly, we learned to handle it practically by what is now called "medical orgone therapy." In the preface to the second edition, I pointed out that "character-analysis" is still valid in the realm of depth-psychology where it originated and where it still belongs. We no longer practice character-analysis as described in this book. However, we still use the character-analytic method in certain situations; we still proceed from character attitudes to the depths of human experience. But in orgone therapy, we proceed *bio-energetically* and no longer psychologically.

Why then publish a third edition of this book, in its original form? The main reason is the fact that one cannot easily find one's way toward an understanding of orgonomy and medical orgone therapy without being well acquainted with their development from the study of human emotional pathology of 20 or 25 years ago.

Character-analysis is still valid and helpful in psychiatry, but it is far from being sufficient to cope with the *bio-energetic core* of emotional functions. It is indispensable for the medical orgone therapist who, without having studied psychoanalysis, comes directly to orgone biophysics of the 1940s. The psychiatrist who has not studied the bio-energetic functions of the emotions is apt to overlook the organism as such and to remain stuck in the psychology of words and associations. He will not find his way to the *bio-energetic* background and origin of every type of emotion. The orgone therapist, on the other hand, trained to see a patient first of all as a biological organism, may easily forget that, besides muscular armoring, bodily sensations, orgonotic streamings, anorgonotic attacks, diaphragmatic or pelvic blocks, etc., there is a vast field of functioning such as marital distrust, specifically distorted ideas about genital functions in puberty, certain social insecurities and anxieties, unconscious intentions, rational social fears, etc. Although the "psychic realm" of the emotions is much narrower than their "bio-energetic realm"; although certain diseases, such as vascular hypertension, cannot be attacked by psychological means; although language and thought association cannot possibly penetrate more deeply than to the phase of speech development, that is, about the second year of life, the psychological aspect of emotional disease remains important and indispensable; however, it is no longer the foremost aspect of orgonomic biopsychiatry.

The third edition of CHARACTER-ANALYSIS has been considerably enlarged. I have added "The Emotional Plague," previously published as an article in the *International Journal of Sex-economy and Orgone Research*, 1945. Also, a paper on "The Expressive Language of the Living," not previously published. It deals with the realm of *biophysical* emotional expressions, the main realm of medical orgone therapy. Finally, an extensive case history of a paranoid schizophrenia will introduce the student of human nature to the new field of *biopathology* which was opened up only a few years ago by the discovery of the organismic orgone energy ( = bio-energy). This case history will convince the reader that the organismic orgone energy is the *physical reality* which corresponds to the classical, merely psychological, concept of "psychic energy."

The old term "vegetotherapy" has been replaced by "orgone therapy." Otherwise, the book remains unchanged in its main structure. It represents the essential first step, taken 1928 to 1934, from psychoanalysis toward the bio-energetic study of the emotions (orgone biophysics) and deserves to be preserved as such.

The discovery of the atmospheric (cosmic) orgone energy has forced major revisions in our basic physical as well as psychological concepts. These are not dealt with in this book. It will take many years of painstaking work to elucidate the main trends which have developed since the discovery of the orgone. Such things as a "psychic idea," for example, appear today in an entirely different light, as a result of disclosures made by orgonomic experiments. But this should not distract the psychotherapist and orgone therapist from his everyday task with emotionally sick people. At present, it is mainly the natural scientist and the natural philosopher who are being challenged by the disclosure of a universal primordial energy: orgone energy.

W. R.

*December, 1948*

# TRANSLATOR'S PREFACE TO SECOND EDITION

The publication of Reich's CHARAKTERANALYSE in 1933 was a milestone in psychoanalysis. Here—at a time when psychoanalysis was becoming more and more involved in metapsychological speculation—was a book based on sound psychoanalytic principles and strict clinical observation. It represented the first real step beyond the customary symptom– and interpretation analysis, both theoretically and practically.

Theoretically, it took the concept of "character" out of the realm of moral philosophy and made it the object of scientific investigation. Up to that time, psychoanalysis had only investigated the historical background of some individual character traits; the "character" as such was regarded as an unwelcome complication and was adjudged as "good" or "bad" in the usual sense rather than investigated scientifically. A scientific characterology which would answer the questions as to the mode and function of character formation and the conditions for character differentiation, that is, the development of definite character types, had never been attempted.

Practically, the new insights into the function of the character led inevitably to fundamental changes in therapeutic technique. The emphasis shifted from the unconscious material obtained by "free association" to the patient's character, that is, to his "characteristic" behavior in defending himself against analytic insight and unconscious material. The importance of this change in technique can be appreciated only by those therapists who have themselves undergone a character-analysis and who have mastered the technique in their own practice. It made patients accessible for treatment who had previously remained inaccessible. It put an end to those depressing analyses of many years' duration, particularly in compulsion neuroses, where a wealth of unconscious material had been recovered without any therapeutic result because the analysis had not succeeded in mobilizing the patient's affects; this was due to the fact that the affects were bound up mostly in the character armor from which they could be released only by the character-analytic technique. It made unnecessary the therapeutic alibis that "the patient did not want to get well" because he had an "unconscious need for punishment," a "death instinct," etc., because now these phenomena could be understood and therapeutically handled.

The book was enthusiastically received by many psychoanalysts. Its technical instructions were called one of the "clearest and most unequivocal contributions that have yet appeared in psycho-analytic literature . . . ," "the best and most mature that has been said about psychotherapy." "This desire [for technical advice] must indeed have been very strong, judging from the eagerness with which Reich's book and ideas were absorbed by the younger German analysts." Nevertheless, to judge from the psychoanalytic publications and from discussions with psychoanalysts, there has been little *real* comprehension of character-analysis. The main reason for this is the fact that one cannot—as many have tried to do—accept and apply character-analysis without accepting the orgasm theory. One cannot argue, as so many psychoanalysts do, "Yes, character-analysis is correct, but the orgasm theory is not." Since the therapeutic goal of character-analysis is —unequivocally—the establishment of orgastic potency, it follows that character-analysis and the orgasm theory are inseparable. Yet, the concepts of "orgastic potency" and "orgastic impotence" have not yet found their way into psychoanalytic thinking to any appreciable degree; a man is still considered "potent" when he is erectively and ejaculatively potent. One then often hears the argument that theory and practice are not necessarily inseparable, that one can have one kind of theoretical concept and another kind of practice. This is a dangerous fallacy and a self-deception. For if one has not accepted the orgasm theory, if one does not recognize that the basis of the neurosis is sexual stasis due to orgastic impotence, this has an inevitable result in practice: the practical therapeutic goal then is not the establishment of orgastic potency, and the sexual energies liberated in the therapeutic process must find another outlet. This in turn necessitates the formulation of a corresponding theory: that of "sublimation" and "renunciation." Theory and practice are as inseparable as the orgasm theory and character-analysis. A particular way of "accepting" character-analysis deserves special mention: that of applying the name of "character-analysis" to a technique which has nothing whatsoever to do with it. This is an insidious way of doing away with new discoveries which has many parallels in the history of science.[1]

These few remarks may indicate why the book was a milestone in psychoanalysis. It was also a milestone in sex-economy. It appeared at a time when political events in Europe were coming to a head. Like many previous publications of Reich, it was to be published in the publishing house of the International Psycho-analytic Association, the Internationaler Psychoanalytischer Verlag. It was already in page proof when Hitler came to power and the Verlag refused to publish it under its imprint: Reich had become too well known as an antifascist. At the same time, the Association planned Reich's exclusion, which became effective the following year, 1934. The first edition of his MASSENPSYCHOLOGIE DES FASCHISMUS appeared in 1933, the second in 1934. The years around 1933 were the time of a turning-point in sex-economy, the time when the breakthrough succeeded from psychology into biology. The theoretical necessity of this had been formulated by Freud, and its practical realization had been foreshadowed in Reich's DIE FUNKTION DES ORGASMUS, 1927, where he formulated, for the first time, the connections between sexuality and anxiety on the one hand and the vegetative system on the other. Thus, it is not due to a sudden change in concepts but the result of a gradual and inevitable development that, after the CHARAKTERANALYSE, Reich's publications were no longer of a psychological nature, but of a biological, and more recently, a biophysical nature. The development over the past ten years has been so rapid that the tempo was often rather uncomfortable even for those who watched it closely; to most people who have not followed the

---

[1] Cf. "Character-analysis." *Internat. Journal of Sex-economy and Orgone-Research* 1, 1942, 90ff.

development step by step there may even seem to exist a gap difficult to understand. This difficulty has been taken into account by appending to the present edition a translation of PSYCHISCHER KONTAKT UND VEGETATIVE STRÖMUNG, a monograph published in 1935. The essential contents of EXPERIMENTELLE ERGEBNISSE ÜBER DIE ELEKTRISCHE FUNKTION VON SEXUALITÄT UND ANGST, a monograph published in 1937, will be found in THE FUNCTION OF THE ORGASM, 1942, as well as the major parts of ORGASMUSREFLEX, MUSKELHALTUNG UND KÖRPERAUSDRUCK, published also in 1937, introducing the technique of character-analytic vegetotherapy. Thus, taking into account the more recent publications in our JOURNAL, there is sufficient material in print in the English language to enable the serious student to follow, theoretically at least, the steps which led from the character-analysis of 1933 to the orgone therapy and orgone biophysics of today.

T. P. W.

*New York, January, 1945.*

# PREFACE TO SECOND EDITION

During the 12 years since the appearance of the first edition of this book, character-analysis has developed into orgone therapy. In spite of the fact that this means a far-reaching change in technique as well as in concepts, the book—which is presented here for the first time in the English language—appears without changes. There is a special reason for this: During the time when the character-analytic technique was being worked out—between 1925 and 1933—sex-economy was still in its early development. It was then only a few years that the individual and social significance of the function of the orgasm had been recognized. This had, of course, a great influence on the theory and technique of psychoanalytic therapy. Character-analysis still belongs, as it did 12 years ago, in the framework of Freud's psychoanalysis. It was in this framework that the book was written and that it is still valid today. It was meant for psychoanalysts in practice and in training, and cannot be taken out of this framework. For this reason, I have left it unchanged.

However, the comprehension of character formation, in particular, of the *character armor,* led far beyond the character-analysis of 1933. It was the starting point of present-day *orgone biophysics* and the corresponding therapeutic techniques, *vegetotherapy* and *orgone therapy.* These are described in my book, THE FUNCTION OF THE ORGASM ( THE DISCOVERY OF THE ORGONE, VOL. 1, 1942), and in special orgone-physical articles. The problem of character formation, originally a psychiatric problem, opened an avenue of approach to the problems of biological energy and of the biopathies. Orgone biophysics did not bring about a refutation or revision of the findings of character-analysis; on the contrary, it put them on the sound foundation of natural science.

The present edition contains as an appendix the translation of the monograph, PSYCHISCHER KONTAKT UND VEGETATIVE STRÖMUNG, which was based on the last paper I read before the International Psychoanalytic Association, at the 13th Congress in

Lucerne, 1934. This paper presented the transition from Freud's depth psychology to biology and later orgone biophysics. The problems of the orgone are not touched upon in this book. Those acquainted with my later publications, however, will have no difficulty in finding the places where orgone biophysics meets the problems of character structure. In a few instances, I have tried to indicate these places by the addition of footnotes.

By excluding sex-economy and the orgasm theory from the organization of the psychoanalysts, those of its representatives who were responsible for this step have *themselves* drawn the dividing line for which I was to be blamed later, erroneously and out of a bad conscience. It is important to state here unequivocally the following: Sex-economy has never taken any stand against the basic scientific findings of Freud. Rather, the psychoanalytic movement, motivated by mistaken social considerations—considerations which have become meaningless as a result of the social revolutions of the past 10 years—took a stand against sex-economy. Sex-economy is no more a rival of psychoanalysis than, say, Newton's law of gravitation is a rival of Kepler's law of harmony. Sex-economy is the continuation of Freud's psychoanalysis and provides it with a foundation in natural science, in the realms of biophysics and social sexology. In particular, sex-economy of today can claim the triumph of having led to the discovery of the biological energy, the *orgone,* that energy which, according to definite physical laws, is the basis of the sexual functions first described by Freud. Freud's "psychoneuroses," studied by a psychological method, found their organic correlate in the "biopathies," studied by an orgone-physical method.

Character-analysis, then, as described in this volume, is still fully valid in the framework of depth-psychological thinking and of the *psycho*therapeutic techniques which correspond to it. It is also valid as an indispensable auxiliary technique in biophysical orgone therapy. But as a result of the developments over the past decade, the sex-economist and orgone therapist of today is essentially a *biotherapist* and no longer merely a psychotherapist.

*New York, January, 1945.*                                    **W. R.**

# PREFACE TO FIRST EDITION

The present character-analytic studies deal with problems which I tried to sketch in the preface to my book, DER TRIEB-HAFTE CHARAKTER, nine years ago. Those who are familiar with psychoanalytic research work will not be surprised to see that almost a decade had to pass between the formulation of the problem and a partial solution. When I took over for treatment a number of psychopaths of the impulsive type at the Vienna Psychoanalytic Clinic it was found that they presented technical problems for the solution of which the insights into the ego structure of the impulsive was fairly adequate. On the other hand, there were problems which seemed important also for the theory and therapy of the instinct-inhibited character-neuroses as contrasted to the impulsive characters. These were: a genetic-dynamic theory of character; a strict differentiation of the contents and the form of the resistances; and, finally, a clinically well-founded differentiation of character types.

The technical discussions and the dynamic-economic concepts of the character in its total functioning were essentially derived from the Vienna Seminar for Psychoanalytic Therapy which I directed for six years with the enthusiastic collaboration of a number of young colleagues. Here, too, I must ask the reader to expect neither an exhaustive presentation of the relevant problems nor their complete solution. Today as nine years ago we are still far from a comprehensive and systematic psychoanalytic characterology. This book will serve, however, to decrease that distance a considerable stretch.

The technical sections were written during the winter of 1928-1929 and thus could be checked for four years; nothing essential in them had to be changed. The theoretical sections—with the exception of Chapter IX—represent expansions and in part revisions of papers which appeared during the past few years in the *Internat. Zeitschr. f. Psychoanalyse.*

For a number of reasons, time being one of them, I was not able to fulfil the wish of many of my colleagues that I should write an extensive book on psychoanalytic technique. The task I have set myself here is only that of presenting the technical principles as they result from character-analysis. Analytic technique cannot be learned from books anyhow because in practice things are ever so much more complicated; what is necessary is a thorough study of cases in seminars and control analyses.

An objection is likely to be made which needs some discussion. It is the following: Does not this publication as such signify a tremendous and one-sided overevaluation of individual psychotherapy and characterology? In a city like Berlin there are millions of people who are neurotically ruined in their psychic structure, in their ability to work and to enjoy life; every hour of the day, familial education and social conditions create thousands of new neuroses. Under these circumstances, is there any sense in a book which discusses individual analytic technique, structure and dynamics of the character, and such things? This all the more as it cannot give any useful directions for a mass therapy of the neuroses, for brief and reliable treatment? For a long time, I was impressed with the seeming validity of this objection. Finally I had to realize that such a standpoint is short-sighted and, in the long run, even worse than the current exclusive preoccupation with questions of individual psychotherapy. It may sound paradoxical but it is true: it was precisely the insight into the socially hopeless position of individual psychotherapy as it results from the social mass production of neuroses which led to an even more intensive occupation with the problems of individual psychotherapy. I have endeavored to show that the neuroses are a result of patriarchal, authoritarian education with its sexual suppression and that the real issue is the *prevention* of the neuroses. In our present social system, all prerequisites for a practical program of prevention are absent; they will first have to be created by a basic revolution in the social institutions and ideologies, a change which will depend on the outcome of the political struggles of our century. It goes without saying that a prevention of the neuroses is not possible unless a theoretical groundwork has been laid for it; that is, the study of the dynamic and economic factors in the human structure is the most important prerequisite. What has that to do with the technique of individual therapy? In order to study human structure with a view to the prevention of the neuroses our analytic technique must be improved. Our presentation will show why the previous state of technical knowledge was insufficient for such a task. The first prerequisite for a future prevention of the neuroses is a *theory of technique and therapy* based on the dynamic and economic processes in the psychic apparatus. First of all we need therapists who know what enables them to change structures or why they fail in this task. If we try to fight a plague in any other branch of medicine, we will examine typical cases of the disease with the best possible methods in order to be able to point the way to the epidemiologist. We do not concentrate on individual technique because we overestimate the importance of individual therapy but because only a good technique can provide us with those insights which are necessary for the wider goal of understanding and changing structure.

There is another aspect of our clinical investigations which has to be considered here. Unlike other branches of medical science, we are dealing not with bacteria or tumors but with human reactions and psychic illnesses. Though derived from medicine, our science has gone far beyond it. If, as has been said, man himself makes his history, dependent on certain economic conditions, if the materialistic[1] concept of history has to proceed from the basic premise of sociology, the natural and psychic organization of man, then it is clear that our investigation, at a certain point, will gain decisive sociological importance. The most important productive power, the *productive power, working power,* depends on the psychic structure. Neither the so-called "subjective factor" of history nor the productive power, working power, can be comprehended without a natural-scientific psychology. This presupposes the rejection of those psychoanalytic concepts according to which culture and history of human society

[1] *Footnote, 1945:* Today we would say "functional" concept.

are explained by the instincts. The fact has to be realized that human needs first have to be influenced and changed by social conditions before the altered drives and needs begin to act as historical factors. The best-known characterologists of today try to understand the world from "values" and the "character," instead of trying to comprehend, conversely, character and the setting of definite values from the social process.

In connection with the sociological function of character formation we must study the fact that certain social orders go with certain average human structures, or, to put it differently, that every social order creates those character forms which it needs for its preservation. In class society, the ruling class secures its position with the aid of education and the institution of the family, by making its ideologies the ruling ideologies of all members of the society. But it is not merely a matter of imposing ideologies, attitudes and concepts on the members of society. Rather, it is a matter of a deep-reaching process in each new generation, of the formation of a psychic structure which corresponds to the existing social order, in all strata of the population. Natural-scientific psychology and characterology, then, has a sharply defined task: It has to discover the means and mechanisms by way of which social existence is transformed into psychic structure and with that, into ideology. One has to distinguish the social production of ideologies from their reproduction in the members of the society. To study the former is the task of sociology and economics, to study the latter that of psychoanalytic characterology. Characterology has to study the effects of the immediate economic situation (food, housing, clothing, work process) as well as the effects of the so-called social superstructure, that is, of morality, laws and institutions, on the instinctual apparatus; it must define, as completely as possible, the many intermediate links between "material basis" and "ideological superstructure." It cannot be a matter of indifference to sociology how well psychology does this job, for, to begin with, man is the *object* of his needs and of the social system which regulates the gratification of needs in one way or the other. But at the same time he is the *subject* of history and the social process which he "makes himself," although not quite as he would like to, but under certain definite economic and cultural conditions which determine the content and effect of human action.

Ever since society was split into the owners of the means of production and the owners of the commodity working power, every social order has been established by the former, with disregard or against the will of the latter. Because this order forms the psychic structure of all members of society, it *reproduces itself* in people. Since this is done by utilizing and altering the instinctual apparatus, it also becomes affectively *anchored* in people. The first and most important place of reproduction of the social order is the patriarchal family which creates in children a character structure which makes them amenable to the later influences of an authoritarian order. The role played by sexual education in the whole educational system shows that it is primarily *libidinal* interests and energies by way of which the anchoring of the authoritarian social order takes place. The character structures of the people belonging to a certain epoch or a certain social order, then, are not only reflections of this order but, much more importantly, they represent the anchoring of this order. Investigation of the change in sexual morality with the transition from matriarchy to patriarchy (*cf.* my book, DER EINBRUCH DER SEXUALMORAL) shows that this anchoring through adaptation of the character structure to the new social order constitutes the conservative nature of so-called "tradition."

This characterological anchoring of the social order explains the tolerance of the suppressed toward the rule of an upper class, a tolerance which sometimes goes as far as the affirmation of their own subjugation. This is much more obvious with regard to the suppression of sexuality than with regard to the gratification of economic and cultural needs. However, the anchoring of a social order which frustrates the gratification of needs to a considerable extent goes with the development of psychic factors which tend to undermine this characterological anchoring. Gradually, with the development of the social process, there develops an ever increasing discrepancy between enforced renunciation and increased libidinal tension; this discrepancy undermines "tradition" and forms the psychological core of attitudes which threaten the anchoring.

The conservative element in the character structure of the people of today cannot be equated with what is called the "super-ego." True, the moral inhibitions in the person derive from certain prohibitions of society, represented by the parents. But even the first changes of the ego and the instincts which take place on the occasion of earliest frustrations and identifications, long before the formation of a super-ego, are, in the last analysis, determined by the economic structure of society; they are already the first reproductions and anchorings of the social system, and determine the first contradictions. If the small child develops an anal character, it will also develop the corresponding stubbornness. The significance of the super-ego for this anchoring lies in the fact that its core is the infantile incestuous genital demands; it is here that the most vital energies are bound and character formation is determined.

The dependence of character formation on the historico-economic situation in which it takes place is most clearly shown in the changes taking place among the members of primitive societies at a time when they come under foreign economic and cultural influences or when, for intrinsic reasons, they begin to develop a new social order. Malinowski's reports show that character changes take place rapidly when the social structure changes. For example, he found the inhabitants of the Amphlett islands distrustful, shy and hostile, while the neighboring Trobianders were simple, natural and open. The former already have a patriarchal order with a strict familial and sexual morality, while the latter still enjoy most of the freedoms of matriarchy. These findings confirm the clinical finding[1] that the socio-economic structure of society influences character formation not directly, but in a very complicated indirect manner: The socio-economic structure of society creates certain family forms; these, however, not only presuppose certain forms of sexual life but also produce them by a definite influence on the instinctual life

---

[1] *Cf.* DER EINBRUCH DER SEXUALMORAL, 1932, and DIALEKTISCHER MATERIALISMUS UND PSYCHOANALYSE, 1929.

of the children and adolescents; this results in different attitudes and modes of reaction. *The character structure, then, is the crystallization of the sociological process of a given epoch.* The ideologies of a society can become a material power only on the condition that they actually alter the character structures. The investigation of character structure, therefore, is of more than clinical interest. It leads to the question why it is that ideologies change so much more slowly than the socio-economic basis, why man, as a rule, lags far behind that which he creates and which should and could change him. The reason is that the character structure is acquired in early childhood and undergoes little change. The socio-economic situation which originally created it, however, changes rapidly as the productive powers develop; after it has changed, it makes different demands and necessitates different modes of adaptation. True, it also creates new attitudes and modes of reaction; these, though they permeate the old ones, do not replace them. The two attitudes, corresponding, as they do, to different sociological situations, now come in conflict with each other. For example: the woman brought up in the family of 1900 developed a mode of reaction which corresponded to the socio-economic situation of 1900; in 1925, however, the familial situation, as a result of the changes in the modes of production, have changed in such a manner that the woman, in spite of superficial adaptation, finds herself in the most severe contradictions. Her character requires, for example, a strictly monogamous sexual life while in the meantime compulsive monogamy has become undermined socially and ideologically. Intellectually, the woman can no longer demand monogamy either of herself or of her husband, but structurally she is in conflict with the new conditions and with the demands of her own intellect.

Similar problems are obvious in the difficulties encountered in the attempts to change individual farming into collectivistic farming in Soviet Russia. The difficulties lie not only in economic circumstances but also in the structure of the Russian peasant which he has acquired during Tsarism and the period of individualistic agriculture. The reports show the role of the replacement of the family by the collective and, particularly, of the changes in sexual

living. The old structures not only lag behind the new developments, very often they resist them vigorously. If the old ideology,
which corresponds to an earlier sociological situation, were not
anchored in the character structure as a chronic and automatic
mode of reaction, with the aid of libidinous energy, the adaptation to the economic changes would be relatively easy. It goes
without saying that a thorough knowledge of the mechanisms
which relate economic situation, instinctual life, character formation and ideology would lead to many practical measures, particularly in education, possibly also in practical mass psychology.

All these things wait to be worked out. Psychoanalytic science,
however, cannot expect practical and theoretical recognition on
a social scale unless it masters the fields in which it can show its
value and where it can show that it no longer wishes to remain
aloof from the decisive historical events of our century. For the
time being, psychoanalytic characterology will have to restrict
itself to the clinical field. The investigations described in Part Two
will show where the connections to more-inclusive sociological
problems are to be looked for. They are discussed elsewhere.

W.R.

*Berlin, January, 1933.*

# PART ONE

# TECHNIQUE

CHAPTER I

# SOME PROBLEMS OF PSYCHOANALYTIC TECHNIQUE

The practising psychoanalyst is confronted every day by problems which he is unable to solve either by his theoretical knowledge alone or by his practical experience alone. All problems of technique converge in the one basic question whether and how an unequivocal technique of analytic therapy can be derived from the theory of the neuroses; it is the question of the possibilities and limitations of the application of theory to practice. In reality, it is analytic practice which, by the problems it presents, leads to a theory of the psychic processes; thus we have to explore the paths which lead from purely empirical practice, over theoretical considerations, to a theoretically well-grounded practice. Ample experience in the Vienna Technical Seminar as well as control-analyses have shown that we have hardly made a beginning at this task. True, there are Freud's fundamental works on technique, its ABC, as it were, as well as many scattered remarks on technique in many of his writings; the works by Ferenczi and others on technique have taught us much about individual technical problems. On the whole, nevertheless, one finds that there are just about as many individual techniques as there are individual psychoanalysts, apart from the technical rules laid down by Freud which are few compared with the wealth of problems presented by everyday practice.

These general rules which have become a matter of course among analysts are derived from the basic theoretical concepts of the neurotic process. Every neurosis is due to a conflict between repressed instinctual demands—which always include early infantile sexual demands—and the repressing forces of the ego. The unresolved conflict expresses itself in the neurotic symptom

3

or neurotic character trait. The technical requirement for the solution of the conflict, therefore, is the "resolution of the repression," in other words, the making conscious of the unconscious conflict. Since, however, certain psychic forces act like a rigorous censor with regard to the patient's own thoughts and wishes and thus keep them from becoming conscious, it is necessary to eliminate the selecting of material which is necessary in ordinary thinking and to let the thoughts wander freely, without critical selection. Among the material then coming up, one finds more and more repressed, unconscious and infantile elements which, with the aid of the analyst, have to be translated into the language of the conscious. The so-called "fundamental rule," the rule of "free association" with the elimination of critical selection of material, is the indispensable prerequisite of analytic technique. It is aided by the force of the unconscious drives which urge to consciousness and to action; it is hampered, on the other hand, by an also unconscious force, the defense of the ego, which makes it difficult or impossible for the patient to follow the fundamental rule. This force makes itself felt as a "resistance" against the dissolution of the repression. This theoretical insight determines another practical rule: the rule that the making conscious of the unconscious has to take place not directly, but by the elimination of the resistances. That is, the patient must first find out *that* he defends himself, then by what means, and, finally, against what. This work of making things conscious is called "interpretation." It consists either in the disclosure of disguised expressions of the unconscious or in the re-establishment of connections which had been lost by repressions. The repressed wishes and fears of the patient seek constantly for discharge, that is, they tend to become attached to real persons and situations. The most important reason for this is the lack of libidinous gratification in the patient; thus, he attaches his unconscious demands and fears also to the analyst and the analytic situation. This results in the "transference," that is, the establishment of relationships of love, hatred or anxiety with the analyst. These attitudes toward the analyst are nothing but repetitions of earlier, chiefly infantile attitudes toward people in the early environment which had been

of importance and which had become unconscious. These transferences must be treated as such, that is, they must be "resolved"
by discovering their meaning in terms of infantile relationships.
Since every neurosis is based on unresolved conflicts which occurred before the fourth year of life, and since these conflicts
become reactivated in the transference, the analysis of the transference, together with the resolution of the resistances, forms the
most important aspect of the analytic work. Since, further, the
patient, in the transference, attempts to replace the interpretation
work by the gratification of the unsatisfied old love or hate impulses and also defends himself against recognizing these attitudes, the transference usually becomes a resistance, that is, it
impedes the progress of the treatment. The negative transference,
that is, the transferred hate impulses, are from the beginning
recognizable as resistances, while the transference of love impulses turns into a resistance only when, as a result of disappointment, it turns into negative transference or anxiety.

It was only as long as there was little and unsystematic discussion of analytic technique that one could believe that analysts,
on the basis of a common groundwork of technique, had also
developed a technique which was common to all. This was shown,
for example, in the discussion of such concepts as "analytic passivity" which was interpreted in many different ways. The extreme—and certainly the most erroneous—interpretation was that
one only had to keep silent, and the rest would come by itself. As
to the role of the analyst in the treatment there were—and are—
the most confused concepts. True, one knows generally that he
has to dissolve resistances and has to "handle" the transference.
But how and when this is to take place, how his actions have to
differ according to the different cases and situations, that had
never been systematically discussed. Thus, there was a wide
divergence of opinion even with regard to everyday problems
of analytic practice. If, for example, a certain resistance situation
is presented in the Seminar, one analyst will say it calls for this
measure, a second, another, and a third, still another. If the
analyst then, provided with all this advice, again approaches his
case, there appear innumerable other possibilities, and the con-

fusion often is worse than before. And yet, one must assume that one definite analytic situation—given certain conditions and situations—admits of only one optimal technical procedure, that there is one definite procedure which in this situation is better than any other. This applies not only to an individual situation, but to analytic therapy as a whole. We have to find out, therefore, what characterizes this one correct technique, and how one arrives at it.

It took a long time before it came clear what is the crux of the matter: *to derive the situation technique from each respective analytic situation itself by way of an exact analysis of its details.* This method of developing analytic technique was strictly adhered to at the Vienna Technical Seminar and proved highly valuable. Instead of giving advice, one discussed the difficulty, say, a resistance situation, until the discussion itself spontaneously revealed the necessary measure; then one had the feeling that only that could be the right thing and nothing else. Thus we had won a method of applying the analytic material to analytic technique; if not in every case, certainly in a great many cases, and, more importantly, in principle. Our method is not a principle based on fixed procedures; it is a method which is based on certain basic theoretical principles but really determined by the individual case and the individual situation. For example, a basic principle is that all manifestations of the unconscious have to be made conscious by interpretation. But does that mean that one should immediately interpret this unconscious as soon as it shows itself only halfway clearly? Or, a basic principle is that all transference phenomena should be reduced to their infantile sources. But when and in what manner should this be done? One is confronted, at one and the same time, with negative and positive transference phenomena. In principle, either has to be "dissolved"; but should one not ask, which has to be dissolved first, and what determines that choice?

An easy objection to the attempt to derive the sequence, emphasis and depth of an interpretation from the respective total situation would be that one interprets whatever comes up. But when innumerable experiences and their subsequent theoretical evaluation show that interpretation of the material as it comes up usually does not fulfil its therapeutic function, then one must ask oneself: what are the conditions that make an interpretation therapeutically effective? They are different from case to case, and although they lead to certain valid technical generalizations, these mean little compared with the basic principle that the technique in every individual case has to be derived from the individual case and each individual situation, while at the same time one does not lose sight of the total analytic process. Such pieces of advice as that this or that should be "analyzed" or that one should "analyze properly" are phrases but not technical principles. What that means, to "analyze," remains obscure. Neither can one seek consolation in the duration of the treatment. Time alone does not do it. To put one's trust in the duration of the treatment makes sense only if and when the analysis is developing, that is, when one understands the resistances and can guide the analysis correspondingly. Then, of course, time is of no concern. But it is senseless to expect success from just waiting.

We will have to show how essential for the logical development of the treatment is the correct comprehension and handling of the *first* transference resistance. It is important in which detail, in which layer, the transference neurosis is first attacked analytically; whether from the wealth of the material presented one picks out this or that part, whether one first interprets the unconscious material which has become manifest or the respective resistance, etc. If one interprets the material in the sequence in which it presents itself, one proceeds from a preconceived idea: that "material" is always analytically usable, that is, therapeutically effective material. What matters, however, is its dynamic value. My efforts to develop a theory of technique and therapy have precisely the aim of gaining criteria for the *consistent application* of the material to the technical handling of the case, criteria which enable one to know exactly, in the case of each interpretation, why and to what effect it is given, rather than giving interpretations at random. If one interprets the material in the sequence in which it appears—no matter whether the patient may be deceiving one, whether he hides an attitude of hatred, whether he has

a secret attitude of derision, whether he is affect-blocked, etc.—
then hopeless situations at a later time are inevitable. Proceeding
thus, one works according to a schema which is imposed upon
every case, without consideration of the *individual* constellation
of the case which makes it necessary to individualize interpretations as to time and depth. Only if one strictly adheres to the
rule of deriving the technique from every situation will one at
least approximately fulfil the requirement of being able to tell
why one has or has not cured a case. Unless one can do this, at
least in the average case, our therapy cannot claim the name of
a scientific, causal therapy. If one asks oneself the reasons for the
failure of an analysis, one cannot take recourse to such statements
as that the patient "did not want to get well" or that he was inaccessible. For our question is precisely that: *why* did the patient
not want to get well, or why was he inaccessible?

I shall not present a "system" of technique. It is not a matter of
drawing a schema which would be applicable to all cases. Rather,
it is a matter of creating a basis for the comprehension of our
therapeutic task, a framework with sufficient space for the individual application of the fundamental principles.

I have nothing to add to Freud's principles of the interpretation
of the unconscious or to his general formula that the analytic
work consists in the elimination of the resistances and the handling of the transference. The following exposition makes the
claim, however, of being the consistent application of basic
psychoanalytic principles, an application which also opens new
fields for analytic work. If our patients, from the beginning of
the treatment, followed the fundamental rule even to a reasonable
degree, there would be no reason for writing a book on character-
analysis. Unfortunately, only the fewest of our patients are accessible to analysis from the very beginning; they are incapable of
following the fundamental rule until such time as a loosening
of their resistances has succeeded. We shall deal, therefore, only
with the introductory phase of the analysis, up to that point where
the course of the analysis can be left to the patient without danger;
the first problem is the "analytic education to analysis." The
second problem is that of the termination of the analysis, of the

dissolution of the transference and of the education to reality. The middle part of the analysis will occupy us only insofar as it develops out of the introductory phase and into the terminal phase.

But first we need a brief theoretical consideration of the libido-economic basis of analytic therapy.

## Chapter II

# THE ECONOMIC VIEWPOINT IN THE THEORY OF ANALYTIC THERAPY

When Freud gave up cathartic therapy and hypnosis as an adjuvant of analysis, when he assumed the standpoint that what the patient could tell the physician in his sleep he should also be able to tell him in the waking state, he attempted, for some time, to make the patient understand the unconscious meaning of his symptoms by direct interpretation of the derivatives of the unconscious. He soon discovered that the success of this method depended on the degree of the patient's readiness to accept such interpretations. He found that the patient opposed the interpretations with a—usually unconscious—"resistance," and altered his technique accordingly. That is, he gave up direct interpretation and tried, instead, to make the unconscious conscious by the elimination of the resistances which were put up against the repressed material.

This fundamental change in theoretical concept and technique was the turning-point in the history of analytic therapy at which the therapy of today began to develop. This was never understood by those of Freud's pupils who turned away from him; even Rank returned to the old method of direct symptom-interpretation. The present attempt is nothing but a consistent application of the newer method of resistance analysis to the analysis of the character, corresponding to the progress of analytic therapy from symptom-analysis to the analysis of the total personality.

In the period of catharsis the concept was that the symptom would disappear if one succeeded in "releasing the repressed affect from repression." Later, in the period of resistance analysis, the concept was—perhaps a hangover from the period of direct interpretation of the meaning of the symptom—that the symptom would *of necessity* disappear if the corresponding repressed idea was made conscious. Later, when the untenability of this concept had become obvious after one had found that symptoms often persist in spite of the consciousness of the previously repressed idea, Freud, in a meeting of the Vienna Psychoanalytic Society, changed the previous formula. He said now that the symptom *could* disappear after its unconscious content had been made conscious, but that it did *not necessarily* do so. Now one was confronted with a new and difficult problem. If the becoming conscious alone did not bring about cure, then, the question was, what has to be added, what further circumstances determine whether or not the becoming conscious of the repressed idea leads to cure? True, the making conscious of the repressed remained the indispensable prerequisite of cure, but it did not specifically determine it. Now one began to wonder whether perhaps those opponents of psychoanalysis were right after all who had always warned that analysis should be followed by "synthesis." Yet, this was no more than a phrase, and Freud had already answered this objection when, at the Budapest Congress, he pointed out that analysis is at the same time synthesis, since every impulse which is freed from one connection immediately establishes another. Was this perhaps where the answer to the problem lay hidden? *What* impulses, and what new connections, came into consideration here? Is it not important with what kind of libidinous structure the patient leaves the analysis? As an analyst, one had to give up perfectionism and had to be content with finding a solution which was in keeping with the demands of the average individual. It was a failing of all of psychotherapy to neglect the primitive biological as well as the sociological basis of what is called the "higher things." Again Freud's libido theory, neglected though it was, pointed the way. Yet, there was a wealth of unanswered questions. Let us arrange them according to metapsychological points of view.

The *topical* viewpoint brought no solution. More than that, such an attempt had proved a failure: the making conscious of an unconscious idea was not sufficient for cure. There was more to be expected from the *dynamic* point of view. But this, too, proved inadequate, notwithstanding the efforts of Ferenczi and Rank in their ENTWICKLUNGSZIELE DER PSYCHOANALYSE. The release of the affect connected with an idea, it is true, almost regularly brings about an improvement, but this is usually only temporary. In addition, apart from certain forms of hysteria, this release can rarely be brought about in such intensity as would bring about the desired result. Thus, the only remaining point of view was the *economic* one: The patient suffers from a disturbed libido economy; the biological functions of his sexuality are partly pathologically distorted, partly repressed. Whether or not the libido economy of an individual is normal or disturbed must depend on his libidinal structure. In other words, one had to make a fundamental distinction between such libidinal structures which allowed a normal libido economy and others which made it impossible. Our later differentiation of the "genital character" and the "neurotic character" was a formulation of this distinction.

The topical and the dynamic point of view were easy to handle in everyday practice; it was a matter of consciousness or unconsciousness of an idea, or of the intensity of an affective breakthrough of the repression, respectively. It was less clear, however, in which manner the economic point of view should find its practical application. Here, we were dealing with the quantitative factor of psychic life, with the libido quantity which was dammed up or discharged. What were we to do about this difficulty determined by quantity, in view of the fact that in analysis we deal, in an immediate way, only with qualities? First of all, one had to understand why, in our theory of the neuroses, we keep coming up against the quantitative factor, and why, in explaining psychic phenomena, the qualities of psychic life proved insufficient. While, thus, experience as well as theoretical considerations in questions of analytic therapy kept pointing to the question of quantity, clinical experience unexpectedly shed light on the problem.

Practical experience showed that many cases, in spite of extensive and intensive analysis, remain refractory, while others, in spite of incomplete exploration of the unconscious, may attain permanent health. In comparing these two groups,[1] it was found

---

[1] *Cf.* Reich, "Über Genitalität," *Internat. Zeitschr. f. Psychoan.* 10, 1924, and "Die therapeutische Bedeutung der Genitallibido," *ibid.*, 11, 1925.

that those patients who remained refractory or who relapsed after a short time, had not been able, after the analysis, to establish a normal sex life or had continued to live in sexual abstinence, while the others, enabled by a partial analysis, had soon established a satisfactory sex life. A study of the prognosis of average cases showed, furthermore, that, other things being equal, the prognosis is the better the more completely the primacy of the genital was established in childhood and adolescence; that, conversely, the prognosis was poorer the less libido had been attached to the genital in childhood; those cases proved more or less inaccessible who had altogether failed to establish genital primacy in infancy and who had used their genitals exclusively in the sense of oral, anal or urethral eroticism.[2] Genitality being shown to be such an important prognostic criterion, it was necessary to examine the patients as to their genitality, their potency. This examination revealed the fact that there were no women at all without a disturbance of vaginal potency, and almost no men without disturbances of erective and ejaculative potency. The patients who had no disturbance of potency in the usual sense, that is, the small number of erectively potent neurotics, seemed to invalidate the importance of genitality for the understanding of the economic factor in therapy.

Finally one had to arrive at the consideration that it does not matter whether erective potency is present or not, for this does not make any difference as far as the libido *economy* is concerned. What matters is whether the *ability for adequate sexual gratification* is present. In the case of the vaginally anesthetic women it was clear where the symptoms derived their energy from, in other words, what maintained the libido stasis, the specific source of energy of the neurosis. The economic concept of *orgastic* impotence, that is, the inability to discharge an amount of sexual energy corresponding to the sexual tension, was revealed only through an exact exploration of the male patients with erective potency. The cardinal importance of genitality, or orgastic impotence, for the etiology of the neuroses was presented in my book, Die Funk-

---

[2] Since that time, it has become possible to bring about considerable improvement even in these patients.

TION DES ORGASMUS.[3] It attained theoretical importance, for characterological investigations also, through its connections with the
theory of the "actual neuroses." Thus it became suddenly clear
where the problem of quantity lay: it could be nothing else but
the somatic basis, the "somatic core of the neurosis," the actual
neurosis (stasis neurosis) which develops from the dammed-up
libido. That is, the economic problem of the neurosis as well as the
therapy of the neurosis was largely in the somatic realm and not
accessible except over the somatic contents of the libido concept.[4]

Now one was better prepared to tackle the question as to what
has to be added to the making conscious of the unconscious in
order to eliminate the symptom. What becomes conscious is only
the *meaning*, the ideational content of the symptom. Dynamically
speaking, the process of becoming conscious brings in itself a
certain relief because of the emotional release connected with it
and because it makes unnecessary a certain amount of repression.
But these processes alone produce very little change as far as the
*source* of energy of the symptom or neurotic character trait is
concerned; in spite of the consciousness of the meaning of the
symptom, the libido stasis continues to exist. True, the pressure
of the dammed-up libido can be somewhat relieved by intensive
work, but definitive release from the sexual tension requires
*genital* sexual gratification; pregenitality cannot provide orgasm.
Only the establishment of orgastic potency will result in a decisive
change, economically speaking. As I formulated it once: the
analysis, by eliminating the sexual repressions, creates the possibility of a *spontaneous organotherapy* of the neuroses. That is, in
the final analysis the therapeutic agent is an organic process in
the sexual metabolism. This process is based on sexual gratification in the genital orgasm. By eliminating the actual neurosis
(stasis neurosis), the somatic core of the neurosis, it also eliminates the psychoneurotic superstructure. Originally, when the
neurosis developed, the following process took place: An external

---

[3] *Translator's note: Cf.* also THE FUNCTION OF THE ORGASM, Orgone Institute
Press, 1942, 1948.

[4] *Cf.* Reich, "Die Rolle der Genitalität in der Neurosentherapie." *Allg. ärztl.
Zeitschr. f. Psychotherapie,* 1.

inhibition, which then became internalized, created the libido stasis; this in turn invested the experiences of the Oedipus age with energy; the libido stasis, continuing to exist as a result of sexual repression, constantly kept providing energy for the psychoneurosis; there is a vicious circle. Therapy reverses this process: by working on the psychoneurosis through making conscious of the unconscious inhibitions and fixations it creates the possibility of eliminating the libido stasis; once this has succeeded, repression and psychoneurosis become unnecessary; more, they become impossible.

This is roughly the concept about the role of the somatic core of the neurosis as I presented it in the book just mentioned. It gives the analysis a definite therapeutic goal: if the patient is to get well and stay well he must become able to establish a *satisfactory genital sex life*. No matter how short of that goal one will have to stop in many cases, the dynamics of libido stasis definitely show this to be the real therapeutic goal. It would be dangerous to make effective sexual gratification a less strict therapeutic requirement than sublimation; if for no other reason, because the ability to sublimate is an as yet not understood gift, while the capacity for sexual gratification, even though considerably restricted by social factors, can, in the average case, be established. It goes without saying that shifting the emphasis from sublimation to direct sexual gratification as a therapeutic goal vastly increases the field of our therapeutic possibilities. On the other hand, this shift also brings us face to face with social difficulties which should not be underestimated.

The technical discussions which are to follow will show that this goal cannot be reached by education, "synthesis" or suggestion, but only by a thorough analysis of the sexual inhibitions *in the character*. But first a few remarks about Nunberg's presentation of the theory of psychoanalytic therapy, in his book, ALLGEMEINE NEUROSENLEHRE. He considers the first therapeutic task that of "helping the instincts to discharge and to gain access to consciousness." He further considers it important that "peace is established between the two parts of the personality, the ego and the id, in the sense that the instincts no longer lead a separate existence outside of the organization of the ego and that the ego regains its synthetic power." This is, though incomplete, essentially correct. But Nunberg adheres to the old concept, since proved erroneous by practical experience, that in the act of remembering psychic energy is discharged, "spent." That is, in his explanation of the dynamics of therapy, he stops short at the becoming conscious of the repressed, without asking himself whether the small affect quantities discharged in this process can be sufficient to discharge the total amount of dammed-up libido and to bring about a well-regulated energy economy. To counter this objection, he might argue that the total energy is discharged in the course of all the innumerable acts of becoming conscious. But clinical experience shows that only a small part of the affect connected with a repressed idea is discharged in the act of making conscious; by far the larger part is, very soon, shifted to another unconscious activity; or, there is no discharge of affect at all, if, for example, the affect is contained in a character attitude; in that case, the becoming conscious of unconscious material remains without therapeutic effect. That is, it is impossible to derive the dynamics of therapy from the process of making conscious alone.

This leads to another necessary criticism of Nunberg's formulations. He states that the repetition compulsion works independently of the transference and that it is based on the attractive forces of the repressed infantile ideas. This would be correct if the repetition compulsion were a primary fact. Clinical experience shows, however, that the attraction of the unconscious and infantile ideas is based on the strength of the unsatisfied sexual needs and that it retains its compulsive repetitive character only as long as the path to mature sexual gratification is blocked. That is, the neurotic repetition compulsion depends on the libido-economic situation. Thus the peace between ego and id which Nunberg rightly postulates can be established only on a certain sex-economic basis: first, by the replacement of pregenital strivings by genital ones, and second, by effective gratification of the genital needs, which also definitely solves the problem of stasis.

Nunberg's theoretical concept leads to a technical attitude which we cannot consider the real analytic one. Nunberg states that the resistances should not be directly attacked. Instead, the analyst should mobilize the positive transference against them, by "sneaking into" the ego of the patient and by destroying the resistances from that position. In this way, he thinks, a similar situation is established as between a hypnotized person and the hypnotist. "Since the analyst is now surrounded with libido in the ego, he sort of neutralizes the strictness of the super-ego." In this way, Nunberg thinks, the analyst becomes capable of bringing about the reconciliation of the two estranged parts of the neurotic personality. The objections to these views are the following:

a) Precisely this "sneaking in into the ego" is dangerous in a great many cases, for in the beginning of the treatment there never exists a genuine positive transference. It is always a matter of narcissistic attitudes, such as infantile dependence which may rapidly turn into hatred because the disappointment reaction is stronger than the positive object-relationship. Such a "sneaking in" for the purpose of circumventing the resistances and of "destroying them from within" is dangerous insofar as it allows the resistances to be camouflaged; what is even more important is that the old condition or, worse, violent reactions of disappointment will set in as soon as the weak object-relationship becomes still weaker or is replaced by other kinds of transference. It is precisely this procedure which produces the most difficult manifestations of negative transference, manifestations which appear too late and in a disorderly fashion. The result is often sudden breaking off of the treatment by the patient, or suicide. The latter is most likely to occur when the establishment of such an artificial positive, hypnoid attitude has particularly well succeeded; on the other hand, an open and clear working out of the destructive and narcissistic reactions can prevent the breaking-off as well as the suicide.

b) The artificial establishment of a positive transference—instead of its being crystallized out of the infantile fixations—creates the danger of a superficial acceptance of interpretations which may deceive the patient as well as the analyst about the real state of affairs until it is too late to correct the situation. Unfortunately, a sort of hypnotic situation is only too often established; but it should be unmasked as a resistance and should be eliminated.

c) If in the beginning of the treatment the anxiety subsides, this proves only that the patient has invested a part of his libido in the transference, the negative included; it does not mean that he has dissolved any anxiety. It may be necessary at times, in order to continue the treatment, to alleviate acute anxiety, but, on the whole, one has to make the patient understand that he can get well only when a maximum amount of destructiveness and anxiety is mobilized.

I am very familiar, from my own experience, with the description of the typical course of an analysis as given below by Nunberg. I can only add that I make every effort to prevent such a course and that for that reason I pay so much attention to the technique of analyzing resistances in the beginning of the treatment. The following is the common result of neglecting the negative transference in the beginning of the treatment and of misjudging the strength of the positive transference:

For some time, there is complete agreement between patient and analyst; more, the patient depends completely on him, also for the interpretations, and if that were possible, he would also do it as far as the remembering goes. But soon this harmony is disturbed. As I said before, the deeper the analysis goes, the stronger become the resistances; this is increasingly so the closer one gets to the original pathogenic situation. Added to this difficulty is the element of frustration in the transference which sooner or later inevitably must occur since the personal demands which the patient makes on the analyst cannot be satisfied. To this frustration, most patients react with a slackening in analytic work, with acting out; that is, they behave as they once behaved in analogous previous situations. One could think that in doing so they express a certain activity; . . . on the contrary, they evade it, they behave basically passively. That is, the repetition compulsion, which is a factor in bringing about the fixations, also governs the psychic expressions of the repressed in the transference situation. Now, the patient leaves a piece of active work to the analyst: that of guessing what he wants to say and cannot express. Usually, it is a matter of being loved. The omnipotence of the means of expression (which may be wordless) as well as the supposed omnipotence of the therapist are put to an extreme test. In part the analyst succeeds in unmasking these resistances, in part it is impossible to guess what it is about. The conflict which no longer is an internal one but one between the patient and the analyst thus comes to a point. *The analysis threatens to go on the rocks, that is, the patient is confronted with the choice of losing the analyst and his love or to take up active work again* [italics are mine. W.R.]. If the transference is strong, that is, if the patient has available a minimum of object-libido which is already loosened from its fixations, he becomes afraid of the loss. In such cases, something peculiar often happens. At a time when the analyst has already given up hope and has lost interest in the case, there suddenly appears a wealth of material which promises a rapid termination of the analysis. (Nunberg, ALLGEMEINE NEUROSENLEHRE, p. 305).

No doubt, a systematic and consistent resistance analysis is not possible in every case. But where it succeeds, such hopelessness does not occur in an analysis. Where it does not succeed, such situations are quite common; all the more reason to pay the closest attention to the technique of analyzing resistances.

CHAPTER III

# ON THE TECHNIQUE OF INTERPRETATION
# AND OF RESISTANCE ANALYSIS *

## 1. SOME TYPICAL ERRORS IN THE TECHNIQUE OF INTERPRETATION
## AND THEIR RESULTS

In the analytic work, we must distinguish two parts: first, the cure of the patient, and second, his immunization, to the extent to which it can take place during the treatment. The cure itself consists of two parts, the introductory phase and the process of cure proper. True, this distinction is artificial; even the first resistance interpretation has a good deal to do with the cure. Nevertheless, even the preparations for a voyage to which Freud likened an analysis, have much to do with the voyage itself and may decide its success or failure. In analysis, at any rate, everything depends on how it is started. A case which has been started in a wrong or confused manner is usually lost. Most cases present the greatest difficulties in the introductory period, no matter whether they "go well" or not. It is precisely the cases which seemingly go smoothly in the beginning who later present the greatest difficulties, because the smooth course in the beginning makes difficult the early recognition and elimination of the difficulties. Errors made in the introduction of the analysis are all the more difficult to eliminate the longer the analysis proceeds without their correction.

Now, which are these special and typical difficulties of the introductory period?

The goal of the analysis in the introductory period is that of penetrating to the energy sources of the symptoms and of the neurotic character, in order to set the therapeutic process in mo-

* First presented in the Vienna Technical Seminar for Psychoanalytic Therapy, June, 1926. Published in *Internat. Zeitschr. f. Psychoan.*, 1927.

tion. This task is impeded by the resistances of the patient, among which the most stubborn are those arising out of transference conflicts. They have to be made conscious, interpreted and to be given up by the patient. Thus he progresses, ever more deeply, to the affectively important recollections from early infancy. The much-discussed question as to what is more important, affective re-living (acting out) or remembering, is of no significance to us. Clinical experience confirms Freud's demand that the patient who tends to repeat his experiences by acting out must, in order to really solve his conflicts, not only understand what he is acting out, but must also remember with affect.[1] I mention this only because I did not want to give the impression that we considered our work as consisting of nothing but resistance– and transference analysis, merely because in this section we discuss nothing but the principles of resistance analysis.

Now, what happens in ever so many cases instead of remembering with affect?

There are the cases which fail because the analyst, as a result of the many heterogeneous transferences, gets lost in the wealth of the material produced by the patient. We call this a "chaotic situation" and find that it is caused by certain mistakes in the technique of interpretation. Then there are the many cases in which the negative transference is overlooked because it is hidden behind manifest positive attitudes. Finally, there are the many cases which show no progress in spite of deep-reaching recollection work, because no attention was paid to their affect-lameness or because it was not made the focal point of the analysis. In contrast to these cases which seem to run a normal course but end in a chaotic situation, we have those others which "do not go," that is, do not produce associations and oppose our efforts with passive resistance.

I am going to outline a few of my own bad failures and we shall soon see that they are due to typical errors. The similarity of most

---

[1] *Footnote, 1945:* This technical problem of psychoanalysis has since found its complete solution: In orgone therapy, the pathogenic memories appear *spontaneously* and *without effort* when the somatic emotions break through the muscular armor.

of these failures points to typical errors committed in the introductory period, errors which no longer can be counted among the
gross beginner's sins. This is no reason for despair; as Ferenczi
once said, every new experience costs us a case. All that matters
is to see the error and to learn from it. It is no different in any
other branch of medicine; only the hushing up of and the alibi-ing
for the failures we shall leave to the others.

A patient suffering from inferiority feelings and self-consciousness acted out his impotence in the form of not having any associations ("I can't do anything"). Instead of recognizing the nature of this resistance and making conscious the tendencies to
deprecation hidden behind it, I kept telling him that he did not
want to work and did not want to get well. Although I was not
altogether wrong in this, I made the mistake of not working on his
"not wanting to" and of not trying to understand the reasons for
his inability; instead, my own inability led me to make these
senseless reproaches. Every patient has the tendency to remain
ill, and I know that the phrase, "You don't want to get well,"
without any further explanation, is often used as a reproach by
many analysts in unclear situations. It should be eliminated from
the analyst's vocabulary and be replaced by self-scrutiny. For we
must realize that every unresolved stoppage in an analysis is the
fault of the analyst.

Another case, in the course of three years of analysis, had remembered the primal scene in all details. But not a single time
had his affect-lameness subsided, not a single time had he made
the analyst the reproaches which were—without affect, it is true—
in his mind against his father. He was not cured. I had not known
how to develop his repressed hatred. Ah, many will triumph:
finally the admission that the recovery of the primal scene does no
good therapeutically! They are wrong. Without analysis of early
infantile experiences there is no real cure. What matters is that
these recollections occur with the corresponding affects.

In another case it happened that the incest phantasy came up
clearly in connection with a dream in the second week of the
analysis and the patient himself realized its meaning. For a whole
year, I heard nothing more about it; the result was correspond-

ingly poor. I had learned that sometimes it is necessary to suppress material which comes up too soon, until such time as the patient is ready to assimilate it.

A case of erythrophobia resulted in failure because I painstakingly interpreted all material as it was presented without having first carefully eliminated the resistances. They came later, but then very intense and in chaotic disorder; I had shot my bolt, my explanations remained without effect, it was impossible to restore order. I may say that at that time, in the third or fourth year of my analytic practice, I was no longer such a beginner that I would have interpreted the unconscious unless it had shown itself in a clear and unequivocal manner and the patient had been near the solution himself, which is when Freud said interpretations should be given. Obviously, however, this precaution is insufficient, for this chaotic situation was of the very kind which one meets in seminars and control-analyses.

A case of classical hysteria with twilight states could have made an excellent recovery, to judge from later experiences in similar cases. But I failed to comprehend and treat in time the patient's reactions to the analysis of the positive transference, that is, her reactive hatred. I let myself be lured into a chaos by her recollections and found no way out. She kept having twilight states.

A number of bad experiences due to erroneous handling of the transference at the time of the disappointment reaction taught me to properly evaluate the danger to the analysis of the negative transference, be it the original negative transference or that originating from the disappointment of transference love. Not until a patient who had, in good positive transference, produced a wealth of recollections and yet had failed to get well, told me many months after breaking off the analysis that he had never trusted me, did I really know the danger of a negative transference which is allowed to remain latent. This made me, successfully, seek for the means of always getting the negative transference out of its hiding places.

In the Technical Seminar, also, we were mostly occupied with the problem of negative transference, particularly the latent. In other words, it was not a matter of an individual blind spot; the overlooking of the negative transference seems to be quite general. No doubt, this is due to our narcissism which makes us willing to listen to complimentary things but blind to negative attitudes unless they are expressed in more or less gross forms. It is striking that "transference" in the psychoanalytic literature always refers to positive attitudes; apart from the article on "Passive Technik" by Landauer, the problem of the negative transference is essentially neglected.

The overlooking of the negative transference is only one of the many mistakes which confuse the course of the analysis. We all experience what we have called the "chaotic situation," so I can limit myself to some of the main points.

One situation is the following: Memories and actions are very numerous but fail to show any logical sequence; the patient brings much material from all strata of his unconscious, from all age periods; all this lies there in a big heap, as it were; nothing is worked through in the sense of the therapeutic goal; in spite of the wealth of material the patient has no feeling of its importance. The analyst has given many interpretations, but these have never deepened the analysis in one or the other direction. It seems clear that everything the patient has presented was in the service of a secret, unrecognized resistance. What makes such chaotic analyses dangerous is that the analyst continues to believe, for a long time, that they are running very well, simply because the patient "brings material." This goes on until the analyst—usually too late— recognizes that the patient has been going around in a circle and has kept presenting the same material, only in different aspects. In this manner, he could fill his analytic hours for years on end without ever undergoing any real change.

Here is a characteristic case which I took over from a colleague. He had been in analysis for eight months for a multiple perversion. During treatment, he had continually talked and produced material from the deepest layers. This was constantly interpreted. The more the material was interpreted, the more ample was the flow of associations. Finally, the analysis had to be interrupted for external reasons and the patient came to me. At that time I was already partly acquainted with the dangers of latent resist-

ances. I was struck by the fact that the patient produced unconscious material uninterruptedly and was able, for instance, to
present the finest details of the simple and double Oedipus complex. I asked the patient whether he really believed what he was
saying and what he had heard. "But not in the least," he said,
"with all this, I cannot help smiling inside." When I asked him
why he had not told this to the first analyst, he said he had not
thought it necessary. There was nothing to be done, in spite of
vigorous analysis of his smile, for he had already learned too much.
The interpretations had all gone up in thin air, and my own
interpretations bounced back from his attitude of smiling. After
four months I gave him up, richer by another experience. It is
possible, though, that a longer and more consistent analysis of his
narcissistic defense might have brought a result after all. But at
that time I had not had as yet the good results which one can
achieve by consistent work on such attitudes.

In investigating the causes of such chaotic situations we soon
find that the following errors in the technique of interpretation
are to be blamed:

1. *Too early* interpretation of the meaning of the symptoms or
of other manifestations of the deepest layers of the unconscious,
particularly of symbols. The patient uses the analysis in the service of resistances which remain hidden and one finds out too late
that, completely untouched by the analysis, the patient has been
going around in a circle.

2. Interpretation of the material in the sequence in which it
presents itself, without consideration of the structure of the neurosis and the stratification of the material. The error consists in
interpreting for the sole reason that the material presents itself
clearly ( *unsystematic* interpretation of meaning).

3. The analysis becomes confused not only through interpretation of the material as it presents itself but also because the interpretations were given before work was done on the main
resistances. That is, the interpretation of meaning preceded the
interpretation of the resistance. The situation became further
complicated by the fact that the resistances soon became linked
with the relationship to the therapist, and thus the *unsystematic*

*resistance interpretation* also complicated the transference situation.

4. The interpretation of the transference resistances was not only unsystematic, but also *inconsistent*. That is, the fact was overlooked that the patient has the tendency of again hiding his resistances, of masking them by sterile productions or acute reaction formations. The latent transference resistances were mostly overlooked or the analyst was afraid to let them fully develop or to bring them into the open when they were hidden in one form or another.

These errors are probably based on a misconception of Freud's rule that the course of the analysis should be left to the patient. This rule can only mean that one should not disturb the work of the patient as long as it proceeds aecording to the patient's wish to get well and to our therapeutic intentions. But of course we must take action as soon as the patient's fear of meeting his conflicts and his tendency to stay ill disturb this course.

## 2. SYSTEMATIC INTERPRETATION AND RESISTANCE ANALYSIS

The reader will ask now: What, then, is the correct technique? He will have gained sufficient insight into the difficulty of the subject to realize that I can give no more than very generalized conclusions from the errors described. There is another difficulty in the discussion of this subject: We are dealing with living, ever-changing psychic life which inevitably becomes more or less rigid when we put it into words. What follows may give the impression of a rigid schema, and yet it is nothing but a rough sketch of a field which still has to be surveyed and thoroughly studied. It is only a matter of establishing a common language. Whatever in the following presentation appears schematic is no more than a means of orientation. The schema which automatically develops as soon as one separates one phenomenon from the other and views it separately, is nothing but a scientific makeshift. For the rest, we do not impute the schema, the rule, or the principle to the patient, but we view the patient without preconceived ideas and gain our orientation from *his* material, *his* behavior, from what he hides or misrepresents. Only then do we turn to the question, How do I best use what I have learned from *this* case in the technique of *that* case? It would be easier if, as Freud suggested at the Budapest Congress, we could formulate different resistance types; but even then we would have to find out in each case whether he shows this or that type of typical resistance. The latent negative transference is only *one* of these typical resistances, and we should not overlook others. The orientation can be gained only from the material of the individual patient.

We have seen that deep-reaching interpretations must be avoided as long as the first front of the cardinal resistances has not become clear and has not been eliminated, no matter how ample, clear and interpretable the material may be. The more memory material a patient presents without having produced the corresponding resistances the more one has to be on one's guard. At any rate, confronted with the choice of interpreting unconscious material or working on manifest resistances, one will decide in favor of the latter. Our principle is: *No interpretation of meaning when a resistance interpretation is needed.* The reason for this is simple enough. If one interprets the meaning *before* eliminating the corresponding resistance, the patient either accepts the interpretation for reasons of the transference, or he completely depreciates it at the first appearance of a negative attitude, or the resistance comes afterwards. In either case, the interpretation has lost its therapeutic effectiveness and it is difficult if not impossible to correct the situation. The way to the deep unconscious which the interpretation has to take has been blocked.

It is important not to disturb the patient during the first few weeks in the development of his "analytic personality." The resistances, too, cannot be interpreted before they have fully developed and are essentially understood by the analyst. Of course, the time at which the interpretation of resistance is begun will largely depend on the experience of the analyst; the experienced will need no more than slight signs, while the beginner, in the same case, will need more or less gross actions. It takes a good deal of experience to recognize the signs of a *latent* resistance. If one has grasped the meaning of such resistances, one will make them conscious through consistent interpretation; that is, one will show the patient first, that he has a resistance; then, which means it uses; and finally, against what the resistance is directed.

If the first transference resistance has not been preceded by sufficient production of memory material, its resolution meets with a difficulty which, it is true, becomes less with increasing experience of the analyst. This difficulty consists in the fact that, in order to resolve the resistance, one must know the unconscious material it contains, while, on the other hand, one cannot get at this material because the resistance blocks it. Just like a dream, every resistance has a historical meaning (an origin) and a present-day meaning. The difficulty can be overcome in the following manner: from the present situation—the development of which one has been watching—and from the form and the means of the resistance one finds the present meaning and purpose of the resistance. One then can influence it by interpretation sufficiently so that the infantile material makes its appearance; only with the help of this infantile material can the resistance be fully resolved. As far as the finding of the resistances and the divining of their present meaning is concerned, there can, of course, be no hard and fast rules; it is largely a matter of intuition; this is where the non-teachable analytic art begins. The subtler and the more secret the resistances are, the more the patient deceives, the more reliable will the intuitive acts of the analyst have to be. In other words, the analyst must be free of inhibitions and must have a special gift in addition.

What is a "latent resistance"? Attitudes of the patient which are not expressed directly and immediately as in the case of doubt, distrust, being late, silence, spite, lack of associations, etc., but indirectly in the mode of analytic production. Thus, extreme compliance or complete lack of manifest resistances always points to a latent and, for that reason, all the more dangerous passive resistance. I tackle such latent resistances as soon as I perceive them and do not hesitate to interrupt the patient's communications as soon as I have heard enough to understand the resistance. For experience shows that the therapeutic effect of the patient's communications is lost if they are made in the presence of unresolved resistances.

The onesided and consequently erroneous evaluation of the analytic material and the misinterpretation of Freud's thesis that one has to proceed from the surface often lead to dangerous misunderstandings and technical difficulties. To begin with, what does that mean, "analytic material"? The usual concept is: the patient's communications, dreams, associations, slips. True, there is often a theoretical realization of the fact that the total behavior of the patient also has analytic significance; but clear-cut experiences in the Seminar show that the behavior of the patient, his look, manner of speech, facial expression, dress, handclasp, etc., that all these things are not only underestimated in their analytic significance, but usually completely overlooked. At the Innsbruck Congress, Ferenczi and I, independently, stressed the significance of these formal elements for therapy; to me they have become, in the course of the years, the most important point of departure for the analysis of the character. The overestimation of the content of the material usually goes with an underestimation if not with a complete neglect of the manner in which the patient tells these things. If one, however, overlooks the mode of behavior of the patient or fails to consider it as at least as important as the content, one arrives, unawares, at a concept of the "psychic surface" which is therapeutically dangerous. If, for instance, a patient is very polite, while at the same time he brings ample material, say, about his relationship with his sister, one is confronted with two simultaneous contents of the "psychic surface": his love for his sister, and his behavior, his politeness. Both have unconscious roots. This view of the psychic surface puts a different face on the rule that "one should always proceed from the surface." Analytic experience shows that behind this politeness and niceness there is *always* hidden a more or less unconscious critical, distrustful or deprecatory attitude; that is, the stereotyped politeness of the patient is in itself a sign of negative criticism, of distrust or deprecation. This being the case, is it admissible to interpret the incestuous love for the sister when a corresponding dream or association appears? No. There are good reasons for choosing one part of the psychic surface to work on first, and not the other. Were one to wait until the patient himself begins to talk about his politeness and its reasons, one would make a serious mistake. Since such a character trait immediately becomes a resistance in the analysis, the same is true of it as of any resistance: the patient will never talk about it himself, it is up to the analyst to unmask it as a resistance. Here, an important objection might be made: that my contention that the politeness immediately turns into a resistance is incorrect, otherwise the patient would not produce material. But the point is just that, particularly in the beginning, the important thing is not the content, but the formal aspect of the material. To remain with the example of politeness: the neurotic, as a result of his repressions, has every reason to value highly his politeness and all social conventions and to use them as protection. True, it may be more pleasant to treat a polite patient than an impolite, very candid one, one who tells the analyst that he is too young or too old, that he has a shabby apartment or an ugly wife, that he looks stupid or too Jewish, that he behaves neurotically and better go for analysis himself, etc. Such things are not necessarily transference phenomena: in reality, the analyst never is a "blank screen"; the personal characteristics of the analyst are a fact which, to begin with, has nothing to do with transference. And our patients have an extraordinary ability to sense our weak points; more, in scenting them, many patients take revenge for the fundamental rule being forced upon them. There are some few patients, mostly sadistic characters, who derive their sadistic pleasure from the candor which is asked of them. Therapeutically this behavior is valuable although at times it becomes a resistance. But the overwhelming majority of our patients are much too inhibited and anxious, too much laden with guilt feelings, to develop such candor spontaneously. In disagreement with many of my colleagues, I must maintain my contention that every case, without exception, begins the analysis with a more or less explicit attitude of distrust and criticism which, as a rule, *remains hidden*. In order to convince oneself of this, it is necessary to make the patient discuss, first of all, all the matter-of-course factors making for distrust and criticism inherent in the situation (new kind of situation, unknown person, public opinion about analysis, etc.); only through this candor on the part of the analyst can the patient's confidence be gained. The technical question as to when these, not necessarily neurotic, attitudes of distrust and criticism should be discussed is not a difficult one; it is merely a matter of avoiding any deep-reaching interpretations of the unconscious as long as the wall of conventional politeness between patient and analyst continues to exist.

We cannot continue the discussion of the technique of interpretation without including the development and treatment of the transference neurosis. In a correctly carried-out analysis, it is not long before the first strong transference resistance makes its appearance. We will have to understand first why it is that the first significant resistance against the continuation of the analysis becomes automatically, and in a manner which is determined by the structure of the individual case, connected with the analyst; what is the motive for what Ferenczi called "transference compulsion"? Our insistence on following the fundamental rule has begun to dislodge forbidden things. Sooner or later, the patient puts up an accentuated defense against their becoming conscious. At first, this defense is directed exclusively against the repressed material; but the patient knows neither that he has these forbidden things in himself nor that he is defending himself against them. As Freud has shown, the resistances themselves are unconscious. Yet, the resistance is an emotional process, and for this reason cannot remain hidden. Like everything else which has an irrational basis, this affect also seeks a rational causation, an anchoring in an actual situation. Thus the patient projects; he projects to the one who, by his insistence on the fundamental rule, has stirred up the whole conflict. The displacement of the defense from the unconscious to the therapist brings with it a displacement of the unconscious content also: the content also is displaced to the analyst. He becomes, for example, the strict father or the loving mother. It is clear that this defense can result at first only in a negative attitude. As the disturber of the neurotic equilibrium, the analyst automatically becomes the enemy, no matter whether the projected impulses are impulses of love or of hatred; for in either case there is, at the same time, defense against these impulses.

If it is hate impulses which are projected first, the transference resistance is unequivocally negative. If it is love impulses, the real transference resistance is preceded by a manifest but not conscious positive transference. This, however, turns regularly into reactive negative transference, partly because the disappointment is inevitable, resulting in the "disappointment reaction," partly because the patient defends himself against it as soon as, under the pressure of sensual impulses, it tends to become conscious; and every defense results in negative attitudes.

The technical problem of the latent negative transference is so important that it necessitates a separate presentation of its many forms and its treatment. Now, I shall only enumerate a few typical disease pictures in which we are most likely to meet a latent negative transference. They are:

1. The over-obedient, over-friendly, too trusting, that is, the "*good patients*"; those cases who are forever in positive transference and never show a disappointment reaction. Usually, they are passive-feminine characters or female hysterias with nymphomanic trends.

2. Those who are always *conventional and correct*. Usually, they are compulsive characters who have converted their hatred into "politeness at all cost."

3. The *affect-lame* patients. Like the "correct" patients, they are characterized by an intensive but blocked aggressivity. Usually, they are compulsive characters, but female hysterias also often show a superficial affect-lameness.

4. Patients complaining about a lack of genuineness in their feelings and their expressions, that is, who suffer from *depersonalization*. Among these are to be counted such patients who—consciously and at the same time compulsively—"play-act," that is, who somehow in the background of their mind know that they deceive the therapist. Usually, they belong to the group of narcissistic neuroses of the hypochondriac type. They regularly show an "*inward smile*" about everything and everybody, something which they themselves begin to feel as painful and which presents a very difficult therapeutic task.

The form and stratification of the first transference resistance are conditioned by the individual infantile love experiences. For this reason, we can achieve an orderly, not unnecessarily complicated analysis of the infantile conflicts only if in our interpretations we pay the strictest attention to this stratification. True, the contents of the transferences are not determined by our interpretations, but the sequence in which they become acute depends on our interpretation technique. It is important not only that the transference neurosis develops but that in developing it follows the same paths as its prototype, the original neurosis, and that it shows the same dynamic stratification. Freud has taught us that the original neurosis is only accessible through the transference neurosis. Clearly, the therapeutic task is all the easier the more completely and orderly the original neurosis unfolds in the transference neurosis. Of course, this takes place in the reverse order. It is easy to understand that a faulty analysis of the transference, such as the interpretation of an attitude from a deeper layer—no matter how clear the attitude and how correct the interpretation in itself— must blur the copy of the original neurosis and bring disorder into the transference neurosis. Experience teaches us that the transference neurosis develops spontaneously according to the structure of the individual neurosis if we avoid one mistake: that of giving too early, too deep-reaching and unsystematic interpretations.

To illustrate by a schematic example: If a patient first loved his mother, then hated his father, then, for fear, gave up his mother and converted his hatred of the father into passive-feminine love toward him, then his first transference, in a correctly carried-out resistance analysis, will be his passive-feminine attitude, the latest result of his libidinal development. A systematic resistance analysis will bring out the hatred of the father which hides behind it; only after this will a new cathexis of the mother occur, at first in the form of the love for the mother as transferred to the analyst. From there, it can be transferred to a woman in reality.

Remaining with this simplified example, we shall consider a possible less favorable outcome. Say, the patient shows manifest positive transference and produces dreams showing his passive-feminine attitude as well as dreams which show his attachment to his mother. Both are equally clear and interpretable. If the analyst recognizes the true layering of the positive transference; if he realizes that in the positive transference the reactive love of the father is the most superficial layer, the hatred of the father the second, and the transferred love of the mother the deepest layer, then, certainly, he will let the latter attitude alone, no matter how obvious it may be. If he did not, if, instead, he were to pick out first the transferred love of the mother, then there would be, between his interpretations of the incest love and the experience of the patient, the latent hatred of the father in the form of reactive transference love. This would present an impenetrable block of resistance. The interpretation which should have passed through the topically higher layer of distrust, unbelief and defense, would be seemingly accepted. But seemingly only; it would remain in-effective therapeutically and would have only one result: the patient, frightened by this interpretation and put on his guard, would even more industriously hide the hatred of the father and, because of intensified guilt feelings, would become still more "good." The analytic situation would be chaotic.

It is a matter, then, of picking, out of the material which flows from many psychic layers, that part which in the present or preceding transference resistance assumes a central position and which is not covered up by other attitudes. As theoretical as this may sound, it is possible of execution in any average case.

What, then, happens to all the rest of the material which at present is less important? Usually it is sufficient not to enter upon it; with that, it automatically recedes. However, it happens very often that a patient puts an attitude or certain experiences into the foreground, in order to hide other things which are of more immediate importance. Clearly, such a resistance must be elimi-nated by *constantly pointing to that which is being hidden* while no attention is being paid to the "red herring." A typical example is the behavior of the patient in latent negative transference: he tries to hide his latent criticism and aversion by forcedly laudatory comments about the analyst and the analysis. If one analyzes this resistance, one easily arrives at the patient's motive, his fear of expressing criticism.

Only rarely is it necessary to suppress material which flows all too rapidly, as in the case when unconscious perverse or incestuous tendencies become conscious too early and too massively, at a time when the patient is as yet not ready to deal with them. If neglecting the material is not sufficient, one will have to divert the patient.

In this manner, the central content of the transference resistances remains in constant close contact with the memories, and the affects aroused by the transference become automatically associated with the memories. Thus one avoids the dangerous situation where memories appear without affects. The chaotic situation, on the other hand, is characterized by a latent resistance which remains unresolved for months and binds all affects, while at the same time the memories appear in wild disorder, concerning, say, today castration anxiety, then oral phantasies and then again incest phantasies.

By the proper selection of the material for interpretation we achieve a *continuity* in the analysis. We thus not only understand the present-day situation at any given time but can follow, like a red thread, the logical development of the transference. Our work is facilitated by the fact that the resistances which, after all, are nothing but individual bits of the neurosis, make their appearance in a logical sequence which is determined by the history and structure of the neurosis.

### 3. CONSISTENCY IN RESISTANCE ANALYSIS

Thus far, we have dealt with the technique of interpretation of meaning and resistance; we saw that it must be ordered and systematic corresponding to the individual structure of the neurosis. In enumerating the errors in interpretation, we distinguished systematic from inconsistent interpretation. For we found that many cases become chaotic in spite of systematic interpretation because of a lack of *consistency in the working through of resistances which had already been interpreted.*

If one has happily gotten past the barrier of the first transference resistance, the memory work usually proceeds quickly and penetrates to childhood. But soon the patient will meet new layers of forbidden material which he now tries to ward off with a second front of transference resistances. The same process of resistance analysis starts again, with the difference that this time it has a somewhat different character. Then, it was a matter of the first difficulty; the new resistance has already an analytic past which has not remained without influence on it. One would expect that the patient, having learned from the first resistance analysis, would now cooperate in the elimination of the difficulty. But practical experience teaches us differently: in almost all cases, the patient reactivates, alongside the new resistance, the old one; sometimes he even relapses into the old resistance without showing the new one. The whole situation is complicated by this layering. The patient again takes recourse to the old resistance position which had apparently been eliminated. If, now, one tackles the new resistance first or exclusively, one neglects an interposed layer, namely, the reactivated old resistance and runs the risk of squandering one's interpretations. One can spare oneself disappointments and failures if one always goes back to the old resistance—no matter whether it is more or less manifest—and begins the work of resolving the resistance from there. In this way, one gradually penetrates to the new resistance and avoids the danger of gaining a new piece of territory while the enemy again settles down in that which was previously gained.

It is important to undermine the neurosis from the cardinal resistance, from a definite strong-point, as it were, instead of focusing one's attention on detail resistances, that is, attacking the neurosis at many different points which have no immediate connection. If one deploys the resistances and the analytic material consistently from the strong-point of the first transference resistance, one never loses sight of the total situation, past and present; this guarantees the indispensable continuity of the analysis and its thorough working through. Provided that one is dealing with already known typical disease pictures and provided that the resistance analysis was correctly carried out, it is even possible to foresee the sequence in which certain tendencies will appear as acute transference resistances.

No argument could convince us that haphazard interpretations of meaning or treatment of all patients according to the same schema could solve the enormous problems of psychotherapy. Those who attempt such things only show that they have not comprehended the real problems of psychotherapy and do not know what the "cutting of the Gordian knot" really means: the destruction of the possibilities of analytic cure. An analysis carried out in such fashion is beyond repair. Interpretation may be likened to a valuable drug which has to be used sparingly if it is not to lose its efficacy. Our experience shows that the laborious unraveling of the knot is still the shortest way to real success.

Then there are those who misinterpret the concept of analytic passivity and become past masters in waiting. They can give us ample case material to illustrate the chaotic situation. In resistance phases, it is up to the analyst to direct the course of the analysis; it is in the hands of the patient only in resistance-free periods. Nothing else can have been Freud's meaning. The danger of staying silent on principle or of letting the patient "float along" is no less than that of haphazard interpretations or interpretations according to a theoretical schema, for the patient as well as for the development of psychoanalytic therapy.

In certain forms of resistance, this kind of passivity is a very serious mistake. Say, a patient evades a resistance or the discussion of the corresponding material. He touches on quite a different subject, until there, too, he develops resistances, whereupon he switches to a third subject, etc. This "zigzag technique" may go on indefinitely, no matter whether one watches it "passively" or follows the patient step by step with interpretations. Since the patient is obviously in constant flight and since his efforts to satisfy the analyst with substitute productions remain sterile, the task of the analyst is that of *again and again bringing him back to the first resistance position* until he finds the courage to tackle it analytically.[2]

---

[2] *Footnote, 1945:* Many patients present a resistance in the form of compulsive talking. This compulsion is, to begin with, nothing but a *biological manifestation* of a chronic spasm of the deep muscles of neck and throat. There is a need for talking, irrespective of the content. In orgone therapy, one asks such patients to keep silent; then, after some time, the anxiety appears which causes this compulsive symptom. The cure of the compulsive talking is brought about by the elimination of the muscular armoring in the throat.

Or the patient may take flight into the infantile, may give away what otherwise would be well-guarded secrets, only in order to hold the one position. These communications have, at best, no therapeutic value. Unless one prefers to interrupt, one may listen to them; the important thing is to work on the one position from which the patient escaped. The same is true in the case of the flight into actuality. The ideal is the development and analysis of the transference neurosis in a straight line, corresponding to the original neurosis; in this case, the patient unfolds his resistances systematically and in between produces memories with the corresponding affects.

The much-discussed question whether an "active" or a "passive" attitude in analysis is better, is, put that way, senseless. Generally speaking, one *cannot act too early in analyzing resistances, and one cannot be too reserved in the interpretation of the unconscious, apart from resistances*. The customary procedure is the reverse: one is too courageous in giving interpretations of meaning and becomes hesitant as soon as a resistance makes its appearance.

## Chapter IV

# ON THE TECHNIQUE OF CHARACTER-ANALYSIS *

## 1. INTRODUCTORY REVIEW

Our therapeutic method is determined by the following basic theoretical concepts. The *topical* standpoint determines the technical principle that the unconscious has to be made conscious. The *dynamic* standpoint determines the rule that this has to take place not directly but by way of resistance analysis. The *economic* standpoint and the psychological structure determine the rule that the resistance analysis has to be carried out in a certain order according to the individual patient.

As long as the topical process, the making conscious of the unconscious, was considered the only task of analytic technique, the formula that the unconscious manifestations should be interpreted *in the sequence in which they appeared* was correct. The dynamics of the analysis, that is, whether or not the making conscious also released the corresponding affect, whether the analysis influenced the patient beyond a merely intellectual understanding, that was more or less left to chance. The inclusion of the dynamic element, that is, the demand that the patient should not only remember things but also experience them, already complicated the simple formula that one had to "make the unconscious conscious." However, the dynamics of the analytic affect do not depend on the contents but on the resistances which the patient puts up against them and on the emotional experience in overcoming them. This makes the analytic task a vastly different one. From the topical standpoint, it is sufficient to bring into the patient's consciousness, one after the other, the manifest elements of the unconscious;

---

* First presented at the X. International Psychoanalytic Congress, Innsbruck, 1927.

in other words, the guiding line is the *content* of the material. If one also considers the dynamic factor one has to relinquish this guiding line in favor of another which comprehends the content of the material as well as the affects: that of the *successive resistances*. In doing so we meet, in most patients, with a difficulty which we have not yet mentioned.

## 2. CHARACTER ARMOR AND CHARACTER RESISTANCE

*a) The inability to follow the fundamental rule.*

Rarely are our patients immediately accessible to analysis, capable of following the fundamental rule and of really opening up to the analyst. They cannot immediately have full confidence in a strange person; more importantly, years of illness, constant influencing by a neurotic milieu, bad experiences with physicians, in brief, the whole secondary warping of the personality have created a situation unfavorable to analysis. The elimination of this difficulty would not be so hard were it not supported by the character of the patient which is part and parcel of his neurosis. It is a difficulty which has been termed "narcissistic barrier." There are, in principle, two ways of meeting this difficulty, in especial, the rebellion against the fundamental rule.

One, which seems the usual one, is a direct education to analysis by information, reassurance, admonition, talking-to, etc. That is, one attempts to educate the patient to analytic candor by the establishment of some sort of positive transference. This corresponds to the technique proposed by Nunberg. Experience shows, however, that this pedagogical method is very uncertain; it lacks the basis of analytic clarity and is exposed to the constant variations in the transference situation.

The other way is more complicated and as yet not applicable in all patients, but far more certain. It is that of *replacing the pedagogical measures by analytic interpretations*. Instead of inducing the patient into analysis by advice, admonitions and transference manoeuvres, one focuses one's attention on the actual behavior of the patient and its meaning: *why* he doubts, or is late, or talks in a haughty or confused fashion, or communicates only

every other or third thought, why he criticizes the analysis or produces exceptionally much material or material from exceptional
depths. If, for example, a patient talks in a haughty manner, in
technical terms, one may try to convince him that this is not good
for the progress of the analysis, that he better give it up and behave less haughtily, for the sake of the analysis. Or, one may relinquish all attempts at persuasion and wait until one understands
why the patient behaves in this and no other way. One may then
find that his behavior is an attempt to compensate his feeling of
inferiority toward the analyst and may influence him by consistent
interpretation of the meaning of his behavior. This procedure, in
contrast to the first-mentioned, is in full accord with the principle
of analysis.

This attempt to replace pedagogical and similar active measures
seemingly necessitated by the characteristic behavior of the patient, by purely analytic interpretations led unexpectedly to the
analysis of the *character.*

Certain clinical experiences make it necessary to distinguish,
among the various resistances we meet, a certain group as *character resistances.* They get their specific stamp not from their content
but from the patient's specific way of acting and reacting. The
compulsive character develops specifically different resistances
than does the hysterical character; the latter different resistances
from the impulsive or neurasthenic character. The *form* of the
typical reactions which differ from character to character—though
the contents may be the same—*is determined by infantile experiences just like the content of the symptoms or phantasies.*

### b) Whence the character resistances?

Quite some time ago, Glover worked on the problem of differentiating character neuroses from symptom neuroses. Alexander
also operated on the basis of this distinction. In my earlier writings, I also followed it. More exact comparison of the cases
showed, however, that this distinction makes sense only insofar as
there are neuroses with circumscribed symptoms and others without them; the former were called "symptom neuroses," the latter,
"character neuroses." In the former, understandably, the symp-

toms are more obvious, in the latter the neurotic character traits. But, we must ask, are there symptoms without a neurotic reaction basis, in other words, without a neurotic character? The difference between the character neuroses and the symptom neuroses is only that in the latter the neurotic character also produced symptoms, that it became concentrated in them, as it were. If one recognizes the fact that the basis of a symptom neurosis is always a neurotic character, then it is clear that we shall have to deal with character-neurotic resistances in *every* analysis, that every analysis must be a character-analysis.

Another distinction which becomes immaterial from the standpoint of character-analysis is that between chronic neuroses, that is, neuroses which developed in childhood, and acute neuroses, which developed late. For the important thing is not whether the symptoms have made their appearance early or late. The important thing is that the neurotic character, the reaction basis for the symptom neurosis, was, in its essential traits, already formed at the period of the Oedipus phase. It is an old clinical experience that the boundary line which the patient draws between health and the outbreak of the disease becomes always obliterated during the analysis.

Since symptom formation does not serve as a distinguishing criterion we shall have to look for others. There is, first of all, insight into illness, and rationalization.

The lack of insight into illness is not an absolutely reliable but an essential sign of the character neurosis. The neurotic symptom is experienced as a foreign body and creates a feeling of being ill. The neurotic character trait, on the other hand, such as the exaggerated orderliness of the compulsive character or the anxious shyness of the hysterical character, are organically built into the personality. One may complain about being shy but does not feel ill for this reason. It is not until the characterological shyness turns into pathological blushing or the compulsion-neurotic orderliness into a compulsive ceremonial, that is, not until the neurotic character exacerbates symptomatically, that the person feels ill.

True enough, there are also symptoms for which there is no or only slight insight, things that are taken by the patient as bad habits or just peculiarities (chronic constipation, mild ejaculatio praecox, etc.). On the other hand, many character traits are often felt as illness, such as violent outbreaks of rage, tendency to lie, drink, waste money, etc. In spite of this, generally speaking, insight characterizes the neurotic symptom and its lack the neurotic character trait.

The second difference is that the symptom is never as thoroughly rationalized as the character. Neither a hysterical vomiting nor compulsive counting can be rationalized. The symptom appears meaningless, while the neurotic character is sufficiently rationalized not to appear meaningless or pathological. A reason is often given for neurotic character traits which would immediately be rejected as absurd if it were given for symptoms: "he just is that way." That implies that the individual was born that way, that this "happens to be" his character. Analysis shows this interpretation to be wrong; it shows that the character, for definite reasons, had to become that way and no different; that, in principle, it can be analyzed like the symptom and is alterable.

Occasionally, symptoms become part of the personality to such an extent that they resemble character traits. For example, a counting compulsion may appear only as part of general orderliness or a compulsive system only in terms of a compulsive work arrangement. Such modes of behavior are then considered as peculiarities rather than as signs of illness. So we can readily see that the concept of disease is an entirely fluid one, that there are all kinds of transitions from the symptom as an isolated foreign body over the neurotic character and the "bad habit" to rational action.

In comparison to the character trait, the symptom has a very simple construction with regard to its meaning and origin. True, the symptom also has a multiple determination; but the more deeply we penetrate into its determinations, the more we leave the realm of symptoms and the clearer becomes the characterological reaction basis. Thus one can arrive—theoretically—at the characterological reaction basis from any symptom. The symptom has its immediate determination in only a limited number of unconscious attitudes; hysterical vomiting, say, is based on a repressed fellatio phantasy or an oral wish for a child. Either expresses itself also characterologically, in a certain infantilism and maternal attitude. But the hysterical character which forms the basis of the symptom is determined by many—partly antagonistic—strivings and is expressed in a specific attitude or *way of being*. This is not as easy to dissect as the symptom; nevertheless, in principle it is, like the symptom, to be reduced to and understood from infantile strivings and experiences. While the symptom corresponds essentially to a single experience or striving, the character represents the specific way of being of an individual, an expression of his total past. For this reason, a symptom may develop suddenly while each individual character trait takes years to develop. In saying this we should not forget the fact that the symptom also could not have developed suddenly unless its characterological neurotic reaction basis had already been present.

The totality of the neurotic character traits makes itself felt in the analysis as a compact *defense mechanism* against our therapeutic endeavors. Analytic exploration of the development of this character "armor" shows that it also serves a definite economic purpose: on the one hand, it serves as a protection against the stimuli from the outer world, on the other hand against the inner libidinous strivings. The character armor can perform this task because libidinous and sadistic energies are consumed in the neurotic reaction formations, compensations and other neurotic attitudes. In the processes which form and maintain this armor, anxiety is constantly being bound up, in the same way as it is, according to Freud's description, in, say, compulsive symptoms. We shall have to say more later about the economy of character formation.

Since the neurotic character, in its economic function of a protecting armor, has established a certain *equilibrium*, albeit a neurotic one, the analysis presents a danger to this equilibrium. This is why the resistances which give the analysis of the individual case its specific imprint originate from this narcissistic protection mechanism. As we have seen, the mode of behavior is the result of the total development and as such can be analyzed and altered; thus it can also be the starting point for evolving the technique of character-analysis.

## c) The technique of analyzing the character resistance.

Apart from the dreams, associations, slips and other communications of the patients, their attitude, that is, *the manner* in which they relate their dreams, commit slips, produce their associations and make their communications, deserves special attention.[1] A patient who follows the fundamental rule from the beginning is a rare exception; it takes months of character-analytic work to make the patient halfway sufficiently honest in his communications. The manner in which the patient talks, in which he greets the analyst or looks at him, the way he lies on the couch, the inflection of the voice, the degree of conventional politeness, all these things are valuable criteria for judging the latent resistances against the fundamental rule, and understanding them makes it possible to alter or eliminate them by interpretation. The *how* of saying things is as important "material" for interpretation as is *what* the patient says. One often hears analysts complain that the analysis does not go well, that the patient does not produce any "material." By that is usually meant the content of associations and communications. But the manner in which the patient, say, keeps quiet, or his sterile repetitions, are also "material" which can and must be put to use. There is hardly any situation in which the patient brings "no material"; it is our fault if we are unable to utilize the patient's behavior as "material."

That the behavior and the form of the communications have analytic significance is nothing new. What I am going to talk about is the fact that these things present an avenue of approach to the analysis of the character in a very definite and almost perfect manner. Past failures with many cases of neurotic characters have taught us that in these cases the form of the communications is, at least in the beginning, always more important than their content. One only has to remember the latent resistances of the affect-lame, the "good," over-polite and ever-correct patients; those who

---

[1] *Footnote, 1945:* The *form* of expression is far more important than the *ideational content.* Today, in penetrating to the decisively important infantile experiences, we make use of the form of expression *exclusively.* Not the ideational contents but the form of expression is what leads us to the biological reactions which form the basis of the psychic manifestations.

always present a deceptive positive transference or who violently and stereotypically ask for love; those who make a game of the analysis; those who are always "armored," who smile inwardly about everything and everyone. One could continue this enumeration indefinitely; it is easy to see that a great deal of painstaking work will have to be done to master the innumerable individual technical problems.

For the purpose of orientation and of sketching the essential differences between character-analysis and symptom-analysis, let us assume two pairs of patients for comparison. Let us assume we have under treatment at the same time two men suffering from premature ejaculation; one is a passive-feminine, the other a phallic-aggressive character. Also, two women with an eating disturbance; one is a compulsive character, the other a hysteric.

Let us assume further that the premature ejaculation of both men has the same unconscious meaning: the fear of the paternal penis in the woman's vagina. In the analysis, both patients, on the basis of their castration anxiety which is the basis of the symptom, produce a negative father transference. Both hate the analyst (the father) because they see in him the enemy who frustrates their pleasure; both have the unconscious wish to do away with him. In this situation, the phallic-sadistic character will ward off the danger of castration by insults, depreciation and threats, while the passive-feminine character, in the same case, will become steadily more passive, submissive and friendly. In both patients, the character has become a resistance: one fends off the danger aggressively, the other tries to avoid it by a deceptive submission. It goes without saying that the character resistance of the passive-feminine patient is more dangerous because he works with hidden means: he produces a wealth of material, he remembers all kinds of infantile experiences, in short, he seems to cooperate splendidly. Actually, however, he camouflages a secret spitefulness and hatred; as long as he maintains this attitude he does not have the courage to show his real self. If, now, one enters only upon *what* he produces, without paying attention to his way of behavior, then no analytic endeavor will change his condition. He may even remember the hatred of his father, but he will not *ex-*

*perience* it unless one interprets consistently the meaning of his deceptive attitude *before* beginning to interpret the deep meaning of his hatred of the father.

In the case of the second pair, let us assume that an acute positive transference has developed. The central content of this positive transference is, in either patient, the same as that of the symptom, namely, an oral fellatio phantasy. But although the positive transference has the same content in either case, the form of the transference resistance will be quite different: the hysterical patient will, say, show an *anxious* silence and a shy behavior; the compulsive character a *spiteful* silence or a cold, haughty behavior. In one case the positive transference is warded off by aggression, in the other by anxiety. And the form of this defense will always be the same in the same patient: the hysterical patient will always defend herself anxiously, the compulsive patient aggressively, no matter what unconscious content is on the point of breaking through. That is, *in one and the same patient, the character resistance remains always the same and only disappears with the very roots of the neurosis.*

In the character armor, the *narcissistic defense* finds its concrete chronic expression. In addition to the known resistances which are mobilized against every new piece of unconscious material, we have to recognize a constant factor of a *formal* nature which originates from the patient's character. Because of this origin, we call the constant formal resistance factor "character resistance."

In summary, the most important aspects of the character resistance are the following:

The character resistance expresses itself not in the content of the material, but in the formal aspects of the general behavior, the manner of talking, of the gait, facial expression and typical attitudes such as smiling, deriding, haughtiness, over-correctness, the *manner* of the politeness or of the aggression, etc.

What is specific of the character resistance is not *what* the patient says or does, but *how* he talks and acts, not *what* he gives away in a dream but *how* he censors, distorts, etc.

The character resistance remains the same in one and the same patient no matter what the material is against which it is directed.

Different characters present the same material in a different manner. For example, a hysteric patient will ward off the positive father transference in an anxious manner, the compulsive woman in an aggressive manner.

The character resistance, which expresses itself formally, can be understood as to its content and can be reduced to infantile experiences and instinctual drives just like the neurotic symptom.[2]

During analysis, the character of a patient soon becomes a resistance. That is, in ordinary life, the character plays the same role as in analysis: that of a psychic protection mechanism. The individual is "characterologically armored" against the outer world and against his unconscious drives.

Study of character formation reveals the fact that the character armor was formed in infancy for the same reasons and purposes which the character resistance serves in the analytic situation. The appearance in the analysis of the character as resistance reflects its infantile genesis. The situations which make the character resistance appear in the analysis are exact duplicates of those situations in infancy which set character formation into motion. For this reason, we find in the character resistance both a defensive function and a transference of infantile relationships with the outer world.

*Economically* speaking, the character in ordinary life and the character resistance in the analysis serve the same function, that of avoiding unpleasure, of establishing and maintaining a psychic equilibrium—neurotic though it may be—and finally, that of absorbing repressed energies. One of its cardinal functions is that of binding "free-floating" anxiety, or, in other words, that of absorbing dammed-up energy. Just as the historical, infantile element is present and active in the neurotic symptoms, so it is in the character. This is why a consistent dissolving of character resistances provides an infallible and immediate avenue of approach to the central infantile conflict.

What, then, follows from these facts for the technique of char-

---

[2] By the realization of this fact, the formal element becomes included in the sphere of psychoanalysis which, hitherto, was centered primarily on the content.

acter-analysis? Are there essential differences between character-analysis and ordinary resistance analysis? There are. They are related to

a) the selection of the sequence in which the material is interpreted;

b) the technique of resistance interpretation itself.

As to a): If we speak of "selection of material," we have to expect an important objection: some will say that any selection is at variance with basic psychoanalytic principles, that one should let oneself be guided by the patient, that with any kind of selection one runs the danger of following one's personal inclinations. To this we have to say that in this kind of selection it is not a matter of neglecting analytic material; it is merely a matter of *safeguarding a logical sequence* of interpretation which corresponds to the structure of the individual neurosis. All the material is finally interpreted; only, in any given situation this or that detail is more important than another. Incidentally, the analyst always makes selections anyhow, for he has already made a selection when he does not interpret a dream in the sequence in which it is presented but selects this or that detail for interpretation. One also has made a selection if one pays attention only to the content of the communications but not to their form. In other words, the very fact that the patient presents material of the most diverse kinds forces one to make a selection; what matters is only that one select *correctly* with regard to the given analytic situation.

In patients who, for character reasons, consistently fail to follow the fundamental rule, and generally where one deals with a character resistance, one will be forced *constantly to lift the character resistance out of the total material* and to dissolve it by the interpretation of its meaning. That does not mean, of course, that one neglects the rest of the material; on the contrary, every bit of material is valuable which gives us information about the meaning and origin of the disturbing character trait; one merely postpones the interpretation of what material does not have an immediate connection with the transference resistance until such time as the character resistance is understood and overcome at least in its essential features. I have already tried to show (*cf.* Chapter III) what are the dangers of giving deep-reaching interpretations in the presence of undissolved character resistances.

As to b): We shall now turn to some special problems of character-analytic technique. First of all, we must point out a possible misunderstanding. We said that character-analysis begins with the emphasis on and the consistent analysis of the character resistance. It should be well understood that this does not mean that one asks the patient, say, not to be aggressive, not to deceive, not to talk in a confused manner, etc. Such procedure would be not only un-analytic but altogether sterile. The fact has to be emphasized again and again that what is described here as character-analysis has nothing to do with education, admonition, trying to make the patient behave differently, etc. In character-analysis, we ask ourself *why* the patient deceives, talks in a confused manner, why he is affect-blocked, etc.; we try to arouse the patient's interest in his character traits in order to be able, with his help, to explore analytically their origin and meaning. All we do is to lift the character trait which presents the cardinal resistance out of the level of the personality and to show the patient, if possible, the superficial connections between character and symptoms; it is left to him whether or not he will utilize his knowledge for an alteration of his character. In principle, the procedure is not different from the analysis of a symptom. What is added in character-analysis is merely that we isolate the character trait and confront the patient with it repeatedly until he begins to look at it objectively and to experience it like a painful symptom; thus, the character trait begins to be experienced as a foreign body which the patient wants to get rid of.

Surprisingly, this process brings about a change—although only a temporary one—in the personality. With progressing character-analysis, that impulse or trait automatically comes to the fore which had given rise to the character resistance in the transference. To go back to the illustration of the passive-feminine character: the more the patient achieves an objective attitude toward his tendency to passive submission, the more aggressive does he become. This is so because his passive-feminine attitude was essentially a reaction to repressed aggressive impulses. But with the aggression we also have a return of the infantile castration anxiety which in infancy had caused the change from aggressive to passive-feminine behavior. In this way the analysis of the character resistance leads directly to the center of the neurosis, the Oedipus complex.

One should not have any illusions, however. The isolation of such a character resistance and its analytic working-through usually takes many months of sustained effort and patient persistence. Once the breakthrough has succeeded, though, the analysis usually proceeds rapidly, with *emotionally* charged analytical experiences. If, on the other hand, one neglects such character resistances and instead simply follows the line of the material, interpreting everything in it, such resistances form a ballast which it is difficult if not impossible to remove. In that case, one gains more and more the impression that every interpretation of meaning was wasted, that the patient continues to doubt everything or only pretends to accept things, or that he meets everything with an inward smile. If the elimination of these resistances was not begun right in the beginning, they confront one with an insuperable obstacle in the later stages of the analysis, at a time when the most important interpretations of the Oedipus complex have already been given.

I have already tried to refute the objection that it is impossible to tackle resistances before one knows their *infantile* determination. The essential thing is first to see through the *present-day* meaning of the character resistance; this is usually possible without the infantile material. The latter is needed for the *dissolution* of the resistance. If at first one does no more than to show the patient the resistance and to interpret its present-day meaning, then the corresponding infantile material with the aid of which we can eliminate the resistance soon makes its appearance.

If we put so much emphasis on the analysis of the *mode* of behavior, this does not imply a neglect of the contents. We only add something that hitherto has been neglected. Experience shows that the analysis of character resistances has to assume first rank. This does not mean, of course, that one would only analyze character resistances up to a certain date and then begin with the interpretation of contents. The two phases—resistance analysis and analysis of early infantile experiences—overlap essentially; only in the beginning, we have a preponderance of character-analysis, that is, "education to analysis *by* analysis," while in the later stages the emphasis is on the contents and the infantile. This is, of course, no rigid rule but depends on the attitudes of the individual patient. In one patient, the interpretation of the infantile material will be begun earlier, in another later. It is a basic rule, however, not to give any deep-reaching interpretations—no matter how clear-cut the material—as long as the patient is not ready to assimilate them. Again, this is nothing new, but it seems that differences in analytic technique are largely determined by what one or the other analyst means by "ready for analytic interpretation." We also have to distinguish those contents which are part and parcel of the character resistance and others which belong to other spheres of experiencing. As a rule, the patient is in the beginning ready to take cognizance of the former, but not of the latter. Generally speaking, our character-analytic endeavors are nothing but an attempt to achieve the greatest possible security in the introduction of the analysis and in the interpretation of the infantile material. This leads us to the important task of studying and systematically describing the various forms of characterological transference resistances. If we understand them, the technique derives automatically from their structure.

*d) Derivation of the situational technique from the structure of the character resistance (interpretation technique of the defense).*

We now turn to the problem of how the situational technique of character-analysis can be derived from the structure of the character resistance in a patient who develops his resistances right in the beginning, the structure of which is, however, completely unintelligible at first. In the following case the character resistance had a very complicated structure; there were a great many coexistent and overlapping determinations. We shall try to describe the reasons which prompted me to begin the interpretation work with one aspect of the resistance and not with any other. Here also we will see that a consistent and logical interpretation of the defenses and of the mechanisms of the "armor" leads directly into the central infantile conflicts.

### A CASE OF MANIFEST INFERIORITY FEELINGS

A man 30 years of age came to analysis because he "didn't get any fun out of life." He did not really think he was sick but, he said, he had heard about psychoanalysis and perhaps it would make things clearer to him. When asked about symptoms, he stated he did not have any. Later it was found that his potency was quite defective. He did not quite dare approach women, had sexual intercourse very infrequently, and then he suffered from premature ejaculation and intercourse left him unsatisfied. He had very little insight into his impotence. He had become reconciled to it; after all, he said, there were a lot of men who "didn't need that sort of thing."

His behavior immediately betrayed a severely inhibited individual. He spoke without looking at one, in a low voice, haltingly, and embarrassedly clearing his throat. At the same time, there was an obvious attempt to suppress his embarrassment and to appear courageous. Nevertheless, his whole appearance gave the impression of severe feelings of inferiority.

Having been informed of the fundamental rule, the patient began to talk hesitatingly and in a low voice. Among the first communications was the recollection of two "terrible" experiences. Once he had run over a woman with an automobile and she had died of her injuries. Another time, as a medical orderly during the war, he had had to do a tracheotomy. The bare recollection of these two experiences filled him with horror. In the course of the first few sessions he then talked, in the same monotonous, low and suppressed manner about his youth. Being next to the youngest of a number of children, he was relegated to an inferior place. His oldest brother, some twenty years his senior, was the parents' favorite; this brother had traveled a good deal, "knew the world," prided himself on his experiences and when he came home from one of his travels "the whole house pivoted around him." Although the content of his story made the envy of this brother and the hatred of him obvious enough, the patient, in response to a cautious query, denied ever having felt anything like that toward his brother. Then he talked about his mother, how good she had been to him and how she had died when he was 7 years of age. At this, he began to cry softly; he became ashamed of this and did not say anything for some time. It seemed clear that his mother had been the only person who had given him some love and attention and that her loss had been a severe shock to him. After her death, he had spent 5 years in the house of this brother. It was not the content but the tone of his story which revealed his enormous bitterness about the unfriendly, cold and domineering behavior of his brother. Then he related in a few brief sentences that now he had a friend who loved and admired him very much. After this, a continuous silence set in. A few days later he related a dream: *He saw himself in a foreign city with his friend; only, the face of his friend was different.* The fact that the patient had left his own city for the purpose of the analysis suggested that the man in the dream represented the analyst. This identification of the analyst with the friend might have been interpreted as a beginning positive transference. In view of the total situation, however, this would have been unwise. He himself recognized the analyst in the friend, but had nothing to add to this. Since he either kept silent or else expressed his doubts that *he* would be able to carry out the analysis, I told him that he had something against me but did not have the courage to come out with it. He denied this categorically, whereupon I told him that he also never had had the courage to express his inimical impulses toward his brother, not even to think them consciously; and that apparently he had established some kind of connection between his older brother and myself. This was true in itself, but I made the mistake of interpreting his resistance at too deep a level. Nor did the interpretation have any success; on the contrary, the inhibition became intensified. So I waited a few days until I should be able to understand, from his behavior, the more important present-day meaning of his resistance. What was clear at this time was that there was a transference not only of the hatred of the brother but also a strong defense against a feminine attitude (*cf.* the dream about the friend). But an interpretation in this direction would have been inadvisable at this time. So I continued to point out that for some reason he defended himself against me and the analysis, that his whole being pointed to his being blocked against the analysis. To this he agreed by saying that, yes, that was the way he was generally in life, rigid, inaccessible and on the defensive. While I demonstrated to him his defense in every session, on every possible occasion, I was struck by the monotonous expression with which he uttered his complaints. Every session began with the same sentences: "I don't feel anything, the analysis doesn't have any influence on me, I don't see how I'll ever achieve it, nothing comes to my mind, the analysis doesn't have any influence on me," etc. I did not understand what he wanted to express with these complaints, and yet it was clear that here was the key to an understanding of his resistance.[3]

Here we have a good opportunity for studying the difference between the character-analytic and the active-suggestive education to analysis. I might have admonished him in a kindly way to tell me more about this and that; I might have been able thus to establish an artificial positive transference; but experience with other cases had shown me that one does not get far with such procedures. Since his whole behavior did not leave any room for doubt that he refuted the analysis in general and me in particular, I could simply stick to this interpretation and wait for further reactions. When, on one occasion, the talk reverted to the dream, he said the best proof for his not refuting me was that he identified me with his friend. I suggested to him that possibly he had expected me to love and admire him as much as his friend did; that he then was disappointed and very much resented my reserve. He had to admit that he had had such thoughts but that he had not dared to tell them to me. He then related how he always only *demanded* love and especially recognition, and that he had a very *defensive*

---

[3] *Footnote, 1945:* The explanation given here is insufficient, although it is psychologically correct. Today we know that such complaints are the immediate expression of muscular armoring. The patient complains about affect-lameness because of a block in his plasmatic currents and sensations. The disturbance, then, is primarily of a *biophysical* nature. Orgone therapy eliminates the block in motility not with psychological but with biophysical means.

attitude toward men with a particularly masculine appearance. He said he did not feel equal to such men, and in the relationship with his friend he had played the feminine part. Again there was material for interpreting his feminine transference but his total behavior warned against it. The situation was difficult, for the elements of his resistance which I already understood, the transference of hatred from his brother, and the narcissistic-feminine attitude toward his superiors, were strongly warded off; consequently, I had to be very careful or I might have provoked him into breaking off the analysis. In addition, he continued to complain in every session, in the same way, that the analysis did not touch him, etc.; this was something which I still did not understand after about four weeks of analysis, and yet, I felt that it was an essential and acutely active character resistance.

I fell ill and had to interrupt the analysis for two weeks. The patient sent me a bottle of brandy as a tonic. When I resumed the analysis he seemed to be glad. At the same time, he continued his old complaints and related that he was very much bothered by thoughts about death, that he constantly was afraid that something had happened to some member of his family; and that during my illness he had always been thinking that I might die. It was when this thought bothered him particularly badly one day that he had sent me the brandy. At this point, the temptation was great to interpret his repressed death wishes. The material for doing so was ample, but I felt that such an interpretation would be fruitless because it would bounce back from the wall of his complaints that "nothing touches me, the analysis has no influence on me." In the meantime, the secret double meaning of his complaint, "nothing touches me" ("*nichts dringt in mich ein*") had become clear; it was an expression of his most deeply repressed transference wish for anal intercourse. But would it have been justifiable to point out to him his homosexual love impulse— which, it is true, manifested itself clearly enough—while he, with his whole being, continued to protest against the analysis? First it had to become clear what was the meaning of his complaints about the uselessness of the analysis. True, I could have shown him that he was wrong in his complaints: he dreamed without interruption, the thoughts about death became more intense, and many other things went on in him. But I knew from experience that that would not have helped the situation. Furthermore, I felt distinctly the armor which stood between the unconscious material and the analysis, and had to assume that the existing resistance would not let any interpretation penetrate to the unconscious. For these reasons, I did no more than consistently to show him his attitude, interpreting it as the expression of a violent defense, and telling him that we had to wait until we understood this behavior. He understood already that the death thoughts on the occasion of my illness had not necessarily been the expression of a loving solicitude.

In the course of the next few weeks it became increasingly clear that his inferiority feeling connected with his feminine transference played a considerable role in his behavior and his complaints. Yet, the situation still did not seem ripe for interpretation; the meaning of his behavior was not sufficiently clear. To summarize the essential aspects of the solution as it was found later:

a) He desired recognition and love from me as from all men who appeared masculine to him. That he wanted love and had been disappointed by me had already been interpreted repeatedly, without success.

b) He had a definite attitude of envy and hatred toward me, transferred from his brother. This could, at this time, not be interpreted because the interpretation would have been wasted.

c) He defended himself against his feminine transference. This defense could not be interpreted without touching upon the warded-off femininity.

d) He felt inferior before me, because of his femininity. His eternal complaints could only be the expression of this feeling of inferiority.

Now I interpreted his inferiority feeling toward me. At first, this led nowhere, but after I had consistently held up his behavior to him for several days, he did bring some communications concerning his boundless envy, not of me, but other men of whom he also felt inferior. Now it suddenly occurred to me that his constant complaining could have only one meaning: "The analysis has no influence on me," that is, "It is no good," that is, "the analyst is inferior, is impotent, cannot achieve anything with me." *The complaints were in part a triumph over the analyst, in part a reproach to him.* I told him what I thought of his complaints. The result was astounding. Immediately he brought forth a wealth of examples which showed that he always acted this way when anybody tried to influence him. He could not tolerate the superiority of anybody and always tried to tear them down. He had always done the exact opposite of what any superior had asked him to do. There appeared a wealth of recollections of his spiteful and deprecatory behavior toward teachers.

Here, then, was his suppressed aggression, the most extreme manifestation of which thus far had been his death wishes. But soon the resistance reappeared in the same old form, there were the same complaints, the same reserve, the same silence. But now I knew that my discovery had greatly impressed him, which had *increased* his feminine attitude; this, of course, resulted in an intensified defense against the femininity. In analyzing the resistance, I started again from the inferiority feeling toward me; but now I deepened the interpretation by the statement that he did not only feel inferior but that, because of his inferiority, he felt himself in a female role toward me, which hurt his masculine pride.

Although previously the patient had presented ample material with regard to his feminine attitude toward masculine men and had had full insight for this fact, now he denied it all. This was a new problem. Why should he now refuse to admit what he had previously described himself? I told him that he felt so inferior toward me that he did not want to accept any explanation from me even if that implied his going back on himself. He realized this to be true and now talked about the relationship with his friend in some detail. He had actually played the feminine role and there often had been sexual intercourse between the legs. Now I was able to show him that his defensive attitude in the analysis was nothing but the struggle against the surrender to the analysis which, to his unconscious, was apparently linked up with the idea of surrendering to the analyst in a female fashion. This hurt his pride, and this was the reason for his stubborn resistance against the influence of the analysis. To this he reacted with a confirmatory dream: he lies on a sofa with the analyst, who kisses him. This clear dream provoked a new phase of resistance in the old form of complaints that the analysis did not touch him, that he was cold, etc. Again I interpreted the complaints as a depreciation of the analysis and a defense against surrendering to it. But at the same time I began to explain to him the economic meaning of this defense. I told him that from what he had told thus far about his infancy and adolescence it was obvious that he had closed himself up against all disappointments by the outer world and against the rough and cold treatment by his father, brother and teachers; that this seemed to have been his only salvation even if it demanded great sacrifices in happiness.

This interpretation seemed highly plausible to him and he soon produced memories of his attitude toward his teachers. He always felt they were cold and distant—a clear projection of his own attitude—and although he was aroused when they beat or scolded him he remained indifferent. In this connection he said that he often had wished I had been more severe. This wish did not seem to fit the situation at that time; only much later it became clear that he wished to put me and my prototypes, the teachers, in a bad light with his spite. For a few days the analysis proceeded smoothly, without any resistances; he now remembered that there had been a period in his childhood when he had been very wild and aggressive. At the same time he produced dreams with a strong feminine attitude toward me. I could only assume that the recollection of his aggression had mobilized the guilt feeling which now was expressed in the passive-feminine dreams. I avoided an analysis of these dreams not only because they had no immediate connection with the actual transference situation, but also because it seemed to me that he was not ready to understand the connection between his aggression and the dreams which expressed a guilt feeling. Many analysts will consider this an arbitrary selection of material. Experience shows, however, that the best therapeutic effect is to be expected when an immediate connection is already established between the transference situation and the infantile material. I only ventured the assumption that, to judge from his recollections of his aggressive infantile behavior, he had at one time been quite different, the exact opposite of what he was today, and that the analysis would have to find out at what time and under what circumstances this change in his character had taken place. I told him that his present femininity probably was an avoidance of his aggressive masculinity. To this the patient did not react except by falling back into his old resistance of complaining that he could not achieve it, that the analysis did not touch him, etc.

I interpreted again his inferiority feeling and his recurrent attempt to prove the analysis, or the analyst, to be impotent; but now I also tried to work on the transference from the brother, pointing out that he had said that his brother always played the dominant role. Upon this he entered only with much hesitation, apparently because we were dealing with the central conflict of his infancy; he talked again about how much attention his mother had paid to his brother, without, however, mentioning any subjective attitude toward this. As was shown by a cautious approach to the question, the envy of his brother was completely repressed. Apparently, this envy was so closely associated with intense hatred that not even the envy was allowed to become conscious. The approach to this problem provoked a particularly violent resistance which continued for days in the form of his stereotyped complaints about his inability. Since the resistance did not budge it had to be assumed that here was a particularly acute rejection of the person of the analyst. I asked him again to talk quite freely and without fear about the analysis and, in particular, about the analyst, and to tell me what impression I had made on him on the occasion of the first meeting.[4] After much hesitation he said the analyst had appeared to him so masculine and brutal, like a man who is absolutely ruthless with women. So I asked him about his attitude toward men who gave an impression of being potent.

This was at the end of the fourth month of the analysis. Now

---

[4] Since then I am in the habit of soon asking the patient to describe my person. This measure always proves useful for the elimination of blocked transference situations.

for the first time that repressed attitude toward the brother broke through which had the closest connection with his most disturbing transference attitude, the envy of potency. With much affect he now remembered that he had always condemned his brother for always being after women, seducing them and bragging about it afterwards. He said I had immediately reminded him of his brother. I explained to him that obviously he saw in me his potent brother and that he could not open up to me because he condemned me and resented my assumed superiority just as he used to resent that of his brother; furthermore, it was plain now that the basis of his inferiority feeling was a feeling of impotence.

Then occurred what one always sees in a correctly and consistently carried-out analysis: *the central element of the character resistance rose to the surface.* All of a sudden he remembered that he had repeatedly compared his small penis with the big one of his brother and how he had envied his brother.

As might have been expected, a new wave of resistance occurred; again the complaint, "I can't do anything." Now I could go somewhat further in the interpretation and show him that he was acting out his impotence. His reaction to this was wholly unexpected. In connection with my interpretation of his distrust he said for the first time that he had never believed anyone, that he did not believe anything, and probably also not in the analysis. This was, of course, an important step ahead, but the connection of this statement with the analytic situation was not altogether clear. For two hours he talked about all the many disappointments which he had experienced and believed that they were a rational explanation of his distrust. Again the old resistance reappeared; as it was not clear what had precipitated it this time, I kept waiting. The old behavior continued for several days. I only interpreted again those elements of the resistance with which I was already well acquainted. Then, suddenly, a new element of the resistance appeared: he said he was *afraid of the analysis because it might rob him of his ideals.* Now the situation was clear again. He had transferred his castration anxiety from his brother to me. He was afraid of me. Of course, I did not touch upon his castration anxiety but proceeded again from his inferiority feeling and his impotence and asked him whether his high ideals did not make him feel superior and better than everybody else. He admitted this openly; more than that, he said that he was really better than all those who kept running after women and lived sexually like animals. He added, however, that this feeling was all too often disturbed by his feeling of impotence, and that apparently he had not become quite reconciled to his sexual weakness after all. Now I could show him the neurotic manner in which he tried to overcome his feeling of impotence: he was trying to recover a feeling of potency in the realm of ideals. I showed him the mechanism of compensation and pointed out again the resistances against the analysis which originated from his secret feeling of superiority. I told him that not only did he think himself secretly better and cleverer than others; it was for this very reason that he resisted the analysis. For if it succeeded, he would have taken recourse to the aid of somebody else and it would have vanquished his neurosis, the secret pleasure gain of which had just been unearthed. From the standpoint of the neurosis this would be a defeat which, furthermore, to his unconscious, would mean becoming a woman. In this way, by progressing from the ego and its defense mechanisms, I prepared the soil for an interpretation of the castration complex and of the feminine fixation.

The character-analysis had succeeded, then, in penetrating from his mode of behavior directly to the center of his neurosis, his castration anxiety, the envy of his brother because of his mother's favoritism, and the disappointment in his mother. What is important here is not that these unconscious elements rose to the surface; that often occurs spontaneously. What is important is the logical sequence and the close contact with the ego-defense and the transference in which they came up; further, that this took place without any urging, purely as the result of analytic interpretation of the behavior; further, that it took place with the corresponding affects. This is what constitutes a consistent character-analysis; it is a thorough working through of the conflicts assimilated by the ego.

In contrast, let us consider what probably would have happened without a consistent emphasis on the defenses. Right at the beginning, there was the possibility of interpreting the passive-homosexual attitude toward the brother, and the death wishes. Undoubtedly, dreams and associations would have provided further relevant material for interpretation. But without a previous systematic and detailed working through of his ego-defense, no interpretation would have affectively penetrated; the result would have been an intellectual knowledge of his passive desires alongside with a violent affective defense against them. The affects belonging to the passivity and the murderous impulses would have continued to remain in the defense function. The final result would have been a chaotic situation, the typical hopeless picture of an analysis rich in interpretations and poor in results.

A few months' patient and persistent work on his ego-defense, particularly its form (complaints, manner of speech, etc.) raised the ego to that level which was necessary for the assimilation of the repressed, it loosened the affects and brought about their displacement in the direction of the repressed ideas. One cannot say, therefore, that in this case two different techniques would have been feasible; there was only one possibility if one was to alter the patient *dynamically*. I trust that this case makes clear the different concept of the application of theory to technique. The most important criterion of an orderly analysis is the giving of *few* interpretations which are to the point and consistent, instead of a great many which are unsystematic and do not take into consideration the dynamic and economic element. If one does not let oneself be led astray by the material, if, instead, one evaluates correctly its dynamic position and economic role, then one gets the material later, it is true, but more thoroughly and more charged with affect. The second criterion is a continuous connection between present-day situation and infantile situation. While in the beginning the various elements of the content co-exist side by side without any order, this changes into a logical sequence of resistances and contents, a sequence determined by the dynamics and structure of the individual neurosis. With unsystematic interpretation, one has to make one new start after another, guessing rather than knowing one's way; in the case of character-analytic work on the resistances, on the other hand, the analytic process develops as if by itself. In the former case, the analysis will run smoothly in the beginning only to get progressively into more and more difficulties; in the latter case, the greatest difficulties are met in the first few weeks and months of the treatment, to give way progressively to smooth work even on the most deeply repressed material. The fate of every analysis depends on its introduction, that is, the correct or incorrect handling of the resistances. The third criterion, then, is that of tackling the case not in this or that spot which happens to be tangible but at the spot which hides the most essential ego-defense; and the systematic enlarging of the breach which has been made into the unconscious; and the working out of that infantile fixation which is affectively most important at any given time. A certain unconscious position which manifests itself in a dream or an association may have a central significance for the neurosis and yet may at any given time be quite unimportant with regard to its technical significance. In our patient, the feminine attitude toward the brother was of central pathogenic significance; yet in the first few months the technical problem was the fear of the loss of the compensation for the impotence by high ideals. The mistake which is usually made is that of attacking the central pathogenic point of the neurosis which commonly manifests itself somehow right at the beginning. What has to be attacked instead are the respective important present-day positions which, if worked on systematically, one after the other, lead *of necessity* to the central pathogenic situation. It is important, therefore, and in many cases decisive, *how, when* and from which side one proceeds toward the central point of the neurosis.

What we have described here as character-analysis fits without difficulty into Freud's theory of resistances, their formation and dissolution. We know that every resistance consists of an id-impulse which is warded off and an ego-impulse which wards it off. Both impulses are unconscious. In principle, then, one would seem to be free to interpret first either the id-impulse or the ego-impulse. For example: If a homosexual resistance in the form of keeping silent appears right at the beginning of the analysis, one can approach the id-impulse by telling the patient that he is occupied with thoughts about loving the analyst or being loved by him; one has interpreted his positive transference, and if he does not take flight it will, at best, take a long time before he can come to terms with such a forbidden idea. The better way, then, is to approach first the *defense of the ego* which is more closely related to the conscious ego. One will tell the patient at first only that he is keeping silent because—*"for one reason or another,"* that is, without touching upon the id-impulse—he is defending himself against the analysis, presumably because it has become somehow dangerous to him. In the first case one has tackled the id aspect, in the latter case the ego aspect of the resistance, the defense.

Proceeding in this manner, we comprehend the negative transference in which every defense finally results, as well as the character, the armor of the ego. The superficial, more nearly conscious layer of *every* resistance must of necessity be a negative attitude toward the analyst, no matter whether the warded-off id-impulse is hatred or love. The ego projects its defense against the id-impulse to the analyst who has become a dangerous enemy because, by his insistence on the fundamental rule, he has provoked id-impulses and has disturbed the neurotic equilibrium. In its defense, the ego makes use of very old forms of negative attitudes; it utilizes hate impulses from the id even if it is warding off love impulses.

If we adhere to the rule of tackling resistances from the ego side, we always dissolve, at the same time, a certain amount of negative transference, of hatred. This obviates the danger of overlooking the destructive tendencies which often are extremely well hidden; it also strengthens the positive transference. The patient also comprehends the ego interpretation more easily because it is more in accordance with conscious experience than the id interpretation; this makes him better prepared for the latter which follows at a later time.

The ego defense has always the same form, corresponding to

the character of the patient, whatever the repressed id-impulse may be. Conversely, the same id-impulse is warded off in different ways in different individuals. If we interpret only the id-impulse, we leave the character untouched. If, on the other hand, we always approach the resistances from the defense, from the ego side, we include the neurotic character in the analysis. In the first case, we say immediately *what* the patient wards off. In the latter case, we first make clear to him *that* he wards off "something," then, *how* he does it, what are the means of defense (character-analysis); only at last, when the analysis of the resistance has progressed far enough, is he told—or finds out for himself—what it is he is warding off. On this long detour to the interpretation of the id-impulses, all corresponding attitudes of the ego have been analyzed. This obviates the danger that the patient learns something too early or that he remains affectless and without participation.

Analyses in which so much analytic attention is centered upon the attitudes take a more orderly and logical course while the theoretical research does not suffer in the least. One obtains the important infantile experiences later, it is true; but this is more than compensated for by the emotional aliveness with which the infantile material comes up *after* the analytic work on the character resistances.

On the other hand, we should not fail to mention certain unpleasant aspects of a consistent character-analysis. It is a far heavier burden for the patient; he suffers much more than when one leaves the character out of consideration. True, this has the advantage of a selective process: those who cannot stand it would not have achieved success anyhow, and it is better to find that out after a few months than after a few years. Experience shows that if the character resistance does not give way a satisfactory result cannot be expected. The overcoming of the character resistance does *not* mean that the character is altered; that, of course, is possible only after the analysis of its infantile sources. It only means that the patient has gained an objective view of his character and an analytic interest in it; once this has been achieved a favorable progress of the analysis is probable.

*e) The loosening of the character armor.*

As we said before, the essential difference between the analysis of a symptom and that of a neurotic character trait consists in the fact that the symptom is, from the beginning, isolated and objectively looked at while the character trait has to be continually pointed out so that the patient will attain the same attitude toward it as toward a symptom. Only rarely is this achieved easily. Most patients have a very slight tendency to look at their character objectively. This is understandable because it is a matter of loosening the narcissistic protection mechanism, the freeing of the anxiety which is bound up in it.

A man of 25 came to analysis because of some minor symptoms and because he suffered from a disturbance in his work. He showed a free, self-confident behavior but often one had the impression that his demeanor was artificial and that he did not establish any genuine relationship with the person to whom he talked. There was something cold in his manner of talking, something vaguely ironical; often he would smile and one would not know whether it was a smile of embarrassment, of superiority or irony.

The analysis began with violent emotions and ample acting out. He cried when he talked about the death of his mother and cursed when he described the usual upbringing of children. The marriage of his parents had been very unhappy. His mother had been very strict with him, and with his siblings he had established some sort of relationship only in recent years. The way in which he kept talking intensified the original impression that neither his crying nor his cursing or any other emotion came out really fully and naturally. He himself said that all this was not really so bad after all, that he was smiling all the time about everything he was saying. After a few hours, he began to try to provoke the analyst. For example, he would, when the analyst had terminated the session, remain lying on the couch ostentatiously for a while, or would start a conversation afterwards. Once he asked me what I thought I would do if he should grab me by the throat. Two days later, he tried to frighten me by a sudden hand movement toward my head.

I drew back instinctively and told him that the analysis asked of him only that he say everything, not that he do things. Another time he stroked my arm in parting. The deeper meaning of this behavior which could not be interpreted at this time was a budding homosexual transference manifesting itself sadistically. When, on a superficial level, I interpreted these actions as provocations, he smiled and closed up even more. The actions ceased as well as his communications; all that remained was the stereotyped smile. He began to keep silent. When I pointed out the defensive character of his behavior, he merely smiled again and, after some period of silence, repeated, obviously with the intention of making fun of me, the word "resistance." Thus the smiling and the making fun of me became the center of the analytic work.

The situation was difficult. Apart from the few general data about his childhood, I knew nothing about him. All one had to deal with, therefore, were his modes of behavior in the analysis. For some time, I simply waited to see what would be forthcoming, but his behavior remained the same for about two weeks. Then it occurred to me that the intensification of his smile had occurred at the time when I had warded off his aggressions. I tried to make him understand the meaning of his smile in this connection. I told him that no doubt his smile meant a great many things, but at the present it was a reaction to the cowardice I had shown by my instinctive drawing back. He said that may well be but that he would continue to smile. He talked about unimportant things, and made fun of the analysis, saying that he could not believe anything I was telling him. It became increasingly clear that his smile served as a protection against the analysis. This I told him repeatedly over several sessions but it was several weeks before a dream occurred which had reference to a machine which cut a long piece of brick material into individual bricks. The connection of this dream with the analytic situation was all the more unclear in that he did not produce any associations. Finally he said that, after all, the dream was very simple, it was obviously a matter of the castration complex, and—smiled. I told him that his irony was an attempt to disown the indication which the unconscious had given through the dream. Thereupon he produced a screen memory which proved of great importance for the further development of the analysis. He remembered that at the age of about five he once had "played horse" in the backyard at home. He had crawled around on all fours, letting his penis hang out of his pants. His mother caught him doing this and asked what on earth he was doing. To this he had reacted merely by smiling. Nothing more could be learned for the moment. Nevertheless, one thing had been learned: his smile was a bit of mother transference. When I told him that obviously he behaved in the analysis as he had behaved toward his mother, that his smile must have a definite meaning, he only smiled again and said that was all well and good but it did not seem plausible to him. For some days, there was the same smile and the same silence on his part, while I consistently interpreted his behavior as a defense against the analysis, pointing out that his smile was an attempt to overcome a secret fear of me. These interpretations also were warded off with his stereotyped smile. This also was consistently interpreted as a defense against my influence. I pointed out to him that apparently he was always smiling, not only in the analysis, whereupon he had to admit that this was his only possible way of getting through life. With that, he had unwillingly concurred with me. A few days later he came in smiling again and said: "Today you'll be pleased, Doctor. 'Bricks,' in my mother-tongue, means horse testicles. Swell, isn't it? So you see, it is the castration complex." I said that might or might not be true; that, in any case, as long as he maintained this defensive attitude, an analysis of the dreams was out of the question; that, no doubt, he would nullify every association and every interpretation with his smile. It should be said here that his smile was hardly visible; it was more a matter of a feeling and an attitude of making fun of things. I told him he need not be afraid of laughing about the analysis openly and loudly. From then on, he was much more frank in his irony. His association, in spite of its fun-making implication, was nevertheless very valuable for an understanding of the situation. It seemed highly probable that, as happens so often, he had conceived of the analysis in the sense of a danger of castration; at first he had warded off this danger with aggression and later with his smile. I returned to the aggressions in the beginning of the analysis and added the new interpretation that he had tried to test me with his provocations, that he wanted to see how far he could go, how far he could trust me. That, in other words, he had had a mistrust which was based on an infantile fear. This interpretation impressed him visibly. He was struck for a moment but quickly recovered and again began to disavow the analysis and my interpretations with his smiling. I remained consistent in my interpretations; I knew from different indications that I was on the right track and that I was about to undermine his ego defense. Nevertheless, he remained equally consistent in his smiling attitude for a number of sessions. I intensified my interpretations by linking them up more closely with the assumed infantile fear. I told him that he was afraid of the analysis because it would revive his infantile conflicts which he thought he had solved with his attitude of smiling but that he was wrong in this belief because his excitation at the time when he talked about his mother's death had been genuine after all. I ventured the assumption that his relationship with his mother had not been so simple; that he had not only feared and ridiculed but also loved her. Somewhat more serious than usually, he related details concerning the unkindness of his mother toward him; one time when he had misbehaved she even hurt his hand with a knife. True, he added, "Well, according to the book, this is again the castration complex, isn't it?" Nevertheless, something serious seemed to go on in him. While I continued to interpret the manifest and latent meaning of the smiling as it appeared in the analytic situation, further dreams occurred. Their manifest content was that of symbolical castration ideas. Finally he produced a dream in which there were horses, and another where a high tower arose from a fire truck. A huge column of water poured from the tower into a burning house. At this time, the patient suffered from occasional bedwetting. The connection between the "horse dreams" and his horse game he realized himself, although accompanied by smiling. More than that, he remembered that he had always been very much interested in the long penes of horses; he thought that in his infantile game he had imitated such a horse. He also used to find a great deal of pleasure in urinating.

He did not remember whether as a child he used to wet his bed.

On another occasion of discussing the infantile meaning of his smile he thought that possibly his smile on the occasion of the horse game had not been derisive at all but an attempt to reconcile his mother, for fear that she might scold him for his game. In this way he came closer and closer to what I had now been interpreting for months from his behavior in the analysis. The smiling, then, had changed its function and meaning in the course of time: originally an *attempt at conciliation,* it had later become a *compensation of an inner fear,* and finally, it also served as a means of *feeling superior.* This explanation the patient found himself when in the course of several sessions he reconstructed the way which he had found out of his childhood misery. The meaning was: "Nothing can happen to me, I am proof against everything." It was in this last sense that the smile had become a defense in the analysis, as a protection against the reactivation of the old conflicts. The basic motive of this defense was an infantile fear. A dream which occurred at the end of the fifth month revealed the deepest layer of his fear, the fear of being left by his mother. The dream was the following: "I am riding in a car, with an unknown person, through a little town which is completely deserted and looks desolate. The houses are run down, the windowpanes smashed. Nobody is to be seen. It is as if death had ravaged the place. We come to a gate where I want to turn back. I say to my companion we should have another look. There is a man and a woman kneeling on the sidewalk, in mourning clothes. I approach them to ask them something. As I touch them on the shoulder they jump and I wake up, frightened." The most important association was that the town was similar to that in which he had lived until he was four years of age. The death of his mother and the infantile feeling of being left alone were clearly expressed. The companion was the analyst. For the first time, the patient took a dream completely seriously, without any smiling. The character resistance had been broken through and the connection with the infantile had been established. From then on, the analysis proceeded without any special difficulty, interrupted, of course, by the relapses into the old character resistance as they occur in every analysis.

It goes without saying that the difficulties were far greater than may appear from this brief synopsis. The whole resistance phase lasted almost six months, characterized by derision of the analysis for days and weeks on end. Without the necessary patience and the confidence in the efficacy of consistent interpretation of the character resistance, one often would have been inclined to give up.

Let us see whether the analytic insight into the mechanism of this case would justify some other technical procedure. Instead of putting the emphasis consistently on the mode of behavior, one might have thoroughly analyzed the patient's scarce dreams. Possibly he might have had associations which one could have interpreted. It may not be important that previous to the analysis the patient did not dream or forgot all his dreams and did not produce any dreams with a content relevant to the analytic situation until after the consistent interpretation of his behavior. One might object that the patient would have produced these dreams spontaneously anyhow; this cannot be argued because it cannot be proved one way or the other. At any rate, we have ample experience which teaches us that such a situation as presented by our patient can hardly be solved by passive waiting alone; if so, it happens by accident, without the analyst having the reins of the analysis in his hand. Let us assume, then, that we had interpreted his associations in connection with the castration complex, that is, tried to make him conscious of his fear of cutting or of being cut. *Perhaps* this would have finally also led to a success. But the very fact that we cannot be sure that it would have happened, that we must admit the accidental nature of the occurrence, forces us to refute such a technique which tries to circumvent an existing resistance as basically un-analytic. Such a technique would mean reverting to that stage of analysis where one did not bother about the resistances, because one did not know them, and where, consequently, one interpreted the meaning of the unconscious material directly. It is obvious from the case history that this would mean, at the same time, a neglect of the ego defenses.

One might object again that while the technical handling of the case was entirely correct one did not understand my argument; that all this was self-evident and nothing new, that this was the way all analysts worked. True, the general principle is not new; it is nothing but the consistent application of resistance analysis. Many years of experience in the Technical Seminar showed, however, that analysts generally know and recognize the principles of resistance technique, while in practice they use essentially the old technique of the direct interpretation of the unconscious. This discrepancy between theoretical knowledge and practical action was the source of all the mistaken objections to the systematic attempts of the Vienna Seminar to develop the consistent application of theory to therapy. If they said that all this was trite and nothing new, they had their theoretical knowledge in mind; if they objected that it was all wrong and not "Freudian" analysis, they thought of their own practice, which, as we have said, was quite different.

A colleague once asked me what I would have done in the following case: For the past four weeks he had been treating a young man who kept consistently silent but was otherwise very nice and showed a very friendly behavior before and after the analytic session. The analyst had tried all kinds of things, had threatened to break off the analysis and finally, when even dream interpretation failed, had set a date for the termination of the analysis. The scarce dreams had been filled with sadistic murder. The analyst had told the patient that, after all, he should realize from his dreams that in his phantasy he was a murderer. But it did not help. The colleague was not satisfied with my statement that it was incorrect to interpret such deep material in the presence of an acute resistance, no matter how clearly the material might appear in a dream. He thought there was no other way. When I told him that, first of all, the silence should have been interpreted as a resistance, he said that could not be done, for there was no "material" available to do it with. Is not the behavior itself, the silence during the hour in contrast to the friendly attitude outside, "material" enough? Does not this situation show clearly the one thing at least, that the patient expresses, with his silence, a negative attitude or a defense? And that, to judge from his dreams, it is a matter of sadistic impulses which, by his over-friendly behavior, he tried to compensate and camouflage? Why does one dare to deduce certain unconscious processes from a slip such as a patient's forgetting some object in the consultation room, and why does one not dare to deduce the meaning of the situation from his behavior? Is the total behavior less conclusive material than a slip? All this did not seem plausible to my colleague; he continued to insist that the resistance could not be tackled because there was "no material." There could be no doubt that the interpretation of the murderous impulses was a technical error; it could only have the effect of frightening the patient and of putting him all the more on his guard.

The difficulties in the cases presented in the Seminar were of a very similar nature: It was always the same underestimation or the complete neglect of the behavior as interpretable material; again and again the attempt to remove the resistance from the id side instead of by analysis of the ego defense; and finally, almost always, the idea—which was used as an alibi—that the patient simply did not want to get well or that he was "all too narcissistic."

In principle, the loosening of the narcissistic defense is not different in other types than in the one described. If, say, a patient is always affectless and indifferent, no matter what material he may be presenting, then one is dealing with the dangerous affect-block. Unless one works on this before anything else one runs the danger of seeing all the material and all the interpretations go to waste and of seeing the patient become a good analytical theorist while otherwise he remains the same. Unless one prefers in such a case to give up the analysis because of "too strong narcissism" one can make an agreement with the patient to the effect that one will continue to confront him with his affect-lameness but that, of course, he can stop whenever he wants to. In the course of time—usually many months, in one case it took a year and a half—the patient begins to experience the continued pointing out of his affect-lameness and its reasons as painful, for in the meantime one has acquired sufficient means of undermining the protection against anxiety which the affect-lameness presents. Finally the patient rebels against the danger which threatens from the analysis, the danger of losing the protective psychic armor and of being confronted with his impulses, particularly with his aggression. This rebellion activates his aggressivity and before long the first emotional outburst in the sense of a negative transference occurs, in the form of an attack of hatred. That achieved, the road becomes clear. When the aggressive impulses make their appearance, the affect-block is breached and the patient becomes capable of being analyzed. The difficulty consists in bringing out the aggressivity.

The same is true when narcissistic patients express their character resistance in their way of talking; they will talk, for example, always in a haughty manner, in technical terms, always highly correctly or else confusedly. Such modes of talking form an impenetrable barrier and there is no real experiencing until one analyzes the mode of expression itself. Here also, the consistent interpretation of the behavior results in narcissistic indignation, for the patient does not like to be told that he talks so haughtily, or in technical terms, in order to camouflage his feeling of inferiority before himself and the analyst, or that he talks so confusedly because he wants to appear particularly clever and is unable to put his thoughts into simple words. In this manner, one makes an important breach in the neurotic character and creates an avenue of approach to the infantile origin of the character and the neurosis. Of course, it is insufficient to point out the nature of the resistance at one time or another; the more stubborn the resistance, the more consistently does it have to be interpreted. If the negative attitudes against the analyst which are thus provoked are analyzed at the same time the risk of the patient's breaking off the analysis is negligible.

The immediate effect of the analytic loosening of the character armor and the narcissistic protection mechanism is twofold: First, the loosening of the affects from their reactive anchoring and hiding places; second, the creation of an avenue of approach to the central infantile conflicts, the Oedipus complex and the castration anxiety. An enormous advantage of this procedure is that one not only reaches the infantile experiences as such, but that one analyzes them in the specific manner in which they have been assimilated by the ego. One sees again and again that one and the same piece of repressed material is of different dynamic importance according to the stage which has been reached in the loosening of the resistances. In many cases, the affect of the infantile experiences is absorbed in character defenses; with simple interpretation of the contents, therefore, one may be able to elicit the memories but not the corresponding affects. In such cases, interpretation of the infantile material without *previous* loosening of the affect energies which are absorbed in the character is a serious mistake. It is responsible, for example, for the hopelessly long and relatively useless analyses of compulsive characters.[5] If, on the other hand, one first frees the affects from the defense formations of the character, a new cathexis of the infantile impulses takes place automatically. If the line of character-analytic resistance interpretation is followed, remembering without affect is practically out of the question; the disturbance of the neurotic equilibrium which goes with the analysis of the character from the very beginning makes it practically impossible.

In other cases, the character has been built up as a solid protective wall against the experiencing of infantile anxiety and has served well in this function, although at the expense of much happiness. If such an individual comes to analysis because of some symptom, this protective wall serves equally well as character resistance and one realizes soon that nothing can be done unless this character armor which covers up and absorbs the infantile anxiety is destroyed. This is the case, for example, in

[5] The following case illustrates the decisive importance of the neglect of a mode of behavior. A compulsive character who had been in analysis for twelve years without any appreciable result and knew all about his infantile conflicts, such as his central father conflict, talked in the analysis in a peculiarly monotonous, sing-song intonation and kept wringing his hands. I asked him whether this behavior had ever been analyzed, which was not the case. One day it struck me that he talked as if he were praying, and I told him so. He then told me that as a child he had been forced by his father to go to the synagogue and to pray. He had prayed, but only under protest. In the same manner he had also prayed—for twelve long years—before the analyst: "Please, I'll do it if you ask me to, but only under protest." The uncovering of this seemingly incidental detail of his behavior opened the way to the analysis and led to the most strongly hidden affects.

"moral insanity" and in many manic, narcissistic-sadistic characters. In such cases one is often confronted with the difficult question whether the symptom justifies a deep-reaching character-
analysis. For one must realize that the character-analytic destruction of the characterological compensation temporarily creates a
condition which equals a breakdown of the personality. More than
that, in many extreme cases such a breakdown is inevitable
before a new, rational personality structure can develop. One may
say, of course, that sooner or later the breakdown would have
occurred anyhow, the development of the symptom being the
first sign. Nevertheless, one will hesitate about undertaking an
operation which involves so great a responsibility unless there is
an urgent indication.

In this connection another fact must be mentioned: character-
analysis creates in every case violent emotional outbursts and
often dangerous situations, so that it is important always to be
master of the situation, technically. For this reason, many analysts
will refuse to use the method of character-analysis; in that case,
they will have to relinquish the hope for success in a great many
cases. A great many neuroses cannot be overcome by mild means.
The means of character-analysis, the consistent emphasis on the
character resistance and the persistent interpretation of its forms,
ways and motives, are as potent as they are unpleasant for the
patient. This has nothing to do with education; rather, it is a
strict analytic principle. It is a good thing, however, to point out
to the patient in the beginning the foreseeable difficulties and
unpleasantness.

*f) On the optimal conditions for the analytic reduction of the
present-day material to the infantile.*

Since the consistent interpretation of the behavior spontaneously opens the way to the infantile sources of the neurosis, a
new question arises: Are there criteria to indicate *when* the reduction of the present-day modes of behavior to their infantile
prototypes should take place? This reduction, we know, is one
of the cardinal tasks of analysis, but this formulation is too general
to be applied in everyday practice. Should it be done as soon as

he first signs of the corresponding infantile material appear, or
are there reasons for postponing it until a certain later time?
First of all it must be pointed out that in many cases the purpose
of the reduction—dissolution of the resistance and elimination
of the amnesia—is not fulfilled: either there is no more than
an intellectual understanding, or the reduction is refuted by
doubts. This is explained by the fact that—as is the case with the
making conscious of unconscious ideas—the topical process is
complete only if combined with the *dynamic-affective* process
of the becoming conscious. This requires the fulfilment of two
conditions: first, the main resistances must be at least loosened
up; second, the idea which is to become conscious—or, in the case
of the reduction, is to enter a new association—must become
charged with a certain minimum of affect. Now, we know that
the affects are usually split off from the repressed ideas, and
bound up in the acute transference conflicts and resistances. If,
now, one reduces the resistance to the infantile situation before
it has fully developed, as soon as there is only a trace of its infantile origin, then one has not fully utilized its affective energies;
one has interpreted the content of the resistance without also
having mobilized the corresponding affect. That is, dynamic considerations make it necessary not to nip the resistance in the bud,
but, on the contrary, to bring it to full development in the transference situation. In the case of chronic, torpid character incrusta-
tions there is no other way at all. Freud's rule that the patient
has to be brought from acting out to remembering, from the
present day to the infantile, has to be complemented by the
further rule that *first* that which has become chronically rigid
must be brought to new life in the actual transference situation,
just as chronic inflammations are treated by first changing them
into acute ones. With character resistances this is always necessary. In later stages of the analysis, when one is certain of the
patient's cooperation, it becomes less necessary. One gains the
impression that with many analysts the immediate reduction of
as yet completely immature transference situations is due to the
fear of strong and stormy transference resistances; this fits in
with the fact that—in spite of better theoretical knowledge—

resistances are very often considered something highly unwelcome and only disturbing. Hence the tendency to circumvent the resistance instead of bringing it to full development and then treating it. One should not forget the fact that the neurosis itself is contained in the resistance, that with the dissolution of every resistance we dissolve a piece of the neurosis.

There is another reason why it is necessary to bring the resistance to full development. Because of the complicated structure of each resistance, one comprehends all its determinations and meanings only gradually; the more completely one has comprehended a resistance situation, the more successful is its later interpretation. Also, the double nature of the resistance—present-day and historical—makes it necessary first to make fully conscious the forms of ego defense it contains; only after its present-day meaning has become clear should its infantile origin be interpreted. This is true of the cases who have already produced the infantile material necessary for an understanding of the resistance *which follows*. In the other, more numerous cases, the resistance must be brought to full development for no other reason than that otherwise one does not obtain enough infantile material.

The resistance technique, then, has two aspects: *First, the comprehension of the resistance from the present-day situation through interpretation of its present-day meaning; second, the dissolution of the resistance through association of the ensuing infantile material with the present-day material.* In this way, one can easily avoid the flight into the present-day as well as into the infantile, because equal attention is paid to both in the interpretation work. Thus the resistance turns from an impediment of the analysis into its most potent expedient.

*g) Character-analysis in the case of amply flowing material.*

In cases where the character impedes the process of recollection from the beginning, there can be no doubt about the indication of character-analysis as the only legitimate way of introducing the analysis. But what about the cases whose character admits of the production of ample memory material in the beginning? Do they, also, require character-analysis as here described? This question could be answered in the negative if there were cases without a character armor. But since there are no such cases, since the narcissistic protection mechanism always turns into a character resistance—sooner or later, in varying intensity and depth—there is no fundamental difference between the cases. The practical difference, though, is this: In cases such as described above, the narcissistic protection mechanism is at the surface and appears as resistance immediately, while in other cases it is in deeper layers of the personality so that it does not strike one at first. But it is precisely these cases that are dangerous. In the former case one knows what one is up against. In the latter case, one often believes for a long period of time that the analysis proceeds satisfactorily, because the patient seems to accept everything very readily, shows prompt reactions to one's interpretations, and even improvements. But it is just in these patients that one experiences the worst disappointments. The analysis has been carried out, but the final success fails to materialize. One has shot all one's interpretations, one seems to have made completely conscious the primal scene and all infantile conflicts; finally the analysis bogs down in an empty, monotonous repetition of the old material, and the patient does not get well. Worse still, a transference success may deceive one as to the real state of affairs, and the patient may return with a full relapse soon after his discharge.

A wealth of bad experiences with such cases suggested as a rather self-evident conclusion that one had overlooked something. This oversight could not refer to the contents, for in that respect these analyses left little to be desired; it could only be an unrecognized latent resistance which nullified all therapeutic endeavor. It was soon found that these latent resistances consisted precisely in the great willingness of the patients, in the lack of manifest resistances. In comparing them with successful cases, one was struck by the fact that these analyses had shown a constantly even flow, never interrupted by violent emotional outbursts; more importantly, they had taken place in almost constant "positive" transference; rarely, if ever, had there been violent negative impulses toward the analyst. This does not mean that the hate impulses had not been analyzed; only, they did not appear in the transference, or they had been remembered without affect. The prototypes of these cases are the narcissistic affect-lame and the passive-feminine characters. The former show a luke-warm and even, the latter an exaggerated "positive" transference.

These cases had been considered "going well" because they procured infantile material, that is, again because of a one-sided overestimation of the contents of the material. Nevertheless, all through the analysis, the character had acted as a severe resist-ance in a form which remained hidden. Very often, such cases are considered incurable or at least extremely difficult to handle. Before I was familiar with the latent resistances of these cases, I used to agree with this judgment; since then, I can count them among my most gratifying cases.

The character-analytic introduction of such cases differs from others in that one does not interrupt the flow of communications and does not begin the analysis of the character resistance until such time as the flood of communications and the behavior it-self has unequivocally become a resistance. The following case will illustrate this as it will again show how character-analysis leads of itself into the most deeply repressed infantile conflicts. We shall follow this analysis farther along than those previously described, in order to show the logical development of the neu-rosis in the transference resistances.

### A CASE OF PASSIVE-FEMININE CHARACTER

*Anamnesis.*

A 24-year-old bank employee came to analysis because of his anxiety states; these had set in a year previously on the occasion of his going to a hygiene exhibit. Even before that he had had *hypochondriac* fears: he thought he had a *hereditary* taint, he would go *crazy* and would *perish in a mental institution.* For these fears, he seemed to have rational grounds: his father had acquired syphilis and gonorrhea ten years previous to his marriage. The paternal grandfather also was supposed to have had syphilis. A paternal uncle was very nervous and suffered from insomnia. The maternal heredity was even more serious: the mother's father committed suicide, as did one of her brothers. A great-aunt was "mentally abnormal." The patient's mother was an anxious and nervous woman.

This double "heredity" (syphilis on the paternal, suicide and psychosis on the maternal side) made the case all the more interesting in that psychoanalysis—in contradistinction to orthodox psychiatry—considers heredity only one of many etiological factors. As we shall see, the patient's idea about his heredity had also an irrational basis. He was cured in spite of his heredity and did not relapse during a follow-up period of five years.

This presentation covers only the first seven months of the treatment which were taken up with the analysis of the character resistances. The last seven months are presented only very briefly because, from the standpoint of resistance and character-analysis, they presented little which would be of interest. What is to be presented here is chiefly the introduction of the treatment, the course of the resistance analysis, and the way it established the contact with the infantile material. We shall follow the red thread of the resistances and their analysis. In reality, of course, the analysis was not as simple as it may appear here.

The patient's anxiety attacks were accompanied by palpitations and a paralysis of all initiative. Even in the intervals between the attacks he was never free of a feeling of malaise. The anxiety attacks often occurred spontaneously but also were precipitated by his reading about mental diseases or suicides in the newspaper. In the course of the past year his working capacity had begun to suffer and he was afraid that he might be discharged because of inefficiency.

Sexually he was severely disturbed. Shortly before the visit to the hygiene exhibit, he had attempted coitus with a prostitute and had failed. He said that this had not bothered him particularly. There was very little conscious sexual desire: he said he did not suffer from his sexual abstinence. A few years earlier, he had succeeded in carrying out the sexual act, although he had suffered from a premature and pleasureless ejaculation.

Asked whether his anxiety states had not had any precursors, he related that already as a child he had been very apprehensive, and particularly during puberty he had been *afraid of world catastrophes*. Thus he was very much afraid when in 1910 the end of the world through a collision with a comet was predicted; he was surprised that his parents could talk about it so calmly. This "fear of catastrophe" gradually subsided, being completely replaced by his fear of the hereditary taint. Severe anxiety states he had had since childhood, although less frequently.

Apart from the hypochondriac idea of the hereditary taint, the anxiety states and the sexual weakness, there were no symptoms. Awareness of illness was at first present only with regard to the anxiety states which was the symptom which bothered him most. The idea of the hereditary taint was too well rationalized and the sexual weakness produced too little suffering to produce insight into their pathological character. Symptomatologically speaking, then, we were dealing with the hypochondriac form of anxiety hysteria with a particularly marked actual-neurotic core (stasis neurosis).

The diagnosis was hysterical character with hypochondriac anxiety hysteria. The diagnosis "hysterical character" is based on the analytic findings concerning his fixations. Phenomenologically, he was a typical passive-feminine character: he was always over-friendly and humble; he kept apologizing for the most trifling things; on arriving and on leaving he made several deep bows. In addition, he was *awkward, shy and circumstantial*. If he was asked, for example, whether his hour could be changed, he did not simply say, Yes, but assured me at length that he was completely at my disposal, that he was agreeable to any change I wished to make, etc. When he asked for something, he would stroke the analyst's arm. When I first mentioned the possibility of a distrust of the analysis, he returned on the same day, highly perturbed, saying that he could not stand the thought of my thinking him distrustful; he asked repeatedly for forgiveness in case he should have said something that could have given me any such impression.

*The development and analysis of the character resistance.*

The analysis developed according to the resistances which were determined by this kind of character, as follows:

After being told the fundamental rule, he talked rather fluently about his family and the hereditary taint. He asserted that he loved both his parents equally well but had more respect for his father whom he described as an energetic, clear-thinking person. The father had always *warned him against masturbation and extramarital sexual intercourse*. He had told him about his own bad experiences, his syphilis and gonorrhea, of his relationships with women which had come to a bad end; all this with the intention of saving the patient from similar experiences. The father had never beaten him but had always gotten his way by telling him, "I'm not forcing you, I only advise you to . . ."; this, however, had been done very forcefully. The patient described the relationship with his father as very good and his father as his very best friend in whom he had the greatest confidence.

Soon he switched to an extensive description of the relationship with his mother. She was always very solicitous and kind. He was also very kind to her; on the other hand he let her wait on him hand and foot. She took care of his laundry, brought breakfast to his bed, sat beside him until he went to sleep, even now, she combed his hair, in a word, he led the life of a pampered mother's boy.

After six weeks, he was *close to becoming conscious of the wish for coitus*. Apart from this, he had been fully conscious of the tender relationship with his mother, in part he had known it even before the analysis: he had often thrown his mother on his bed to which she had reacted with "bright eyes and flushed cheeks." When she would come in in her nightgown to say good night to him, he would embrace her and press her against him. Though he always tried to emphasize the sexual excitation on the part of his mother—undoubtedly in order to give away less of his own intentions—he mentioned several times, parenthetically as it were, that he himself had definitely felt sexual excitation.

A very cautious attempt to make him understand the real significance of these things, however, led to a violent resistance: he could assure me, he said, that he felt exactly the same thing with other women. I had made this attempt by no means in order to interpret the incest phantasy to him but only in order to see whether I was correct in surmising that this straight advance of his in the direction of the historically important incest love was actually a manoeuvre to divert attention from something that *at present* was much more important. The material about his mother was unequivocal; it really appeared as if he needed only one more step to arrive at the core. But something militated against the interpretation of this material: the content of his communications was in striking contrast to the content of his dreams and to his over-friendly behavior.

For this reason, I centered my attention more and more on his behavior and on his dream material. He produced no associations to his dreams. During the session, he enthused about the analysis and the analyst, while outside he was very much concerned about his future and ruminated about his hereditary taint.

The content of the dreams was of a twofold nature: On the one hand, they also contained incest phantasies; what he did not express during the day he expressed in the manifest dream content. For example, in one dream he went after his mother with a knife, or crept through a hole before which his mother was standing. On the other hand, there was often some obscure *murder story*, the hereditary taint, a crime which somebody committed or *derisive remarks made by somebody,* or *distrust* expressed by somebody.

During the first 4 to 6 weeks of the analysis, we had obtained the following material: his statements regarding the relationship with his mother; his anxiety states and the heredity idea; his over-friendly, submissive behavior; his dreams, those which continued the incest phantasy and those of murder and distrust; and certain indications of a positive mother transference.

Confronted with the choice of interpreting his clear-cut incest material or to emphasize the signs of his distrust, I chose the latter. For there could be no doubt that here was a *latent resistance* which for many weeks did not become manifest because it consisted precisely in that the patient presented too much and was too little inhibited. As was shown later, it was also the first important transference resistance the specific form of which was determined by the patient's character. *He was deceiving:* by offering up all the material on his experiences, which was therapeutically useless, by his over-friendly behavior, by his many clear-cut dreams, by his seeming confidence in the analyst. He tried *to please* the analyst, as he had tried to please his father all along, and for the same reason: because he was *afraid of him.* If this had been my first case of this nature I could not possibly have known that such behavior was a decisive and dangerous resistance. Previous experience in such cases had shown, however, that such patients are incapable of producing a manifest resistance, over periods of months or even years; and further, that they do not react therapeutically in the least to the interpretations which, prompted by the clear-cut material, one gives them. One cannot say, therefore, that in such cases one should wait until the transference resistance makes its appearance; it is, in fact, present from the very first moment in a fully developed, but typically *hidden* form.

Clearly, the presented heterosexual incest material could not really be material which had broken through from the depths. If one pays any attention to the actual function of the presented material one often finds that deeply repressed impulses are temporarily used for the purpose of warding off *other* contents, without any change in the state of repression taking place. This is a peculiar fact, not easily understood depth-psychologically. It is obvious from this fact, though, that the direct interpretation of such material is a definite mistake. Such interpretation not only has no therapeutic effect; more than that, it interferes with the maturing of the respective repressed contents for later interpretation. Theoretically one might say that psychic contents appear in consciousness under two totally different conditions: either born by the affects which specifically belong to them, or born by extraneous interests. In the first case, it is the result of the inner pressure of dammed-up excitation, in the latter case it occurs in the service of defense. It is the same difference as that between freely flowing love and manifestations of love which serve to compensate for hatred, that is, reactive love.

In our patient, the handling of the resistance was, of course, far more difficult than it is in the case of manifest resistances. The meaning of the resistance could not be deduced from the patient's communications, but it could be deduced from his behavior and from the seemingly incidental details of many of his dreams. From these it was evident that, for fear of rebelling against his father, he had camouflaged his spite and distrust by reactive love and had escaped anxiety by being submissive.

The first resistance interpretation was given on the fifth day on the occasion of the following dream:

My handwriting is submitted to a graphologist for an opinion. His opinion was: "This man belongs in a mental institution." My mother is completely desperate. I want to commit suicide. Then I wake up.

To the graphologist, he associated Professor Freud. He added that the Professor had told him that analysis cured such diseases as his with "absolute certainty." I called his attention to the following contradiction: since in the dream he was afraid of having to be committed to a mental institution, he apparently did not believe that the analysis would help him. This he could not see; he refused to accept the interpretation and kept insisting that he had the fullest confidence in the analysis.

Until the end of the second month he dreamt much, though little that would have lent itself to interpretation, and continued talking about his mother. I let him talk, without urging him on and without giving interpretations, being careful all the time not to miss any indication of distrust. After the first resistance interpretation, however, he had camouflaged his secret distrust even more thoroughly, until finally he produced the following dream:

A crime, possibly *a murder, has been committed.* Somehow and against my will, I have been implicated in it. *I am afraid of discovery and punishment.* One of my fellow employees, who impresses me with his courage and decision, is there. I am keenly aware of his superiority.

I emphasized only the fear of discovery and related it to the analytic situation, telling him that his whole attitude indicated that he was hiding something. As early as the following night, he had the following confirmatory dream:

*A crime is going to be committed in our apartment.* It is night and I am on the dark stairs. I know that *my father* is in the apartment. I want to go to his aid but *I am afraid of falling into the hands of the enemies.* I want to call the police. I have a roll of paper with me which has all the details of the intended crime on it. I need *a disguise,* otherwise *the leader of the gang,* who has placed a lot of spies, will prevent me. I take a large cape and a false beard and leave the house, bent over like an old man. The leader of the gang stops me and asks one of his men to search me. He finds the roll of paper. I feel that I am going to be lost if he reads its contents. *I act as innocently as possible* and tell him that they are notes which don't mean anything. He says he'll have to have a look anyhow. There is a moment of painful tension, then, in desperation, a look for a weapon. I find a revolver in my pocket and fire it. The man has disappeared, and suddenly I feel myself very strong. The leader of the gang has changed into a woman. I am seized by a desire for this woman. I pick her up and carry her into the house. I am overcome by a pleasurable feeling, and wake up.

At the end of the dream, we have the whole incest motif before us, but earlier in the dream unmistakable allusions to the patient's masquerading in the analysis. I entered only upon the latter because the patient would have to give up his attitude of deceit before deeper interpretations could be given. This time, however, I went a step further in the resistance interpretation. I told him that not only was he distrustful of the analysis; that, furthermore, by his behavior, he pretended the exact opposite. Upon this, the patient became highly excited, and through six sessions he produced three different hysterical actions:

1. He thrashed around with arms and legs, yelling: "Let me alone, don't come near me, I'm going to kill you, I'm going to squash you!" This action often changed into another:

2. He grabbed his throat and whined in a rattling voice: "Please let me alone, please, I'm not going to do anything any more!"

3. He behaved not like one who is violently attacked but like

a girl who is sexually attacked: "Let me alone, let me alone." This, however, was said without the rattling voice and, while during the action of the second type he pulled up his legs, he now spread them apart.

During these six days he was in a manifest resistance, and continued to talk about his hereditary taint, from time to time falling back into the actions just described. Peculiarly enough, as soon as the actions would cease he would continue to talk calmly as if nothing had happened. He only remarked, "Certainly something queer goes on in me, Doctor."

Without entering upon the content I merely told him that apparently he was acting something in front of me which earlier in his life he had experienced or at least fantasied. This explanation pleased him evidently and from now on he acted out much more frequently than before. My resistance interpretation, then, had stirred up an important part of his unconscious which now expressed itself in the form of these actions. The patient, however, was far from understanding these actions analytically; rather, he utilized them in the sense of his resistance: he thought he would please me particularly if he produced these actions very frequently. Later I found out that in his nightly anxiety attacks he behaved just as he did in the second and third action. Although I understood the meaning of the actions and could have told him the meaning in connection with the murder dream, I stuck consistently to the analysis of his character resistance which his actions had made so much more intelligible.

The following picture presented itself of the *layering of the contents of his characterological transference resistance:*

The first action represented his murderous impulses toward his father and, in transference, toward me (deepest layer).

The second action contained the fear of the father because of the murderous impulse (middle layer).

The third action represented his hidden, grossly sexual feminine attitude, the identification with the (violated) woman, and at the same time the passive-feminine defense against the murderous impulses.

He gave himself, then, in order to keep the father from carrying out the punishment (castration).

But even the interpretation of the actions of the most superficial layer was as yet not admissible. The patient might have *seemingly* accepted each and every interpretation, in order to "please" the analyst, but they would have had no therapeutic effect. For the real understanding of the presented unconscious material would have been made impossible by the *transferred feminine defense against a similarly transferred fear of me*. This fear in turn was due to a *hatred* and distrust transferred to me from the father. That is, hatred, fear and distrust were hidden behind his submissive, trusting attitude, a wall from which every interpretation of unconscious material would have bounced back.

For this reason, I continued to interpret only his unconscious deception, telling him that he was producing his actions so frequently in order to please me. I added, however, that in themselves the actions were highly significant, but that we could not get closer to understanding them until he had gained insight into the meaning of his behavior. He objected less to the resistance interpretation but he could still not agree with me. The following night, however, he dreamed for the first time *openly* about his distrust of the analysis:

Dissatisfied because of the failure of the analysis thus far, I go to Professor Freud. As a means of curing my illness, he gives me a long rod in the shape of an ear-spoon. I feel gratified.

During the analysis of this dream he admitted for the first time that he had been somewhat distrustful of the Professor's prognostic optimism and that, on coming to me, he had been disagreeably surprised to find such a young man. I told him I was struck by two things: first, that he had told me this again in order to please me, and second, that he was suppressing something. Somewhat later I found out that he had cheated me in the question of the fee.

During this consistent work on his character resistance, on his deception through obedience and submission, there flowed increasingly rich material from different age periods, about his infantile relationship with his mother, his relationships with young men, his infantile anxiety, the pleasure he had found as a child in being sick, etc. Of all this, nothing was interpreted except what had an immediate connection with his character resistance.

The dreams about his distrust and his hidden derisive attitude became more frequent. A few weeks later, for example, he had the following dream:

My father remarks that he never dreams. I say to him that certainly is not true, that obviously he forgets his dreams because they consist largely of forbidden wishes. *He laughs scornfully.* I get excited, saying that this is the theory of no less a man than Professor Freud. But while I say this I am somehow worried.

I showed him that he let his father laugh scornfully because he himself did not dare do so and pointed out the worry in the dream which I interpreted as the sign of a bad conscience.

He accepted this interpretation, and during the next 10 days the question of the fee was discussed. It turned out that during the initial interview he had consciously lied to me, "in order to protect himself," that is, because he distrusted my honesty. Without being asked about it, he mentioned the amount of money which he had at his disposal, a lower amount than what he actually had. As usual, I had told him my average fee and my minimum fee. On the basis of his statements, I took him at the minimum fee. He was perfectly able to pay more, however; not only because he had more savings and a better salary than he had said but also because his father defrayed half the expense of the analysis.

*The reduction of the present-day material to the infantile.*

During the discussion of the "money affair," always in connection with his character resistance, his secret fear and distrust, he once made a slip of the tongue, saying, "I had wished my money in the bank to become steadily bigger" [instead of "more"]. With that, he betrayed the connection between money and penis and *the fear of losing the money and the fear of losing his penis.* I did not interpret the slip because I did not want to interpret the castration anxiety as such too early; I only remarked that his tendency to economize must have something to do with his fear of catastrophe, that apparently he felt more secure when he had more money. He accepted this with real understanding and brought confirming associations from childhood: Very early, he had begun to save up pennies. He had never forgiven his father for having once taken his savings, without asking him, and having spent them. *For the first time he uttered spontaneously a reproach to the father;* this reproach referred consciously to the money, unconsciously, of course, to the castration danger. In this connection I said that his father, in suppressing the patient's sexuality as he did, had acted with the best intentions, but unwisely. The patient admitted that he had often had thoughts along this line but had never dared to contradict his father who, he thought, acted only in the patient's best interests. It was yet too early to tell him that this acquiescence of his was based on a deep guilt feeling and a fear of the father.

From now on the analysis of the transference resistance proceeded hand in hand with the analysis of the hidden negative attitude toward the father. Every aspect of the transference situation was related to 'the father and was understood by the patient who at the same time produced a wealth of material about his real attitude toward him. True, all his productions were still strongly censored, not yet accessible to deep interpretation, but the analysis of his childhood was correctly begun. He no longer produced the material as a fence in order to evade other things, but, as a result of the analysis of the character defense, in the growing conviction that his relationship with his father had not been what he had believed it to be, and that it had had a harmful influence on his development.

Every time he came close to the murder phantasy his anxiety increased. The dreams became shorter and less frequent but clearer and the connection with the analytic situation closer. The material which previously had been used as a fence no longer appeared. Everything else was in close connection with his father complex: his phantasy of being a woman, and his incest wish. In the course of the next six weeks, undisguised castration dreams appeared for the first time, without any corresponding interpretation or hint on my part:

1. I am lying in my bed, suddenly get scared and see that my former school principal sits on me. I wrestle with him and get him under me, but he gets one hand free and *threatens my penis*.

2. My older brother climbs through a window into our apartment. He tells somebody to bring him a sword because *he wants to kill me. But I get the start of him and kill him.*

We see, then, how the basic conflict with the father unfolds more and more clearly, without any specific effort on my part, merely as the result of correct resistance analysis.

In this phase, there were repeated blocks and definite manifestations of distrusting the analysis. The resistance was now connected with the fee question: he distrusted my honesty. The doubts and the distrust always appeared when he came closer to the hatred of his father, the castration complex and the murder phantasy. True, the resistances were still sometimes masked by feminine surrender, but now it was no longer difficult to get behind this mask.

After a five weeks' vacation, the analysis was resumed. The patient, who had not taken a vacation, had lived with a friend during this time, because his parents had been out of town and he had been afraid of being alone. His anxiety states had not subsided; on the contrary, they had become more intense after my leaving. In this connection he told me that as a child he was always afraid when his mother left, that he always wanted to have her around, and that he was angry with his father when he took her to a concert or the theatre.

It was rather clear, then, that besides his negative father transference he had developed a strong tender mother transference. This had existed from the very beginning, alongside with the reactive, passive-feminine attitude; the patient, comparing the vacation period with the preceding months, stated that he had felt very secure with me. He found out for himself that with me he felt as safe and secure as with his mother. I did not enter upon this, for the tender mother transference was as yet no interference; on the other hand, it was too early for an analysis of the mother transference, and his reactive-feminine father transference, as a result of the interruption, was again as strong as before. He talked again in a humble and submissive manner as he had done in the beginning of the analysis, and largely about his relationship with his mother.

On the third and fourth day after the resumption of the analysis he had two dreams about the *incest wish, his infantile attitude toward his mother, and the phantasy of the maternal womb.* In connection with these dreams, he remembered bathroom scenes with his mother. She had washed him until he was 12 years old, and he could never understand why his pals teased him about it. Then he remembered his childhood fear of criminals who might break into the apartment and kill him. In other words, the analysis already revived the infantile anxiety hysteria, without any corresponding interpretations or hints having been given. A deep-reaching analysis of these dreams was avoided because his whole attitude was again a deceptive one. A dream of the next night was still more explicit:

1. I am hiking through the Arnbrechtthal, where I spent my summer vacations when I was five or six, with the intention of reviving childhood impressions. Suddenly I get to a place one cannot get out of except through a castle. The doorkeeper opens the gate and says that I cannot visit the castle at this time. I say that this was not my intention; I merely wanted to get into the open through the castle. The proprietress of the castle appears, an elderly lady who seeks to win me with her coquettish behavior. I want to retire, but suddenly notice that I have forgotten my key (which opens my trunks and seems to be otherwise of great importance to me) in the private box of the castle lady. I have a feeling of discomfort which disappears when the box is opened and the key is returned to me.

2. My mother calls me from upstairs. I grab a newspaper, roll it into the shape of a penis, and go to my mother.

3. I am in a large room with my cousin and her mother. My cousin, whose looks please me, is dressed only in a shirt, and so am I. I embrace her. Suddenly I find that I am much smaller than she, for my penis is halfway between her knees and her genital. I have an ejacu-

lation and am very much embarrassed because there might be stains on my shirt which would give me away.

In the cousin, he himself recognized his mother. In connection with being undressed, he mentioned that he never took off his clothes on the occasions of his attempts at coitus, that he had some vague fear of doing so.

In this dream, the incest phantasy (in part 2 and 3) and the castration anxiety (part 1) were clearly expressed. Why did he censor so little? In view of his obvious deception manoeuvres I avoided interpretations or making attempts to get further associations. I first wanted the theme to unfold itself more; more importantly, it should not be discussed *before the next transference resistance had become manifest and had been eliminated.*

This resistance was not long in coming. It came in connection with a remark about the second dream part which I had let slip against my better knowledge. I had called his attention to the fact that once before he had dreamt about a paper penis. This remark was unnecessary, and he reacted to it—in spite of the clear-cut manifest dream content—with one of his typical resistances: "Yes, surely, but . . ." That night, he had a violent anxiety attack and two dreams. One concerned his "money resistance" (transferred castration anxiety), the other brought forth, *for the first time, the primal scene,* which, in the last analysis, motivated the money resistance:

1. I am in a crowd in the Prater, standing in front of an amusement stand. Suddenly I notice that a man behind me tries to steal my wallet from my hip pocket. I reach for it, and at the last moment prevent the theft.

2. I am in the last car of a train in the region south of the Wörthersee. In a curve, I suddenly notice that on the one-track line another train comes toward us. The catastrophe seems inevitable; in order to save myself, I jump off.

Here it was shown that I had done well not to interpret his incest dreams, for a strong latent resistance was in the way. We also see that the resistance dream had a close connection with his infantile anxiety (fear of castration—fear of the primal scene). Between his third and sixth year, he used to spend his summer vacation at the Wörthersee.

He had no associations to the dream. Relating the man in the first dream to myself, I brought up again his whole attitude, his secret fear of me and his hidden distrust in the money matter, without, for the time being, mentioning the connection with the fear of catastrophes. From the second dream, I emphasized only the "inevitable catastrophe" and reminded him that to him money meant a protection against catastrophes, that he was afraid I might rob him of this protection.

He did not quite agree, seeming rather horrified at the idea of seeing a robber in me; but he also did not refute the interpretation. In the next few days he produced dreams in which he assured me of his attachment and his trust; I also appeared as his mother. In addition, there was a new element: *his mother as a man.* She appeared as a Japanese. This we did not understand until many months later when the significance of his infantile phantasies about the Russo-Japanese War became clear. The Russian was the father, the Japanese—because of his smallness— the mother. Furthermore, his mother had at that time worn Japanese pyjamas: the mother in pants. Repeatedly, he made a slip of the tongue, speaking of "mother's penis." The "school pal" in many dreams also represented the cousin who resembled his mother.

The clear-cut incest dreams had been resistance dreams: they were to hide his fear of the woman, the woman with the penis.

From then on, for about six weeks, the analysis took a peculiar zigzag-like course: Dreams and communications regarding his money resistance alternated with others about his desire for his mother, about the mother as man, the dangerous father and the castration anxiety in its various forms. In the interpretation work, I always took the money resistance (= castration anxiety) as the starting point, and kept deepening the analysis of the infantile situation from there, every day. This was not difficult because *the infantile material was always in closest connection with the transference situation.* Not all the infantile fears and desires which came up now, however, also appeared in the transference; rather, the transference revolved completely about the castration anxiety which became more and more acute. Only the core of the infantile situation had appeared in the transference resistance. Since I was certain that the analysis proceeded in order, I could postpone deep interpretations until the proper time; all I did was to work consistently on the fear of me, by constantly relating it with the fear of the father.

What I was trying to do was to penetrate to the infantile incest phantasies by eliminating the transferred father resistance as thoroughly as possible in order to obtain them as free of resistance as possible. This would avert the danger of wasting the most important interpretations. Thus I did not yet interpret the incest material which came to the fore increasingly clearly and consistently.

Schematically, the topical layering of the resistance and the material at the beginning of this phase was the following:

1. The foreground was occupied by his castration anxiety in the form of his money resistance.

2. This he tried continually to ward off by means of a feminine attitude toward me; this was, however, much less successful than at the beginning.

3. The feminine attitude covered up a sadistic-aggressive attitude toward me (i.e., the father) and was accompanied by

4. a deep tender mother attachment which also was transferred to me.

5. With these ambivalent attitudes which were centered in the transference resistance were connected the incest wishes which had appeared in dreams, the masturbation anxiety, his longing for the maternal womb and the violent fear originating from the primal scene. Of all this, nothing had been interpreted except his deception and its motives, and the fear and hatred of the father.

During the fifth month of the analysis he had his first incestuous masturbation anxiety dream:

I am in a room. A young woman with a round face sits at the piano. I can see only the upper part of her body, the rest is hidden by the piano. I hear the voice of the analyst beside me: "You see, that's the cause of your neurosis." I feel more close to the woman but then I suddenly get frightened and yell out loudly.

On the previous day, in the course of a dream interpretation, I had said to him, "You see, this is one of the causes of your neurosis." I had been referring to his infantile attitude, his desire to be loved and to be taken care of. As if the patient had known the true cause of his neurosis, he connected this remark with his repressed *masturbation anxiety.* The subject of masturbation came up again in connection with the incest motif. He woke up with anxiety. The fact that the lower part of the woman's body in the dream was not visible expressed his fear of the female genital. Nevertheless, I left the subject alone because he was still at the height of his resistance, and had no associations to the dream.

Then the patient had a dream in which "a naked family" consisting of father, mother and child were enveloped by a gigantic snake. Another dream was the following:

1. I am lying in bed, the analyst sitting beside me. He says: "Now I'm going to show you the cause of your neurosis." I yell with fear— but there is also a pleasurable sensation—and I almost faint. He goes on saying that he is going to analyze me in our bathroom. This idea seems pleasant to me. As we open the door to the bathroom, it is dark inside.

2. I walk through the woods with my mother. I notice that we are being followed by a robber. I notice a revolver in my mother's dress and take it in order to shoot the robber. Walking fast, we reach an inn. As we mount the steps, the robber is on our heels. I fire a shot at him. The bullet, however, *changes into a money bill.* For the time being we are safe but the robber, who sits in the anteroom, may still be planning something bad. *In order to win his favor, I give him another bill.*

That I was correct in not interpreting those dreams—clear-cut as they were—was shown in the fact that the patient, apart from not having any associations, did not refer with one word to the person of the robber. Instead he kept silent or talked excitedly about "all the money" which he had to pay and expressed his doubts as to whether the analysis would help him.

No doubt, this resistance was also directed against a discussion of the incest material. But such an interpretation would not have done any good; I had to wait for the proper opportunity of interpreting his money anxiety as castration anxiety.

In the first part of the "robber dream" the analysis is going to take place in the bathroom. Later we found that, in masturbating, he had felt safest in the bathroom. In the second part of the dream I (the father) appear as robber (= castrator). *His present-day resistance* (distrust in money matters), then, *had the closest connection with his old masturbation anxiety* (castration anxiety).

With regard to the second part of the dream I told him that he was afraid I might do him harm but that this fear really referred to his father. After some hesitation, he accepted this interpretation and began spontaneously to talk about his exaggerated friendliness. He recognized his exaggerated friendliness toward his superiors to be an expression of a vague fear that he might do something wrong; they also should be kept from noticing that secretly he ridiculed them. To the extent to which he took an objective view of his character and began to look through it, he became freer, more candid and open, in the analysis as well as outside. He dared to express criticism and began to be ashamed of his previous behavior. *For the first time, the neurotic character became a foreign-body-like symptom.* With that, the character-analysis had achieved its first success: the character began to be analyzed.

The money resistance continued to exist, and in the dreams, in connection with the primal scene, the fear for his penis came more and more to the fore; this *without the slightest help on my part.*

This fact deserves special emphasis. With systematic and consistent analysis of the character resistance, one need not make any effort to obtain the infantile material. It flows spontaneously, increasingly clear-cut and closely associated with the actual resistance—provided, of course, that one has not disturbed this process by premature interpretations of the infantile material. The less one tries to penetrate into childhood, the more correctly one works on the resistances, the faster does one get there.

This was again exemplified after the interpretation that he was afraid of being harmed. The following night he dreamed that he passed a chickenyard and saw a chicken killed. A woman was stretched out on the ground and another woman repeatedly stuck a big fork into her. Then he embraced a girl; his penis was *half-way between her knees and her genital,* and he had an ejaculation.

Since the money resistance had somewhat subsided, an attempt was made to interpret the dream. To the chickenyard he associated that as a child, during the summer in the country, he had often watched animals having sexual intercourse. At that time, we had as yet no idea how important the detail "summer in the country" was. In the first woman he recognized his mother, without, however, being able to explain her position. Only about the dream with the ejaculation he had more to say. In the dream, he had appeared as a child; he remembered that he used to press against women until he had an ejaculation.

It seemed a good sign that the patient, in spite of the undisguised material, did not offer any interpretations. If I had interpreted symbols or important unconscious contents *before* the analysis of his resistances, he would have immediately accepted the interpretations for reasons of resistance, and we would have gone from one chaotic situation to the other.

My interpretation of his fear of being harmed had set the analysis of his character in full motion. For days, the money resistance was absent, he constantly discussed his infantile behavior and brought example after example of situations in his life in which he had acted "cowardly" and "slyly," modes of behavior which he now honestly condemned. I tried to convince him that such behavior had been largely the result of his father's influence. This attempt, however, provoked the most violent resistance. *He did not yet dare to reproach his father.*

After a longer interval he dreamed again of that theme behind which I surmised the primal scene:

I am standing at the seashore. Some polar bears tumble about in the water. Suddenly they become anxious, and I see the back of an enormous fish emerge from the water. He chases a bear and injures him with frightful bites. Finally he lets go of the mortally wounded bear. The fish himself, however, is severely wounded; a stream of blood gushes from his gills.

I pointed out that his dreams were always of a cruel nature. For several sessions he related his masturbation phantasies and various cruel acts he used to indulge in before puberty. Most of these were determined by the "sadistic concept of the sexual act." After analysis, I had him write them down:

3rd to 5th year: During summer vacation, I happen to witness the butchering of pigs. I hear the groaning of the animals and see the blood spurt from them. I feel a deep pleasure.

4th to 6th year: The idea of the butchering of animals, especially horses, fills me with pleasure.

5th to 11th year: I like to play with tin soldiers. I arrange battles in which there is always hand-to-hand fighting. I press the bodies of the soldiers against each other; the favored soldiers get the others down.

6th to 12th year: I press two ants together so that they grab each other with their tweezers. Biting into each other, they fight for their lives. I scatter sugar between two ant colonies which then engage in regular battles. I also found pleasure in putting a wasp and a fly together in a waterglass; after a while, the wasp would bear down on the fly and bite off its wings, legs and head.

12th to 14th year: I keep a terrarium and like to watch the animals having sexual intercourse. I also observe this in the chickenyard where I like to see how the stronger cocks chase away the weaker ones.

8th to 16th year: I like to wrestle with the chambermaids. In later years, I used to pick them up, carry them to a bed and throw them down on it.

5th to 12th year: I like to play with railroads, running the trains through the whole apartment, making tunnels of boxes, chairs, etc. I also try to imitate the noise of the locomotive.

15th year, *masturbation phantasies:* Regularly, I am only an *on-looker.* The woman tries to fight off the man *who usually is consider-ably smaller than she.* After a long struggle, the woman is *overpowered.* The man brutally grabs her breasts loins or thighs. *I never think of a male or female genital and never of the sexual act itself.* In the moment in which the woman ceases her resistance I have an orgasm.

The situation at this time was the following: He was ashamed of his cowardice and remembered the sadism in his past. The analysis of the phantasies and actions just summarized lasted until the end of the treatment. It made him much freer in the analysis, and more courageous and aggressive generally, but for the time being there was still an apprehensive note in his behavior. His anxiety states had become less frequent but kept recurring again and again in connection with the money resistance.

We see here again that the production of the genital incest material served mainly the purpose of covering up his infantile sadism, although, of course, it was at the same time an attempt to progress toward a genital object cathexis. His genital striving, however, was intermixed with sadistic strivings; the therapeutic task, therefore, was that of crystallizing it out of this intermixture.

Early in the sixth month of the analysis came the first opportunity of interpreting his *fear for his penis,* on the occasion of the following dreams:

1. I am lying on a sofa in an open field on summer vacation. A girl I know comes toward me and lies on top of me. I get her under me and attempt intercourse. Though I am getting an erection, I notice that *my penis is too short* to have intercourse. This makes me very sad.

2. I am reading a drama. The people in it are 3 Japanese, father, mother and a child of four. I feel that the piece will come to a *tragic ending.* What moves me most is *the fate of the child.*

For the first time, an attempt at coitus appeared in the manifest dream content. The second part, in which there was an allusion to the primal scene (age 4) was not analyzed at this time. In uninterrupted discussion of his cowardice and apprehensiveness, he himself came to talk of his penis. Now I told him that his fear of being harmed or cheated really related to his genital. The question why and of whom he was afraid was not yet discussed, nor was the real meaning of the fear interpreted. The interpretation seemed plausible to him, but now he developed a resistance which lasted for six weeks and which was based on *a passive-feminine, homosexual defense against the castration anxiety.*

That the patient was in a resistant phase could be seen from the following indications: He did not openly rebel or express any doubts; instead, he became again exaggeratedly polite, friendly and submissive. His dreams, which in the course of the resistance analysis had become less frequent, shorter and clearer, became again long and confused. His anxiety states became as frequent and intense as ever; in spite of this, he did not express any distrust of the analysis. The heredity idea also cropped up again; here, his doubt about the outcome of the analysis found a disguised expression. As in the beginning of the analysis, he began again to act a woman who is being raped. In his dreams also, the passive-feminine attitude was predominant. There were no longer any dreams about coitus or ejaculation. We see, then, how —in spite of the fact that the analysis of his character had progressed quite far—the old character resistance reappeared in its full force when a new layer of the unconscious came to be analyzed. This layer was that which was most decisive for his character: his castration anxiety.

Consequently, the subject of the resistance analysis was not the castration anxiety which had provoked the resistance but again his total behavior. For full six weeks, hardly anything was done but exclusive interpretation of his behavior as a protection against dangers. Every detail of his behavior was scrutinized in this light and brought to his attention; with this, we gradually progressed to the core of his behavior, the fear for his penis.

The patient kept trying to evade me by "offering up" infantile material, but the meaning of this was also constantly interpreted to him. Gradually he began to realize that he felt a woman also toward me and said this in so many words, adding that he felt sexual excitation in the perineum. I explained this transference phenomenon: He felt my attempts at explaining his behavior to be reproaches, *felt guilty and tried to expiate his guilt by feminine submission.* The deeper meaning of this behavior—identification with the mother because he was afraid to be a man (the father)—

I left untouched for the present. Then he produced among other things, the following confirmatory dream:

> I'm in the Prater and get to talking with a young fellow. It seems he misunderstands a remark of mine and says that he is willing to give himself to me. In the meantime, we have arrived at our apartment and the fellow gets into my father's bed. His underwear seems to be dirty.

In analyzing this dream I was able again to reduce the feminine transference to the father. Now he remembered for the first time that in his masturbation phantasies he used to imagine himself to be a woman. The dirty underwear led to the analysis of his anal activities and habits (bathroom ceremonials). Another character trait, his circumstantiality, was clarified here.

In resolving the resistance, not only its old form but also its erogenous, anal basis had been discussed. Now I went a step further in the analysis of his character. I explained to him the connection between his submissive behavior and the phantasy of being a woman: his behavior was feminine, that is, exaggeratedly kind, submissive and trusting because he was afraid of being a man. I added that we would have to find out for what reason he was afraid of being a man, that is, in his sense, courageous, open, and honest instead of crawling. Almost as an answer to this question he produced a dream in which the castration anxiety and the primal scene again stood out:

> I am at my cousin's, a young, pretty woman [the mother, W.R.]. All of a sudden I have the feeling of being *my own grandfather*. I get terribly depressed. At the same time I feel somehow that I am *the center of a planetary system* and that planets revolve around me. Simultaneously I suppress—still in the dream—my anxiety and am annoyed by my weakness.

The most important detail of this incest dream was his being his own grandfather. There was no doubt that here his fear of a hereditary taint played an important role. It was also clear that he fantasied of creating himself, in identification with his father, that is, of having intercourse with his mother; this, however, was not discussed at this time.

As to the planetary system, he said, it referred to his egotism: "everything revolved around him." I surmised an additional, deeper meaning, namely the primal scene, but did not mention it. For some days he talked almost exclusively about his egotism, his desire of being a child loved by everyone, and realized that he himself neither wanted to love nor was able to love. I showed him the connection between his egotism and his fear for his beloved self and his penis.[6] His next dreams brought out the infantile background:

1. I am undressed and look at my penis which bleeds at the tip. Two girls walk away and I am sad, because I assume that they will *despise me because of the smallness of my penis.*

2. I am smoking a cigarette through a cigarette holder. I take it off and realize to my surprise that it is a cigar holder. As I put the cigarette back into my mouth, *the tip breaks off.* I have an unpleasant sensation.

Thus, without my doing anything about it, the castration idea began to take definite forms. The patient now interpreted the dreams without my aid and produced a wealth of material concerning his fear of the female genital and his fear of touching his penis or having somebody else touch it. In the second dream, an oral idea is obvious (cigarette holder). He was struck by the fact that in a woman he desired everything *except* the genital; but what he desired most was the breast; with that, he began to talk about the oral fixation to his mother.

I told him it was not sufficient to know about his fear of the genital; that one had to find out why he had this fear. In response to this, he dreamed again of the primal scene, without an inkling that he had entered upon my question:

I am behind the last car of a stationary railroad train, just at a switch. A second train goes by and I get *caught between the two trains.*

---

[6] This, taken in its total setting, should show to some individual psychologists why we psychoanalysts cannot recognize the inferiority feeling as an ultimate factor: because the real problem, and the real work, starts precisely where for Alfred Adler it stops.

Before continuing the presentation of the analysis, I should mention the fact that during the seventh month of the treatment, after the resolution of his passive-homosexual resistance, the patient made a courageous move in the direction of the woman. This took place without my knowledge; he mentioned it later more or less in passing. He made the acquaintance of a girl in the park. His mode of sexual activity was this: He pressed himself against the girl, had a strong erection and an ejaculation. The anxiety states gradually subsided. It did not occur to him to have sexual intercourse. Calling this to his attention, I said that apparently he was afraid of sexual intercourse. This he did not admit, using the lack of opportunity as an excuse, until finally he was struck by the infantile manner of his sexual activity. It had occurred in many of his dreams, and now he remembered that as a child he used to press himself against his mother in this manner.

The subject of his incest love with which—deceptively—he had started the analysis came up again; this time, however, with little resistance, certainly without the previous ulterior motive. Thus the analysis of his attitudes took place corresponding to his experiences.

Again and again he rejected the interpretation that he really had desired his mother. The corresponding material which he had produced in the course of seven months was so clear, and the connections, as he himself admitted, so evident, that I did not try to convince him but started to investigate why he was afraid of admitting the fact to himself.

This question had been discussed together with his fear for his penis; thus there were two problems to be solved:

1. What was the origin of his castration anxiety?

2. Why, in spite of conscious agreement, did he not accept the fact of sexual incest love?

The analysis now progressed rapidly in the direction of the primal scene. This phase was ushered in by the following dream:

I am in the hall of a castle where the king and his entourage are assembled. *I deride the king.* His people pounce on me. I'm being thrown down and I feel that they are inflicting deadly cuts on me. My dead body is being dragged away. Suddenly I feel that I'm still alive, *but I keep very still in order to make the gravediggers believe that I'm dead.* There is a thin layer of soil over me and my breath is impeded. *I keep absolutely still and thus keep from being found out.* A little later, I am free. I go again into the palace, a terrible weapon in each hand, perhaps thunderbolts. Whoever opposes me is killed by me.

He thought that the idea of the gravediggers had something to do with his fear of catastrophes. I was able to show him now that this fear, the fear of heredity and the fear for his penis were one and the same thing. I ventured the assumption that the dream contained that scene in his childhood from which the fear for the penis originated.

He was struck by the fact that he "played dead," in order not to be found out. In this connection, he remembered that in his masturbation phantasies he was always the onlooker and he himself brought up the question whether perhaps he had experiences "something like that" with his parents. However, he rejected the idea immediately, saying that he had never slept in his parents bedroom. This was disappointing, for I was convinced, on the basis of his dream material, that he had actually experienced the primal scene. I pointed out the contradiction and said one should not give up too readily, the analysis would solve it in time. Still in the same session the patient thought he must have seen a certain maid with her friend. Then he remembered two occasions on which he might have watched his parents. He remembered that his bed used to be moved to his parents' bedroom when they had guests. Also, in his preschool years, he had slept in one room with his parents *during summer vacations.* In this connection he recalled the various dreams about the summers in the country and the representation in one of them of the primal scene in the killing of chickens.

In this connection he came back to the acting-out in the beginning of the analysis and his night terrors in childhood. A detail of these fears was now explained: he was afraid of a white female figure coming out from between curtains. Now he remembered that when he used to cry at night his mother would come to his bed, in her nightgown.

Apparently, we had gone too far in this hour, for during the next night he had a definitely derisive resistance dream:

> I am standing on a wharf and am about to get on a large boat, as *companion of a mental patient.* Suddenly the whole thing appears to me to be *a play* in which a certain role has been assigned to me. On the gangplank *I have to say the same thing three times,* which I do.

He himself interpreted the getting-on-the-boat as wish for coitus, but I led him to the more important thing, the "play-acting." That he had to say the same thing three times was a derisive allusion to my consistent interpretations. He had to admit that he had often smiled inside about my efforts. He said further that he intended to look up a woman and to have intercourse three times. "To please me," I added. But I also explained to him that this resistance had another, deeper meaning, his avoiding attempts at coitus because of fear of the sexual act.

The following night he had again dreams of homosexual surrender on the one hand and fear of coitus on the other:

> 1. I meet a young fellow in the street who belongs to the lower classes but looks very healthy and strong. I feel that he is stronger than I and *try to gain his favor.*
>
> 2. I am on a skiing tour with the husband of one of my cousins. Going down a steep slope, I find that the snow is sticky and say that this is bad terrain for skiing because *in going down one is bound to fall down frequently.* We come to a road leading along the slope of a mountain. In a sharp curve *I lose a ski which drops into the abyss.*

He did not enter upon the dream at all. Instead, he began with the theme of the fee: he had to pay so much and did not know whether it was going to help at all, he was dissatisfied, was suffering from anxiety again, and so forth.

Now it was possible to reduce the money resistance to the still unresolved genital anxiety and fear of coitus. Now I could show him the deeper motive of his feminine surrender: *When he ap-*

*proached a woman, he became afraid of the consequences and became a woman himself, that is, homosexual and passive in his character.* The fact that he had made himself into a woman he understood very well, but he could not understand why and of what he was so afraid. It was perfectly clear to him that he was afraid of sexual intercourse. But what, was the question, could happen to him?

He was now constantly occupied with this question, but instead of discussing the fear of the father he discussed the fear of the woman. As we know, in his infantile anxiety hysteria he had also been afraid of the woman; he used to say, "the penis of the woman." Up until puberty he had believed that the woman also had a penis. He himself connected this idea with the primal scene the reality of which he was now convinced of.

At the end of the seventh month he dreamed that he saw how a girl lifted her skirt so that her underwear became visible. He turned away like somebody "who sees something that he shouldn't." Now I told him that he was afraid of the female genital because it looked like an injury, a wound, and that he must have been frightened by the first sight of it. This interpretation seemed plausible to him inasfar as he felt the female genital to be not only disgusting but frightening. However, he could not recall an actual experience.

The situation at this time was the following: The core of his symptoms, the castration anxiety, had been worked through but not yet resolved in its deepest and ultimate significance because the close individual connections with the primal scene were still lacking and because the latter had been only deduced but not analytically handled.

One time when these things were again discussed in a period free of resistance and there was nothing tangible to work with, the patient said in a low voice, as to himself: "I must have been caught at one time." He said he had the feeling as if he had done something once in a sly manner and had been caught in doing it. Now the patient remembered that even as a small boy he had secretly rebelled against his father. He had made fun of him behind his back while openly playing the obedient son. In puberty, the rebellion against the father had ceased entirely. That is, the patient had repressed the hatred of his father because he feared him.

His idea of the hereditary taint, also, proved to be a reproach to his father. It meant, "my father has damaged me when he made me." Analysis of the phantasies about the primal scene revealed that the patient imagined himself in the maternal womb while his father had intercourse with his mother. The phantasy of being harmed at the genital combined with the phantasy of the womb into the phantasy that *he was castrated by his father in his mother's womb*.

The remaining part of the analysis can be described briefly. It was relatively free of resistance and consisted plainly of two parts.

The first part was taken up by the working through of his infantile masturbation phantasies and his masturbation anxiety. His castration anxiety manifested itself for a long time in the fear of the female genital. The "injury," the "wound," seemed to prove the reality of castration. Finally, the patient dared masturbate. With that, the anxiety states disappeared completely; this shows that they were due to libido stasis and not to the castration anxiety, for the latter continued to exist. Further analysis of infantile material reduced it sufficiently so that he undertook an attempt at coitus in which he was erectively potent. Subsequent sexual acts revealed two disturbances: he was orgastically impotent, that is, he experienced less pleasure than in masturbation, and his attitude toward the woman was one of indifference and contempt. His genitality was still dissociated into tender and sensual components.

The second part was taken up with the analysis of his orgastic impotence and his infantile narcissism. As always before, he wanted to get everything from the woman, the mother, without having to give anything himself. With great understanding, the patient worked himself on his disturbances. He began to experience his narcissism as painful and finally overcame it, when the last remnant of his castration anxiety, which was anchored in his orgastic impotence, was analytically resolved. He was *afraid of the orgasm* because he thought that the excitation connected with it was harmful. The following dream shows this fear:

I visit a picture gallery. I am struck by a picture called "Drunken Tommy." It is of a young, pretty English soldier in the mountains. It storms, he seems to have lost his way. The hand of a skeleton has taken his arm and seems to be leading him, apparently a symbol that he is *going to meet with disaster*. Another picture is called "Hard Profession." It is also in the mountains. A man and a boy fall down a precipice. At the same time, a knapsack empties: the boy is surrounded by a whitish mass.

The fall represented the orgasm,[7] the whitish mass the sperm. The patient talked about the fears he had experienced during puberty with ejaculation and orgasm. His sadistic phantasies about women also were worked through more thoroughly. A few months later, during the summer, he began a relationship with a young girl; the disturbances were now much milder.

The resolution of the transference created no difficulties because it had been worked on systematically from the very beginning, in its positive as well as its negative aspects. He left the analysis full of hope. In the course of the ensuing five years, I saw the patient five times. His apprehensiveness and anxiety states had entirely disappeared. He considered himself completely healthy and expressed his satisfaction about having lost his crawling and sly traits and was now able to meet difficulties courageously. His potency had still increased since the termination of the treatment.

### Summary.

Arrived at the conclusion of this history, we are keenly aware of the difficulty of putting analytic processes into words. But that should not keep us from sketching at least the rough outlines, in order to bring about an understanding in the problems of character-analysis. To summarize:

---

[7] *Cf.* the symbolism of the orgasm in DIE FUNKTION DES ORGASMUS, 1927.
*Translator's note: Cf.* also THE FUNCTION OF THE ORGASM, Orgone Institute Press, 1942, 1948.

1. Our case is the prototype of the passive-feminine character who—no matter what symptoms make him seek analytic help—always presents us with the same type of character resistance. It also demonstrates to us the typical mechanisms of the latent negative transference.

2. Technically, the main emphasis was on the analysis of the passive-feminine character resistance, on the deceiving through exaggerated friendliness and submissive behavior. This procedure made the infantile material develop in the transference neurosis according to its own inner laws. This prevented the patient from gaining mere intellectual insight into his unconscious, for reasons of feminine surrender (in order "to please"), which would have had no therapeutic effect.

3. The case history shows that with systematic and consistent emphasis on the character resistance and with avoidance of premature interpretations, the corresponding infantile material appears increasingly clearly and unequivocally *of itself*. This makes the subsequent interpretations of meaning and of symptoms incontrovertible and therapeutically effective.

4. The case history shows that one can begin to work on the character resistance as soon as one has recognized its present-day meaning and function, that is, without knowing the corresponding infantile material. The emphasis on and the interpretation of its present-day meaning brought the infantile material to the fore, without any necessity for symptom interpretations or suggestions. When the connection with the infantile material was established *the resolution of the character resistance began.* The subsequent symptom interpretations took place under conditions of full cooperation on the part of the patient. The resistance analysis consisted of two typical phases: first, the *emphasis* on its form and present-day meaning, and second, its *resolution* with the aid of the infantile material thus brought to the fore. In this case, the difference between a character resistance and a simple resistance consisted in the difference between politeness and submissiveness on the one hand, and simple doubt and distrust in the analysis on the other. It was only the former which belonged to his character; they were the *form* in which his distrust was expressed.

5. Consistent interpretation of the latent negative transference resulted in the liberation of his repressed and masked aggressivity toward the analyst, superiors and the father. This eliminated the passive-feminine attitude which, of course, was nothing but a reaction formation against the repressed aggressivity.

6. The repression of his aggression against the father brought with it the repression of his genital urge for the woman. Conversely, under analysis, the masculine genital striving reappeared, together with the aggressivity; this led to the cure of the impotence.

7. The apprehensiveness in his character disappeared with the castration anxiety, when the aggressivity became conscious, and the anxiety states disappeared when he gave up his sexual abstinence. The orgastic discharge of the energy which had manifested itself as stasis anxiety resulted in the elimination of the "somatic core of the neurosis."

In conclusion, I trust that the presentation of these cases will shake the opinion of some of my opponents who contend that I impose a "ready-made schema" on every patient. It will make clear the meaning of the contention which I have made for years: that for each and every case there is only *one* technique which has to be derived from its individual structure.

## CHAPTER V

# INDICATIONS AND DANGERS OF CHARACTER-ANALYSIS

The transitions from unsystematic and inconsistent analysis to systematic character-analysis are fluid and so many-sided that they are as yet difficult to define. Nevertheless, some criteria for its applicability can already be defined.

Since the character-analytic dissolution of the narcissistic defense mechanisms not only mobilizes violent affects but also results in a temporary condition of helplessness on the part of the patient, character-analysis is not a technique for beginners.[1] It can be practised without danger only by therapists who have already mastered analytic technique, who, in particular, know how to handle transference reactions. The temporary helplessness of the patient is due to the fact that the characterological stabilization of his infantile neurosis has been eliminated whereby the infantile neurosis regains its full strength. True, the infantile neurosis becomes reactivated without systematic character-analysis also. But since, in this case, the armorings remain relatively intact, the affective reactions are weaker and consequently more easily handled. There is no danger in the practice of character-analysis *if* one gains an early and thorough insight into the structure of the case. Thus far, I have not had a suicide happen in my

---

[1] *Footnote, 1945:* This caution was justified in the early days of character-analytic research, about 18 years ago. Even at that time, the objection was rightly raised that if character-analysis was superior to symptom analysis then it ought to be learned by beginners and not only by experienced analysts. Today, at a time when the technique of character-analysis is based on ample experience, the reasons for this caution are no longer valid. The technique can be taught and is preferable to symptom analysis, for beginners also. Similarly, the reasons for limiting the indication of character-analysis are no longer valid. It has been shown that the use of character-analysis is not only feasible in every case of psychoneurosis but *indispensable* if one wishes to eliminate the *character-neurotic reaction basis.* Whether character-analysis can be carried out without orgone therapy is another question.

practice—with the exception of a desolate case of acute depression where the patient broke off treatment after two or three hours, even before I could have taken any decisive measures. It is only seemingly paradoxical that since I have been practising character-analysis, that is, during about eight years, I have lost only three cases through their breaking off treatment prematurely, while this occurred much more frequently before. This is explained by the immediate analysis of negative and narcissistic reactions; this, usually, makes flight impossible, although it is much harder on the patient.

Character-analysis is applicable in every case, but not indicated in every case. More than that, there are circumstances which make its application strongly contra-indicated. First, for the indications. They are all determined by the degree of character rigidity, that is, by the degree and intensity of the neurotic reactions which have become chronic and assimilated by the ego. In compulsive neuroses—particularly in cases where there is a predominance not of symptoms but of general impairment of functioning, where the character traits form not only the object of the treatment but also its main obstacle—character-analysis is always indicated. The same is true of phallic-narcissistic characters who, without character-analysis, always succeed in frustrating every therapeutic effort, and of cases of moral insanity, impulsive characters and pseudologia phantastica. In schizoid or early schizophrenic patients a very careful but very consistent character-analysis is necessary for the prevention of premature and uncontrollable emotional breakthroughs; it strengthens the ego functions before the deeper strata of the unconscious are activated.

In serious acute anxiety hysterias, an early and consistent analysis of the ego defenses is not indicated, because here the unconscious impulses are all stirred up while the ego lacks the character traits to defend itself against them and to bind the free-floating energies. Severe acute anxiety, we must remember, indicates that the armoring has broken down on a wide front. Thus, work on the character defenses is not necessary in the early stages. In later stages, when anxiety has been replaced by an intense attachment to the analyst and when the first signs of a disappointment reaction appear, it will become necessary. But it is not the main part of the work in the initiation of the treatment.

In melancholias and severe depressions, the use of character-analysis will depend on whether we are dealing with an acute exacerbation such as acute suicidal impulses or acute anxiety, or with emotional indolence; further, it will depend on how much of a genital object-relationship has been maintained. If one wants to avoid analyses of ten years' duration, cautious but thorough character-analytic work on the ego defense (against repressed aggression) is indispensable in the indolent forms.

On the whole, it goes without saying that the loosening of the armorings can be controlled in intensity, not only according to the individual case but also according to individual situations. Some means of doing this are the following: an increase or decrease in the intensity and the consistency of resistance interpretation or of the depth at which the interpretation takes place; the more or less thorough dissolution of the negative or positive aspects of the·transference at any given time; giving the patient free rein occasionally even if he finds himself in an intensive resistance, without resolving the resistance for the time being. The patient must be prepared for violent therapeutic reactions shortly before they occur. If one is sufficiently elastic in one's interpretations and in one's influencing of the patient, if one has overcome the initial apprehensiveness and insecurity and has a great deal of patience, one will not meet too great difficulties.

Character-analysis is very difficult in patients who represent a new type with which one is unacquainted. In such cases one will try gradually, step by step, to understand the ego structure and proceed according to this understanding. One will certainly not —if one wishes to avoid unpredictable and untoward reactions— proceed to the interpretation of deeper strata. If one waits with deep interpretations until the defense mechanisms have disclosed themselves, one has lost some time, temporarily, but has gained a secure way of guiding the analysis.

Colleagues, in and out of control analysis, have often asked me whether a character-analysis can still be instituted in patients who had already produced a chaotic situation over a period of months. Experiences from the technical seminars are not yet conclusive, but it seems that in many cases, nevertheless, the change in technique is successful.

It is worth noting that, with consistent character-analysis, it is irrelevant whether the patient has much or little intellectual analytic knowledge. Since one does not give any deep interpretations before the patient has loosened his central defensive attitude and has allowed himself to feel his emotions, he has no opportunity to bring up his knowledge. If he tries to do so, nevertheless, in the interest of his resistance, this behavior is only a part of his general defensive behavior and can be unmasked in the framework of his other narcissistic reactions. If, for example, the patient uses technical analytic terms, he is not told not to do so; instead, it is treated as defense and as narcissistic identification with the analyst.

Another question frequently asked is, in how many per cent of the cases character-analysis can be successfully initiated and carried out. Certainly not in all cases; it also depends on the indications, and the intuitive abilities and the experience of the analyst. In the past few years, however, always more than half of the patients were accessible to character-analysis.

To what extent is an alteration of the character necessary in analysis? And to what extent can it be brought about?

To the first question there is, in principle, only one answer: The neurotic character must be altered to the extent to which it forms the characterological basis of neurotic symptoms and to the extent to which it produces disturbances of working ability and capacity for sexual gratification.

To the second question there is only an empirical answer. The extent to which the actual result approximates the desired change depends, in each case, on a great number of factors. Qualitative changes of character cannot be achieved by the present-day means of psychoanalysis. A compulsive character will never change into a hysteric character, a choleric does not become phlegmatic or a sanguine character melancholy. What can be achieved are quantitative changes which, if they go beyond a

certain measure, equal qualitative changes. Thus, the slight feminine attitude of compulsion-neurotic patients keeps increasing
during the analysis while the masculine-aggressive attitudes decrease.

In this manner, the whole being of the patient becomes "different," a change which is often more apparent to people who see
the patient only occasionally, at long intervals, than to the analyst.
The inhibited and self-conscious person becomes freer, the apprehensive more courageous, the over-conscientious less scrupulous, the unscrupulous more conscientious. Nevertheless, the person's "personal note" never gets lost and continues to show
through whatever changes have taken place. The formerly over-
scrupulous compulsive character, for example, becomes a realistic,
conscientious worker; the impulsive character, after cure, will
always act more quickly than he; the patient with "moral insanity," after cure, will never take life tragically and will get
through life more easily than the cured compulsive character.
But though these character traits, as such, persist, they remain,
after character-analysis, within limits which do not impair the
ability to work or to obtain sexual gratification.

## CHAPTER VI

# ON HANDLING THE TRANSFERENCE

## 1. THE CRYSTALLIZING OUT OF THE GENITAL OBJECT LIBIDO

The task of "handling the transference" arises from the fact that infantile attitudes are transferred to the analyst; this transference takes on diverse forms and functions in the course of the treatment. The attitudes toward the analyst are not only of a positive but also of a negative nature. The analyst must keep in mind that any kind of transference, sooner or later, turns into a resistance which the patient is unable to solve by himself. In particular, as Freud pointed out, an initial positive transference is apt to turn into a negative one. What makes the transference particularly important is the fact that the essential parts of the neurosis make their appearance only in the transference. For this reason, the dissolution of the "transference neurosis" which gradually takes the place of the original neurosis, becomes one of the essential tasks of analytic technique. The positive transference is the main vehicle of the treatment. However, it is not the therapeutic factor in itself, but the most important prerequisite for establishing those processes which finally—independent of the transference—lead to cure. The purely technical tasks which Freud discusses in his works on transference are the following:

1. The establishment of an effective positive transference;

2. Utilization of this transference for the overcoming of the neurotic resistances;

3. Utilization of the positive transference for the production of the repressed contents and of dynamically effective emotional breakthroughs.

From the standpoint of character-analysis, we have two additional tasks, a technical and a libido-economic one.

The technical task has to do with the requirement of establishing an effective positive transference. Clinical experience shows that only the fewest patients are capable of spontaneously establishing such a positive transference. But our character-analytic considerations lead to another question. If it is correct that all neuroses arise on the basis of a neurotic character; if, further, a narcissistic armoring is a typical aspect of the neurotic character, then the question arises whether patients, in the beginning of the treatment, are capable of a *genuine* positive transference at all. By "genuine" we mean a strong, non-ambivalent erotic object-relationship which could provide the basis for a relationship with the analyst which would be strong enough to withstand the storms of the analysis. In looking over our cases, we must answer this question in the negative: there is in the early phases of the analysis no genuine positive transference. More than that, there cannot be, because of the existing sexual repression, the lack of object-libidinal strivings, and because of the character armor. True enough, manifestations which *look like* positive transference are seen in great numbers. But what is the unconscious background of these transference manifestations? Are they genuine or not? The discussion of this problem is necessitated precisely by the unfortunate experiences made on the assumption that these were genuine object-libidinal strivings. It is part of the wider question whether a neurotic character can be capable of love at all, and if so, in what sense. An exact study of these first manifestations of so-called positive transference, that is, of object-libidinal sexual strivings toward the analyst, proved them to be—apart from a small remainder which corresponds to a reflection of rudimentary genuine love—one of three things:

1. "Reactive positive transference." In this case, the patient compensates for a transferred hatred by seeming manifestations of love. The background here is a *latent negative transference*. If one interprets the resistances which result from this kind of transference as the expression of a relationship of love, one overlooks the negative transference which is hidden behind it and runs the danger of leaving the core of the neurotic character untouched.

2. *Submissiveness* to the analyst as it results from a *guilt feeling*

or from moral masochism, behind which is again nothing but repressed and compensated hatred.

3. The transference of *narcissistic desires,* of the narcissistic expectation that the analyst will love or admire the patient. No other kind of transference collapses more rapidly than this, no other changes more easily into bitter disappointment and hateful narcissistic hurt. If one interprets this kind of transference as positive transference ("You love me") one has again made a serious mistake. For the patient does not love at all: he *wants to be loved,* and he loses interest the moment he realizes that his desires cannot be fulfilled. True, there are libidinal strivings in connection with this kind of transference but they cannot provide an effective positive transference because of their strong narcissistic component, as in the case of oral demands.

These three types of seemingly positive transference—undoubtedly, further study will reveal others—drown out such rudiments of genuine object love as have not yet been consumed by the neurosis. They are in themselves results of the neurotic process, in that the frustration in love has given rise to hatred, narcissism and guilt feelings. They are sufficient to keep the patient in analysis until such time as they can be dissolved; but if they are not unmasked in time, they will provide the patient with strong motives for breaking off the analysis.

It was precisely the wish for the establishment of an intensive positive transference which made me pay so much attention to the negative transference. The early and thorough making conscious of negative, critical or deprecatory attitudes toward the analyst does not intensify the negative transference, but dissolves it and crystallizes out the positive attitudes. What might give the impression that I "work with the negative transference" is the fact that the analytic dissolution of the narcissistic defense apparatus brings the latent negative transferences into the open so that the analyses are often characterized by defense manifestations for months at a time. After all, I do not put anything into the patient that had not been there before. I only set into focus what previously was hidden in the patient's mode of behavior (such as over-politeness, indifference, etc.) and which was nothing but a latent defense against being influenced by the analyst.

At first I called every form of ego defense negative transference. This was correct insofar as the ego defense, sooner or later, makes use of existing hate impulses. It is also correct that one always provokes hatred if, in interpreting the resistance, one proceeds from the ego defense. It was only incorrect to call the ego defense in itself negative transference. Rather, it is a narcissistic defense reaction. Narcissistic transference, too, is not a negative transference in the strict sense of the word. I was at that time strongly impressed by the fact that every ego defense, if consistently analyzed, results so quickly and easily in negative transference. A latent negative transference exists from the beginning only in the transference of the passive-feminine character and in the affect block; here we are dealing with an active but repressed hatred.

I shall illustrate the transference technique in the case of seeming positive transference with the story of a woman of 27 who came to analysis because of her sexual fickleness. She had divorced two husbands and had had a long series of lovers. She knew herself the reason for this nymphomanic tendency: sexual intercourse left her unsatisfied because of orgastic impotence. For an understanding of her resistance and its interpretation it is necessary to mention that the patient was exceptionally pretty and was quite conscious of her female charms. During the first interview I noticed a certain self-consciousness: she kept looking at the floor although she talked and answered questions fluently.

During the first and most of the second hour she talked, rather freely, about the painful circumstances of her second divorce and about the disturbances of sensation in the sexual act. Toward the end of the second hour, a disturbance set in: the patient turned silent and after a while she said that she had nothing more to say. It was clear that the transference had already become a disturbance. Now there were two possibilities: either to try, by encouragement and admonition, to move the patient to go on talking, or to tackle the resistance itself. The first would have meant to circumvent the resistance; the second was possible only if one understood the inhibition at least in part. Since, in such situations, one is always dealing with an ego defense, the resistance could be approached from this angle. I explained the meaning of such blocks to her, saying that they are due to something which is being held back, something against which she defended herself unconsciously. I added that it is usually thoughts about the analyst which give rise to such blocks, and that the success of the treatment depended on her ability to be absolutely honest about such thoughts also. Now she said, with much hesitation, that the day before she had still been able to talk freely, but that since certain thoughts had come up which really had nothing to do with the treatment. Finally it turned out that she had wondered what would happen if the analyst started to "feel a certain way" about her and whether he would not despise her because of her experiences with men. This was at the end of the hour. The next day, the block continued. I called it again to her attention and pointed out that she was again warding off something. It turned out that she had completely repressed what had come up during the previous session. I explained the meaning of this to her whereupon she related that she had been unable to sleep the night before because she was so much afraid that the analyst might develop personal feelings for her. This one might have interpreted as a projection of her own love impulses, but the patient's personality, her intense female narcissism and her past did not fit this interpretation. I felt somehow that she distrusted my dependability as a physician and feared that I might misuse the analytic situation for sexual purposes. There was no doubt that she, on her part, had already transferred sexual wishes to the analytic situation. Confronted with the choice of discussing first these manifestations of the id or those fears of the ego, one had to decide in favor of the latter. So I told her as much as I had guessed with regard to her fears. Thereupon she related a wealth of bad experiences with physicians: sooner or later, all of them had made propositions to her or had misused the therapeutic situation even without asking her. She thought that, under these circumstances, her distrust of physicians was only natural, and said that she had no way of knowing whether I was any different. This had a liberating effect for the time

being; she was again able to talk freely about her actual conflicts. She talked much about her love relationships, and from
this material two facts stood out: First, she usually chose younger
men, and second, she soon got tired of them. It was clear, of
course, that her love life was determined by *narcissistic* conditions: she wanted to dominate men, which was easier in younger
men, and she lost interest as soon as a man had given her his
full measure of admiration.

One might have told her the meaning of this behavior; it would
not have done any harm because it was not a matter of anything
that was deeply repressed. But the consideration of the dynamic
effectiveness of the interpretation made it seem wiser not to do
so. Since it was certain that her chief character trait would very
soon become a major resistance in the analysis, it seemed more
advantageous to wait until this would happen, in order to connect the emotions of the transference experience with her consciousness. The resistance soon made its appearance, but in an
unexpected form.

The patient kept silent again, and after my repeated interpretation that she was undoubtedly holding back something, she
said, after much hesitation, that what she had been afraid of
had happened, only that now she was troubled not by my possible
feelings toward her, but by her attitude toward me. She said she
kept thinking about the analysis all the time; that the day before
she had even masturbated with the phantasy of having sexual
intercourse with the analyst. I told her that such phantasies were
not unusual, that patients always transferred their feelings to
the analyst, which she understood very well. I then pointed out
the narcissistic background of this transference. True, there could
be no doubt that the phantasy was also in part the expression
of a beginning breakthrough of object-libidinal wishes. To interpret this as a transference, however, was contraindicated for
several reasons. The incest wish was still deeply repressed; although the phantasy already contained infantile elements, it
could, therefore, not stem from this wish. On the other hand,
the patient's personality and the total situation in which the
transference phantasy appeared provided ample material for

the study of other aspects and motives of the phantasy. She had anxiety states before and during the analysis which corresponded in part to dammed-up sexual excitation and in part to the necessity of dealing with a difficult situation. Thus, in interpreting the transference resistance, I proceeded again from the ego side. I told her that her strong inhibitions in talking about these things were due to the fact that she was too proud to admit such feelings to a man. This she admitted immediately, adding that everything in her shrank from it. Asked whether she had ever spontaneously loved or desired a man, she said, no, that had never happened to her; it was always the men who desired her, and she only reciprocated. I explained the narcissistic character of this behavior to her which she understood very well. As to the transference, I explained that it was not a matter of a genuine love impulse at all; that, rather, she had merely been irritated by the fact that here a man was quite unimpressed by her charms, a situation which was difficult to take—for her. I told her the phantasy had corresponded to the desire to make the analyst fall in love with her. This she confirmed by the statement that in the phantasy *the conquest of the analyst had played the greatest role and had been the real source of satisfaction.* Now I could point out to her the danger connected with this attitude: the danger was that she could not stand the rebuff for any length of time and would sooner or later lose interest in the analysis. She had already thought of this possibility herself.

This is a point which should be emphasized. If one fails to unmask the narcissistic background of such transferences at an early time, it happens very often that the patient, in an unforeseen reaction of disappointment, breaks off the analysis in negative transference. A number of such cases were reported in the technical seminar during the past few years. It had always been the same thing: Such manifestations had been taken at their face value, they had been interpreted as love instead of as the desire to be loved, the tendency to disappointment had been overlooked and the patients, sooner or later, had broken off the analysis.

In our patient, the transference interpretation opened the way to an analysis of her narcissism, of her contempt for the men who ran after her, and of her general incapacity for love which was one of the main reasons for her difficulties. She understood very well that first she had to unearth the reasons for her incapacity for love. In this connection she mentioned, in addition to her vanity, her extreme stubbornness and finally her lack of inner participation in people and things, the superficiality of her interest and the resulting feeling of emptiness. Thus the analysis of the transference resistance had led directly to the analysis of her character which from now on occupied the center of the analysis. She had to admit that the analysis, too, did not really touch her inside, in spite of her earnest will to get well. The further course of the analysis in this case does not interest us here. I only wanted to show how a handling of the transference which corresponds to the patient's character leads immediately to the problem of the narcissistic defenses.

There are other things which point to the fallacy of making the rudiments and beginnings of a genuine positive transference conscious at an early stage instead of first working on the narcissistic and negative tendencies which are superimposed. These are considerations of the economic point of view in analytic therapy.

To my knowledge, it was Landauer who first pointed out that every interpretation of a transferred emotional attitude first decreases its intensity and increases that of the opposite tendency. The goal of analytic therapy is that of crystallizing out the genital object libido, of liberating it from repression and from its admixture with narcissistic, pregenital and destructive impulses. From this it follows that one must, as long as possible, interpret only, or predominantly, the expressions of a narcissistic and negative transference while letting the signs of a beginning love impulse develop without interference until it is concentrated, without ambivalence, in the transference. Usually, this does not take place until the last stages of the analysis. Particularly in compulsion neuroses it is impossible to eliminate the ambivalence and the doubts unless one isolates the ambivalent impulses by a consistent emphasis on those impulses (like narcissism, hatred, guilt feeling) which oppose the object libido. Unless one does this, one never really gets out of a situation of acute ambivalence and doubt, and all interpretations of unconscious contents are made more or less ineffective by the armor of doubt. This economic consideration is in harmony with the topical one, for the genuine, original object libido, in particular the incestuous genital wish, is always that which is most deeply repressed, while narcissism, hatred, guilt feeling and pregenital impulses are topically and structurally more superficial.

From the economic point of view, the task in handling the transference is that of *concentrating all object libido in a purely genital transference.* This makes necessary not only the liberation of the sadistic and narcissistic energies bound up in the character armor, but also the dissolution of pregenital fixations. When the narcissistic and sadistic drives are loosened from the character armor, the liberated energy flows to pregenital positions. Then we observe, for some time, a positive transference of pregenital, that is, more infantile character. This transference furthers the breakthrough of pregenital phantasies and incest wishes and thus helps to dissolve the pregenital fixations. All libido, however, that is liberated from its pregenital fixations, flows to the genital position where it intensifies the genital Oedipus situation as in hysteria or reactivates it as in compulsion neurosis or depression. This is usually accompanied by more or less acute anxiety and the re-activation of the infantile anxiety hysteria. This is the first sign of a new cathexis of the genital stage. What appears in the analysis at this stage, however, is not the genital Oedipus wish as such, but the defense against it, castration anxiety. Typically, this concentration of the libido on the genital stage is at first only temporary; soon, the castration anxiety makes the libido again flow back temporarily to its narcissistic and pregenital points of fixation. This process usually repeats itself a number of times: every breakthrough to the genital incest desires is followed by a flowing back as a result of castration anxiety. Due to this reactiva-tion of the castration anxiety, the old mechanism of binding anxiety becomes re-established. That is, there is the formation of transitory symptoms, or, more frequently, a full reactivation of the narcissistic defense apparatus. The interpretation work, of course, has always to be done on the defense mechanisms; this unearths infantile material from ever deeper strata and thus dissolves a certain amount of anxiety with every new breakthrough to genitality. This repeats itself until finally the libido remains in the genital position; then anxiety or pregenital and narcissistic drives are replaced by *genital* sensations and transference phantasies.[1]

When I presented these facts, some analysts asked at what point the actual neurosis played a role in the analysis. The answer is: At this stage of the analysis, when the essential fixations of the libido have been dissolved, when the anxiety is no longer bound up in symptoms and in the character, then the core of the neurosis, the stasis neurosis, again makes its appearance. It corresponds to the stasis of the libido which is now free-floating. At this stage the *genuine* positive transference develops in its full strength, not only a tender but also a sensual transference; the patient begins to masturbate with transference phantasies. With the help of these phantasies, it is possible to eliminate the remaining inhibitions and infantile distortions of genitality, and the stage is reached in which the dissolution of the transference becomes necessary. But before discussing this I should like to point out some details which one observes in the course of the concentration of the libido in the transference and to the genital zone.

## 2. SECONDARY NARCISSISM, NEGATIVE TRANSFERENCE AND INSIGHT INTO ILLNESS

The loosening and dissolution of the characterological protection mechanisms which is necessary for the liberation of a maximum amount of libido brings about a temporary condition of complete helplessness. It might be called the *phase of the breakdown of secondary narcissism.* True, in this phase the patient clings to the analysis with the aid of the object libido which has been liberated in the meantime, and this provides him a certain

---

[1] *Footnote, 1945:* In terms of orgone biophysics, the goal of orgone therapy is that of dissolving the armorings in such a manner that finally all biological reflexes and movements become united in the *total orgasm reflex* and lead to sensations of orgonotic current in the genital. This makes possible the establishment of orgastic potency.

protection of an infantile kind. But the fact should be kept in mind that the breakdown of the reaction formations and of the illusions which the ego had created for its preservation mobilizes in the patient the strongest negative feelings toward the analysis;[2] in addition, the instincts regain their original strength with the dissolution of the armor, and the ego feels itself confronted by this newly regained strength. All these things taken together often make this transitional phase a highly critical one; there are often suicidal tendencies and inability to work, and in schizoid characters outspoken autistic regressions. Those who stand this process best are the compulsive characters, due to their anal perseverance and forceful aggression. If one knows how to handle the transference, it is not too difficult to manage the tempo and the intensity of this process by regulating the consistency of interpretation and, particularly, by clearly crystallizing out the negative tendencies in the patient.

In the process of dissolving the reaction formations, what is left of potency in men breaks down. It is a good thing to prepare patients who come to analysis with erective potency for this eventuality. In order to alleviate the shock of suddenly occurring erective impotence, one may advise temporary abstinence as soon as one senses the coming decompensation from such signs as an increase in symptoms and anxiety, increased unrest, or predominance of castration anxiety in dreams. On the other hand, certain narcissistic characters who are incapable of recognizing the compensation of their fear of impotence, must be exposed to the unpleasant experience. This results in violent narcissistic and negative reactions but, by bringing the castration anxiety to the fore, initiates the final decompensation of the secondary narcissism.

The decompensation of potency is the surest indication of the fact that castration anxiety is becoming an *affective experience*, which also means that the armor is being dissolved. For this

---

[2] Undoubtedly, many of the objections I hear in the discussions about negative transference stem from the fact that one usually leaves the narcissistic protection mechanism of the patients relatively untouched and therefore does not obtain any stormy hate transference.

reason, the failure of a potency disturbance to occur in the analysis of erectively potent neurotics indicates that they have not really been touched by the analysis. In most cases, of course, this problem does not exist because the patients come to the analysis with a potency disturbance to begin with. Nevertheless, there are a great number of patients who either maintain an erective potency on a sadistic basis or who have a disturbance of potency of which they are unaware, such as weak erections or premature ejaculation.

Up to the point where the patient realizes the full significance of his sexual disturbance, the analysis has to struggle more or less against the total personality of the patient. True, the analysis has the patient as an ally to the extent to which it is dealing with symptoms, for which the patient has insight and from which he suffers. But he has little interest in the analysis of the neurotic reaction basis, the neurotic character. At this point, however, his attitude usually undergoes a thorough change: he feels ill also in respect to his character, he recognizes the basis of his symptoms, develops an interest in changing his character and in getting rid of his sexual disturbance. Subjectively, he will often feel sicker than before the analysis, but also more ready to work analytically on his problems. His main incentive for getting well is now that of becoming capable of a healthy sexual life, the significance of which for psychic health has become clear to him. The incentive to get well is essentially created consciously by the unpleasure accompanying the neurosis, and unconsciously by the natural genital demands.

The increased insight into illness and the intensified feeling of being ill are not only the result of a consistent analysis of the narcissistic protection mechanism which, rather, leads to intensified defense in the form of negative transference, of hatred against the analyst as the disturber of the neurotic equilibrium. But this attitude already contains the germ of an opposite attitude which greatly aids the analysis. The patient is now forced to give himself up completely to the analysis and begins to see in the analyst the only helper, the only one who can get him well. This gives a strong basis to the will to get well. It goes without saying that these attitudes are closely connected with infantile tendencies, with castration anxiety and the infantile need for protection.

### 3. ON HANDLING THE ABSTINENCE RULE

If the dynamic and economic goal is that of establishing a genital transference, the question arises, What is the meaning and content of the abstinence rule? Should every kind of sexual gratification be stopped, and if not, which kind? Many analysts interpret the rule as meaning that the sexual act should be prohibited except perhaps in married people; otherwise, they argue, the necessary stasis of the libido and its concentration in the transference does not come about. The fact should be kept in mind, however, that prohibitions are much more apt to prevent the establishment of a positive transference than to further it. We do not believe that the prohibition of coitus can have the desired effect. One must ask, furthermore, is not such a measure against the general principles of analytic therapy? Will such a prohibition not automatically reinforce the pathogenic situation of the neurosis, genital frustration, instead of eliminating it? In sexually inhibited women and erectively impotent men such a prohibition is a serious mistake. The whole concept of our therapeutic task makes it clear that the frustration of genitality can be indicated only under exceptional circumstances. The neurosis owes its existence to a diversion and regression of the libido from the genital position; the therapeutic task, therefore, is that of liberating it from its pathological anchorings and of concentrating it again on the genital zone. Generally speaking, one will eliminate the pregenital activities by proper interpretation while giving the genital tendencies free rein to develop. To prohibit masturbation in patients who previously did not masturbate and who are just on the point of overcoming their fear of masturbating would be a serious mistake. On the contrary, there is, under the usual circumstances, no reason why genital masturbation should be interfered with. It is only when masturbation or the genital act become resistances that they have to be dealt with. As a rule, this will be done by interpretation, as with any other resistance. Only in rare cases, for example, of excessive masturbation, will prohibition be necessary. The average patient, particularly the female one, should not be exposed to any genital frustration during analysis. It should be remembered that the beginning of genital masturbation is the first sure indication of a new cathexis of the genital stage.

In many cases, the libido stasis even acts as a definite hindrance to the analysis. When the concentration of the libido to the genital zone has progressed far enough, the intense sexual excitations which occur will disturb the analysis. After one has exhausted the content of the phantasies, there is a phase of intense sexual desire without the production of further unconscious material. In this case, periodic relief of the stasis by masturbation or sexual intercourse has a liberating effect and the analysis proceeds again. It is clear, then, that the abstinence rule must be handled extremely elastically and must be subordinated to the principle of the concentration of the libido on the genital zone. Generally speaking: every technical measure is correct which serves to bring about this concentration, every measure is incorrect which hinders it.

The sensual transference which goes with this genital concentration of the libido is, on the one hand, the most potent factor in bringing to the surface unconscious material, and, on the other hand, a hindrance to the analysis. The genital excitation which arises on the basis of the transference reactivates the total sexual conflict; many patients refuse for a long time to recognize the transference character of this situation. The important thing is that in this process they learn to tolerate genital frustration, that, for the first time, they do not react with disappointment, that they do not regress, and that they have concentrated both tender and sensual strivings on one person. Experience shows that *patients who fail to go through such a phase of sensual transference of a genital character do not succeed fully in establishing genital primacy;* from the point of view of libido economy, this means a more or less serious defect in the therapeutic process. In such cases, the analysis has either not succeeded in *really* liberating the sensual genital striving from repression; or it has not succeeded in dissolving the guilt feeling which makes a confluence of tender and sensual strivings possible. The following are signs that this task has fully succeeded:

1. *Genital masturbation without guilt feeling,* with genital transference phantasies and corresponding gratification. Where the analyst is of the same sex as the patient: masturbation with phantasies of the incest object in the person of the analyst.

2. *Phantasies of incest without guilt feeling* sometimes occur. The renunciation is easiest if the wish is *fully conscious.*

3. *Genital excitation during the analysis,* indicating that the castration anxiety has been overcome.

It goes without saying that this activation of genitality, which initiates the final dissolution of the neurotic character and the establishment of the genital character, can never be achieved by some kind of suggestion but only analytically, that is, by the handling of the transference with the goal of the concentration of the libido on the genital. This is made difficult by such factors as age and the chronicity of the neurosis, and cannot be achieved in all cases, though often enough to make it a practical goal. From the libido-economic point of view, the attainment of this goal is indispensable because it is the basis of an orderly libido economy regulated by the genital function.

The danger that the patient may get into difficult situations as a result of one's giving his genitality free rein during the analysis is negligible. If he is about to get himself into trouble for neurotic motives, thorough analysis of the situation will keep him from doing so; such analytic procedure makes prohibitions unnecessary. This is possible only if one has handled the transference correctly from the beginning. Of course, much room is left here for the subjective evaluation of the situation by the analyst. One analyst will see nothing wrong in a young man's engaging in a sexual act while he will take strong measures in the case of a girl (double sexual morality). Another analyst will, rightly, not make any such distinction, unless the socially more dangerous step is to be prevented in the case of the girl in the interest of the analysis.

#### 4. ON THE "DISSOLUTION" OF THE POSITIVE TRANSFERENCE

The last task of the analyst, according to Freud, is the solution of the positive transference. The question arises immediately whether this process is analogous to the other solutions of transferred emotions by reduction to the infantile, whether, in other words, it is a matter of a "dissolution" of the positive transference. Obviously, this cannot be so. Rather, the object libido, now freed from all the impediments of hatred, narcissism, spite, tendency to disappointment, etc., has to be "transferred" from the analyst to another object, one that corresponds to the patient's needs. While all pregenital and sadistic transferences can be dissolved by reducing them to their infantile background, this is not possible in the case of genitality because the genital function is part of the general reality function. True, it is not easy to see why the reduction of the genital transference to the genital incest wishes does not dissolve it but, on the contrary, liberates it from the incest fixation, makes it urge for gratification. We are helped here by the consideration that the reduction of, say, an anal transference to the infantile situation does not dissolve it either; what happens is that the corresponding libido quantity is shifted from the anal to the genital. This is how the progression from pregenitality to genital primacy takes place. In the reduction of the genital transference to the primal situation, such a qualitative shift can no longer take place, because the genital stage represents the highest stage. The only possibility here is a "transference of the transference" to a real object.

In this process one often meets considerable difficulties, particularly in patients of the opposite sex, in the form of a stickiness of the libido which often makes a detachment impossible for months. Investigation of the reasons for this stickiness reveals the following:

1. *Unresolved guilt feelings* corresponding to sadistic impulses toward a childhood object which have not become fully conscious.

2. *A secret hope* that the analyst will finally fulfil the patient's love demands after all. One has to be on the lookout for this hope because patients almost never express it spontaneously.

3. A remnant of a non-genital, *infantile fixation to the analyst as the representative of the protecting mother*. This is where Rank's concept of the analytic situation as a fantasied situation of the mother's womb applies in many cases. Just as the analysis of the fixation due to guilt feelings eliminates the last remnants of sadistic impulses, so does the analysis of the stickiness due to infantile mother fixation eliminate the remnants of a libidinous fixation of a pregenital character.

4. Finally, one finds in these last stages of the analysis, particularly in girls and unhappily married women, a great fear of a sexual life, partly in the form of primitive fear of coitus, partly in the form of an adherence to the social norms of monogamous ideology and demand for chastity. Particularly the latter demands most thorough analysis. This usually shows either a strong identification with the monogamous mother or the mother who demands chastity, or a feeling of inferiority with regard to the female sexual function. There is, in addition, the fear—fully rational—of the difficulties which a sexual life presents in a society in which sexuality is so much debased. In men the difficulty is often that now, that they have become capable of concentrating both tenderness and sensuality in one object, they also are incapable of intercourse with prostitutes or kept women. If they do not marry immediately, the finding of a sexual partner who satisfies the tender as well as the sensual needs is difficult.

These and many other circumstances make the detachment from the analyst difficult. It happens often that the patient satisfies his sensuality with an object he does not love, or, rather, cannot love, because his tenderness is bound to the analyst. Although this fixation makes the right object choice during the analysis difficult, nevertheless, the best results are seen if the patient finds his appropriate sexual object before the termination of the analysis. This has the great advantage that one can observe the behavior in the new relationship and can analyze possible neurotic residues.

If the finding of an object during the analysis does not take place too early, that is, not *before* the working through of the positive transference, and if one is careful to avoid influencing the patient, for example, urging him into an object choice, then such a termination of the treatment has its undoubted advantages. On the other hand, one now meets difficulties of a social nature; these are discussed elsewhere.[3]

## 5. A NOTE ON COUNTER-TRANSFERENCE

It is easy to see that the individuality of the therapist is a more or less important factor, according to the individual case. The analyst must attune his own unconscious, like a receiving apparatus, to the unconscious of the patient, and he must approach each patient according to the patient's individuality. This has to do with the analyst's theoretical and practical knowledge only insofar as his receptivity for the patient's unconscious and his ability to adapt to any analytic situation will enable him to widen and deepen his theoretical and practical knowledge.

First we must set straight a possible misunderstanding. Freud recommended an unbiased attitude, an attitude in which one lets oneself be surprised by every new turn the analysis takes. This seems to be at variance with our demand for a systematic analysis of the resistances and for deducing the special technique from the individual structure of the patient. How, one will ask, can one have a passive, receptive, unbiased attitude and at the same time proceed in a logical and systematic fashion?

The contradiction is only a seeming one. If one has developed the attitude which Freud demands, then the handling of the resistances and the transference will take place automatically as a reaction to the process going on in the patient, without much thinking about the structure of the case. For example, if material of different dynamic value from different strata is presented at the same time, one will spontaneously choose that which is more important dynamically; without giving it much thought, one will analyze the ego defense *before* the repressed contents, etc. The necessity of thinking much about the structure of the case and

3 *Cf.* GESCHLECHTSREIFE, ENTHALTSAMKEIT, EHEMORAL, 1930, and DER SEXUELLE KAMPF DER JUGEND, 1931.

*Translator's note:* A second edition of the first of these two books appeared in 1936 under the title DIE SEXUALITÄT IM KULTURKAMPF. The English translation of this is entitled THE SEXUAL REVOLUTION. Orgone Institute Press, 1945.

about technical measures always indicates either that the patient presents a new and unaccustomed type or that the analyst's own unconscious is somehow blocked against the material presented. True, as Freud said, one must always expect the unexpected, but one must also be able to fit it into the total context of the therapeutic process. If the analysis has been unrolled from the beginning according to the structure of the case, by way of correct handling of the transference resistances; if, furthermore, one has avoided confusing the situation by premature and too deep interpretations, then the new material fits as of itself. The most important reason for this is that the unconscious material does not emerge haphazardly, but in a sequence which is determined by the analysis itself. This is the case only in a systematic resistance analysis.

The technical discussions of cases which can be only intellectual may give one the erroneous impression that character-analytic work is the result of an intellectual dissection of the case during treatment. Treatment, however, rests largely on intuitive comprehension and action. Once one has overcome the typical tendency of the beginner immediately to "sell" his knowledge of the case, if one lets oneself flow freely, then the essential basis for analytic work is established.

This ability of the analyst to let himself flow freely in the work, instead of clinging to his intellectual knowledge, the ability to comprehend the individual case itself, depends, of course, on certain conditions of a characterological nature; just as the ability of the patient to let go depends on the degree to which his character armor has been loosened up.

Without discussing the whole complex of relevant questions, we shall illustrate the problem of *counter-transference* with a few typical examples. The course which a case takes usually shows where the attitude of the analyst is defective, that is, disturbed by his own difficulties. In many patients who never produce an affective negative transference this is due not so much to their own blocking as to that of the therapist. If the analyst has not resolved the repression of his own aggressive impulses he will not be able to do it satisfactorily in his patients; he may even

develop an affective aversion toward a correct intellectual evaluation of the analysis of the negative transference. In such cases the
hidden aggression of the patient means a provocation of the
repressed aggression of the analyst. The analyst will be inclined
to overlook negative tendencies in the patient, or he will prevent
their open manifestation in one way or another, or he will even
reinforce their repression by exaggerated friendliness toward the
patient. The patients are very quick to sense such attitudes on
the part of the analyst and utilize them for purposes of defense.
Affect-block or apprehensively over-polite behavior on the part
of the analyst are the most important signs of repressed aggression on his part.

The counterpart is the inability to tolerate the sexual manifestations of the patient, his positive transference. Control analyses show that the analyst's fear of the patient's sensual manifestations not only interferes seriously with the treatment but often
prevents the patient from establishing genital primacy. It is
normal for the patient to develop his demands for genital love
in the transference. If, now, the analyst is not sexually healthy, or
if he does not have at least intellectually an unequivocally sex-
affirmative attitude, the analysis must inevitably suffer. It goes
without saying that, without sexual experiences of one's own, one
cannot comprehend the actual difficulties in a patient's sexual life.
One of the most important requirements of a training analysis,
therefore, should be that the young analysts fulfil at least the
same requirement as the patient: establishment of genital primacy
and of a healthy, satisfactory sex life. The sexually disturbed or
unsatisfied analyst not only has more difficulty in handling his
positive counter-transferences and may have to repress his own
impulses; he also will, in the long run, not be able to stand the
provocation of his own sexual demands by the patient's sexual
manifestations and will inevitably get into neurotic difficulties. In
this respect, the therapeutic work makes the highest demands on
us; it would be senseless to deny them. It does not make any
difference whether the analyst acknowledges or denies such difficulties in himself: every average patient will sense the unconscious sex-negation in the analyst and will, as a result, be unable

to get rid of his sexual inhibitions. But the consequences of such attitudes go even farther. The analyst may himself live as he thinks is right, but if he adheres—*unconsciously*—to rigid moralistic principles which the patient always senses, if, for example, he has, *without knowing it,* repressed in himself, say, polygamous behavior or certain kinds of love play, he will not be a match for his patients and will have an inclination to accuse a patient of "infantile" behavior when such behavior may in itself be quite normal.

Analysts who experience the transference of their patients essentially narcissistically have a tendency to interpret any real falling-in-love as a being-in-love with the analyst. For the same reason, the patient's criticism and distrust is often not brought into the open.

Analysts who are unable to control their own sadism easily fall into the famous "analytic silence." To them, the enemy is not the patient's neurosis, but the patient himself who "does not want to get well." Threats to break off the analysis are often not so much the result of lacking technical knowledge as of lacking patience, a lack which, of course, has its effect on the technique.

Finally, it is a mistake to interpret the general analytic rule that one has to approach the patient as a blank screen onto which he projects his transferences in such a manner that one assumes, always and in every case, an unalive, mummy-like attitude. Under such circumstances, few patients can "thaw out," and this leads to artificial, un-analytic measures. It should be clear that one approaches an aggressive patient unlike a masochistic one, a hyperactive hysteric unlike a depressive one, that one changes one's attitude in one and the same patient according to the situation, that, in brief, one does not behave neurotically oneself, even though one may have to deal with some neurotic difficulties in oneself.

One cannot give up one's own individuality, a fact which one will consider in the choice of patients. But one should be able to expect that this individuality is not a disturbing factor and that the training analysis should establish the necessary minimum in plasticity of character.

In brief, the demands which must be made on the analyst are as great as the difficulties encountered in practice. He will have to know that his work is in conflict with most of the heavily defended positions of conservative society and that for this reason he will be exposed to enmity, contempt and slander—unless he prefers, at the expense of his theoretical and practical convictions, to make concessions to a social order which is in direct and insoluble conflict with the demands of the therapy of neuroses.

PART TWO

# THEORY OF CHARACTER FORMATION

In our presentation thus far, we have followed the path pointed out by analytic practice. Our starting point was the question as to the economic principle of analytic therapy; this led to the character-analytic problems of the "narcissistic barrier," the solution of certain technical problems and to new theoretical questions. The study of case histories revealed the fact that the narcissistic armor has a typical connection with the infantile sexual conflicts. While this corresponds entirely to our analytic expectations, it imposes the task on us of following up these connections in detail. We also found that the changes which the pathological character attitudes undergo in the course of treatment follow a definite course. It is the development from the neurotic structure to another one characterized by the establishment of genital primacy; for this reason, we call it "genital character." Finally, we shall have to describe certain typical characters. One among these, the masochistic character, will lead to a critique of a more recent analytic theory of the instincts.

CHAPTER VII

# THE CHARACTEROLOGICAL MASTERY OF THE INFANTILE SEXUAL CONFLICT[1]

Psychoanalytic investigation is in a position to provide characterology with fundamentally new points of view and, based on these, with new findings. This is made possible by three of its characteristics:

1) Its theory of unconscious mechanisms; 2) its historical, genetic point of view; and 3) its comprehension of the dynamics and the economy of psychic functioning.

By penetrating from phenomenological manifestations to their nature and development and by comprehending the processes of the "depth personality" in cross section and longitudinal section, it automatically opens the way to the ideal of character research, a "genetic typology." This could provide not only the natural-scientific comprehension of human modes of reaction but also of their specific developmental history. The merit of taking character research out of the realm of so-called Geisteswissenschaft in the sense of Klages, and of making it part of natural-scientific psychology, would be in itself something not to be underestimated. But the clinical investigation of this field is not simple; a preliminary clarification of the facts to be discussed is, therefore, in order.

## 1. THE CONTENT AND THE FORM OF PSYCHIC REACTIONS

In studying character, psychoanalysis, from the beginning, struck out on new paths corresponding to its methods. First, Freud[2] discovered that certain character traits are to be explained

---

[1] First read at a meeting of the Deutsche Psychoanalytische Gesellschaft, Dresden, September 28, 1930.
[2] Freud: "Charakter und Analerotik." Ges. Schr., Bd. V.

143

historically as the socially conditioned derivative and continuations of primitive instinctual impulses, that, for example, parsimony, pedantry and orderliness are derivatives of anal-erotic impulses. Later it was, in particular, Jones[3] and Abraham[4] who added fundamental findings to characterology by reducing character traits to their infantile instinctual basis (e.g., envy and ambition to urethral eroticism). In these first characterological attempts it was a matter of explaining the *instinctual basis* of individual character traits. The problems presented by the demands of everyday practice, however, go much further. We are confronted with the following alternative: Either we understand the *character as a total formation* historically and dynamico-economically, in general as well as in its typological variations— or we must relinquish the possibility of success in a great many cases, the cases in which the elimination of the character-neurotic reaction basis is the main therapeutic task.

During the analysis, the character of the patient, in the form of his typical mode of reaction, becomes the most important resistance against the uncovering of the unconscious (*character resistance*). It can be shown that this function of the character during treatment reflects its development: The circumstances which, in everyday life and in the analysis, give rise to the typical reaction of an individual are the same which conditioned the character formation originally, which maintained the typical mode of reaction once it was established and formed it into an automatic mechanism which became independent of the conscious will.

Our problem, then, is not the content or the nature of this or that character trait, but the origin and the meaningful working of the typical mode of reaction in general. Up to now, we have been able to understand genetically the experiential contents, the neurotic symptoms and character traits. Now we arrive at a clarification of the formal problem, of the manner in which an experience takes place and in which neurotic symptoms are pro-

---

[3] Jones: Über analerotische Charakterzüge. *Internat. Zeitschr. f. Psychoan.* 5, 1919.
[4] Abraham: PSYCHOANALYTISCHE STUDIEN ZUR CHARAKTERBILDUNG. Internat. Psychoan. Verlag, 1924.

duced. This paves the way to an understanding of what one might call the *basic trait of a personality.*

Popularly, people are referred to as hard and soft, proud and humble, cold and warm, etc. Analysis of these different characters shows that they are merely different forms of *armoring of the ego* against the dangers threatening from the outer world and from the repressed inner impulses. Exaggerated politeness in one person is no less motivated by anxiety than is harsh or brutal behavior in another person. The difference is merely that different environmental influences led one person to deal with his anxiety in one way, the other person in another way. When we speak of such clinical classifications as passive-feminine, paranoid-aggressive, compulsive, hysterical, phallic-narcissistic characters, etc., we have roughly characterized different reaction types. The task now is to comprehend not only "character formation" in general but also the fundamental conditions which lead to such a typical differentiation.

## 2. THE FUNCTION OF CHARACTER FORMATION

The next question is what causes character formation. In order to answer it, we must first remind ourselves of some attributes of characterological reactions in general. The character consists in a *chronic* alteration of the ego which one might describe as a rigidity. It is the basis of the becoming chronic of a person's characteristic mode of reaction. Its meaning is the protection of the ego against external and internal dangers. As a protection mechanism which has become chronic it can rightly be called an *armor.* This armor inevitably means a reduction of the total psychic mobility. This reduction is alleviated by relationships with the outer world which are not conditioned by the character and thus are atypical. There are "gaps" in the armor through which libidinal and other interests are put out and pulled back like pseudopodia. The armor, however, is to be thought of as mobile. It operates according to the pleasure-unpleasure-principle. In unpleasurable situations the armoring increases, in pleasurable situations it decreases. The degree of character mobility, the ability to open up to a situation or to close up against it, constitutes the difference between the healthy and the neurotic character structure. The prototype of a pathologically rigid armoring is the affect-blocked compulsive character and schizophrenic autism which tend in the direction of catatonic rigidity.

The character armor developed as the chronic result of the conflict between instinctual demands and the frustrating outer world; the continuing actual conflicts between instinct and outer world give it its strength and continued reason for existence. It is the sum total of those influences of the outer world on instinctual life which, by reason of their similarity, form a historical unit. One only has to think of well-known character types such as "the bourgeois," "the official," "the proletarian," etc. The place where the armor is formed is the ego, that part of the personality which forms the boundary between instinctual life and outer world. We can call it, therefore, the character of the ego.

At the beginning of the final formation of character, analysis always reveals the conflict between the genital incest wishes and their actual frustration. Character formation begins as a definite form of the solution of the Oedipus complex. The conditions which lead to this particular form of the solution of conflicts are specific for character formation. (These conditions correspond to the social conditions of today and their influence on infantile sexuality. With the change of these social conditions, the conditions of character formation will also change, and with that, the character structures). For there are also other ways of dealing with the Oedipus complex which determine the future personality to a lesser degree, such as simple repression or the formation of an infantile neurosis. What these conditions of character formation have in common are intense genital desires and a relatively weak ego which, for fear of punishment, protects itself first by repressions. The repression leads to a damming up of the impulses. This in turn threatens the simple repression with a breakthrough of the repressed impulse. This leads to an alteration of the ego, say, to the development of apprehensive attitudes, of shyness. Such an attitude, it is true, means a limitation of the ego but also a strengthening of it, for it presents a protection against situations which would provoke the repressed impulses.

This first alteration of the ego, such as shyness, is not sufficient to master the instinct; on the contrary, it leads to the development of anxiety and is always the basis of the infantile phobia. In order to maintain the repression, a further alteration of the ego is necessary: The repressions must become consolidated, the ego must harden, the defense must assume a chronically active, automatic character. In addition, the repressed manifests itself in the infantile anxiety which is simultaneously produced, and the anxiety itself threatens to weaken the ego; for this reason, a protection must be formed against the anxiety also. The motive behind all these measures of the ego is conscious or unconscious fear of punishment, a fear which, as we know, is constantly being kept alive by the actual behavior of parents and educators.

The hardening of the ego takes place essentially on the basis of three processes:

1. Identification with frustrating reality, specifically, with the main person who represents this reality. This process gives the armoring its meaningful contents. For example, the affect-block of a compulsive patient had the following meaning: "I must exercise self-control, as my father always said I should." At the same time it meant: "I must preserve my pleasure possibilities and therefore become indifferent toward my father."

2. The aggression which was mobilized against the frustrating person and which caused anxiety is turned against the self. This process immobilizes the greatest part of the aggressive energies, blocks them off from motor expression and thus creates the inhibiting aspect of the character.

3. The ego forms reactive attitudes toward the sexual impulses and utilizes their energies in warding them off. This process withdraws certain amounts of libido from the repressed libidinal impulses, thus making them less capable of breaking through.

The armoring of the ego, then, takes place as a result of fear of punishment, at the expense of id energies, and contains the prohibitions of early education. In this way, character formation serves the economic purpose of alleviating the pressure of the repressed and of strengthening the ego. But the whole process has also another aspect. While the armoring was successful, at least for the time being, against the inner forces, it means, at the same time, a more or less far-reaching insulation against stimuli from the outside and against further influences of education. This does not preclude an external submissiveness, except in cases of outspoken stubbornness. The fact should also not be overlooked that superficial compliance, as seen, for example, in the passive-feminine character, may be combined with tenacious inner resistance. Moreover, the armoring may take place at the surface of the personality, or in the depth. In the case of deep-seated armoring, the manifest appearance of the personality is not the real expression of the personality but only a seeming one. Superficial armoring is typical of the affect-blocked compulsive character and the paranoid-aggressive character, deep armoring is typical of the hysterical character. The depth of the armoring depends on the conditions of regression and fixation and is a detail question in the problem of character differentiation.

Character armoring is, on the one hand, a *result* of the infantile sexual conflict and a mode of solving it. On the other hand, it also becomes the *basis* of later neurotic conflicts and symptom neuroses; it becomes the *character-neurotic reaction basis*. This will be discussed in some detail later; here I shall only give a brief résumé of the relevant facts:

The prerequisite of a later neurotic illness is a character structure which does not admit of the establishment of a sex-economic regulation of energy. The basic pathogenic factor, therefore, is not the infantile sexual conflict and the Oedipus complex as such, but the manner in which these conflicts were solved. This solution, however, is to a far-reaching extent determined by the nature of the family conflict itself, that is, by such things as the intensity of the fear of punishment, the degree to which instinctual gratification is permitted, character of the parents, etc. For this reason, the development of the child up to and through the Oedipus phase determines whether the further development will result in a neurosis or in a sex-economic regulation of the energies which alone provides a basis for social and sexual potency.

The presence of the character-neurotic reaction basis means that the ego has become rigid in a fashion which makes an orderly sexual life and a full sexual experience impossible. As a result, the damming up of sexual energy, the sexual stasis, not only becomes permanent but keeps increasing. The next consequence of this is the increasing development of reaction formations such as an ascetic ideology. In a vicious circle, this increases the stasis which in turn leads to new reaction formations. However, the stasis always increases more rapidly than the armoring process progresses, until finally the reaction formations can no longer keep the tension in check. Now, the repressed sexual desires break through and are immediately warded off by symptom formation.

In this neurotic process, the various defense positions of the ego permeate each other and become interlinked; thus we find, in the cross section of the personality, character reactions which, historically, belong to different periods of development. In the phase of the final breakdown of the ego, this cross section resembles a strip of country after a volcanic eruption which produces various geological strata in complete disorder. Yet it is possible to find the cardinal meaning and mechanism of all character reactions in this disorder; once they are found and understood, they provide the shortest path to the central infantile conflict.

### 3. CONDITIONS OF CHARACTER DIFFERENTIATION

What conditions for the establishment of a healthy and of a pathological armor are descernible at our present state of knowledge? As long as we cannot give concrete answers to this question which will point to new ways in education, our characterological investigation remains sterile theory. Considering our present sexual order, the results of such investigation are highly inconvenient for the educator who wishes to bring up people to be healthy.

To begin with, the fact must be pointed out that character formation depends not merely on the fact that instinct and frustration create a conflict; it depends also on the nature of this conflict, on the period at which the character-forming conflicts occur, and on what impulses are involved. If we try, for the purpose of orientation, to draw a schema of the conditions involved, we find the following possibilities. The result of character formation depends on the following factors:

The time at which an impulse is frustrated;

The extent and the intensity of the frustrations;

Against which impulses the central frustration is directed;

The ratio between permission and frustration;

The sex of the main frustrating person; and

The contradictions in the frustrations themselves.

All these conditions are determined by the social order of education, morality and gratification of needs, that is, in the last analysis, by the economic structure of society at any given time.

The goal of a future prevention of the neuroses can only be that of creating character structures which allow of the sexual and social mobility necessary for psychic economy. For this reason, we must first try to understand the results of any denial of instinctive gratification in the child.

Every frustration of the kind of present-day educational measures results in a withdrawal of libido from the outside, that is, an intensification of secondary narcissism;[5] this already alters the character in the sense of a heightened sensitivity which expresses itself, say, as shyness or apprehensiveness. If, as is usually the case, the frustrating person was loved by the child, it develops an ambivalent attitude which leads to an identification: in addition to the denial, the child also takes over certain character traits of this person, specifically, those which are directed against the impulse in question. The final result, as far as the impulse is concerned, is its repression or some other kind of neurotic outcome.

The effect of the frustration, as far as the *character* is concerned, is different according to the time at which the impulse meets it. At an early stage of instinctual development the frustration results in a repression which is only too successful. True, the

---

[5] *Footnote, 1945:* In terms of orgone biophysics: The lasting frustration of primary, natural needs leads to a chronic contraction of the biosystem (muscular armor, sympatheticotonia, etc.). The conflict between inhibited primary impulse and armor leads to the formation of *secondary,* antisocial impulses (sadism, etc.). Primary biological impulses break through the armor; in doing so, they are changed into destructive-sadistic impulses.

victory over the impulse is complete, but, as a result of this, the energies of the impulse are available neither for sublimation nor for conscious gratification. An all too early repression of anal eroticism, for example, impedes the development of the anal sublimations and lays the groundwork for severe anal reaction formations. What is more important from the point of view of character is that the disconnection of the impulses from the total personality results in an impairment of the total activity. This can be readily seen, for example, in children whose aggression and pleasure in motor activity were inhibited at an early time. This results later in a reduction of working ability.

Once an impulse is fully developed, on the other hand, it can no longer be fully repressed. At this stage, a denial can only produce an *insoluble* conflict between instinctual urge and prohibition. If the fully developed impulse meets a sudden unaccustomed frustration, the basis is laid for the development of an impulsive character.[6] The child does not fully take over the prohibition but develops, nevertheless, strong guilt feelings; these, in turn, give the impulsive actions the character of compulsive impulses. Thus we find, in impulsive psychopaths, a largely unformed character structure, the opposite of a thorough armoring toward the inside and the outside. In the impulsive characters it is not the reaction formations which are used as a defense against the impulses; rather, the impulses themselves, especially, sadistic impulses, are utilized as a defense against imaginary dangers, including the danger threatening from the impulses. Since the disorganized genital structure prevents an orderly libido economy, the sexual stasis increases the anxiety and character reactions and often leads to excesses of all kinds.

The opposite of the impulsive character is the instinct-inhibited character. The former shows in his history the impact of fully developed instinct and sudden frustration; the latter, constant frustration from the beginning to the end of instinctual development. Correspondingly, the character armoring tends to be rigid, it greatly reduces the psychic mobility of the individual and forms the reaction basis for depressive states and compulsion

---

[6] *Cf.* Reich: DER TRIEBHAFTE CHARAKTER. Internat. Psychoan. Verlag, 1925.

symptoms which correspond to inhibited aggression; on the other hand—and this is its sociological meaning—it makes people submissive and lacking critical faculties.

What is most significant in determining the kind of later sexual life is the sex and the character of the person who exerts the main educational influences. The influences which authoritarian society exerts on the child are extremely complicated; we shall reduce them here to the fact that the father and the mother are the essential executive organs of this social influence. The usually unconscious sexual attitude of the parents to the children results in the fact that the father prefers the daughter, the mother the son; consequently, they also restrict them less. For this reason alone it is the rule that the parent of the same sex is the one who exerts the main educational influence. True, during the first few years of the child, and among the masses of the working population, this relationship shifts in favor of the mother as the main educating person. Nevertheless, the identification with the parent of the same sex is the predominant one: the daughter develops an ego and super-ego according to that of her mother, the son according to his father. Special family constellations or character traits of the parents result in frequent exceptions to this rule. We shall discuss some of the typical backgrounds for such atypical identifications.

First, the boy. Ordinarily, that is, if he has developed a simple Oedipus complex, if his mother loved him more and frustrated him less than the father, he will identify himself with his father. Provided that the father himself was of an active masculine character, he will develop in the direction of masculine activity. If, however, the mother was a strict, "masculine" personality, if the main frustrations originated with her, the boy will identify himself largely with her. In this case, depending on the stage of libidinal development during which he met the main maternal frustration, he will develop a *mother identification either on a phallic or on an anal basis*.

On the basis of a *phallic* mother-identification a phallic-narcissistic character usually develops, whose narcissism and sadism is directed especially toward women (vengeance on the strict mother). This attitude is the character defense against the deeply repressed original love of the mother which could not continue to exist in the face of her frustrating influence and thus ended in disappointment. To be more precise: this love changed into the character attitude, from where it can be freed again analytically.

In the case of a mother-identification on an *anal* basis a passive-feminine character develops who displays this attitude not toward men but toward women. Such a character is often the basis of a masochistic perversion with the phantasy of the strict woman. This character formation usually serves to ward off phallic wishes which during infancy—for a short period but intensely—had been directed toward the mother. In these cases, there is fear of castration with *the mother* as the castrating person; this intensifies the anal identification with her. The erogenous basis of this character formation is, specifically, anality.

The passive-feminine character in the man is always based on an identification with the mother. In the type just mentioned, the mother is the frustrating person and thus also the object of the fear and of the passive behavior occasioned by it. There is, however, another type of passive-feminine character, which developed on the basis of exaggerated severeness of *the father*. In this case, the boy, afraid of realizing his genital desires, gives up the masculine-phallic position and retreats to the feminine-anal position where he identifies himself with his mother and develops a passive-feminine attitude toward the father, later on to all persons in authority. This type is characterized by exaggerated politeness and compliance, softness and tendency to cunning; this attitude wards off the active masculine tendencies and especially the repressed hatred toward the father. While he has a mother-identification in the ego and thus is actually passive-feminine, he has a father-identification in the super-ego and ego ideal without, however, being able to practically realize this identification, because of the lack of a phallic position. He always *is* feminine and always *wants to be* masculine. This tension between a female ego and a masculine ego-ideal results in a severe feeling of inferiority and gives the individual the stamp of being oppressed or humble. This has a rational justification in a severe disturbance of potency which is always present in these cases.

Comparing this type with that of phallic mother-identification, we see that the phallic-narcissistic character wards off his inferiority feeling successfully so that it is visible only to the trained observer, while the passive-feminine character openly portrays his inferiority feeling. The difference lies in the basic erogenous structure: Phallic libido enables the individual to compensate completely all attitudes which do not correspond to the masculine ego-ideal, while such a compensation is impossible if the anal libido is in the center of the male sexual structure.

Now, to the girl. Here we see, conversely, that a father who exerts little frustration will contribute more to the formation of a feminine character than will a stern or brutal father. The typical reaction of the girl to a brutal father is the formation of a masculine, hard character. Penis envy is activated and leads, characterologically, to a masculinity complex. In this case, the hard, masculine-aggressive armoring serves as a defense against the infantile-feminine attitude toward the father which had to be repressed because of his hardness and lovelessness. If the father is mild and loving, the girl can retain and develop her object-love; she does not need to identify herself with her father. True, she also is likely to have acquired penis envy; but, as there were no serious frustrations of heterosexual tendencies, it remained harmless as far as character formation is concerned. We see, then, that to say that this or that woman has penis envy does not mean anything. What matters is its influence on character or symptom formation. The decisive factor in this type is that a mother-identification in the ego took place; it expresses itself in those character traits which are called "feminine."

Whether or not this character structure can be maintained depends on whether, in puberty, vaginal eroticism comes to form a lasting basis of femininity. Disappointments in the father or in father images at this age may give rise to a masculine identification which failed to materialize in childhood and may activate dormant penis envy and initiate the change from the feminine to the masculine character. This is often seen in girls who repress their heterosexual desires for moralistic reasons (identification with the authoritarian moralistic mother) and who provoke disillusioning experiences with men. In most cases, such female types tend to develop hysterical characteristics. One then finds an ever-repeated approach to genitality (coquetry) and shrinking back when the situation threatens to become serious (hysterical genital anxiety). The hysterical character in the woman serves the function of a protection against her own genital desires and against the male aggression of the object.

One sees in analyses the special case that severe, hard mothers produce daughters who, characterologically speaking, are neither masculine nor feminine; rather, they are infantile. Such mothers give their child too little love, thus creating a hatred in the child against the dangers of which the child retreats to the position of the infant. The child hates the mother on the genital level, represses the hatred and changes it, after having assumed an oral attitude, into reactive love and a paralyzing dependence on the mother. Such women develop a peculiarly sticky attitude toward older and married women to whom they are attached in a masochistic manner; they have a tendency to passive homosexuality (and to cunnilingus if a perversion develops); they let themselves be taken care of by older women, develop hardly any interest in men and generally present a "babyish" behavior. This character attitude, like any other, serves as an armor against repressed impulses and against stimuli from the outer world. It is an oral warding-off of intensive hatred against the mother behind which it is often very difficult to find the normal feminine attitude toward the man which is also repressed.

Thus far we have emphasized the role of the sex of the frustrating person for character formation and mentioned the character of that person only insofar as we discussed a "mild" or "severe" influence. The character formation in the child depends, however, on the character of the parents in more than one decisive way. With a sufficiently deep-reaching analysis, much of what official psychiatry considers "hereditary" can be shown to be the result of early identifications.

We do not deny a hereditary factor in the modes of reacting;

even the newborn infant has its "character." But we maintain that the environment is the decisive factor. It determines whether an anlage is developed and intensified, or not. The strongest argument against the concept of the heredity of character is provided by those patients in whom analysis shows that up to a certain age they had certain modes of reacting, at which time they began to show a completely different development of character; for example, they were first lively, later depressive, or first active and aggressive, later quiet and inhibited. True, it is likely that certain basic qualities of the personality are given at birth which allow of little alteration. Nevertheless, the importance of the hereditary factors is generally overestimated; this is undoubtedly due to the unconscious fear of the criticism of education which must result from a correct evaluation of environmental factors. The question could be decided by the mass experiment of isolating, say, a hundred children of psychopathic parents right after birth and bringing them up in the same environment, and by comparing the result with that in a hundred other children who remained in a psychopathic environment.

In looking over the basic character structures we have sketched so far, we find that they all have one thing in common: their formation was initiated by the conflicts of the child-parent relationship, they are a way of dealing with these conflicts and at the same time they perpetuate them. When Freud said that the Oedipus complex vanishes as a result of castration anxiety we have to add the following: True, it vanishes, but it arises anew in the form of character reactions which, on the one hand, perpetuate its main features in a distorted form and are, on the other hand, reaction formations against its basic elements.

We find further that the neurotic character, exactly like the symptom, has the form of a compromise, with regard to its contents as well as with regard to its form. It contains the infantile instinctual demand as well as the defense; the latter may belong to the same or to a different stage of development. The basic infantile conflict continues to exist, *transformed into chronic attitudes,* into chronic automatic modes of reaction from which the infantile conflict must be analytically uncovered.

These insights make it possible to answer a question once asked by Freud: In what form does the repressed continue to exist? It seems that those parts of infantile experience which do not enter into character formation are retained as affective memories, and those which do enter character formation as actual modes of reacting. As obscure as this process may be, the continued existence of the repressed in the form of a specific kind of functioning cannot be doubted; for analytic therapy succeeds in reducing such character functions to their origin. We understand now why in many cases of severe character neurosis we do not succeed in uncovering the Oedipus complex if we analyze only the contents; the reason is that it can be reached only by an analysis of the formal modes of reacting.

The discussions of character differentiations which are to follow and which are based on a differentiation of the specifically pathogenic from the specifically healthy psychic dynamisms are far from being theoretical pastimes. They are made with the goal of a *theory of psychic economy* in mind, a theory which could provide signposts for practical education. Whether such a theory is furthered or repudiated depends, of course, on society. Present-day society, with its sex-negative morality and its inability to secure even a minimum of material security for the masses of its members, is as far from the recognition of such possibilities as from their practical application. Parental fixation and prohibition of infantile masturbation, the demand for abstinence in puberty and the strangling of sexual needs by the institution of compulsive marriage, all these things represent the exact opposite of the conditions which are necessary for a sex-economic regulation of biological energy. The present sexual order creates of necessity the characterological basis of the neuroses; sexual and psychic economy is incompatible with that kind of morality which today is defended tooth and nail. This is one of the inexorable consequences of the psychoanalytic investigation of the neuroses.

## Chapter VIII

# THE GENITAL CHARACTER AND THE NEUROTIC CHARACTER. THE SEX-ECONOMIC FUNCTION OF THE CHARACTER ARMOR

## 1. CHARACTER AND SEXUAL STASIS

We now turn to the questions as to why a character is formed at all and what is its economic function. Study of the dynamic function and the meaning of the character reactions shows that *the character is essentially a narcissistic protection mechanism.* Just as today, say, during the analytic situation, it serves as a protection for the ego, so it developed earlier as a protection mechanism against dangers. If character-analysis penetrates back into the period of definitive character formation, that is, the Oedipus phase, one finds that the character was formed under the influence of the threatening outer world and the instinctual impulses which urged for expression.

It is necessary here to differentiate our concepts from Alfred Adler's formulations about character formation.

a) Adler began his defection from psychoanalysis and the libido theory with the thesis that the important point was not the analysis of the libido but of the nervous character. The postulate of an antithesis between libido and character, and the exclusion of the former from all consideration, was completely at variance with psychoanalysis. Our starting-point is the same, the meaningful functioning of what is called total personality or character, but our theory and our method is totally different. In asking what forces the psychic organism to form a character, our point of view is causal; only secondarily do we arrive at a purpose. The cause is unpleasure, the purpose is protection from unpleasure. Adler's point of view, on the other hand, is finalistic.

b) We try to explain character formation from the point of view of *libido economy* and thus arrive at entirely different results from Adler who uses the principle of the "will to power" as an explanation and who overlooks the dependence of the "will to power," and individual narcissistic striving, on the fates of the total narcissism and the object libido.

c) Adler's formulations concerning the workings of the inferiority feeling and its compensations, while correct, fail to show the connection with the deep-lying processes of the libido. In contradistinction to Adler, we try to understand and dissolve the inferiority feeling itself and its effects through an understanding of its connections with the libidinal processes.

Following up the theory of Lamarck, Freud and Ferenczi distinguished an autoplastic and an alloplastic adaptation in psychic life. The latter means that the organism, in order to exist, changes the outer world (technic, civilization), the former means that it changes itself. Biologically speaking, character formation is an autoplastic function. In the conflict between instinct and frustrating outer world, and motivated by the anxiety arising from this conflict, the organism erects a protection mechanism between itself and the outer world. We shall consider this process for a moment not from the dynamic or economic but from the topical point of view.

The ego, the part of the personality which is exposed to the outer world, is where character formation takes place; it is a buffer in the struggle between id and outer world. In the interest of self-preservation, the ego, attempting to mediate between the two sides, introjects the frustrating objects of the outer world which then form the super-ego. The morals of the ego, then, do not derive from the id, from the narcissistic-libidinal organism; rather, they are a foreign body taken from the threatening and prohibiting outer world. According to the psychoanalytic theory of the instincts, there is at first nothing in the psychic organism but most primitive needs based on somatic excitation. Between these primitive needs on the one hand and the outer world on the other, the ego gradually develops through differentiation of part of the psychic organism. One is reminded here of certain protozoa. There are many among them who protect themselves against the outer world by means of an armor of inorganic material. The motility of these armored protozoa is considerably restricted compared with the plain ameba; the contact with the outer world is limited to the pseudopodia which can be put out through small openings in the armor and pulled back again. In the same way, the character of the ego can be thought of as the armor which protects the id from the outer world. The ego in Freud's sense is a structural element. By character we mean here not only the external manifestation of this element, but also the sum total of the modes of reactions which are specific of this or that personality, that is, a factor which is essentially functionally determined and expresses itself in the characteristic ways of walking, facial expression, posture, manner of speaking, etc. This character of the ego consists of various elements of the outer world, of prohibitions, instinct inhibitions and identifications of different kinds. The contents of the character armor, then, are of an external, social origin. Before entering upon the question as to what holds these contents together, what is the dynamic process which consolidates the armor, we must realize that while protection against the outer world was the main reason for the formation of the character, this does not constitute its chief function later on. Against the actual dangers of the outer world, civilized man has a wealth of means at his disposal, the social institutions in all their forms. Being a highly developed organism, he has at his disposal a muscular apparatus to flee or to fight with, and an intellect to enable him to foresee and avoid dangers. The protection mechanisms of the character typically come into action when a danger from the inside, from an instinctual impulse, is threatening. Then it is the task of the character to master the stasis anxiety (actual anxiety) caused by the energies of the impulses which are barred from expression.

The relationship between character and repression is the following: The necessity of repressing instinctual demands gives rise to character formation. On the other hand, the character, once formed, makes a great deal of repression unnecessary; this is possible because instinctual energies which are free-floating in the case of simple repression, are absorbed in the character formations themselves. The establishment of a character trait, therefore, indicates the solution of a repression problem: it either makes the process of repression unnecessary or it changes a repression, once it is established, into a relatively rigid, ego-accepted formation. The processes of character formation thus correspond entirely to the tendency of the ego to bring about a unification of different psychic strivings. These facts explain why it is so much more difficult to eliminate repressions which have led to the formation of well-established character traits than repressions which led to a symptom.

There is a definite relationship between the starting-point of character formation, that is, the protection against actual dangers, and its final function, that is, protection against internal instinctual dangers and stasis anxiety, and the absorption of instinctual energies. The development from a primitive state to the civilization of today demanded a considerable restriction of libidinal and other gratification. Human development has been characterized by increasing sexual suppression; in particular, the development of patriarchal society went hand in hand with an increasing disruption and restriction of genitality. With the progress of civilization, the number and intensity of external dangers decreased progressively, at least for the individual; socially speaking, the dangers to life for the individual have increased. Imperialistic wars and the class struggle more than make up for the dangers of primitive eras. In order to avoid real anxiety (occasioned by actual external dangers) people had to inhibit their impulses: aggression has to be held down even if people, as a result of the economic crisis, are at the point of starvation, and the sexual instinct is shackled by social norms and prejudices. A transgression against the norms means actual danger, such as punishment for "theft" or infantile masturbation, jail for incest or homosexuality. To the extent to which real anxiety is avoided the stasis of libido and with that the stasis anxiety increases. Stasis anxiety and real anxiety are in mutual interaction: the more real anxiety is avoided the more intense becomes stasis anxiety, and vice versa. The unafraid individual satisfies his strong libidinal needs even at the risk of social ostracism. Animals, due to their lack of social organization, are more exposed to the conditions of real anxiety, but, except under conditions of domestication, do not suffer from stasis of libidinal energy.

We have mentioned two economic principles of character formation: the *avoidance of (real) anxiety,* and the *absorption of (stasis) anxiety.* There is a third: the pleasure principle. Character formation is set in motion by the motive of avoiding the dangers involved in instinctual gratification. Once the character is formed, however, the pleasure principle further works in the sense that the character, like the symptom, serves not only defensive purposes, but also that of a disguised instinctual gratification. The genital-narcissistic character, for example, not only protects himself against the influences of the outer world; he also satisfies a good deal of his libido in the narcissistic relation of his ego to his ego-ideal. The energy of the warded-off instinctual impulses, in particular, the pregenital and sadistic ones, is largely consumed in the establishment and maintenance of the protection mechanism. True, this is not an instinctual gratification in the sense of direct, undisguised pleasure, but, like the disguised gratification in the symptom, it leads to a decrease of the instinctual tension. While this decrease of tension is phenomenologically different from direct gratification, it is almost equally valuable economically in that it, also, decreases the tension. The instinctual energy is used up in the process of connecting and solidifying the contents of the character (identifications, reaction formations, etc.). In the affect-block of many compulsive characters, for example, it is mainly sadism which is consumed in the formation and maintenance of the wall between id and outer world; in the exaggerated politeness and passivity of many passive-feminine characters, it is anal homosexuality.

Those impulses which are not consumed in character formation urge for direct gratification, unless they are repressed. The nature of the direct gratification is determined by the form of the character. What impulses are used for the formation of the character and what impulses are allowed direct gratification determines not only the difference between healthy and sick but also the difference between the various types of character.

Besides the quality of the character armoring, we also have to consider its quantity or degree. If the armoring against the outer world and the biological inner world has reached a degree corresponding to the libidinal development at any given time, there remain "gaps" in the armor which provide the means of contact with the outer world. Through these gaps, the available libido is sent out to the outer world and retracted from it. Now, the armoring may reach such a degree that these gaps are "too narrow," so that the communication with the outer world is too small to guarantee a normal libido economy and normal social adaptation. A more or less complete armoring is exemplified in the catatonic stupor, a completely insufficient armoring in the structure of the impulsive character. It must be assumed that every lasting conversion of object libido into narcissistic libido results in an intensification and hardening of the armor. The affect-blocked compulsive character has a rigid, unalterable armor which leaves slight possibilities of establishing affective contact with the world; everything bounces back from his smooth, hard surface. The querulous aggressive character, on the other hand, has an armor which, though mobile, is always in the same way "bristling," and his relationships with the outer world are largely limited to his paranoid-aggressive reactions. The passive-feminine character seems soft and yielding, but in the analysis this proves to be a kind of armoring which is very difficult to dissolve.

Every character formation is typical not only in what it wards off but also in what impulses are used in the defense. Generally speaking, the ego forms the character by taking over a certain impulse which itself had been repressed and by using it as a defense against another impulse. The phallic-sadistic character, for example, uses an exaggerated masculine aggression to ward off feminine, passive and anal tendencies. In doing so, he changes himself more and more in the direction of chronically aggressive behavior. Others, conversely, ward off their repressed aggression by "sucking up," as such a patient once expressed it, to any person who incites their aggression. They develop a smooth, "slimy" behavior; they avoid any straightforward reaction and are difficult to get at; their way of talking is soft, cautious and ingratiating.

The ego, in taking over anal interests for the purpose of warding off the aggressive tendencies, has itself become "slimy." This undermines self-confidence (one such patient felt himself to be "stinky") which in turn leads to all kinds of attempts to gain the favor of people. Since such people are incapable of genuine contact, they usually experience one rejection after the other; this increases their aggression and this, in a vicious circle, necessitates increased anal-passive defense. In such cases, character-analysis discloses not only the function of the defense but also its means, in this case, anality.

The final quality of the character is determined in two ways. First, *qualitatively* by the stage of libido development in which the process of character formation was most decisively influenced, in other words, by the specific fixation point of the libido. Accordingly, we distinguish depressive (oral), masochistic, genital-narcissistic (phallic), hysterical (genital-incestuous) and compulsive (sadistic-anal fixation) characters. Second, *quantitatively* by the libido economy which, in turn, depends on the qualitative factors. The qualitative determination of the character form might be called the historical one, the quantitative the present-day one.

## 2. THE LIBIDO-ECONOMIC DIFFERENCE BETWEEN THE GENITAL AND THE NEUROTIC CHARACTER

If the character armoring exceeds a certain degree, if in its formation mostly such impulses have been used which normally serve the contact with reality, if, thus, the possibility of sexual gratification has been reduced considerably, then all the conditions for the formation of a neurotic character are given. In comparing character formation and character structure of neurotic people with that of individuals capable of work and love, one finds a qualitative difference in the means with which the dammed-up libido is bound in the character. One finds that there are adequate and inadequate means of binding anxiety. *Adequate* means are *genital orgastic gratification,* and *sublimation; inadequate* means are all kinds of *pregenital gratification,* and *reaction formations.* This qualitative difference also expresses itself in a quantitative one: The neurotic character suffers from an ever-increasing libido stasis, for the very reason that his means of gratification are not adapted to the instinctual needs. The genital character, on the other hand, keeps alternating between libido tension and adequate libido gratification; that is, he has an *orderly libido economy*. The term "genital character" is justified by the fact that only genital primacy and orgastic potency (which is itself determined by a definite character structure) guarantee an orderly libido economy.

The historically determined *quality* of the character-forming forces and contents, then, determines the *quantitative* regulation of the libido economy and with that the difference between "healthy" and "sick." With regard to their qualitative differences, the genital and the neurotic character are ideal types. The real characters are mixed types and whether libido economy is possible or not depends on the degree of admixture. With regard to the quantity of possible direct libido gratification, the genital and the neurotic character are to be considered average types: Either the libidinal gratification is such that it eliminates the stasis of libido, or it is not; in the latter case, symptoms or neurotic character traits develop which impair social and sexual capacity.

We shall now try to present the *qualitative* differences between the two ideal types, taking up separately the structure of the id, of the super-ego and finally the qualities of the ego which depend on both the others.

### a) Structure of the Id.

The genital character has fully reached the post-ambivalent genital stage,[1] the wish for incest and the wish to eliminate the father (the mother) have been given up, the genital interests have been transferred to a heterosexual object which does not, as in the case of the neurotic character, actually represent the incest object but has taken its place. *The Oedipus complex no longer exists in actuality;* it is not repressed, but free of cathexis. Pregenital tendencies, such as anality, oral eroticism, voyeurism, etc., are not repressed but are partly anchored in cultural sublima-

---

[1] *Cf.* Karl Abraham: Psychoanalytische Studien zur Charakterbildung, 1925.

tions, and partly gratified directly in the forepleasure acts; at any rate, they are subordinated to genitality. The sexual act is the most important sexual goal and that which provides the greatest pleasure. Aggression also is sublimated in social achievement to the extent to which it is not a part of normal genitality; it never urges for direct and exclusive gratification. This distribution of instinctual drives provides the basis for orgastic gratification which, it is true, is possible only genitally but which also gratifies the pregenital and aggressive tendencies. The fewer pregenital demands are repressed, that is, the more the two systems of pregenitality and genitality communicate with each other, the more complete is the satisfaction and the less the pathogenic stasis of libido.

The neurotic character, on the other hand, is incapable of orgastic discharge of his free, unsublimated libido.[2] He is always more or less orgastically impotent, for the following reasons: The incestuous objects have an actual cathexis or the corresponding libido is consumed in reaction formations. If there is any sexual life at all, its infantile nature can be readily seen: the woman represents the mother or sister and the love relationship carries the stamp of all the anxieties, inhibitions and neurotic peculiarities of the infantile incest relationship. Genital primacy is either not established or, as in the hysterical character, genital functioning is disturbed by the incest fixation. There is either abstinence, or sexual activity is largely confined to forepleasure acts. A vicious circle is established: The infantile fixation disturbs the orgastic function which disturbance in turn leads to libido stasis; the dammed-up libido in turn intensifies the pregenital fixations, and so forth. As a result of this overcharge of pregenitality, libidinal impulses enter into every cultural and social activity. This must needs lead to a disturbance, because the activity becomes associated with repressed and prohibited impulses; more than that, in many cases it becomes a distorted sexual activity as, say, in

---

[2] *Footnote, 1945:* The regulation of sexual energy depends on orgastic potency, that is, on the capacity of the organism to tolerate fully the clonic contractions and expansions of the orgasm reflex. The *armored* organism does not admit of these orgastic contractions and expansions; here, the biological excitation is inhibited by muscular spasms in various places of the body.

musician's cramp. The libidinal component of social achievement is not available because it is repressed in association with infantile instinctual goals.

### b) Structure of the Super-ego.

The super-ego of the genital character is *sex-affirmative;* for this reason, there is a high degree of harmony between id and super-ego. Since the Oedipus complex has lost its cathexis, the counter-cathexis in the super-ego has become superfluous. Practically speaking, there are no super-ego prohibitions of a sexual nature. The super-ego is not sadistic, not only for the reason just mentioned but also because there is no libido stasis to activate sadism.[3] The genital libido, being gratified directly, is not hidden in the ego-ideal strivings. Social achievements, therefore, are not a proof of potency as in the neurotic character but they provide a natural narcissistic gratification which does not serve the purpose of compensation. Since there is no potency disturbance, there are no feelings of inferiority. The ego-ideal and the real ego do not differ greatly from each other; there is, consequently, no appreciable tension between the two.

In the neurotic character, on the other hand, the super-ego is *sex-negative;* correspondingly, there is a marked conflict between id and super-ego. Since the Oedipus complex has not been overcome, the core of the super-ego, the incest prohibition, is also fully maintained, disturbing any kind of sexual relationship. The sexual repressions and the resulting libido stasis intensify the sadistic impulses which express themselves, among other things, in a brutal morality. Since there is always a more or less conscious feeling of impotence, social achievement becomes primarily a compensating proof of potency. This, however, does not decrease the feelings of inferiority. The compensating proofs of potency in social achievement cannot in any way replace the genital potency feeling; for this reason the neurotic character never gets rid of an inner emptiness and feeling of incapacity, no matter

---

[3] Concerning the relationship between sadism and libido stasis, *cf.* Chapter VII of my book, DIE FUNKTION DES ORGASMUS, 1927.

*Translator's note: Cf.* also THE FUNCTION OF THE ORGASM, 1942, 1948.

how much he tries to compensate for it. Thus it comes to pass that the positive ego-ideal demands are steadily increased, while the ego, impotent and doubly paralyzed by inferiority feelings (impotence and high ego-ideal) becomes more and more incapable.

#### c) *Structure of the Ego.*

In the genital character, periodic orgastic discharges of libidinal tension reduce the instinctual demands of the id on the ego; the id is essentially satisfied and thus there is no reason for the development of a sadistic super-ego; the super-ego, thus, exerts no particular pressure on the ego. The ego takes over, *without any guilt feeling*, the genital libido and certain pregenital tendencies of the id for gratification; it sublimates natural aggression and certain parts of the pregenital libido in social action. The ego has no negative attitude toward the id as far as genitality is concerned and can all the more easily impose inhibitions on it as it does not interfere in the main respect, libidinal gratification. This seems to be the only condition under which the id can be held in check by the ego without recourse to repression. An existing homosexual tendency, for example, will have little significance if at the same time heterosexuality is satisfied; it will be important, however, if there is libido stasis at the same time. This is easy to understand economically: in heterosexual gratification—provided that homosexuality is not repressed, provided, in other words, that it is not excluded from the communication system of the libido—energy is withdrawn from the homosexual strivings also.

Since the ego, as a result of sexual gratification, is under little pressure from the id as well as the super-ego, it does not have to defend itself against the id as must the ego of the neurotic character; this leaves ample energies for affective experience and realistic action in the outside world; action and experience are intensive, free-flowing; the ego is accessible to a high degree to pleasure as well as unpleasure. True, the ego of the genital character also has an armor, but it has the armor at its command instead of being at its mercy. This armor is pliable enough to allow adaptation to the various situations of life; the genital character can be very gay but also intensely angry; he reacts to an object-loss with depression but does not get lost in it; he is capable of intense love but also of intense hatred; he can, under appropriate conditions, be childlike but he will never appear infantile; his seriousness is natural and not stiff in a compensatory way because he has no tendency to show himself grown-up at all cost; his courage is not a proof of potency but directed toward a rational goal; thus he will not try to avoid the reproach of cowardice, say, in a war which he is convinced is unjustified, but will stand up for his conviction. Since infantile wishes have lost their cathexis, his love as well as his hatred has a rational goal. The pliability as well as the solidity of his armor are shown in the fact that he can open up to the world as intensely in one case as he can shut himself off from it in another. His ability to give himself is most clearly shown in his sexual experience: In the sexual act with the loved partner the ego is practically reduced to the function of perception, the armor is temporarily dissolved almost completely, the whole personality is engulfed in the pleasurable experience, without any fear of getting lost in it, for the ego has a solid narcissistic foundation which does not serve any compensatory function. His self-confidence derives its most potent energies from the sexual experience. From the way he solves his everyday conflicts it is easy to see that these conflicts are rational, not burdened by infantile admixtures; this is again because a normal libido economy makes a cathexis of the infantile experiences and wishes impossible.

As the genital character is not stiff and rigid in any respect, we find the same thing in the forms of his sexuality. Since he is capable of gratification, he is capable of monogamy without compulsion or repression; on the other hand, if rational grounds are given, he is also capable, without suffering harm, of a change of object or of polygamy. He does not stick to his sexual object out of guilt feelings or for moralistic reasons; he maintains a sexual relationship only because the sexual partner gives him pleasure. He can overcome polygamous wishes without repression if they are in conflict with his relationship with the loved object;

but he is also capable of giving in to them if they are all too disturbing. The resulting conflict he will solve in a realistic manner.

Neurotic guilt feelings are practically absent. His sociality is based not on repressed but on sublimated aggression and on his realistic orientation in life. That does not mean, however, that he always bows to external reality. On the contrary, it is precisely the genital character who—due to his structure which is at variance with the present-day moralistic and antisexual culture—is capable of criticizing and altering the social situation. His lack of fear of life guards him against concessions to the outer world which conflict with his convictions.

If the primacy of the intellect is the goal of social development, it is inconceivable without the primacy of genitality. For the primacy of the intellect presupposes an orderly libido economy, that is, genital primacy. Genital and intellectual primacy have the same mutual interrelationship as have sexual stasis and neurosis, guilt feeling and religion, hysteria and superstition, pregenital sexual gratification and present-day sexual morality, sadism and ethics, sexual repression and societies for the rehabilitation of fallen women.

In the genital character, an ordered libido economy, borne by the capacity for full sexual experience, is the basis of the character traits just described. In the same way, everything the neurotic character is and does is determined by his disturbed libido economy.

The ego of the neurotic character is either ascetic or allows sexual activity only with guilt feelings. It is under a twofold pressure: that of the ungratified id with its dammed-up libido, and that of the brutal super-ego. It is inimical toward the id and submissive toward the super-ego while at the same time exhibiting the opposite tendencies of flirting with the id and secretly rebelling against the super-ego. It's sexuality, unless repressed, is predominantly of a pregenital nature; corresponding to present-day sexual morality, genitality has an anal and sadistic admixture, the sexual act being considered something dirty and sadistic. Since most of the destructive impulses are anchored partly in the character armor, partly in the super-ego, social achievement is impaired. The ego is armored against both pleasure and unpleasure (affect-block), or open only to unpleasure, or pleasure turns very soon into unpleasure. The armor of the ego is rigid, lacking pliability, the "communications" with the outer world are insufficient, with regard to object-libido as well as to aggression. The function of the armor is directed mainly against the inside; this results in a more or less outspoken weakening of the reality function. The relationships with the outer world are unnatural, unalive and contradictory, lacking the harmonious participation of the total personality. There is an inability to experience things and people fully. The genital character is able to change, reinforce or relax his protection mechanisms. The neurotic character, on the other hand, is completely at the mercy of the unconscious mechanisms of his character; he cannot act differently even if he wants to. He would like to be gay or angry but cannot. He cannot love intensely because his sexuality is essentially repressed. Nor can he hate appropriately because his ego is incapable of handling the hatred which has grown violent as a result of libido stasis, and therefore has to repress it. And even when the neurotic character loves or hates, his reactions do not correspond to the rational situation; unconscious infantile reactions largely determine the measure and the kind of the reactions. The rigidity of his armor makes it impossible for him to open himself up to an experience or to close himself up against others where it would be rational to do so. Sexually, he is either abstinent or disturbed in the forepleasure acts so that there is no satisfaction at all or, finally, so incapable of giving himself that the gratification achieved is not sufficient to regulate the libido economy. An exact analysis of the experience during the sexual act shows definite types. There is the narcissistic individual who is not concentrated on the pleasure but on impressing the woman with his potency; or the hyperesthetic individual who thinks only of not touching any part of the body that could offend his esthetic feelings; or the individual with repressed sadism who cannot get rid of the compulsive thought that he might hurt the woman or is tormented by the guilty feeling of misusing her; the sadistic character to whom the sexual act means torturing the woman, etc. Where such disturbances are not clearly manifest, one finds the corresponding inhibitions in the total attitude toward sexuality. Since the super-ego of the neurotic character does not contain sex-affirmative elements, it turns away from sexual experience (H. Deutsch, erroneously, also postulates this for the normal individual); this means that only half the personality participates in the experience.

The feeling of impotence forces the ego to form narcissistic compensations. Present-day conflicts are permeated by irrational motives which make it impossible for the neurotic character to arrive at rational decisions; infantile attitudes and wishes always make themselves felt.

Sexually unsatisfied and incapable of satisfaction, the neurotic character finally becomes ascetic, or he lives in rigid monogamy— as he believes, for moral reasons or out of consideration for his partner; in reality, because he is afraid of sexuality and incapable of regulating it. Since sadism is not sublimated and the super-ego is overly severe while the id continues to press for the gratification of its needs, the ego develops guilt feelings which it calls social conscience and a self-punitive attitude of wanting to do to the self what it really wants to do to others.

It is easy to see that the finding of these mechanisms provides the basis of a fundamental criticism of all theories of morals. We are dealing here with a decisive question of social culture formation. To the extent to which the gratification of needs becomes underwritten by society, and human structure changes accordingly, *moral* regulation of social life will become unnecessary. The final decision does not lie in the psychological but in the social realm. Every analytic treatment which succeeds in changing the neurotic character structure into the genital structure automatically replaces moral regulation by a self-regulation based on a sound libido economy. When many analysts speak of the "dissolution of the super-ego" through psychoanalytic treatment, we must add that it is a matter of withdrawing energy from the moral inhibitions and their replacement by libido-economic self-regulation. How this process conflicts with the present-day interests of the state, of moral philosophy and religion will be discussed elsewhere. What it all means is that the individual who is satisfied in his sexual and his primitive biological and cultural needs does not need moral inhibitions for self-control; the unsatisfied individual, on the other hand, suffers from an increased inner excitation which would seek discharge in all kinds of antisocial and violent action unless his energies were kept in check and absorbed by moral inhibitions. The extent and the intensity of moralistic ascetic ideologies in any society are the best yardstick of the extent and intensity of the suppression of the vital needs in the average mass individual of that society. Both are determined by the relationship of the productive forces and the mode of production on the one hand and the needs which have to be gratified on the other.

The discussion of the larger consequences of sex-economy and analytic characterology cannot escape these problems unless one prefers, at the expense of one's natural-scientific integrity, to stop at the artificial boundary line between what is and what should be.

### 3. SUBLIMATION, REACTION FORMATION AND NEUROTIC REACTION BASIS

We shall now turn to the differences between the social achievements of the genital and the neurotic character, respectively. We said that orgastic gratification and sublimation are the adequate means, pregenital gratification and reaction formation the inadequate means of discharging the sexual energies. Like orgastic gratification, sublimation is specific of the genital character, while reaction formation is typical of the neurotic character. That does not mean, however, that the neurotic individual does not sublimate or that the healthy individual does not have any reaction formations.

Let us try first to describe the relationship between sublimation and sexual gratification. According to Freud, sublimation consists in the diversion of a libidinal tendency from its original goal to a "higher," socially valuable goal. The drive which is sublimated, then, must have given up its original object or goal. This first formulation of Freud's has led to the misunderstanding that sublimation and instinctual gratification are opposites, mutually exclusive. Clinical experience shows, however, that the two are not antithetical; more than that, a sound libido economy is *the* prerequisite of successful and lasting sublimations. It is only necessary that those drives on which our social achievements are based are not gratified directly; this does not apply to libidinal gratification in general. Analysis of work disturbances shows that the sublimation of the pregenital libido is all the more difficult the greater the stasis of the total libido. Sexual phantasies absorb a great deal of psychic interest, withdrawing it from work, or else the cultural achievements themselves become sexualized and with that, subject to repression. Observation of the sublimations in the genital character shows that the orgastic gratification of the libido again and again makes sublimations possible: it liberates energies for increased activity because sexual ideas temporarily have no longer any libidinal cathexis. We see in successful analyses that the maximal capacity for achievement is reached only when the patient becomes capable of full sexual gratification. The durability of the sublimations also is dependent upon a sound libido economy: patients who lost their neurosis merely by way of sublimations are in a much more labile condition and tend much more to a relapse than those who also achieve direct sexual gratification. Incomplete, particularly pregenital libido gratification, interferes with sublimation, orgastic genital gratification furthers it.

Let us now compare sublimation and reaction formation. The latter is of a compulsive and rigid character, while sublimation is spontaneous. In sublimation, it is as if the id had a direct connection with reality, in harmony with ego and ego-ideal; with reaction formation, it looks as if all actions were dictated by a severe super-ego to a rebellious id. In sublimation, the accent is on the effect of the action, even though the action has also a libidinal component. In reaction formation, the action itself is the important thing and the effect more or less incidental; the action is determined not by a libidinal striving, but negatively: it must be carried out. The sublimating individual can interrupt his work for considerable periods of time; rest is as welcome to him as work. If reactive work is interrupted, however, restlessness will appear sooner or later which may increase to irritability and even anxiety. The sublimating individual also is sometimes irritated and tense, but not because he does not achieve anything but because he is in the throes of achieving something. The sublimating individual *wants to* work and derives pleasure from it. The reactively working individual *must* work; as a patient put it, he must "robot." When he has finished one piece of work he must immediately begin another, because his work is a flight from rest. Occasionally, the final effect of a reaction formation may be the same as that of sublimation. Usually, however, the achievements based on reactive work are inferior to those based on sublimation. Certainly, the same individual will be much more effective under the conditions of sublimation than under those of reaction formation.

The differential between *working capacity* (latent working ability) and absolute achievement in work is far less in the case of sublimation than in the case of reaction formation; that is, the sublimating individual works more nearly according to his full capacities than does the reactively working individual. Inferiority feelings often correspond to the inner perception of this differential. Clinical experience shows that achievements based on sublimation change relatively little when unconscious connections are uncovered; reactive work, on the other hand, either breaks down completely, or, if changed into sublimations, increases tremendously in effectiveness.

The average individual in our culture works much more frequently according to the mechanism of reaction formation than that of sublimation. His structure, as it results from present-day education, combined with the social conditions of work, makes him incapable of an effective achievement in work which would correspond to his working capacity.

In the case of sublimation, there is no change in the direction of the drive; the drive is taken over by the ego and merely diverted to a different goal. In the case of reaction formation, the drive is turned against the self, and it is taken over by the ego only to the extent to which this takes place. In this process, the cathexis of the drive turns into a counter-cathexis against the unconscious goal of the drive. In reaction formation, the original goal retains its unconscious cathexis; the original object of the drive was not given up but merely repressed. Reaction formation, then, is characterized by the retention and repression of the goal and object of the drive, and by the turning back of the drive with the formation of a counter-cathexis. Sublimation, on the other hand, is characterized by the renunciation (not repression) and replacement of the original goal and object of the drive, without the formation of a counter-cathexis.

The most important economic aspect of reaction formation is the necessity of a counter-cathexis. Since the original instinctual goal was retained it keeps absorbing libido; consequently, the ego must continually use a counter-cathexis in order to keep the drive in check. The reaction formation is not a process which takes place just once but one which continues to take place and which spreads.

In reaction formation the ego is constantly occupied with itself; it is its own vigilant watchman. In sublimation, the ego has its energies available for achievement. Simple reaction formations, such as disgust or shame, are part of the character formation of everyone. They do not interfere with the development of the genital character and remain within physiological limits because there is no libido stasis which would reinforce pregenital strivings. If, on the other hand, sexual repression has gone very far, if, in particular, it includes the genital libido, thus resulting in libido stasis, then the reaction formations receive a great deal of libidinal energy and tend to spread in the manner which we observe in phobias.

We shall illustrate with the case of an official who, like all compulsive characters, did his office work in an extremely conscientious manner. As the years went by, he worked more and more, although he did not enjoy his work in the least. At the time he came for analysis he worked not infrequently until midnight or even until 3 o'clock in the morning. Analysis soon showed, first, that sexual phantasies kept interfering with his work which was one reason why it took so long ("dawdling"), and second, that he could not allow himself even a minute of quiet, particularly in the evening, otherwise he was swamped with sexual phantasies. True, in his night work he discharged a certain amount of libido; but a large part of his libido could not be taken care of in this manner, and he finally had to acknowledge his work disturbance.

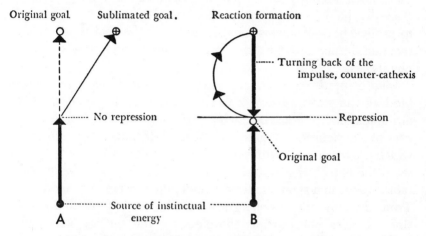

Original goal.    Sublimated goal.    Reaction formation

Turning back of the impulse, counter-cathexis

No repression    Repression

Original goal

Source of instinctual energy

A    B

*Schematic presentation of sublimation as compared with reaction formation*

A: Repression lacking; impulse merely diverted; original instinctual goal lacking cathexis.

B: Repression present; original goal has retained its full cathexis; impulse not diverted, but directed by the ego against itself. At the place where the turning back occurs we find the achievement (reaction formation).

The spreading of the reaction formations and of reactive activities, then, corresponds to a steadily increasing libido stasis. When, finally, the reaction formations no longer suffice to master the libido stasis, when, in other words, the character fails in its task of absorbing the libido, undisguised neurotic anxiety makes its appearance or neurotic symptoms are formed to bind the excess of libido or anxiety.

Reactive activities are always being rationalized. Thus our patient claimed that there was too much work to be done. His exaggerated and mechanical activity served not only the economic function of discharge and that of taking his mind off his sexual phantasies; it also was a reaction formation against his repressed hatred of his chief (father). Analysis showed that his seeming endeavors to be particularly helpful to his chief were the opposite of his unconscious intentions. Such "roboting" cannot be interpreted as being, in the last analysis, a self-punishment. Self-punishment is only one of many meanings of the symptom. Basically, he did not want to punish himself, but, on the contrary, to protect himself against punishment. For the real cause of his reaction formations was the fear of the results of his sexual phantasies.

Like compulsive work, other reaction formations also cannot bind all the stasis anxiety. Take, for example, the hypermotility of the female hysterical character or the hyperagility and restlessness of the neurotic mountain-climber. Both have a musculature which is overcharged with unsatisfied libido, both keep urging toward the object, the hysterical girl in an undisguised, the mountain-climber in a symbolic form (mountain = woman = mother). True, their motility discharges a certain amount of libido but, since it does not provide end-pleasure, the tension keeps increasing. Thus, the girl finally develops hysterical attacks while the neurotic mountain-climber, in order to master his stasis, will have to undertake ever more strenuous and dangerous climbs. Since there are natural limitations to this, a symptom neurosis finally develops unless, as happens so often, he meets disaster in the mountains.

We call the sum total of all those mechanisms which serve the purpose of absorbing the dammed-up libido and of binding it in character traits the *characterological reaction basis*. If, as a result of excessive sexual restriction, it fails in its economic function, it becomes the *neurotic reaction basis*, the elimination of which is the most important therapeutic task. The spreading reaction formation is only one of the mechanisms of the neurotic reaction basis.

No matter at what period an aggravation of the neurotic character occurs, one always finds that a neurotic character has existed from early childhood, since the time of the Oedipus conflict. As a

rule, the nature of the neurotic symptom sho▓
with its neurotic reaction basis. For example, compul▓
orderliness may increase to a compulsion with regard t▓
the anal character may develop constipation, self-conscious▓
may increase to pathological blushing, hysterical agility and
coquetry to hysterical attacks, ambivalence to incapacity to make
decisions, sex-shyness to vaginismus, overscrupulousness to impulses to murder.

However, the quality of the symptom does not always correspond to its reaction basis. The symptom may represent a defense
against the anxiety on a higher or lower libido stage. Thus, a
hysterical character may develop a washing compulsion, a compulsive character a hysterical anxiety or a conversion symptom. It
goes without saying that in practice one deals mostly with mixed
types in which one or the other character form predominates.
It is advisable, however, to make the diagnosis not according to
the symptoms but according to the underlying neurotic character.
Thus, in spite of a conversion symptom for which the patient
seeks analysis, one will make the diagnosis of compulsion neurosis
if the character shows predominantly compulsive traits.

It should be kept in mind that the distinction between the
neurotic character and the genital character is not a rigid one.
Since the distinction is based on a quantitative criterion—the
extent of either direct sexual gratification or libido stasis—there
are all kinds of transitions between the two ideal types. In spite of
this, a typological investigation is not only justified but impera-
tive because of its heuristic values and of the help it provides in
practical work. Since this is only a small beginning of a genetic
typology, it cannot pretend to answer all the questions of typology.
For the time being, it has achieved its purpose if it has shown
that the only legitimate basis of psychoanalytic typology is
Freud's libido theory, without restricting it, and following it to
its logical conclusions.

## CHAPTER IX

# PHOBIA AND CHARACTER FORMATION

## . AN "ARISTOCRATIC" CHARACTER

This case will illustrate how the character attitude derives from infantile experiences. The presentation follows the path which led from the analysis of the character resistance to its origin in definite infantile situations.

A man of 33 comes to analysis because of marital difficulties and work disturbances. He suffers from severe indecision which makes impossible a rational solution of his marital problem as well as success in his profession. The patient begins the analysis with great understanding and soon produces the typical conflicts of the Oedipus situation which theoretically explain his marital situation. We neglect here the contents relating to the relationships between his wife and his mother, his superiors and his father. Instead, we shall concentrate on his behavior, on the connection between this behavior and his infantile conflict, and the ways in which this behavior manifested itself as a resistance in the treatment.

The patient is good-looking, of medium height; his facial expression is reserved, serious, somewhat arrogant. What is striking is his measured, refined gait. It takes him quite some time to get from the door to the couch; plainly, he avoids—or covers up— any haste or excitation. His speech is measured, quiet and refined; occasionally, he interrupts this with an emphasized, abrupt "Yes," at the same time stretching both arms in front of him, and afterwards stroking his hand over his forehead. He lies on the couch in a composed manner, with his legs crossed. His dignified composure hardly ever changes at all, even with the discussion of narcissistically painful subjects. When, after a while, he discussed his relationship with his mother whom he loved very much it was easy to see how he intensified his dignified attitude in order to master his excitation. In spite of my repeated admonitions to give his feelings free rein he maintained his attitude. One day tears came and his voice began to choke; nevertheless, the manner in which he put the handkerchief to his eyes was composed and dignified.

This much was already clear: his behavior, no matter what was its origin, protected him against violent emotions, against an affective breakthrough. His *character* prevented the free development of analytic experience; *it had already become a resistance.* When, soon after the obvious excitation, I asked him what impression this analytic situation had made on him, he said in his composed manner that all this was very interesting but did not really touch him; that the tears had just "gotten away from him" which had been very embarrassing. My explanation of the necessity and fruitfulness of such excitations was to no avail. His resistance became more intense, his communications superficial; his attitude became even more pronounced, he became even more dignified and composed.

It may have been an accident that one day the term "lordliness" occurred to me as a description of his behavior. I told him he was play-acting an English lord, and that this must have a connection with his youth. I also explained the defensive function of his "lordliness." Thereupon he related that as a child he had never believed that he really was the son of his father, a small Jewish merchant; he thought that he was really of English origin. He had heard rumors that his grandmother had had an affair with a real English lord and he thought of his mother as half English. In his dreams about the future, the phantasy of being sent to England as Ambassador played a considerable role. His attitude of lordliness, then, contained the following:

1. The idea of not being related to his father whom he hated and despised;

2. The idea of being the son of a mother who was half English; and

3. The ego-ideal of growing beyond the narrow milieu of his petty-bourgeois family.

The uncovering of the elements which constituted his behavior shook its foundations. It remained to be seen, however, what were the drives which were being warded off by it. Consistent analysis of the "lordly" behavior showed that it was connected with another character trait which created considerable difficulty in the analysis: his tendency to *deride* everybody and his gloating over others' misfortune. This derision was uttered in a lordly fashion but served at the same time the satisfaction of his intense sadistic tendencies. True, he had related that he had produced a wealth of sadistic phantasies during puberty. But he had only related them. He did not begin to *experience* them until we unearthed them in their actual anchoring place, his tendency to derision. The lordly composure was a protection against the derision as a sadistic activity. The sadistic phantasies were not repressed; they were gratified in the derision and warded off in the lordliness. His arrogant behavior, then, had the structure of a symptom: it served the purpose of warding off a drive as well as its satisfaction. This characterological transformation of his sadism had saved him the necessity of repressing it.

The lord phantasy had developed at the age of about four, the composure, the self-control, somewhat later, motivated by the fear of his father and—an important factor—a contrary identification with his father. The father having constant rows with the mother, the patient formed the ideal, "I'm not going to be like father but the exact opposite." This corresponded to the phantasy, "If I were the husband of my mother, I would treat her altogether differently. I would be kind and would control my anger at her inadequacies." This contrary identification, then, was conditioned by his Oedipus complex, the love of his mother and the hatred for his father.

The character of the boy which corresponded to the lord phantasies was one of daydreams, self-control and active sadistic phantasies. During puberty, he fell in love with a male teacher and began to identify himself with him. This teacher was a personified lord, dignified, composed, self-controlled, immaculately dressed. The identification began with the imitation of the dress, was followed by others, and when the patient was fourteen the character as he presented it at the beginning of the analysis was definitely formed: no longer only lord *phantasies,* but lordliness in the *actual behavior.*

There was a specific reason for the fact that the phantasy was realized in the attitude just at this age. The patient had never consciously masturbated during puberty. The castration anxiety—which manifested itself in diverse hypochondriac fears—was rationalized: "A distinguished person does not do such a thing." The lordliness, then, also served the purpose of warding off the desire to masturbate.

As a lord, he felt himself above all other people and could scoff at them. In the analysis he had to realize soon, however, that his derision was a compensation of an inferiority feeling, just as the lordliness as a whole covered up the inferiority feeling of one who came from a narrow milieu. The deeper significance of the derision was a defense against homosexual relationships: he scoffed mostly at men who attracted him. In the lordliness were combined the opposites, sadism and homosexuality, on the one hand, and refined self-control on the other.

During the analysis the lordliness became intensified with every new approach to unconscious material. Gradually, however, these defense reactions became milder, as did the corresponding behavior in his everyday behavior. The analysis of the lordliness led directly to the uncovery of the central conflicts of childhood and puberty. His pathological positions were thus attacked from two sides: his memories, dreams and other verbal communications, with little affect; and from his character, his lordliness, in which the affects of aggression were bound up.

## 2. THE OVERCOMING OF THE INFANTILE PHOBIA BY CHARACTER ATTITUDES

The display of refined behavior also served to bind an essential amount of genital anxiety. The analysis of this process revealed a hitherto little known fate of the infantile phobia. Between the ages of 3 and 6, the patient had suffered from an intense phobia about mice. In its center was his feminine attitude toward his father, which was a regressive reaction to his castration anxiety. This was connected with the typical masturbation anxiety. The more the boy built up the lord phantasy into the lordly behavior the more did the phobia recede, until finally nothing was left of it except a trace of apprehensiveness at bedtime. When, during analysis, the lordliness was undermined, the mouse phobia and the castration anxiety reappeared in an affective manner. Obviously, part of the libido, or anxiety, of the phobia had been woven into the character attitude.

We are familiar with the transformation of infantile wishes and anxieties into character traits. A special case is the replacement of a phobia by a definite kind of armoring against the outer world and the anxiety; in our case, it was the refined behavior which bound the infantile anxiety. Another typical case is that where the infantile phobia or simpler manifestations of the castration anxiety lead to passive-feminine behavior which may manifest itself, say, as exaggerated and stereotyped politeness. The following case is a further illustration of the transformation of a phobia into a character attitude:

This compulsion-neurotic showed a *complete affect-block.* He was equally impervious to pleasure and unpleasure, a living machine, one might say. Analysis showed this affect-block to be chiefly an armoring against his intense sadism. True, he still had sadistic phantasies, but they were dim and lifeless. The motive of the armoring was an equally intense castration anxiety which, however, did not manifest itself in any other way. The analysis could trace the affect-block back to the day of its origin.

The typical infantile phobia in this case was with reference to horses and snakes. Up to the age of 6, the patient had night terrors almost nightly. Particularly often, he had a nightmare of a horse which bit off one of his fingers (masturbation anxiety, castration). One day he simply decided no longer to be afraid, and the next dream in which a horse bit off one of his fingers was entirely free from anxiety. *At the same time, the affect-block developed;* it took the place of the phobia. It was not until after puberty that he again had occasional anxiety dreams.

Now as to the peculiar decision no longer to be afraid. The dynamic process here could not be fully elucidated. However, his whole life was determined by similar decisions; he could do nothing without making a specific decision. The basis of his decisiveness was his anal tenacity and the strict parental demand for self-control. Anal tenacity was also the energetic basis of his affect-block which, among other things, meant a universal Götz-von-Berlichingen attitude toward the whole world. Not until the patient had been in analysis for six months did we find that before ringing my doorbell he would invariably say the Götz quotation out loud three times in succession, as a magic protection against the analysis. There could have been no better way of putting his affect-block into words.

The most important components of the affect-block, then, were his anal tenacity and his reaction against his sadism; this armoring absorbed his sadistic energy as well as his intense infantile anxiety (stasis anxiety plus castration anxiety). Only when the analysis had penetrated this wall of diverse repressions and reaction formations did it arrive at his intense genital incest desires.

The development of a phobia indicates that the ego was too weak to master certain libidinal strivings. The development of a character trait or typical attitude at the expense of a phobia means a strengthening of the ego in the form of chronic armoring against the id and the outer world. The phobia means a splitting of the personality, the formation of a character trait a unification, a synthetic reaction of the ego to a conflict in the personality which finally becomes intolerable.

In spite of this contrast between phobia and ensuing character formation, the basic tendency of the phobia is continued in the character trait. The lordliness of our patient, the affect-block of the compulsive character, the politeness of the passive-feminine character, etc., are, like the preceding phobia, nothing but *attitudes of avoidance*.

The armoring results in a certain strengthening of the ego, but at the same time in a limitation of action and motility. The more the armoring impairs the capacity for sexual experience, the more closely does the structure resemble that of the neurotic character, and the greater is the likelihood of a new breakdown of the ego. In a later neurotic illness the old phobia breaks through again because the character armor proves insufficient to master the dammed-up libidinal excitations and the stasis anxiety. In the typical neurotic illness, we can distinguish the following phases:

1. Infantile conflict between libido and frustration;

2. Repression of the libidinal striving—strengthening of the ego;

3. Breakthrough of the repressed, phobia—weakening of the ego;

4. Mastery of the phobia by the formation of a neurotic character trait—strengthening of the ego;

5. Adolescent conflict (or a quantitatively analogous process): insufficiency of the character armor;

6. Reappearance of the old phobia or formation of a corresponding symptom;

7. Renewed attempt of the ego to master the phobic anxiety by character armoring.

Among the adult patients seeking analysis one can easily distinguish two types: those who are in the phase of breakdown (phase 6) in which symptoms develop on the neurotic reaction basis (renewed formation of a phobia, etc.); and those who are already in the phase of reconstruction (phase 7) where the ego has begun successfully to incorporate the symptoms. A circumscribed and painful compulsion, for example, looses its acuteness and painfulness when the *total ego* develops rituals which permeate everyday activities in such a manner as to be discernible only to the trained observer. This simulates a self-cure. But it should be remembered that the spreading and dilution of the symptoms damages the ability for action no less than the circumscribed symptom; now, the patient seeks treatment no longer because of a painful symptom but because of general work disturbance, lack of joy in life, etc. Thus there is a continuing struggle between the ego and its symptoms, between symptom formation and symptom incorporation. Every symptom incorporation, however, goes hand in hand with a character change. These later incorporations of the symptoms into the ego only reflect that process in childhood in which an infantile phobia was transformed into character structure.

We have spoken of the phobia because it is the most interesting and libido-economically most important expression of a disturbed personal unity. But the processes we have described may take place in the case of any anxiety in early childhood. For example, the fully rational fear of a brutal father may induce chronic character changes such as stubbornness or hardness which take the place of the anxiety.

Because experiences of infantile anxiety and other conflict situations of the Oedipus complex may determine character structure, an infantile experience may be recorded in two different ways: as to *content*, as unconscious ideas, and as to *form*, in character attitudes. This may be briefly illustrated in the following clinical example:

A narcissistic-masochistic hypochondriac engaged in incessant violent complaints about the strict treatment he had suffered from his father. The whole contents of months of analysis could be summarized thus: "Look what I have suffered from my father. He has ruined me and made me unfit for life." His infantile conflicts with his father had been thoroughly worked through in an analysis of one and a half year's duration with another analyst; in spite of this, there had hardly been any change in his symptoms and his behavior.

Finally, I was struck by a certain aspect of his behavior. His movements were flaccid, his expression tired, his speech monotonous and sombre. His intonation revealed the meaning of his behavior: he talked in a tortured manner, as if dying. I learned that outside of the analysis, too, he assumed, in certain situations, this unconsciously play-acted lethargy. The meaning of this mode of talking was also: "Look what my father has made of me, how he tortures me. He has ruined me." His attitude was a severe reproach.

The effect of my interpreting his "dying," complaining and reproachful mode of talking was surprising. It was as if with the solution of this last, formal fixation point of his relationship with his father all the earlier interpretations of content were becoming effective. As long as his mode of talking had not betrayed its unconscious meaning, it bound a large amount of the affects of his relationship to his father; for this reason, the contents of the relationship, although they had been made conscious, carried too little affect to be therapeutically effective.

One and the same aspect of the unconscious infantile structure is conserved and expressed in two ways: in *what* the individual does, says or thinks, and in *the way* in which the individual acts, talks or thinks. It is to be noted that the analysis of the "what"—in spite of the unity of content and form—leaves the "how" untouched; that this "how" turns out to be the hiding-place of the same psychic contents which already seemed to be dissolved or made conscious by the analysis of the "what"; and finally, that the analysis of the "how" is particularly effective in releasing the affects.

## CHAPTER X

# SOME CIRCUMSCRIBED CHARACTER FORMS

## 1. THE HYSTERICAL CHARACTER

Our investigation of the differentiation of character types proceeds from two facts: First, no matter what the form of the character, its basic function is an armoring against the stimuli of the outer world and against the repressed inner impulses. Second, the external form of this armoring has its specific historical determination. We found that perhaps the most important conditions for character differentiation are the character of the persons who exert the main educational influence, and the stage of development at which the decisive frustrations occur. There must be definite relationships between the external manifestations of the character, its inner mechanisms and its specific history of development.

The hysterical character—as complicated as the corresponding symptoms and reactions may be—represents the simplest type of character armoring. Its most outstanding characteristic is an *obvious sexual behavior,* in combination with a specific kind of *bodily agility* with a definitely sexual nuance. This explains the fact that the connection between female hysteria and sexuality has been known for a very long time. In women, the hysterical character type is evidenced by disguised or undisguised coquetry in gait, gaze and speech. In men, there is, in addition, softness and over-politeness, feminine facial expression and feminine behavior (*cf.* the case history in Chapter IV, *supra,* p. 81ff.).

The traits mentioned appear together with a more or less outspoken apprehensiveness. This becomes particularly evident when the sexual behavior seems close to attaining its goal; then the hysterical character regularly retreats or assumes a passive, anxious attitude. As violent as the hysterical action was before, just so intense is the passivity now. In the sexual act, there is often increased activity without corresponding sexual experience. This activity is an attempt to overcome intense anxiety.

In the hysterical character, facial expression and gait are never hard and heavy as in the compulsive character, or self-confident and arrogant as in the phallic-narcissistic character. In the typical case, the movements are soft, more or less rolling, and sexually provocative. The total impression is one of easy excitability, in contrast, for example, to the self-control of the compulsive character.

While coquetry paired with apprehensiveness as well as bodily agility are immediately evident, the other specific hysterical character traits are hidden. Among these are inconstancy of the reactions, that is, a tendency to unexpected and unintended changes of behavior; a strong suggestibility, always together with a strong tendency to disappointment reactions: as quickly as a hysterical character—in contrast to the compulsive character—lets himself be convinced even of what is most unlikely, as quickly will he give up the conviction and replace it by others which are just as easily acquired. Compliance then is quickly replaced by the opposite: quick depreciation and groundless disparagement. The suggestibility of the hysterical character predisposes him to passive hypnosis, but also to flights of the imagination. It has to do with the extraordinary capacity to form sexual attachments of an infantile character. The vivid imagination easily gives rise to pathological lying because imagined experiences may be conceived of and narrated as actual experiences.

Just as the hysterical character is strongly expressed in bodily behavior, so it tends to represent psychic conflicts in somatic symptoms. This can be easily understood from the libido structure.

The hysterical character is determined by a fixation on the genital phase of infantile development, with its incestuous attachment. From this fixation the hysterical character derives its strong genital aggression as well as its apprehensiveness. The genital incest wishes are repressed but have retained their full cathexis; they are not replaced by pregenital drives as is the case in the compulsive character. To the extent to which, in the hysterical character, pregenital, that is, oral, anal or urethral strivings, play a role, they are representations of genitality or are at least combined with it. In the hysterical character, mouth as well as anus always represent the female genital while in other character forms these zones retain their original pregenital function. As Ferenczi put it, the hysterical character genitalizes everything; the other forms of neuroses replace genitality by pregenital mechanisms or let the genital function as breast, mouth or anus, a mechanism which I called the flooding of the genital with pregenital libido. Since the hysterical character always suffers from a severe sexual disturbance, and since the stasis of genital libido has the most pronounced effects, the sexual agility must be as intensive as the anxiety reactions. The hysterical character, unlike the compulsive character, suffers from direct sexual tension.

This leads us to the nature of the character armor. The armor is much less solidified, much more labile than in the compulsive character. It is simply an apprehensive defense against the genital incest strivings. It seems paradoxical but is a fact that here genital sexuality is in the service against itself: the more apprehensive the total attitude, the more pronounced is the sexual behavior. The meaning of this function is the following: the hysterical character has strong and unsatisfied genital strivings which are inhibited by the genital anxiety; thus he feels constantly exposed to dangers which correspond to his infantile fears; the original genital striving is then utilized for the purpose of feeling out, as it were, the nature and magnitude of the threatening dangers. Thus, when a hysterical woman makes particularly active sexual advances it would be erroneous to assume that this is genuine sexual readiness. On the contrary, with the first attempt to take advantage of this seeming readiness one will find that her behavior immediately turns into the opposite: anxiety or any kind of defense, including motor flight. The sexual behavior, then, serves the purpose of finding out whether and from where the expected dangers will realize. This is quite obvious in the transference reactions during treatment. The hysterical character is always ignorant of the meaning of his sexual behavior, fights against taking cognisance of it, becomes highly indignant at such "suggestions"; in brief, one soon realizes that what appears to be a sexual striving is sexuality in the function of defense. Only after one has unmasked this and has analytically dissolved the infantile genital anxiety does the genital striving for an object appear in its original function; to the same extent to which this happens the patient also loses the exaggerated sexual agility. The fact that this sexual behavior also expresses other, secondary strivings, such as primitive narcissism, or the wish to dominate or to make an impression, is not important in this context.

To the extent to which other than genital mechanisms are found in the hysterical character they no longer belong specifically to this character type. For example, one often finds depressive mechanisms. In these cases one finds that the genital-incestuous fixation was in part replaced by a regression to oral mechanisms. The marked tendency of hysterics to oral regressions is explained by the sexual stasis at this zone and by the fact that the mouth, having assumed the role of the genital, absorbs much libido ("displacement from below upwards"). In this process, melancholia-like reactions which belong to the original oral fixation are also activated. The hysterical character, then, presents itself in pure form if it is agile, nervous and lively; if it is depressive, retiring and autistic it shows mechanisms which are no longer specifically hysterical. Nevertheless, one is justified in speaking of hysterical depressions in contrast to melancholic depressions. The difference lies in the extent to which genital libido and object relationships are present together with the oral attitudes. This accounts for gradual transitions at the extreme ends of which we find pure melancholia and, where genitality is predominant, pure hysteria.

The hysterical character has little tendency to sublimation and intellectual achievement and a much lesser tendency to reaction formations than other character types. This is also due to the fact that the libido is neither discharged in sexual gratification which would reduce the hypersexuality nor do the sexual energies become extensively anchored in the character; rather, they are discharged in somatic innervations or in anxiety or apprehensiveness. The mechanisms of hysteria are often used to prove the alleged antithesis of sexuality and social achievement. What is overlooked is the fact that the outspoken inability to sublimate is a result precisely of the sexual inhibition in the presence of genital libido, and the fact that only the establishment of the capacity for gratification liberates social interest and achievement.

With regard to sex-economy and the prevention of the neuroses one has to ask why it is that the hysterical character cannot somehow transform his genital stasis as other characters do with their pregenital strivings. The hysterical character does not utilize the genital libido for reaction formations or sublimations; more than that, there is not even the formation of a solid character armor. The fact is that fully-developed genital excitations do not lend themselves to anything but direct gratification; their inhibition severely impairs the sublimation of other libidinous strivings also because it endows them with an excess of energy. One might assume that this has to do with a specific quality of genitality; more likely, however, it is because of the quantity of libido involved in the excitation of the genital zone. The genital apparatus can provide *orgastic* discharge, a mechanism which does not exist for any other partial impulse; for this reason, it is vital from the point of view of libido-economy. This may be in conflict with certain ethical concepts but cannot be changed. The aversion against these facts can be readily understood: their recognition would be revolutionary.

## 2. THE COMPULSIVE CHARACTER

The most general function of the character being the defense against stimuli, and the maintenance of psychic equilibrium, it must be particularly easy to demonstrate in the compulsive character, for this is one of the best-studied psychic formations. There are fluid transitions from the well-known compulsion symptoms to the corresponding character attitudes. The neurotic orderliness compulsion may be absent but a *pedantic concern for orderliness* is a typical trait of the compulsive character. His whole life, in all its major and minor aspects, runs according to a preconceived, inviolable program. Any change in the program is experienced unpleasurably, in more pronounced cases it even arouses anxiety. This character trait, because of its accompanying thoroughness, may help the individual to get much done; on the other hand, it also reduces the working capacity considerably because it precludes any rapid change and adaptation to new situations. It may be valuable for the official, but detrimental for the individual trying to engage in creative work or work which depends on new ideas. Thus one will rarely find compulsive characters among great statesmen; they are more likely to be found among scientists. But since pedantry paralyzes all speculation this trait will also make pioneering discoveries impossible. This leads us to another character trait which is never missing: the tendency to *circumstantial, ruminative thinking*. There is an inability to concentrate more here and less there, according to the rational significance of an object; attention is always divided more or less evenly; unessential things are thought through no less thoroughly than others which are in the center of professional interest. The more rigid and pathological this trait is, the more is thinking and attention concentrated on unessential things, the more are the rationally important things excluded from thinking. This is the result of a displacement of unconscious cathexes; that is, ideas which have become unconsciously important are replaced by far-fetched insignificant ideas. It is part of the general process of repression and is directed against repressed ideas. Usually, there are infantile ruminations about forbidden things which are never allowed to penetrate to the real concern. These ruminations also take place according to historically determined schemas; in intellectual workers, they impair intellectual motility considerably. In many cases, this is made up for by an above-average ability for abstract logical thinking. The critical abilities are better developed than the creative ones.

Another character trait which is never absent is *thriftiness* if not *avarice*. Pedantry, circumstantiality, tendency to rumination, and thriftiness derive all from one instinctual source, anal eroticism; they are reaction formations against those tendencies which played a major role during the phase of toilet training. To the extent to which these reaction formations have not been successful one finds traits of exactly the opposite nature which, together with the traits mentioned, are also typical of the compulsive character. More correctly, these are breakthroughs of the original tendencies. Then we find extreme sloppiness, incapacity for dealing with money, etc. The great tendency to *collect* things completes the list of the characterological derivatives of anal eroticism. While the connection here with the interest in the functions of evacuation is obvious, the connection between rumination and anal eroticism remains obscure. Though we always find a connection with the ruminations about where the babies come from, the transformation of the interest in defecation into a specific kind of thinking is difficult to understand. What we know here is found in the relevant articles of Freud, Abraham, Jones and Ophuijsen.

There are other character traits which derive not from the anal but from the sadistic impulses of that particular age period. Compulsive characters always have strong *reactions of sympathy and guilt feelings.* This does not contradict the fact that their other traits are by no means pleasant for other people; more than that, in the exaggerated orderliness, pedantry, etc., hostile and aggressive impulses are often directly gratified. Corresponding to the fixation of the compulsive character on the anal-sadistic stage of libido development, these traits are reaction formations against opposite tendencies. The fact should be emphasized that we can speak of compulsive character only when these traits are present in their totality but not if somebody is merely, say, pedantic, without showing any other traits of the compulsive character. If, for example, a hysterical character also shows tendencies to pedantry or rumination, he cannot be called a compulsive character.

While the character traits mentioned thus far are direct derivatives of certain partial impulses, there are other typical traits which show a more complicated structure and result from the interaction of various forces. Among these are *indecision, doubt and distrust.* In his outward appearance, the compulsive character shows marked *restraint* and *control;* his affective reactions, negative as well as positive, are lukewarm; in extreme cases, this becomes a *complete affect-block.* These latter traits are already of a formal nature, bringing us to our real subject, the dynamics and economy of the character.

The restraint and evenness in living and thinking, coupled with indecision, form the point of departure of our analysis of the character form. They cannot be derived from individual impulses like the contents of the character traits; they give the individual his particular stamp; they form, in analysis, the core of the character resistance. Clinical experience shows that the traits of doubt, mistrust, etc., act as resistance in the analysis and cannot be eliminated as long as one does not succeed in breaking through the affect-block. This, therefore, deserves our special attention. We shall limit ourselves essentially to the formal elements since the others are well known while here we are in new territory.

We shall have to recall first what is known about the libido development of the compulsive character. There was a central fixation on the anal-sadistic level, that is, at about the age of two or three. Toilet training took place too early which led to strong reaction formations such as extreme self-control, even at a very early age. The strict toilet training called forth a strong anal stubbornness which also mobilized the sadistic impulses. In the typical compulsion neurosis, the development proceeds, nevertheless, into the phallic phase. That is, genitality was activated but soon relinquished again, partly because of the strong inhibitions set up at a very early age, partly because of the antisexual attitude of the parents. To the extent to which genitality was developed, it was, corresponding to the previous development of anality and sadism, in the form of phallic-sadistic aggression. It goes without saying that a boy will repress his genital impulses all the more quickly the more aggressive his acquired sexual constitution and the more inhibitions and guilt feelings from an earlier phase of development make themselves felt. Thus it is typical of compulsion neurosis that the repression of genitality is followed by a regression to the earlier stage of anal interests and of aggression. During the so-called latency period[1]—which is particularly well-

---

[1] The sexual development among children of primitive peoples shows that the latency period is not a biological phenomenon, but a sociological one created by sexual suppression.

developed in compulsive characters—the anal and sadistic reaction formations are intensified and form the final character. During puberty, under the influence of the increased sexual urge, the process is repeated in abbreviated form. Usually there are at first violent sadistic impulses toward women (phantasies of rape, of beating, etc.), accompanied by a feeling of affective weakness and inferiority; these call forth narcissistic compensations in the form of ethical and esthetic reaction formations. The anal and sadistic fixations are intensified or—after a brief and usually unsuccessful move in the direction of genital activity—reactivated, which causes a further elaboration of the corresponding reaction formations. As a result of these processes in the depth, the puberty of the compulsive character takes a typical course. There is, first of all, a progressive flattening of affective reactions which may impress the untrained observer as a particularly good social "adjustment" and may be experienced as such by the patient himself. But together with this affect-block there is a feeling of inner emptiness and an intense desire to "start life anew" which is often attempted with the most absurd means. One such patient developed a highly complicated system according to which he was going to carry out every major and minor task in his life. Everything was figured out down to the second so that he would start his new life exactly at a given date. Since he was never able to fulfil the self-imposed conditions of his system, he always had to start all over again.

The best object for a study of the formal disturbances in the compulsive character is the affect-block. It is by no means the passive attitude of the ego which it appears to be. On the contrary, there is hardly any other character formation in which analysis reveals such an active and intense defense work. What, then, is warded off, and by what means? The typical mode of repression in the compulsive character is the dissociation of the affects from the ideas, so that very often highly censorable ideas can appear in consciousness. One such patient dreamed and talked openly about incest with his mother, even about violent rape, but he remained entirely unmoved. Genital as well as sadistic excitation was completely absent. If one analyzes such patients without con-

centrating on the affect-block, one gets, it is true, further unconscious material, perhaps even an occasional weak excitation, but
never the affects which would correspond to the ideas. Where do
they keep hidden? To the extent to which they are not absorbed
by symptoms, they are to be found in the affect-block itself. This
is proved by the fact that when one succeeds in breaking through
the affect-block, the affects spontaneously reappear, usually at first
in the form of anxiety.

It is noteworthy that at first no genital impulses are liberated
but only aggressive impulses. The superficial layer of the armor,
then, consists of aggressive energy. What binds it? The aggressive
energy is bound with the help of anal-erotic energies. The affect-
block is one great spasm of the ego which makes use of somatic
spastic conditions. All muscles of the body, but particularly those
of the pelvis and pelvic floor, of the shoulders and the face, are in
a state of chronic hypertonia. Hence the "hard," somewhat mask-
like physiognomy of compulsive characters, and their physical
awkwardness. The ego takes over anal holding-back tendencies
from the repressed layers and utilizes them for the defense against
the sadistic impulses. While, thus, anality and aggression go together in the unconscious, they assume an antithetical function
in the defense: anality, the holding back, is used as a defense
against aggression, and vice versa. That means that we do not
liberate the anal energies either unless we dissolve the affect-
block. We are reminded of our affect-blocked patient who, every
time he rang my doorbell, would recite the Götz quotation three
times. It is as if he said: "I would like to kill you, but I must control
myself; therefore, you can . . ."

The passive-feminine character also wards off his aggression by
means of anal tendencies, but in a different manner. Here, anality
works in the original direction as an object-libidinous impulse; in
the compulsive character, however, in the form of anal holding
back, that is, as a reaction formation. Correspondingly, passive
homosexuality in the compulsive character is not as superficial and
relatively unrepressed as in the passive-feminine which belongs
to the type of the hysterical character.

How is it possible that the anal holding back in the character can be so powerful that the patients become living machines? Not only because of the anal reaction formation. The sadism which is bound up in the affect-block is not only its object but also its means in the defense against anality. That is, an interest in the anal function is also warded off by means of aggressive energy. Every affective and lively utterance provokes in the unconscious the old unresolved excitations so that there is a conscious fear that an accident may happen, that self-control may be lost. It can readily be seen that this opens the way to the whole infantile conflict between urge to let go and necessity for self-control because of fear of punishment. Correct analysis of the affect-block leads to a breakthrough into this central conflict and the displacement of the corresponding cathexes back to the original positions. This, however, is synonymous with the dissolution of the armor.

From the affect-block one also arrives at the affective anchorings of the first identifications and the super-ego: The demand for self-control, originally imposed from the outside on a resisting ego, was internally accepted. More than that, it became a rigid, chronic, unalterable mode of reaction; this could be achieved only with the aid of repressed id energies.

Systematic resistance analysis leads to the separation of two different sadistic impulses which are contained in the affect-block. What is usually liberated first is *anal* sadism with the goals of beating, kicking, squashing, etc. After these are worked through and the anal fixations are dissolved, *phallic*-sadistic impulses, such as stabbing and piercing, come more and more to the fore. That is, the regression is eliminated and the cathexis of the phallic position begins. At this point, castration anxiety makes its first appearance in an affective manner, and the analysis of the genital repressions begins. In compulsive characters, the old infantile phobia often reappears at this stage.

We find, then, two layers of repressions in the compulsive character: more superficially, the sadistic and anal, more deeply, the phallic ones. This corresponds to the reversal of direction in the process of regression. What was more recently invested with affect in the process of regression lies closer to the surface; the object-libidinal genital impulses are most deeply repressed and covered

up by layers of pregenital positions. These structural relationships make clear how erroneous it would be to try to make the
patient understand affectively the weak manifestations of genital
object-strivings *before* having worked through the pregenital layers. If one were to try to do this, everything would be accepted
coldly or warded off with doubt and distrust.

In this connection, we have to say a few words about ambivalence and doubt. They are the most difficult obstacles unless
one succeeds, from the beginning, in separating from each other
the different impulses which make up the ambivalence. The ambivalence represents a conflict between love and hatred for the
same person, in a deeper layer an inhibition of the libidinal as well
as the aggressive strivings by the fear of punishment. If one analyzes all manifestations simultaneously, without discrimination,
one cannot master the ambivalence and may arrive at the assumption of a biological, that is, unalterable ambivalent "anlage." If, on
the other hand, one proceeds according to structural and dynamic
considerations, the hatred soon becomes predominant; after its
analysis, the libidinal strivings become crystallized out. The best
means for this *splitting up of the ambivalence* is a painstaking
analysis of the distrust right from the beginning of the analysis.

It goes without saying that we could do no more here than point
out the most essential traits of the compulsive character.

### 3. THE PHALLIC-NARCISSISTIC CHARACTER

The formulation of a "phallic-narcissistic character" resulted
from the necessity of defining character forms which stand in between compulsion neurosis and hysteria. They manifest circumscribed forms which differ sharply, both in manifestation and
genesis, from the two others. The term "phallic-narcissistic character" or, less correctly, "genital-narcissistic character," has found
its way into psychoanalytic terminology during the past few years.
I first described this type in a hitherto unpublished paper read
before the Vienna Psychoanalytic Society in October, 1926.

Even in outward appearance, the phallic-narcissistic character
differs from the compulsive and the hysterical character. While
the compulsive character is predominantly inhibited, self-con-

trolled and depressive, and while the hysterical character is nervous, agile, apprehensive and labile, the typical phallic-narcissistic character is self-confident, often arrogant, elastic, vigorous and often impressive. The more neurotic the inner mechanism, the more obtrusive are these modes of behavior. As to bodily type, they belong most frequently to Kretschmer's athletic type. The facial expression usually shows hard, sharp masculine features, but often also feminine, girl-like features in spite of athletic habitus. Everyday behavior is never crawling as in passive-feminine characters but usually haughty, either cold and reserved or derisively aggressive, or "bristly," as one of these patients put it. In the behavior toward the object, the love object included, the narcissistic element always dominates over the object-libidinal, and there is always an admixture of more or less disguised sadistic traits.

Such individuals usually anticipate any expected attack with an attack on their part. Their aggression is very often expressed not so much in what they say or do as in the manner in which they say or do things. Particularly to people who do not have their own aggression at their disposal they appear as aggressive and provocative. The outspoken types tend to achieve leading positions in life and resent subordination unless they can—as in the army or other hierarchic organizations—compensate for the necessity of subordination by exerting domination over others who find themselves on lower rungs of the ladder. If their vanity is hurt, they react either with cold reserve, deep depression or lively aggression. In contrast to other characters, their narcissism expresses itself not in an infantile manner but in the exaggerated display of self-confidence, dignity and superiority, in spite of the fact that the basis of their character is no less infantile than that of others. The comparison of their structure with that of, say, a compulsive character, clearly shows the difference between pregenital and phallic narcissism. In spite of their narcissistic preoccupation with their selves they often show strong attachments to people and things outside. In this respect, they resemble most closely the genital character; they differ from it, however, in that their actions are much more intensively and extensively determined by irrational motives. It is not by accident that this type is most frequently found among athletes, aviators, soldiers and engineers. One of their most important traits is aggressive courage, just as the compulsive character is characterized by cautious hesitation and the passive-feminine character by an avoidance of dangerous situations. The success in achievement is little influenced by the fact that the courage and enterprise of the phallic narcissist differs from that of the genital character by being also compensatory, having to ward off opposite strivings.

The phallic-narcissistic character differs from the compulsive character in the absence of reaction formations against his openly aggressive and sadistic behavior. We will have to show that this aggressive behavior itself fulfils a defense function. In relatively unneurotic representatives of this type, social achievement, thanks to the free aggression, is strong, impulsive, energetic and usually productive; the more neurotic the character, the more peculiar and one-sided the achievement; from here there is every transition to the formation of paranoid systems. The achievement differs from that of the compulsive character by a greater boldness and lesser attention to details.

Phallic-narcissistic men show a high erective potency, although they are orgastically impotent. Relationships with women are disturbed by the contempt for the female sex which is rarely lacking. In spite of this, they are highly desired sexual objects because in their appearance they show all the traits of masculinity. In women, the phallic-narcissistic character occurs much less frequently. The definitely neurotic forms are characterized by active homosexuality and clitoris sexuality; those who are genitally healthier are characterized by great self-confidence, based on physical vigor and beauty.

The phallic-narcissistic character comprises almost all forms of active homosexuality, male and female; most cases of so-called moral insanity, paranoia and allied forms of schizophrenia; also many cases of erythrophobia and manifestly sadistic male perverts. Many productive women also belong to this type.

Now as to the structure and genesis of this character type. Here we must distinguish those impulses which find direct gratification in the phallic-narcissistic behavior from those which form the narcissistic protection apparatus. Typically, analysis reveals an identification of the total ego with the phallus, in women the phantasy of having a penis; also, a more or less open display of this ego. In erythrophobia, this impulse is repressed and breaks through in the form of a strong neurotic feeling of shame, and blushing. These cases have in common a fixation to that phase of infantile development in which the anal-sadistic position had just been left while the genital object-libidinal position had not yet been reached and which, therefore, is characterized by a proud, self-confident concentration on the own genital. This, however, is not a sufficient explanation. The phallic narcissist is characterized not only by this phallic pride, but even more by the motives which force him to remain at this stage of development.

The pride in the real or fantasied phallus goes hand in hand with a strong phallic aggression. To the unconscious of the man of this type, the penis is not in the service of love but is an instrument of aggression and vengeance. This is the basis of his strong erective potency as well as of his inability to experience the orgasm. The infantile history regularly reveals serious disappointments in the object of the other sex, disappointments which occurred precisely at the time when attempts were made to win the object through phallic exhibition. In men, one often finds that the mother was the stronger of the parents, or the father had died early or was otherwise out of the picture.

The frustration of genital and exhibitionistic activity at the height of their development by the very person toward whom the genital interest is displayed results in an identification with that person on the *genital* level. That is, the boy will give up and introject the female object and will turn to the father in an active (because phallic) homosexual role, while the mother is retained as an object with only narcissistic attitudes and impulses of sadistic revenge. In such men, the sexual act has the unconscious meaning of again and again proving to the woman how potent they are; at the same time it means piercing or destroying the woman, in a more superficial layer degrading her. In phallic-narcissistic women, conversely, the leading motive is that of taking vengeance on the

man, of castrating him during the act or of making him impotent
or of making him appear impotent. This is in no way at variance
with the strong sexual attraction which these strongly erotic characters exert on the other sex. Neurotic polygamy, active creating
of disappointments for the partner, and passive flight from the possibility of being left alone are very often found. In other cases,
where narcissistic sensitivity disturbs the compensation mechanism, erective potency is unstable, a fact which the patient is unwilling to admit to himself. The more disturbed potency is, the
more labile is the general mood, and there is often a rapid alternation of hypomanic, self-confident phases and phases of severe
depression. In such cases, the ability to work is also severely disturbed.

The phallic-exhibitionistic and sadistic attitude serves also as a
defense against opposite tendencies. The compulsive character,
after the genital frustration, regresses to the earlier phase of
anality and there forms his reaction formations. The phallic character does not regress. He remains at the phallic stage; more than
that, he exaggerates its manifestations *in order to protect himself
against a regression to passivity and anality.* In the course of the
analysis of such characters, strongly warded-off anal and passive
tendencies come more and more to the fore. They constitute the
character not directly but by the defense which the ego puts up
against them in the form of phallic sadism and exhibitionism. They
represent the exact opposite of the passive-feminine character who
wards off his genital impulses with the aid of anal and passive
surrender. The phallic-narcissistic character, conversely, wards
off his anal and passive-homosexual impulses with the aid of
phallic aggression. Analysts often describe such characters as anal
or passive-homosexual. This is incorrect. The passive-feminine
character cannot be called phallic-sadistic because he wards off
these tendencies; similarly, the phallic-narcissistic character cannot be described as anal-passive because he wards off these tendencies. The character is determined not by what it wards off but
by the manner in which and the impulses with which the defense
is effectuated.

In the case of moral insanity, of active homosexuality and

phallic sadism, as well as in the sublimated forms such as the professional athlete, the defense is highly successful and the warded-off tendencies of passive and anal homosexuality are expressed only in certain exaggerations. In paranoia, the warded-off tendencies fully break through in the form of delusions. Erythrophobia is most closely associated with the paranoid form of this character; it is very frequently found in the history of paranoid schizophrenics. Here, we have a symptomatic breakthrough of the warded-off passive and anal homosexuality; the patient, due to acute castration anxiety, gives up masturbation, and the additional sexual stasis, with its vasomotor manifestations, weakens the defense function of the ego. The active homosexual and the phallic sadist, on the other hand, have a strong ego defense as long as there is effective libidinal gratification. If this, for any reason, is interrupted for any considerable period of time, the passive and anal tendency also will break through, either symptomatically or without disguise.

Among the phallic-narcissistic-sadistic characters one often finds addicts, particularly alcoholics. This not only because of warded-off homosexuality but also because of another specific trait of this type which also derives from phallic frustration. Let us take the case of the man. The frustration of phallic exhibitionism and masturbation by the mother leads to an identification with her and a strengthening of the previously relinquished anal position and tendency to passive-feminine behavior. This is immediately counteracted by an emphasis on phallic-exhibitionistic and aggressive, that is, masculine, attitudes. However, in the identification on the phallic level with the woman she was provided with a fantasied penis, and the own phallus also attained the meaning of breast. For this reason, the sexually active forms of this character in men show a tendency to passive and active fellatio, and a maternal attitude toward younger men; women show such an attitude toward younger and feminine types of women. In alcoholism, there is also a regression to orality; for this reason, the typical traits of the phallic-narcissistic character are not so clear-cut.

There are many more forms of transition from the phallic-narcissistic character to the healthy genital character as well as to the severely pathological, pregenital forms of addiction and chronic depression than can be found in other characters. A good deal has been written about the relationship between genius and criminality. The type that is meant here belongs neither to the hysterical nor to the masochistic character but predominantly to the phallic-narcissistic character. Most of the sex murderers of recent history belonged to it such as Haarmann and Kürten who had suffered the most severe infantile disappointments in love and later on realized their phallic-sadistic vengeance on the love object. Landru as well as Napoleon and Mussolini belong to the phallic-narcissistic characters. The combination of phallic narcissism, phallic sadism and simultaneous compensation of passive and anal homosexual strivings makes for the most energetic characters. Whether such a type turns into a creative genius or a large-scale criminal depends largely on the social atmosphere and the possibilities it provides for an outlet of the energy in a sublimated form. The other determining factor is the measure of genital gratification which in turn determines the amount of energy which is channeled into destructive impulses of revenge. This differentiation of social and libido-economic factors is not meant to obliterate the fact that the inability to reach genital gratification depends also on social and familial factors. Constitutionally speaking, there seems to be, in these types, an above-average production of libidinal energy which makes possible an all the more intense aggression.

The analytic treatment of phallic-narcissistic characters is one of the most thankful tasks. Since the phallic phase has been fully reached and since aggression is relatively free, the establishment of genital and social potency, other things being equal, is easier than in other character forms. The analysis is always successful if one succeeds in unmasking the phallic-narcissistic attitudes as a defense against passive-feminine tendencies and in eliminating the unconscious tendency of revenge against the other sex. If one does not succeed in this, the patients remain in their narcissistic inaccessibility. Their character resistance consists in aggressive deprecation of the analysis and the analyst in more or less disguised forms, a narcissistic taking over of the interpretation work, and in the denial of and defense against any passive or apprehensive tendency and particularly the positive transference. The reactivation of phallic anxiety is possible only by an energetic and consistent dissolution of the reactive narcissistic mechanisms. Superficial signs of passivity and anal homosexual tendencies may not immediately be followed into deeper levels because this is apt to result in complete inaccessibility.

CHAPTER XI

# THE MASOCHISTIC CHARACTER

*Translator's note:* A translation of this chapter was published in the *International Journal of Sex-economy and Orgone Research* 3, 1944, 38ff., preceded by the following editorial comment:

There are several reasons for publishing this chapter from Reich's CHARAKTERANALYSE at this time.

First, there has been, in recent years, an increasing interest in this book and increasing demands for an English translation of it, particularly from psychoanalysts. Unfortunately, it has not been possible thus far to translate and publish the book. The publication of selected chapters in this JOURNAL may meet these recurring demands, at least in part.

Second, it is a good thing from time to time to go back and point out the historical links between sex-economy of today and the psychoanalytic matrix from which it took its origin. The present chapter plays a singularly important role in the history of sex-economy. Before its publication as a chapter of CHARAKTERANALYSE, it was published as an article in the *Internat. Zeitschr. f. Psychoanalyse,* Vol. 18, 1932. It was a milestone in that it provided the clinical refutation of Freud's theory of the death instinct. For the first time in the history of sexual pathology, the following facts were demonstrated on the basis of clinical investigation:

a) The manifestations which were erroneously ascribed to a hypothetical death instinct were actually due to a specific form of orgasm anxiety;

b) masochism is no instinct or drive in the biological sense; it is a *secondary* drive in the sex-economic sense, that is, a result of the repression of natural sexual mechanisms;

c) there is no such thing as a biological striving for unpleasure, there is no death instinct.

In the succeeding years, parts of this clarification of the problem of masochism were taken over by many psychoanalysts, without mention of their source. But none of them even mentioned the *central* aspect of the problem, that is, the *specific* masochistic disturbance of the orgasm function which expresses itself in a *fear of dying* or *fear of bursting*. Thus, the solution of the problem of masochism remained the exclusive achievement of sex-economy.

The publication of this article in 1932 was accompanied by some rather dramatic events. Freud, as the Herausgeber of the *Internat. Zeitschr. f. Psychoanalyse,* wanted to have the article published only on the proviso that he would add a note in which he was going to declare that Wilhelm Reich had written this article against the death instinct theory "in the service" of the Communist party. Certain Berlin psychoanalysts who opposed this nonsense suggested another procedure: Reich's article was to be published together with a reply. This was done. This "reply" was written by Siegfried Bernfeld under the title, *Die kommunistische Diskussion um die Psychoanalyse und Reich's "Widerlegung der Todestriebhypothese,"* and appeared in the same number of the *Zeitschrift.* This article of some 30 pages did not deal with the problem of masochism at all, but with Wilhelm Reich's contributions to Marxist sociology. In other words, since Reich's clinical findings and formulations could not be refuted, an attempt was made to discredit his theory of masochism by the imputation of political, emotional motives. This attempt failed thoroughly. We leave it to the reader of the translation of this article to decide whether it is of a clinical or of a political and philosophical nature.

The fact must again be emphasized that the sex-economic clarification of the problem of masochism—which was identical with the clinical refutation of the death instinct theory—represented an enormous step forward in the understanding of the neuroses. For it showed that human suffering was not due to an unalterable "biological will to suffer," to a "death instinct," but to the disastrous effect of *social* conditions on the biopsychic apparatus. This entailed the necessity of criticizing the social conditions which created the neuroses—a necessity which the hypothesis of a biological will to suffer had circumvented.

The sex-economic solution of the problem of masochism also opened an avenue of approach into the biological basis of the neuroses. It was precisely the specific masochistic fear of "bursting" which opened the way to an understanding of the functioning of the vegetative life apparatus (*cf.* THE FUNCTION OF THE ORGASM, 1942, pp. 221-255).

The publication in translation of the present work at this time, then, is no less pertinent than it was at the time of its original publication 12 years ago. It shows the nature of certain kinds of so-called scientific criticism in that not a single one of the contentions that were used 12 years ago against Reich's theory of masochism could even be published today. That kind of argumentation never had a rational basis and belongs to a dead past.—T. P. W.

## 1. RÉSUMÉ OF CONCEPTS

Sexology before Freud held essentially the view that masochism represented a special instinct tendency to derive satisfaction from suffering physical or moral pain. Since these goals are unpleasurable, the central problem was how it is possible that unpleasure should be striven for or should even provide satisfaction. The use of a technical term was only an evasion; "algolagnia" means nothing but a circumlocution of the fact that an attempt is made to derive pleasure from being hurt or offended. Many writers came closer to the truth when they asserted that being beaten was not the immediate aim but only a link in the experience of pleasurable self-depreciation (Krafft-Ebing). Nevertheless, the fundamental formulation was the same: *What the normal person perceives as unpleasure, the masochist perceives as pleasure or, at any rate, as a source of pleasure.*

Psychoanalytic investigation of the latent content and the dynamics of masochism provided a wealth of new insights. Freud discovered that masochism and sadism do not form an absolute antithesis, that one never occurs without the other. Masochism and sadism can each turn into the other. There is a dialectic antithesis, determined by a change from activity to passivity while the ideational content remains the same.[1] Freud's theory of libidinal development distinguishes three main stages of infantile sexuality, oral, anal and genital. At first, sadism was ascribed to the anal phase. Later it was found that each of the stages of sexual development has a form of sadistic aggression corresponding to it. In following up this problem, I found each of the three forms of sadistic aggression to be a reaction to the frustration of the corresponding partial impulse. According to this concept, the sadism on each level of development results from a mixture of the destructive impulse against the frustrating person with the corresponding sexual demand,[2] in the following way: Sucking, frustration → destructive tendency, biting: *oral sadism;* anal pleasure, frustration → wanting to squash, to step on, to beat: *anal sadism;* genital pleasure, frustration → wanting to pierce; *phallic sadism.* This concept was entirely in harmony with Freud's original formulation that the destructive tendency toward the outer world develops first (usually as a result of frustration) and later turns against the self when it, also, becomes inhibited by frustration and fear of punishment. Sadism, in turning toward the self, becomes masochism; the super-ego, the representation of the frustrating person, of the demands of society on the ego, becomes the punishing agency (conscience). The guilt feeling corresponds to the destructive impulse which comes into conflict with love.

Later, Freud gave up this concept of masochism as a secondary formation. He replaced it by the converse concept that sadism is masochism turned toward the outer world; he assumed the existence of a *primary biological* tendency to self-destruction, a primary or erogenous masochism. This concept later turned into that of the "death instinct," the antagonist of "eros." Primary masoch-

---

[1] Freud, "Triebe und Triebschicksale." Ges. Schr., Bd. V, p. 453.
[2] Reich, W.: "Ueber die Quellen der neurotischen Angst." *Int. Zeitschr. f. Psa.* 11, 1926, 427.

ism was thought of as an expression of a biological death instinct which was based on the processes of dissimilation in every cell of the organism.

The proponents of the theory of the death instinct again and again tried to substantiate their views by pointing to physiological processes of dissimilation. None of these attempts was in any way convincing. A recent paper[3] deserves mention because it approaches the problem clinically and sets forth physiological arguments which at first glance seem convincing. Benedek bases her argument on the findings of Ehrenberg. This biologist found that even in the protozoon an antithetical process can be found. Certain processes in the protoplasm lead not only to the assimilation of the food, but also to a precipitation of previously dissolved substances. This first formation of a structure is irreversible; dissolved substances become solid. What assimilates is alive; what develops by way of assimilation, changes the cell, gives it a higher structure which, from a certain point on, i.e., when it gains preponderance, is no longer life, but death. That sounds logical particularly when we remember the hardening of the arteries with advancing age. But this very argument contradicts the assumption of a *tendency* to death, a death *instinct*. What has become solid and immobile hinders life and its cardinal function, the alternation of tension and relaxation, in the gratification of hunger as well as the sexual needs. This disturbance of the life process is exactly the opposite of what characterizes instinct. The rigidity renders the rhythm of tension and relaxation impossible again and again. If we wanted to see an instinct in these processes, we would have to change our concept of the instinct.

If, furthermore, anxiety is considered the expression of a "death instinct become free," it would have to be explained how "solid structures" can become free. Benedek says herself that the structure, that which has become solid, can be considered inimical to life only when it becomes predominant and hinders the life processes.

Furthermore, if the structure-forming processes are synonymous with the death instinct, if, as Benedek assumes, anxiety corre-

---

[3] Therese Benedek, "Todestrieb und Angst." *Int. Zeitschr. f. Psa.* 17, 1931.

sponds to the inner perception of this increasing solidification, i.e., death, then one would expect children and adolescents not to have any anxiety, while old people would have only anxiety. The exact opposite is the case: anxiety is most pronounced during the periods when sexuality is at its height (i.e., when it is inhibited during these periods). According to this concept, we would find fear of death in the sexually satisfied individual also, since he is subject to the same process of biological dissimilation as the sexually unsatisfied one.

Following up consistently Freud's theory of actual anxiety, I arrived at a modification of his original formula according to which anxiety developed by conversion of libido. I found that anxiety is a manifestation of the same excitation of the vaso-vegetative system which in the sensory system is experienced as sexual pleasure.[4]

Clinical experience shows anxiety to be nothing but the sensation of a constriction (*"angustiae"*), of a stasis; fears (the idea of dangers) become affective anxiety only in the presence of such a stasis. If it should be found later on that the social restriction of sexual gratification accelerates the structure-forming process, that is, dying, this finding would not prove that anxiety is the result of these processes; it would only show the life-inimical effect of sex-negating morality.

The change of the concept of masochism automatically involved a change of the etiological formula of the neurosis. Freud's original concept was that psychic development takes place in the conflict between instinct and outer world. Now the concept came to be that the psychic conflict was the result of a conflict between eros (sexuality, libido) and death instinct (instinct to self-destruction, primary masochism).

The clinical starting point for this dubious hypothesis was the peculiar fact that certain patients seem to be unwilling to relinquish their suffering and keep seeking painful situations. This was in contradiction to the pleasure principle. There seemed to be a hidden inner intention to hold on to the suffering and to experience it again and again. The question was whether this "will

---

[4] Reich: DIE FUNKTION DES ORGASMUS, 1927, p. 63ff.

to suffer" was a primary biological tendency or a secondary psychic formation. There seemed to be a need for punishment which satisfied the demands of an unconscious guilt feeling by the infliction of self-damage. After the publication of *Jenseits des Lustprinzips,* psychoanalytic writers, led by Alexander, Reik, Nunberg and others, without being aware of it, changed the formula of the neurotic conflict.[5] The original formulation was that the neurosis results from the conflict between instinct and outer world (libido—*fear* of punishment). Now they said the neurosis resulted from the conflict between instinct and need for punishment (libido—*wish* for punishment). The exact opposite. This concept was based on the new hypothesis of the antithesis between eros and death instinct, and made the significance of the frustrating and punishing outer world recede more and more into the background. The answer given to the question, Where does suffering come from? was now: "from the biological will to suffer, from the death instinct and the need for punishment." This made one conveniently forget the correct answer which was: from the outer world, from frustrating society. This formulation blocked the avenue of approach to sociology, an avenue which the original formulation of the psychic conflict had opened wide. The theory of the death instinct, of a biological will to self-destruction, leads to a cultural philosophy such as that expressed in Freud's DAS UNBEHAGEN IN DER KULTUR; a philosophy which asserts that human suffering is inevitable because the self-destructive tendencies cannot be mastered. Conversely, the original formulation of the psychic conflict leads inevitably to a criticism of the social order.

Placing thus the source of suffering from the outer world, society, into the inner world, was in conflict with the basic original principle of analytic psychology, the *"pleasure-unpleasure-prin-*

---

[5] The theory of the death instinct dominates psychoanalytic literature at present. Freud, in a talk years ago, called this theory a hypothesis which was outside of clinical experience. In *Jenseits des Lustprinzips* he wrote that "one has to be ready to leave a path one has followed for some time if it does not seem to lead to anything good." In spite of these admonitions, the hypothesis developed into a clinical "theory"; it was not only not given up, it led to no good. Many analysts even contend that they have directly observed the death instinct.

*ciple.*" This is a basic law of the psychic apparatus, according to which man strives for pleasure and tries to escape unpleasure. This principle, according to the original psychoanalytic concepts, determined psychic development and psychic reactions. The *"reality principle"* was not an antithesis to the pleasure principle; it simply meant that reality imposes the necessity of postponing or relinquishing certain pleasures. These "two principles of psychic functioning," as Freud called them, could be valid only as long as the original formulation of masochism was valid, that is, as long as masochism was considered inhibited sadism turned against the self. This was an explanation of masochism within the framework of the pleasure principle, but it still left unanswered the question of how suffering can be a source of pleasure. This was in contradiction to the pleasure function. One could well understand how ungratified and inhibited pleasure could turn into unpleasure, but not the reverse, how unpleasure could turn into pleasure. Thus, the explanation that masochism consisted in experiencing unpleasure pleasurably meant nothing.

Most psychoanalysts felt that the assumption of a "repetition compulsion" solved the problem of suffering satisfactorily. True, it fitted marvelously the theories of the death instinct and of the need for punishment, but it was a more than dubious assumption. First, it was at variance with the pleasure principle. Second, it introduced into the theory of the pleasure-unpleasure-principle, which was clinically well founded, an undoubtedly metaphysical element, a hypothesis which was not only unproven but incapable of proof, and which caused great damage to analytic theory. The assumption was that of a biological compulsion to repeat situations of unpleasure. The "principle of the repetition compulsion" meant nothing because it was only a term, while the formulation of the pleasure-unpleasure-principle was based on the physiological laws of tension and relaxation. As long as the repetition compulsion was interpreted as the law that every instinct strives for the re-establishment of a state of rest, and as the compulsion to experience once-had pleasure again, no objection could be made. In this form, the concept was a valuable amplification of our concept of the mechanism of tension and relaxation. But, interpreted thus, the repetition compulsion is entirely *within* the framework of the pleasure principle; more than that, the pleasure principle explains the compulsion to repeat the experience. In 1923, still awkwardly, I interpreted the instinct as the characteristic of pleasure to have to be repeated.[6] Thus, the repetition compulsion *within* the pleasure principle is an important theoretical concept.

However, it was just the principle of the repetition compulsion *beyond* the pleasure principle which became important in psychoanalytic theory; this concept was used in an attempt to explain phenomena which apparently could not be explained by the pleasure principle. But it was not possible to establish clinical proof of the repetition compulsion as a *primary* tendency. It was supposed to explain a great many things and yet could itself not be demonstrated or explained. It led many analysts to the assumption of a superindividual "ananke." This assumption was superfluous for an explanation of the striving for the re-establishment of a state of rest, for this striving is fully explained by the function of the libido to bring about a relaxation. This relaxation is nothing but the re-establishment of the original state of rest, and is implicit in the concept of the instinct. Incidentally, the assumption of a biological striving for death also becomes superfluous when one remembers that the physiological involution of the organism, its gradual dying, sets in as soon as the function of the sexual apparatus, the source of the libido, begins to decline. Dying, thus, is not necessarily anything but the cessation of the function of the vital apparatus.

It was the clinical problem of masochism which clamored for a solution and which led to the unfortunate assumption that a death instinct, a repetition compulsion and a need for punishment were the *basis* of the neurotic conflict. In a controversy with Alexander,[7] who based a whole theory of personality on these assumptions, I myself still adhered to the original theory of masochism as the last possible explanation. True, the question as to

[6] Reich, W.: "Zur Trieb-Energetik." *Zeitschr. f. Sexualwissenschaft,* 1923.

[7] Reich, W.: "Strafbedürfnis und neurotischer Prozess. Kritische Bemerkungen zu neueren Auffassungen des Neurosenproblems." *Int. Zeitschr. f. Psa.* 13, 1927.

how unpleasure could be striven for, how it could turn into pleasure, was already in the air, but I had as yet nothing to say about it. The assumptions of Sadger, of an erogenous masochism, of a specific disposition of buttocks eroticism and skin eroticism to perceive unpleasure as pleasure, were not satisfactory either. For why should buttocks eroticism plus pain be perceived as pleasure? And why did the masochist experience as pleasure what others, when beaten on the same erogenous zone, experienced as pain and unpleasure? Freud himself unraveled a part of the question when he discovered behind the phantasy, "A child is being beaten," the original pleasurable situation, "Not I, but my rival is being beaten." Nevertheless, the question why being beaten can be accompanied by pleasure remained. All masochists report that the phantasy or the act of being beaten is pleasurable, and that only with this phantasy can they have pleasure or sexual excitation.

Years of study of masochistic patients gave no clue. Only when I began to doubt the correctness and precision of the patients' statements did the light begin to dawn. It was astounding to see how little one had learned, in spite of decades of analytic work, to analyze the experience of pleasure itself. Exact analysis of the pleasure function revealed a fact which at first was completely confusing but which, nevertheless, suddenly explained the sexual economy and, with that, the specific basis, of masochism. What was surprising and confusing was that the formulation, "the masochist experiences unpleasure as pleasure," proved erroneous. It was shown that, rather, the *specific* pleasure mechanism of the masochist consists in the fact that while he strives for pleasure like any other person, a disturbing mechanism causes this striving to fail and causes him to experience as unpleasurable sensations which the normal person experiences as pleasure, when they exceed a certain intensity. The masochist, far from striving for unpleasure, suffers from a specific intolerance for psychic tensions and an overproduction of unpleasure far greater than in any other neurosis.

In discussing the problem of masochism I shall take as my point of departure not the masochistic perversion, as is usual, but its characterological reaction basis. I shall illustrate with the history of a patient who was treated for almost four years and which solved questions which a number of previously treated cases had not answered but which became clear in retrospect from the results of this case.

## 2. THE ARMORING OF THE MASOCHISTIC CHARACTER

Only the smallest minority of masochistic characters also develop a masochistic perversion. The sexual economy of the masochist can be understood only from an understanding of his character reactions. Therefore, in presenting this case, we follow the path which every psychoanalytic treatment has to follow if it is to do more than explain the case theoretically and is to establish genital primacy with orgastic potency.

Every character formation serves two functions. First, the armoring of the ego against the outer world and the inner instinctual demands; second, the economic function of absorbing the excess of sexual energy which results from sexual stasis, or in other words, of keeping this energy from manifesting itself as anxiety. While this is equally true of any character formation, the form in which these functions are fulfilled are specific, that is, different for the various forms of neurosis. Every character type develops its own mechanisms. It is, of course, insufficient to know the basic functions of the character (defense and prevention of anxiety) in a patient; one has to find out quite early in which specific manner the character serves this function. Since the character absorbs the greater part of the libido (and anxiety); since, further, it is our task to liberate essential amounts of sexual energy from its chronic anchoring in the character and to make it available to the genital apparatus and to sublimation, the analysis of the character leads us to the root of the pleasure function.

Let us summarize the main traits of the masochistic character. These traits are found, individually, in all neurotic characters. Together, they form the masochistic character only when they are all present, and when they determine the key to the personality and its typical reactions. Typical masochistic character traits are the following: subjectively, a chronic sensation of *suffering*, which appears objectively as a *tendency to complain;* chronic tendencies to *self-damage* and *self-depreciation* ("moral masochism") and a compulsion *to torture others* which makes the patient suffer no less than the object. All masochistic characters show a specifically *awkward, atactic behavior* in their manners and in their intercourse with others, often so marked as to give the impression of mental deficiency. There may be other traits, but these are the typical and specific ones.

It is important to remember that this character-neurotic syndrome may be obvious on the surface in some cases, while in many other cases it is covered up by a superficial mask.

Like any other character attitude, the masochistic attitude shows not only in interpersonal relationships, but also in the inner life of the person. Attitudes which originally were attached to objects are maintained toward the introjected objects, the super-ego. Frequently, this is of decisive importance. What was originally external and then became internalized, must again be externalized in the analytic transference: in the transference behavior that is repeated which was acquired in infancy in the relationship with the object.

The patient from whose case history excerpts are given here came to analysis with the following complaints: Since the age of 16, he had been completely incapable of working and had no social interests whatsoever. Sexually, there was a severe masochistic perversion. He never had had sexual intercourse, but masturbated every night for hours in a way which is typical of pregenital libidinal structures. He would roll around on his stomach with the phantasy that a man or a woman was beating him with a whip; during this he would squeeze his penis. That is, he did not masturbate like a genital character who will induce sexual excitation by more or less regular friction. Instead, he would knead the penis, squeeze it between his legs or roll it between his palms. *As soon as the ejaculation approached, he would hold back and wait until the excitation had subsided, whereupon he would start anew.* In this way he would masturbate for hours, every night, often also during the day, until he was completely exhausted and finally permitted an ejaculation. The ejaculation did not take place in rhythmical spurts; the semen would simply flow out. Afterwards he felt exhausted, leaden, incapable of doing anything, depressed, tortured, "masochistic." He found it almost impossible to get himself out of bed in the morning. In spite of the most severe guilt feelings, he could not stop this "lazing in bed." The whole thing he later called the "masochistic bog." The more he rebelled against it, the less was he able to work himself out of this "masochistic mood"; on the contrary, he got into it all the more deeply. At the time when he came for treatment, this kind of sexual life had already lasted several years. The effect on his whole being and his emotional life had been disastrous.

The first impression I gained of him was that of an individual barely able, with all his will power, to hold himself together. This was partly covered up by a very refined and poised behavior; he talked about his ambition of becoming a mathematician. In the analysis, this turned out to be a well-developed idea of grandeur. For years he had been wandering alone through the woods of Germany, thinking out a mathematical system which would make it possible to calculate and change the whole world. This superficial compensation disintegrated very soon in the analysis when I made him understand its function. It served the function of counteracting the feeling of his absolute worthlessness which, in connection with his masturbation—which he experienced as "filth" and a "morass"—was constantly being reproduced. The "mathematician," the symbol of the pure scientist and asexual individual, was to cover up the "morass individual." The fact is not important here that the patient gave the definite impression of an incipient schizophrenia of the hebephrenic type. What is important here is only that the "pure" mathematics was a protection against the "filthy" feeling of himself which was due to his anal type of masturbation.

With the dissolution of his superficial mask the masochistic attitude made its full appearance. Every treatment hour began with a complaint. Soon there was frank masochistic provocation of an infantile sort. When I asked him to amplify or explain some statement, he would try to nullify my endeavors by such outcries as "I won't, I won't, I won't." In this connection we found that as a boy of 4 or 5 he had gone through a phase of the most severe spite with attacks of yelling and kicking. These occurred on the slightest provocation and made his parents desperate, helpless and furious. Occasionally, such attacks would last for days, until they ended in complete exhaustion. Later he found out by himself that this phase of spite had ushered in his masochism.

The first phantasies of being beaten appeared at the age of about 7. Not only did he fantasy that he was taken across somebody's knee and beaten; he often went to the bathroom, locked himself in and tried to whip himself. A scene from the third year of life, which did not appear until the second year of the analysis, was undoubtedly a traumatic scene. He had been playing in the garden and had soiled his pants. Since there were guests present, his psychopathic and sadistic father got furious, carried him inside and put him on a bed. The boy *immediately turned on his stomach and waited for the beating with great curiosity, mixed with anxiety.* The blows were heavy, but the boy had a feeling of relief; a typically masochistic experience which was his first.

Had the beating given him pleasure? Further analysis showed unequivocally that he had anticipated something far worse. He had so quickly turned on the stomach in order to protect his genitals from the father,[8] and *for this reason had experienced the blows on the buttocks as a great relief;* they were harmless compared to the anticipated injury to the genital and this relieved him of a good deal of anxiety.

In order to understand masochism as a whole, one must clearly comprehend this basic mechanism. With this, we are ahead of our story, for this did not become fully clear until after one and a half year's treatment. Until then, the time had been mostly taken up with the attempts, at first fruitless, to master the patient's masochistic spite reactions.

Later on, the patient described his masturbatory behavior like this: "As if I were turned with screws from my back to my

---

[8] This mechanism was stressed by Freud in his article, "Das ökonomische Problem des Masochismus" (Ges. Schr., V, p. 378). Its clinical examination, however, does not lead to the hypothesis of a primary masochism, but, on the contrary, to its refutation.

stomach." At first I thought this was a beginning phallic sexuality, until I found that it was a defensive action. *The penis had to be protected; rather suffer blows on the buttocks than have the penis injured.* This basic mechanism also determined the role of the beating phantasy. *What later became a masochistic wish had originally been a fear of punishment.* The masochistic beating phantasy thus anticipates in a milder form an expected heavy punishment. Alexander's formulation that by satisfying the need for punishment one purchases sexual pleasure has to be correspondingly interpreted. One does not punish oneself in order to placate or "bribe" one's super-ego, whereupon pleasure can be experienced without anxiety. Rather, the masochist approaches pleasurable activity like any other person, *but the fear of punishment interferes.* The masochistic self-punishment is *not* the execution of the dreaded punishment, but of a milder substitute punishment. It represents a specific mode of defense against punishment and anxiety. A part of this is the passive-feminine attitude toward the punishing person so frequently found in masochistic characters. Our patient once proffered his buttocks in order to be beaten, as he said. In reality, this wanting-to-be-beaten was an offering of himself as a woman (in the sense of Freud's interpretation of the passive beating phantasy as a substitute for a passive-feminine desire). The nonmasochistic passive-feminine character fulfils this function of defense against the threat of castration by a purely anal attitude, without adding the beating phantasy to ward off anxiety.

This leads in a straight line to the question whether a striving for unpleasure is possible. We shall postpone the discussion of this question until the character-analysis of this patient has provided the necessary basis.

In the analysis, the infantile spiting phase of our patient was reactivated in a completely undisguised and uninhibited manner. The analysis of the crying spells lasted about six months, but it resulted in the complete elimination of this way of reacting. At first it was not easy to induce the patient to reactivate the spiteful actions of his childhod. His reaction was that a refined person, a mathematical genius, could not do such things. However, it was unavoidable. If this layer of the character was to be unmasked as a defense against anxiety and was to be eliminated, it had to be first reactivated to the full extent. When the patient started his "I won't," I first tried interpretation, but my endeavors were completely ignored. So I began to imitate the patient; when I gave an interpretation of his behavior, I immediately added the "I won't" myself. At one time he reacted suddenly with involuntary kicking. I seized the opportunity and asked him to let himself go completely. At first he could not understand how anybody could ask him to do a thing like that. But more and more he began to thrash around on the couch, which behavior turned into highly emotional spiteful yelling and inarticulate, animal-like sounds. A particularly violent attack of this kind occurred one day when I pointed out to him that his defense of his father was only a mask for his tremendous hatred of him. I did not hesitate to grant to him that this hatred had a good deal of rational justification. After this, his actions began to assume an almost frightening character. He yelled so that the people in the house began to get fearful. However, this was the only avenue of approach to his deep emotions; only in this way was he able to relive his infantile neurosis fully and affectively, not just in the form of recollections. Again and again, it was possible to deepen his insight into his behavior. Its meaning was a grandiose *provocation of the adults*, and, in a transferred sense, of my person. But, the question was, *why did he provoke?*

Other masochistic patients try to provoke the analyst with the typical masochistic silence. Our patient did it with infantile spite reactions. It took a long time until I could make him understand that his provocation was an attempt to make me strict and to drive me furious. But this was only the superficial meaning of the behavior. If the deeper meaning is so often overlooked it is because of the erroneous belief that the masochist seeks punishment in itself, for the gratification of a guilt feeling. In reality it is not a matter of punishment at all, but of *placing the analyst, or his prototype, the parent, in a bad light,* of provoking him into a behavior which would rationally justify the reproach, "You see how badly you treat me." This provocation of the analyst is,

without exception, one of the first great difficulties in any masochistic character. Without uncovering this meaning, one will not
get one step further.

What is the meaning of thus provoking the analyst, of placing
him in a bad light? The meaning is: "You are bad, you don't love
me. On the contrary, you are cruel to me, and I have a right to
hate you." The justification of the hatred and the reduction of the
guilt feeling through this mechanism are, however, only intermediate processes. True, if one assumes guilt feeling and need
for punishment to be manifestations of a biological death instinct,
one will be inclined to the belief that with the discovery of the
rationalization of the hatred and the provocation of the object
one has hit rock bottom. But the main problem of the masochistic
character is not his guilt feeling, nor is it his need for punishment,
no matter how important they seem to be. Why, then, does the
masochist try to place his object in a bad light?

Behind the provocation there is a deep *disappointment in love*.
The provocation is directed especially against those objects who
caused a disappointment, that is, objects which were loved intensely and who either actually disappointed or who did not
sufficiently gratify the child's love. The actual disappointments
in the masochistic character are intensified by a particularly high
need for love which makes a real gratification impossible and
which has specific inner reasons which will be discussed later.

As time went on and the patient became convinced that he
could not make me furious, the behavior persisted, but for a
different reason. Now it gave him obvious pleasure to let himself
go. His acting out became a hindrance; the hours were filled with
infantile kicking and yelling. Now I could show him that his
provocation originally had served a second purpose, namely to
see how far he could go with his naughtiness before I would
withdraw my love and proceed to punishment. He had convinced
himself that he need not be afraid; he could be naughty without
being punished. The continued naughty behavior, then, showed
the fear of punishment to be unfounded and thus was a source
of pleasure. It had nothing at all to do with any wish to be punished though I searched assiduously for it. At the same time there

were continued complaints about his condition, about the morass he could not get out of and—implicitly—I did not help him to get out of. Masturbation continued in the same manner and put him daily in the "morass" mood to which he gave vent in complaints, that is, in masked reproaches. Under these circumstances the analysis made no progress. To prohibit the spite reactions was out of the question; it might have stopped everything. So I began to show him a reflection of himself. When I opened the door, he would stand there with a drawn face, in an attitude of utter dejection. I would imitate his attitude. I began to use his infantile language, I lay on the floor and kicked and yelled as he did. At first he was surprised, but one day he began to laugh, in an absolutely adult and unneurotic way; a breakthrough, although only temporary, had succeeded. I repeated these procedures until he himself began to analyze the situation.

What was the meaning of the provocation? It was his way of *demanding love,* as it is the way of all masochistic characters. He needed proofs of love which would reduce his anxiety and inner tension. The more his unfortunate masturbation increased his tension, the more he intensified his demand for love. The more he had the "morass feeling," the more intensive became his masochistic attitude, that is, his demand for love. But why was this demand made in this *indirect, disguised* manner? Why did he fight any interpretation of his affection? Why did his complaints continue?

His complaints had the following layers of meaning, corresponding to the genesis of his masochism. "Look how miserable I am; please love me"—"You don't love me enough, you treat me badly"—"You must love me, I shall force you to; or else I'm going to annoy you." The masochistic torturing, the masochistic complaint, provocation and suffering all explain themselves on the basis of the frustration, fantasied or actual, of a demand for love which is excessive and cannot be gratified. This mechanism is *specific* for the masochistic character and no other form of neurosis; if it occurs in other neuroses, one also finds the corresponding masochistic element in the character.

What is the meaning of the excessive demand for love? The

answer is given by an analysis of the masochistic character's *disposition to anxiety*. The masochistic behavior and the demand for love always increase in proportion to the unpleasurable tension, the readiness to anxiety or the danger of loss of love. It is typical of the masochistic character to avoid anxiety by wanting to be loved. Just as the complaints are a disguised demand for love and the provocation an attempt to force love, so is the total masochistic character an *unsuccessful* attempt to liberate himself of anxiety and unpleasure. It is unsuccessful because, in spite of these attempts, he never gets rid of the inner tension which constantly threatens to turn into anxiety. *The feeling of suffering, then, corresponds to the actual facts of a continuous high inner tension and readiness to anxiety.* This becomes clearer if we compare the masochistic character with the compulsion-neurotic affect block. Here, the assimilation of anxiety has been successful. True, at the expense of psychic motility, but the inner tension is completely consumed by a well-functioning psychic apparatus, with the result that there is no restlessness. If the latter is present it means an insufficiency of the character armor.

The masochistic character attempts to allay the inner tension and the threatening anxiety by an inadequate method, that is, by *demands for love in the form of provocation and spite*. Of course, this has its special reasons, that is, this manner of voicing a demand for love is specifically masochistic. The essential element in the failure is, however, that the spite and the provocation are directed against the very person who is loved and from whom love is demanded. In this way, the fear of losing love is increased; similarly, the guilt feeling, instead of being decreased, increases, because it is the loved person who is being tortured. This explains the peculiar behavior of the masochist: the more he tries to get out of his situation of suffering, the more he gets entangled in it.

The attitudes thus far mentioned are found, individually, in other characters also. Only their combination is specific of the masochistic character. But what causes this combination?

We mentioned the *excessive* demand for love. We have to add that this is based on *fear of being left alone* which the masochist experienced intensely in very early childhood. The masochistic character can tolerate being left alone no more than the threat of losing a love relationship. The fact that masochistic characters so often get lonely is the secondary result of the attitude, "See, how miserable, alone, and deserted I am." Our patient, during a discussion of his relationship with his mother, said once in great excitation: "To be left alone means death, means the end of my life." This content, in different words, I have heard very often from masochistic characters. The masochistic character cannot tolerate giving up an object (hence the masochistic sticking to a love object), any more than he can divest it of its protective role. He does not tolerate the loss of contact and tries to re-establish it in his inadequate way, that is, by showing himself miserable. Many of these characters develop the feeling of being alone in the universe.

A number of psychoanalytic authors (e.g., Sadger and Federn) have pointed out that skin eroticism plays a special role in masochism. They made the mistake, though, of considering skin eroticism the immediate basis of the masochistic perversion; analysis shows, however, that this is the case only under certain conditions and by way of a very complicated development. Only the fear of being left alone is based directly on the fear which may arise when the contact with the skin of the beloved person is lost. Let us summarize the symptoms which, in the erogenous masochist, refer to the skin. There is always some kind of wish for activity at the skin or at least phantasies of it: to be pinched, brushed, whipped, fettered, to make the skin bleed, etc. The buttocks play an important part here, but only indirectly, as a result of an anal fixation. All these wishes have in common that the patient wants to feel the *warmth of the skin,* not pain. If a patient wants to be whipped, it is not because he wants to feel pain; the pain is taken in the bargain because of the "burning." Many masochists fantasy directly that their skin is being burned. Cold, on the other hand, is abhorrent. This also explains the "lazing in bed" as a gratification of the need for skin warmth.

This is easily understood from the physiology of anxiety and pleasure. Contraction of the peripheral vessels increases anxiety (pallor of fright, feeling cold when scared); the sensation of skin warmth which is based on dilatation of the peripheral vessels and a greater blood flow, is a specific part of the pleasure syndrome.

It is not easy to understand why bodily contact with a beloved person relieves anxiety. Probably both the direct body heat as well as the innervation of the peripheral vessels in the expectation of maternal protection alleviate the central tension.[9] In this context it is sufficient to point out that the peripheral vasodilatation, which relieves the inner tension and anxiety, is the erogenous basis of the masochistic character. His later striving to avoid the loss of contact is only the psychic reflection of an actual physiological process. To be left alone in the world means being cold and unprotected, and an intolerable condition of tension.

Oral fixation does not seem to have a specific significance in masochism, though it is always present to a marked degree, as in all pregenital characters. There is no doubt that the oral demands contribute to the insatiable character of the masochistic love demands. But the oral demands in masochism seem to be more the result of a regression to an early disappointment in the love object and consecutive fear of being deserted, than a primary cause of the masochistic need for love.

Several cases disclosed another source of their excessive need for love: the fear of being left alone set in at a time when violent aggression and infantile sex curiosity—unlike the previous oral and anal impulses—met with serious rebuff from the beloved parents. The enormous fear of punishment which prevents the progress to genitality is a result of this contradiction between sexual impulses which are permitted, even encouraged, on the one hand, and impulses which are threatened with severe punishment on the other hand. Our patient was allowed to eat as much as he pleased, in fact, he was encouraged to eat much; he was allowed to lie in bed with his mother, to embrace and

---

[9] *Footnote, 1945:* The orgone energy which was discovered in 1939 provides the explanation for this phenomenon: The alleviation of the child's anxiety by bodily contact with the mother is explained, orgone-biophysically, by the orgonotic expansion of the child's biosystem which reaches out for the mother. There is a contact between the orgone fields of the two organisms.

stroke her; there was much interest in his excretory functions. But when he proceeded to new possibilities of sexual gratification, when he began to show interest in his mother's genital and wanted to touch her, he met the full severity of parental authority.

To the extent to which oral demands play a role in masochism, they determine, as in other forms of neurosis, the depressive tendencies. What is specific for masochism is the combination of skin eroticism, anality and the fear of being left alone which the masochist tries to master by bodily contact. This erogenous disposition is one of the chief causes of the excessive demand for love which has the specific nuance of "warm me" ( = "protect me"). The "beat me" is already a disguised expression of this demand. It looks as if the masochist had received too little love and for this reason had developed such a strong demand for love. This is correct only insofar as he has always suffered severe frustrations of love; but very often the excessive demand is also a result of over-coddling. This excessive character of the love demand is in turn the result of certain harmful educational influences which are characteristic of the patriarchal system.

The question here is what determines the erogenous disposition of the masochistic character. It is not simply an anal or skin-erotic disposition, but the result of a specific combination of external influences upon the erogenicity of the skin as well as upon the total sexual apparatus which creates the basis of the masochistic character. Only when we know these influences can we understand the other character traits of the masochist.

## 3. INHIBITED EXHIBITIONISM AND TENDENCY TO SELF-DEPRECIATION

We shall now turn to the discussion of a few other masochistic character traits, this time in connection with the sexual structure of the masochist. I shall report only those analytic findings which, taken together, are specific for masochism, as well as those which are at the basis of the masochistic disturbance of the pleasure mechanism.

It had taken about a year to break through the character armor of spite, provocation and complaining sufficiently to break through into early childhood and, more importantly, to the point where the patient actively participated in the analytic work. After this, particularly after the repression of his hatred for his father and his fear of him had been dissolved, there was a powerful breakthrough of his genitality. He had erections, his masturbation was no longer masochistic, and he had genital desires for a woman. An initial failure of his genital attempts led to the analysis of his deep, specifically anal love for his mother. While he made rapid progress, the following was striking:

His approach to women was very vigorous, but at the same time he could not get rid of a feeling of an *inner struggle* and *artificiality*. This again and again gave rise to masochistic complaints that, in spite of external improvement, he did not feel well: "Nothing has changed about the masochistic morass."

The slightest incident was enough to cause an immediate disappointment; the least difficulty made him retreat from reality into his masochistic phantasies. This oscillation between attempts to establish genital reality and rapid retreats into masochism lasted for many months. I knew that his castration anxiety had not been worked out and that this was the reason. The concentration of the work on this aspect brought a wealth of interesting results. To begin with, the patient, who previously had shown no trace of genital interest, proved full of genital anxieties. Only a few examples: the vagina is a "morass," full of snakes and worms; the tip of his penis is snipped off; one sinks into an abyss and does not find one's way out. The discussion of all these anxieties, however, did not change his labile condition in the least; for months, every hour began with his masochistically voiced complaint that he was "inwardly broken." An analysis of the transference situation showed again and again his passive-anal tendencies, specifically, the fact that he retreated from the woman as soon as a rival appeared. The idea of having a small penis seemed for some time incapable of correction. His attitude toward a rival was one of envy. This was, however, immediately covered up by a passive-feminine attitude; this is a well-known mechanism of warding off the fear of the father. However, even deep-reaching analysis of these attitudes did not change his feeling that, in spite of external successes, he remained a masochist.

After the first attempts at coitus in which he had been erectively potent, though unsatisfied, he developed a syphilophobia. One day he showed me his penis, asking me whether a small erosion was the sign of syphilitic infection. It was immediately clear that he wanted to exhibit himself. Now, the analysis immediately clarified an important point in his genital development. It turned out that as a child he had reached the genital phase only in the form of exhibiting his penis and that *his mother had rebuffed him severely.* This genital disappointment was all the more severe in that his mother had not only not prohibited his anal exhibition, but encouraged it by the intense interest which she had shown in his excretory functions. In fact, she used to go to the bathroom with him when he was as much as ten years old. The pleasure which he had derived from anal exhibition was the reason for his initiating the genital phase with exhibition of the penis. The analysis showed that his first attempts at a genital approach to his mother had been exhibitionistic. This impulse had soon been repressed and this repression resulted later in a severe inhibition in his general behavior. In his attempts at coitus, he never dared to show himself naked to the woman or to let her touch his penis. After the analysis of this element he seriously began to look for a profession, and decided to become a photographer. He started out by buying a camera and by snapping everything that he came across. This showed again how important the elimination of genital repression is for sublimation. Today he is very good in his profession. But for a long time he still lacked the inner satisfaction in his work: "I don't feel myself, but when I do, masochistically miserable."

Exhibitionistic onset of the genital phase with immediate strict prohibition and repression of exhibitionistic impulses and complete inhibition of further genital development is specific of the masochistic character. It is just as typical and specific as early phallic sadism and its inhibition and anal-sadistic fixation are for compulsion neurosis. This is at the basis of some character traits which determine the awkward, atactic manner of the masochist.

Our patient described this inner situation as follows: "I feel like an officer who, sword drawn, runs far ahead of his troops, suddenly turns around and finds that nobody has followed him."

This feeling is connected with another character trait: Masochistic characters *cannot stand praise* and have a strong tendency to *self-depreciation*. In spite of a great ambition, our patient could not stand being near the top in his class. "If I remained a good student I would feel as if I were standing in front of a crowd, showing my erect penis." This was by no means an incidental remark such as are made so often during an analysis; it went to the core of the matter. The inhibition and repression of genital exhibition leads to a severe impairment of sublimation, activity and self-confidence in later life. In the masochist, this inhibition goes as far as the development of contrary traits. The narcissistic character exhibits in a disguised form; the masochistic character uses a reaction formation, the exact opposite of exhibition: *self-depreciation, in order not to stand out*. He lacks the self-confidence of the genital character.

For these reasons, the masochistic character cannot be a leader, although he usually develops grandiose phantasies of heroism. His anal fixation makes him passive, and in addition, the inhibition of exhibitionism leads to self-depreciation. This structure of the ego is in conflict with an active, phallic ego-ideal which cannot make itself felt. This conflict creates another tension and another source of suffering which reinforces the masochistic process. The picture of the officer illustrates this ego-ideal which the masochist must hide, must be ashamed of, because the ego (the troops) do not—and cannot—follow.

In this connection a character trait needs to be mentioned which is common in masochists and children with masochistic tendencies: *to feel stupid or to make oneself appear stupid*. To exploit every inhibition for the purpose of self-depreciation is in full harmony with the masochistic character. One patient said one day he could not stand praise because it made him feel as if he were standing there with his pants down. One should not underestimate the significance of the anal fixation, of the exhibition of the buttocks, for the genital development of the child.

The feeling of shame acquired in connection with anal activities is later transferred to the genital. Since any praise represents a provocation of exhibitionistic tendencies, since, further, to show oneself is connected with severe anxiety, the masochist must make himself small in order to avoid this anxiety. Having done so, he has an additional reason to feel neglected, which in turn provokes the whole need for love.

"Stupidity" or pretending stupidity also belongs here. Our patient once described an infantile scene in which he pretended stupidity, as follows: "I want something I don't get, then I get annoyed and stupid. But how much do they love me, even though I make myself stupid? When I'm not loved, I'm not worth loving and must make myself all the more ugly and stupid."

Now we can answer the question why the masochistic character expresses his demand for love in such a disguised form, why he is completely incapable of showing or demanding love directly. Another patient would always, when he wanted to win a woman, show himself miserable. He had a panicky fear of showing his love directly because the woman might get angry and might punish or shame him. He had the same inhibited exhibitionism as our patient.

All this taken together causes a feeling of inner ataxy, often a painful embarrassment about appearance. The inhibition of the ability to show and demand love openly brings about all kinds of distorted expressions and makes a person, as our patient put it, "bureaucratic," that is, unnatural and stiff. Behind this there is always a fear of disappointment or rebuff. Our patient once said: "I am confronted with the task of inserting a penis which is not erect into a vagina which is not offered to me."

In the place of frank manifestation of love, the hysterical character develops anxiety; the compulsive character, hatred and guilt feeling; and the masochistic character shows and demands love under the disguise of complaining, provoking and showing himself miserable. These differences correspond fully to the specific genesis: the hysterical character has developed his genitality fully, but it is anxiety-laden; the compulsive character has replaced his genitality by phallic sadism; the masochistic character has reached genitality on the exhibitionistic level, then repressed it and now expresses his love in a specifically distorted form.

## 4. UNPLEASURABLE PERCEPTION OF INCREASE IN SEXUAL EXCITATION: THE SPECIFIC BASIS OF THE MASOCHISTIC CHARACTER

There is no neurotic structure without some form of genital disturbance. In the masochistic character the disturbances of the orgasm are of a specific form. Often they do not become obvious until the impotence or anesthesia have been more or less eliminated; this explains the fact that hitherto they were completely overlooked. We have already seen that the masochistic character has an increased production of unpleasure which gives his feeling of suffering a real basis. We have further seen that the masochist constantly tries to master his tension and disposition to anxiety by inadequate mechanisms; more than that, it is typical of the masochistic character that his attempts to avoid anxiety only cause more tension and unpleasure, which, in a vicious circle, again increases the disposition to anxiety. We have also found that the masochistic punishment, or the phantasy of it, represents a substitute for another punishment which is expected.

Can the experience of an anxiety, such as our patient had at the age of three, produce the masochistic fixation of the phantasy of being beaten? No, for the patient could, as others do, completely relinquish the sexual impulse which provokes the dreaded punishment; in doing so, he could save himself the masochistic solution of the punishment situation which only brings suffering. Thus, there must be something additional at the basis of the specific masochistic mechanism.

This mechanism cannot be detected until the patient has progressed to the genital level, that is, until he develops genital impulses. Then one encounters a new difficulty. The patient develops a strong genital desire which at first eliminates much of his masochistic attitude, but on the occasion of his first actual genital experience he feels unpleasure instead of pleasure; as a result of this, he is thrown back into the masochistic "morass" of his anal and sadomasochistic pregenitality. It was years before it became clear that the "incurability of the masochist, who *wants to* hold on to his suffering" was due only to our defective knowledge of his sexual functioning. The solution could not have been found if I had adhered to the concept that the masochist wants to suffer because of an unconscious guilt feeling or need for punishment due to a death instinct.

This does not mean a denial of the fact, that self-punishment can ease the conscience. But this fact must be properly evaluated. The relief of guilt feelings through punishment is a superficial process which does not touch the core of the personality; it is relatively rare, and, in addition, is a symptom and not the cause of a neurosis. On the other hand, the conflict between sexual desire and fear of punishment is a central fact in every neurosis; without this conflict there is no neurotic process; it is itself not a symptom, but the cause of the neurosis. The recent psychoanalytic evaluation of the need for punishment has resulted in a misleading modification of the psychoanalytic theory of the neuroses and the theory of therapy; it blocked the way to a prevention of the neuroses and obscured the sexual and social origin of the neuroses.

The masochistic character is based on a very peculiar *spastic attitude* not only in his psychic but also in his genital apparatus which *immediately inhibits any strong pleasure sensation and thus changes it into unpleasure.* This constantly nourishes the suffering which is at the basis of the masochistic character reactions. It goes without saying that—no matter how thoroughly we analyze the meaning and genesis of the masochistic character— we will not achieve any therapeutic result unless we penetrate to the genesis of this spastic attitude. Otherwise we cannot establish orgastic potency which alone is capable of eliminating the inner source of unpleasure and anxiety. Let us return to our patient.

On the occasion of his first coitus, he had an erection, but he did not dare move his penis in the vagina. At first we thought this was due to bashfulness or ignorance; it took some time to find the real reason. *He was afraid of an increase in pleasurable excita-*

*tion.* This is certainly, at first glance, a peculiar behavior. We always see it during the cure of orgastic impotence, especially in previously frigid women. In the masochist, however, it has a specific character. This will become clear from the material.

After the patient had had intercourse a few times it became clear that it provided far less pleasure than his masochistic masturbation. Nevertheless, he was able to imagine genital pleasure vividly, which became a powerful incentive in the treatment. The relative absence of genital pleasure was serious. For there is no other way of putting pregenital pleasure out of function than the establishment of the more intense genital pleasure. The absence of pleasure in the act certainly was no incentive to the development of his genitality.

In the course of further attempts, a new disturbance made its appearance: the erection disappeared during the act. Was this due only to castration anxiety, or was there something more? Further analysis of his castration fears failed to change the condition. Finally it turned out that the cramping of the musculature of the pelvic floor before ejaculation took place in masturbation was of greater significance than it had appeared at first. I am going to summarize the infantile material which shows that the masochist—in spite of his seemingly free and excessive anal and urethral gratification—has an *anal and urethral inhibition and anxiety* which goes back to early infancy. This inhibition is later transferred to the genital function and provides the immediate basis for his excessive production of unpleasure.

Between the ages of 3 and 6, our patient developed a fear of the toilet. He had the idea that an animal might crawl into his behind. With this, he began to hold back his stools, which in turn created the fear of soiling his pants. If one soils one's pants, one gets a beating from father. This he had learned from that impressive scene which occurred when he was about three. If father beats one, there is also a danger of castration; in order to avoid injury to the genital, one must divert the blows to the buttocks. Nevertheless, he developed the fear that on these occasions, when he was lying on his stomach, he might get a splinter into his penis.

All this together created a spastic condition of the musculature of the pelvic floor, of the genitals and the rectum. The resulting constipation intensified his mother's concern about his bowel movements, which created another conflict: while the mother showed intense interest in his bowel movements, the father beat him for it. This resulted in the predominantly anal foundation of his Oedipus complex. The patient soon developed the further fear that the bladder or the rectum might burst, that, in other words, the holding back was to no avail and he would again fall victim to his father's beatings. A hopeless situation which certainly was not of biological but of purely social origin. It should be mentioned that the father loved to pinch the buttocks of his children and that he used to threaten that he would "take their hides off" if they did not behave.

The boy had an anal fear of his father, together with an anal fixation to his mother, and a tendency to beat himself. Because of the relaxation and gratification connected with it, he felt his evacuation to be punishable; out of fear of his father's punishment, he began to beat himself. Plainly, this simple process is far more important for the pathology of this case than the identification with the punishing father and the masochistic attitude toward a developing anal super-ego. We have to keep in mind that such pathological identifications are in themselves neurotic formations; they are a result and not a cause of the neurosis.[10] True, we found all the complicated relations between ego and super-ego, but we did not stop there; the more important task was that of strictly differentiating those masochistic findings which corresponded to the actual behavior of the father from those which corresponded to inner erogenous impulses. This case, like many others, showed plainly that our educational methods deserve much more attention; that we distribute our attention very poorly if we turn 98% of it to analytic detail work and only 2% to the

---

[10] The neurosis is caused by the conflict between pleasure (ego) and punishing outer world, and is maintained by the conflict between ego and super-ego. The super-ego continues to function on the basis of the ever-repeated experience that sexual pleasure is punishable. The effect of the childhood inhibition is decisively supported by social actuality.

gross damages which are inflicted on the children *by the parents*. It is in this way that psychoanalytic findings fail to lead to the necessary criticism of patriarchal family upbringing.

In our patient, the infantile conflict situation was mainly due to the conflicting behavior of mother and father, respectively, with regard to anality. This conflict determined not only his feminine attitude toward the man (father) but also his feeling of emptiness and impotence. Later, the patient would feel himself impotent as soon as he got near an adult man; becoming afraid, he would withdraw his interest from the genital and would become anal, passive; this expressed itself in his admiration for these men.

All this allows the following conclusions: The customary training to excremental cleanliness (too early and too strict) leads to the fixation of anal pleasure; the associated idea of being beaten is definitely unpleasurable and at first anxiety-laden. It would be erroneous to say that the unpleasure of being beaten turns into pleasure. Rather, the *fear of being beaten prevents the development of pleasure*. This mechanism, acquired on an anal level, later is transferred to the genital.

As late as puberty, the patient still often slept with his mother in the same bed. At the age of 17, he developed a phobia about his mother becoming pregnant by him. The closeness to his mother and her body warmth stimulated his masturbation. The ejaculation had the meaning of urinating at his mother, as was to be expected in view of his specific development. If the mother should become pregnant, this would be proof of his urethral incest and severe punishment would threaten. At this point he began to hold back the semen and to masturbate with vivid masochistic phantasies. This was the actual onset of his disease. He became incapable of work at school. After an attempt at "self-analysis" which failed, there was a progressive psychic emptiness, together with nightly masturbation of the protracted, anal-masochistic kind.

The final breakdown was ushered in by a severe stasis neurosis with irritability, insomnia and migraine-like headaches. At that time he experienced a strong increase of his genital urge. He was in love with a girl, but did not dare approach her; he was afraid that he would "gas" her, and felt he was dying of shame at the very thought of it. He would follow girls at some distance, having vivid phantasies that they were "pressing their bellies against each other" and that that would result in a pregnancy which would give them away. In this behavior, his fear of being rebuffed because of his anal tendencies, played an important role. We see here a typical puberty situation: inhibition of genitality partly by the social barriers, partly by neurotic fixations resulting from earlier damage to the sexual structure by education.

At first there was, in addition to the genital tension, also an anal tension in the form of an urge to defecate or pass wind which had to be constantly controlled. The patient did not allow genital relaxation to take place. Not until the age of 17 did he succeed in having his first seminal emission; this with the aid of many hours of passive beating phantasies. After this, the stasis neurosis improved. But the first emission itself was experienced traumatically by the patient. He was so afraid of soiling his bed that during the emission he jumped up and grabbed the chamber pot; he was highly distressed because some semen had gotten in the bed.

When, during treatment, his genitality began to develop, the erection would disappear during the act. In this genital phase, masturbation began with normal masculine phantasies; but when the pleasure increased, the masochistic phantasy returned. The analysis of this shift from genitality to masochism *during* the sexual act revealed the following. As long as the pleasure sensations were mild, the genital phantasy persisted. But as soon as the pleasure increased and—as he put it—the "melting sensation" began to appear, he became afraid. Instead of letting himself go, he produced a spasm in the pelvic floor and thus changed the pleasure into unpleasure. He described very clearly how he perceived the "melting sensation"—normally a pleasurable orgastic sensation—as unpleasure and with anxiety. He was afraid that the penis would "melt away." The skin of the penis might dissolve as a result of that sensation, he said: the penis might burst if it went on getting increasingly taut (as it normally does just before the acme). He felt as if the penis were a sac filled with fluid to the bursting point.

Here we had the incontrovertible proof that what characterizes masochism is *not* that unpleasure becomes pleasure. On the contrary. A mechanism which is specific for masochism causes every pleasure sensation, as soon as it exceeds a certain degree of intensity, to be inhibited and thus turned into unpleasure. It is worth mentioning that the patient's castration fear referred to the *skin* of the penis: "I get as hot as a boiled chicken, when you can pull off the skin."

As a result of the fear of punishment, the "melting" sensation of warmth which occurs with the increase of excitation before the acme is experienced as the advent of the anticipated penis catastrophe; thus it inhibits the normal course of the sexual excitation and produces, on purely physiological grounds, unpleasure which may increase to pain. This process takes place in three phases: 1. "I strive for pleasure"; 2. "I begin to 'melt'—this is the punishment I feared"; 3. "I must kill the sensation if I want to save my penis."

At this point, an objection may be raised. It may be pointed out that the inhibition of sexual pleasure by infantile anxiety is found in *every* neurosis, that this cannot be the specific factor in masochism. The question may be raised, Why does not every inhibition of the involuntary increase in pleasure sensations lead to masochism? To this, the following is to be said:

Such an inhibition of the perception of pleasure can come about in two ways. The "melting" pleasure sensation was once experienced without anxiety; later, anxiety inhibited the course of the sexual excitation, but pleasure continued, nevertheless, to be perceived as pleasure. Pleasure and unpleasure are two distinct processes. This mechanism operates in every *non*-masochistic inhibition of the orgasm.

In masochism, on the other hand, the melting sensation of preorgastic pleasure is *itself* perceived as the anticipated threat. The anxiety which was acquired in connection with anal pleasure creates a psychic attitude which makes genital pleasure—which is much more intensive—appear as injury and punishment.

Thus the masochistic character keeps advancing toward the expected pleasure and finds himself meeting unpleasure. It actually looks as if he were striving for unpleasure. What has really happened is that anxiety always comes between, and thus the desired pleasure comes to be perceived as the anticipated danger. End-pleasure is replaced by *end-unpleasure.*

This solves the problem of a repetition compulsion *beyond* the pleasure principle. The masochist gives the impression of wanting to repeat an unpleasurable experience. In reality, *he strives for a pleasure situation, but frustration, anxiety and fear of punishment interfere and cause the original goal to be obliterated or made unpleasurable.* In other words, a repetition compulsion beyond the pleasure principle does not exist; the corresponding phenomena can be explained within the framework of the pleasure principle and the fear of punishment.

To go back to our case, this disturbance of the pleasure mechanism definitely explained the flattening and protraction of his masturbation. *He avoided any increase in pleasure perception.* At the time this became clear, he once said, "It is impossible to let these sensations take their course, it is absolutely intolerable." We understand now why he masturbated for hours on end: he never reached satisfaction because he did not allow any involuntary increase in excitation to take place.

This inhibition has, in addition to fear of the increase, another reason. The masochistic character is used to the anal kind of pleasure which has a flat curve of excitation and has no acme; one might say it is a "lukewarm" kind of pleasure. The masochistic character transfers anal practice and the anal kind of pleasure experience to the genital apparatus which functions entirely differently. The intensive, sudden and steep increase of genital pleasure is not only unaccustomed but for one used only to the mild anal pleasure it is apt to be terrifying. If to this is added an anticipation of punishment, all conditions are given for an immediate conversion of pleasure into unpleasure.

In retrospect, this explained many earlier cases, particularly those who showed a suffering, masochistic mood after unsatisfactory (we would add now, after *specifically* disturbed) sexual activity. It explained, from the point of view of libido economy, the strong masochistic tendencies in the cases of orgastic disturbance described in my books, DER TRIEBHAFTE CHARAKTER and DIE FUNKTION DES ORGASMUS. Concerning a female patient with a masochistic perversion it is stated in the latter: "She masturbated . . . with the masochistic phantasy that she was shackled and completely undressed and put into a cage to starve. At this point the orgasm became inhibited because she suddenly had to think about a piece of apparatus which would automatically remove the feces and urine of the girl who was shackled and not allowed to move. . . . In the analysis, when the transference would take on the form of sexual excitation, she would develop an intense urge to urinate and defecate." If she masturbated with coitus phantasies "masochistic phantasies appeared shortly before orgasm was about to occur."

The masochistic attitude and phantasy, then, stems from the unpleasurable perception of the pleasure sensation; it is an attempt to master the unpleasure through an attitude which is psychically formulated as, "I'm so miserable—love me!" The beating phantasy must come in because the demand for love also contains genital demands which force the patient to divert the punishment from the front to the rear: "Beat me—but don't castrate me!" In other words, the masochistic reaction has a specific stasis-neurotic foundation.

The center of the problems of masochism, then, lies in the specific disturbances of the pleasure function. It became clear that it is the fear of the "melting" preorgastic pleasure sensation which makes the patient adhere to a pleasure of the anal kind. Is this the result of anal fixation or of genital inhibition? It would seem that both factors are equally involved, just as both factors cause the chronic neurasthenic condition. Anality mobilizes the whole libidinous apparatus, without, however, being capable of bringing about a relaxation of the tension. The inhibition of genitality is not only a result of anxiety, but produces anxiety in turn; this increases the discrepancy between tension and discharge. There remains the question why the beating phantasy typically sets in, or becomes intensified, just previous to the acme.

It is interesting to see how the psychic apparatus tries to diminish the discrepancy between tension and discharge, how the urge for relaxation breaks through, after all, in the beating phantasy. Our patient kept maintaining that "being beaten by the woman is exactly the same as secretly masturbating in her ( = the mother's) presence." This, indeed, corresponded exactly to his actual experience: as a child and adolescent he did use to lie in bed with his mother while he masturbated in a masochistic fashion. That is, he would squeeze his penis, prevent ejaculation (because of his pregnancy phobia) and would fantasy that his mother was beating him; only then would ejaculation occur. This had the following meaning which the patient remembered consciously: "My penis seems all boiled to me. With the fifth or sixth blow it is bound to burst, as will my bladder." In other words, *the beatings were to bring about the relaxation which he was prohibited from bringing about in any other way.* If his bladder and his penis burst as a result of the beatings by his mother and an ejaculation took place, it was not his fault, for his tormentor had brought it to pass. The wish for punishment, then, has the following meaning: to bring about the relaxation after all, by way of a detour, and to shift the responsibility to the punishing person. We see the same mechanism in this basic process as in the characterological superstructure. In the latter it is: "Love me, so I won't be afraid"; the complaining means: "*You* are to blame, not I." The beating phantasy means: "Beat me, so I can get relaxation without being responsible for it." This seems to be the deepest meaning of the passive beating phantasy.

Since the time when I first recognized this deepest function of the passive beating phantasy, I have found this mechanism in other patients who had not developed a manifest perversion but who had kept their masochistic tendency latent by way of character changes. To mention only a few examples: A compulsive character developed a masturbation phantasy that he was among primitives who forced him to have coitus and to behave without any inhibitions. A passive-feminine character without a manifest perversion had the phantasy that he was made to have an ejaculation by blows on his penis; the condition was that he was shackled in order to be able to stand the blows and be unable to run away. Here we have to mention also the common masochistic sex attitude of neurotic women, an attitude which by many analysts is considered the normal feminine attitude. This passive rape phantasy in the woman, however, serves no other purpose than that of alleviating her guilt feelings. These neurotic women can engage in intercourse without guilt feeling only if—actually or in phantasy—they are raped, thus shifting the responsibility to the man. The formal resistance of many women in the act has the same meaning.

This takes us to the problem of so-called "*Angstlust*" (pleasure in anxiety) which plays such a big role in masochism. Following is a relevant example from another analysis:

A patient remembered that at the age of about four he consciously used to produce night terrors. He would crawl under the covers, masturbate, develop anxiety and then rid himself of it by suddenly throwing the covers off. How tempting in this case is the assumption of a repetition compulsion: he had had a night terror and now wanted again and again to re-experience the anxiety. There are two things which contradict such an assumption. First, he did not want to re-experience the anxiety, but the pleasure, notwithstanding the fact that the experience of the pleasure always led to anxiety. Second, the liberation from the anxiety was a source of pleasure. The essential point in the process, however, was that the anxiety resulted in anal and urethral sensations for the sake of which he was willing to suffer the anxiety. Anxiety as such is not pleasurable; it only gives rise to a certain kind of pleasure. Very often, children experience sensations of relaxation only in anxiety, sensations which they otherwise suppress for fear of punishment. The relaxation connected with the sudden loss of feces or urine in a situation of anxiety is often the reason for wanting to re-experience anxiety. But to explain these facts on an assumption *beyond* the pleasure principle would be a complete misinterpretation. Anxiety or pain, under certain conditions, becomes the only possibility of experiencing relaxation which otherwise is feared. The expressions of "*Schmerzlust*" or "*Angstlust*" thus can correctly mean only that pain or anxiety can become the occasion of sexual excitation.

The fact that in our patient the "bursting of the penis" seems to be the instinctual goal does in no way contradict our concept of masochism. This idea is on the one hand an idea representing anxiety or punishment; but on the other hand it also represents the desire of end-pleasure, of relaxation. It is due to this double meaning of the idea of bursting that end-pleasure itself comes to be perceived as the execution of dreaded punishment.

## 5. ON THE THERAPY OF MASOCHISM

The establishment of a healthy sex life, of a sound sex-economy, requires two therapeutic processes: the liberation of the libido from its pregenital fixations, and the elimination of genital anxiety. That this takes place by an analysis of the pregenital and genital Oedipus complex is a matter of course. One technical point, however, needs special emphasis: the danger of dissolving the pregenital fixations without, *at the same time,* eliminating the genital anxiety. Since in this case the orgastic discharge of energy remains inhibited, the danger is that of an increase in sexual stasis. This danger may be increased to the point of suicide, just at a time when the analysis of pregenitality has been successful. If, conversely, one eliminates the genital anxiety without eliminating the pregenital fixations, the genital energies remain weak, and the genital function cannot release the total amount of anxiety.

The main problem in the therapy of masochism is that of overcoming the patient's tendency to put the analyst in a bad light. The most important measure is to show the sadistic nature of this masochistic behavior. This reverses the original process of sadism being turned inward, toward the self; passive-masochistic-anal phantasies turn into active-sadistic-phallic phantasies. When in this way infantile genitality is reactivated, it becomes possible to uncover the castration anxiety which previously was covered up by the masochistic reaction.

It goes without saying that these measures do as yet not influence the masochistic character of the patient in the least. His complaining, spiting, self-damaging tendencies and his awkwardness—which presents a rational reason for withdrawing from the world—usually persist until it has become possible to eliminate the above-described disturbance of the pleasure mechanism in masturbation. Once genital orgasm has been achieved the patient usually undergoes a rapid change. Nevertheless, there remains for some time the tendency to take flight back into masochism at the slightest disappointment, frustration or dissatisfaction. Even consistent and thorough work on both the genital anxiety and the pregenital fixation can guarantee success only if the damage to the genital apparatus is not too severe and if, in addition, the patient's environment is not such as to throw him back again and again into his old masochistic groove. Thus, the analysis of a young unmarried man will be much easier than that of a masochistic woman who is at the menopause or economically tied to an unfortunate family situation.

The thorough work on the masochistic character traits has to be continued up to the conclusion of the treatment; otherwise, one is apt to run into most difficult situations during the frequent relapses at the time when genital primacy is being established. One also should not forget that a definite dissolution of the masochistic character cannot take place until the patient has led an economic work and love life for a considerable period of time, that is, until long after the conclusion of the treatment.

One has to view with the greatest scepticism the success of the treatment of masochistic characters, especially those with a manifest perversion, as long as one has not understood every detail of the character reactions and therefore has not really broken through them. On the other hand, one has every reason to be optimistic once one has succeeded in this, that is, once genitality has been established, even though at first only in the form of genital anxiety. Then, one need no longer be perturbed by repeated relapses. We know that the treatment of masochism is one of the most difficult of our therapeutic problems. It is not possible unless one adheres to that psychoanalytic theory which has an empirical foundation. Such hypotheses as are criticized here are often only a sign of therapeutic failure.

For if one explains masochism by a death instinct, one confirms to the patient his alleged will to suffer; what corresponds to reality and alone guarantees therapeutic success is to unmask the will to suffer as a disguised aggression.

We have mentioned two specific tasks in the therapy of masochism: changing masochism back into sadism, and progression from pregenitality to genitality. The third specific task is the elimination of the anal and genital spastic attitude which, as described, is the acute source of the suffering.

It goes without saying that this presentation of the masochistic process is far from solving all problems of masochism. But once the problem of masochism is again seen in the framework in which it belongs, that of the pleasure-unpleasure-principle, the path to a solution of the remaining problems, which was blocked by the hypothesis of the death instinct, is again open.

## Chapter XII

# EMOTIONAL PLAGUE

The term "emotional plague" has no defamatory connotation. It does not refer to conscious malice, moral or biological degeneration, immorality, etc. An organism which, from birth, is constantly impeded in its natural way of locomotion *develops artificial forms of locomotion*. It limps or moves on crutches. Similarly, an individual moves through life by the means of the emotional plague if, from birth, his natural, self-regulatory life manifestations have been suppressed. The individual afflicted with the emotional plague *limps, characterologically speaking. The emotional plague is a chronic biopathy of the organism.* It made its appearance with the first suppression of genital love life on a mass scale; it became an *epidemic* which has tortured the peoples of the earth for thousands of years. There are no grounds for the assumption that it passes, in a hereditary manner, from mother to child. Rather, it is implanted in the child from his first day of life on. It is an epidemic disease, like schizophrenia or cancer, with this important difference: it manifests itself essentially in *social living*. Schizophrenia and cancer are biopathies resulting from the emotional plague in social life. The effects of the emotional plague are to be seen in the organism as well as in social living. Periodically, like any other plague, such as bubonic plague or cholera, the emotional plague takes on the dimensions of a pandemic, in the form of a gigantic break-through of sadism and criminality, such as the Catholic inquisition of the middle ages or the international fascism of the present century.

If we did not consider the emotional plague a disease in the strict sense of the word we would be in danger of mobilizing the policeman's club against it instead of medicine and education. It is characteristic of the emotional plague that it necessitates the policeman's club and thus reproduces itself. Nevertheless, in spite of the threat to life which the emotional plague represents, it will never be mastered by means of the club.

Nobody will feel offended when he is called nervous or a cardiac patient. Nobody can feel offended when he is told that he suffers from an "acute attack of the emotional plague." An orgone therapist is apt to say of himself: "I'm no good today, I have the plague." In our circles, such attacks of the emotional plague, if slight, are handled by one's withdrawing for a while until the attack of irrationalism subsides. In serious cases, where rational thinking and friendly counsel are not enough, one clears up the situation orgone-therapeutically. One finds regularly that such acute attacks are caused by a disturbance in love life, and that they subside when the disturbance is eliminated. To me and the close co-workers, the acute attack of the emotional plague is such a familiar phenomenon that we take it with calm and master it objectively. It is one of the most important requirements in the training of orgone therapists that they learn to perceive acute attacks of the emotional plague in themselves in time, not to get lost in them, not to let them take any effect in the social environment, and to master them by assuming an objective attitude toward them. In this manner, possible harm to common work can be reduced to a minimum. It happens, of course, that such an attack of the emotional plague is not mastered, that the individual afflicted with it does more or less harm or that he withdraws from the work. We take such accidents in the same manner as one takes a serious physical disease or the death of an esteemed co-worker.

The emotional plague is more closely allied to character neurosis than to organic heart disease, but in the long run it may lead to cardiac disease or cancer. Like the character neurosis, it is maintained by secondary drives. It differs from physical defects in being a function of the character and, as such, being strongly *defended*. Unlike, say, a hysterical attack, it is not experienced as ego-alien and pathological. As we know, character-neurotic behavior is usually highly rationalized. In the emotional plague reaction, this is the case even to a far higher degree: the lack of insight is far greater. One may ask what makes it possible to recognize a plague reaction and to distinguish it from a rational reaction. The answer is the same as in the case of distinguishing a character-neurotic reaction from a rational reaction: *As soon as one touches upon the motives of the plague reaction, anxiety or anger inevitably appears.* This we shall discuss in some detail:

An orgastically potent individual, essentially free of the emotional plague, will not develop anxiety but, on the contrary, vivid interest when a physician discusses, say, the dynamics of natural life processes. The individual suffering from the emotional plague, on the other hand, will become restless or angry when the mechanisms of the emotional plague are discussed. Not every orgastic impotence leads to the emotional plague, but everyone afflicted with it is either lastingly impotent, orgastically, or becomes so shortly before the attack. This makes it possible easily to distinguish plague reactions from rational reactions.

Further: A natural, healthy behavior cannot be disturbed or eliminated by any influences of genuine therapy. For example, there is no rational means of "curing," of disturbing, a happy love relationship. On the other hand, a neurotic symptom can be eliminated; similarly, a plague reaction is accessible to genuine character-analytic therapy and can be eliminated by it. Thus, one may be able to cure greediness for money, a typical character trait of the emotional plague, but one cannot cure generosity in money matters. One can cure clever underhandedness, but not openness and honesty. The emotional plague reaction may be likened to impotence, which can be eliminated, that is, cured. Genital potency, on the other hand, is "incurable."

It is an essential characteristic of the emotional plague reaction that *action and the reason given for it are never congruent. The real motive is always covered up and replaced by a seeming motive.* In the natural reaction of the healthy character, *motive, action and goal* form an *organic unity.* Nothing is hidden here; the reaction is immediately understandable. For example: The healthy individual has no other reason for his sexual behavior than his natural need for love and its goal of gratification. The ascetic plague individual, on the other hand, justifies his sexual weakness secondarily with ethical demands. This justification has nothing to do with the way of living. *The attitude of life-negating asceticism is present before the justification.* The healthy individual will not try to impose his way of living on anybody else; but he will give help, therapeutic or otherwise, if he is asked for help and has the means of helping. In no case will a healthy individual *decree* that all people *"must be* healthy." To begin with, such a decree would not be rational, for health cannot be commandeered. Further, the healthy individual has no impulse whatsoever to impose his way of living on other people, for the motives for his way of living have to do with his own way of life and not that of others. The emotional plague individual differs from the healthy individual in that he makes his life demands not only on himself, but *primarily and above all on his environment.* Where the healthy individual advises and helps, where he, with his experiences, simply lives ahead of others and leaves it to them whether they want to follow his example or not, the plague individual imposes his way of living on others *by force.* Plague individuals do not tolerate views which threaten their armorings or which disclose their irrational motives. The healthy individual experiences only pleasure when his motives are discussed; the plague individual becomes furious. The healthy individual, where other views of life disturb his life and work, fights in a rational manner for the preservation of *his* way of living. The plague individual fights against *other* ways of living even where they do not touch him at all. The motive of his fight is the provocation which other ways of living represent by their mere existence.

*The energy which nourishes the emotional plague reactions regularly derives from genital frustration,* no matter whether we are dealing with sadistic war or with the defamation of friends. The stasis of sexual energy is what the plague individual has in common with all other biopathies. As to the differences, I shall soon come to that. The biopathic nature of the emotional plague is seen in the fact that, like any other biopathy, it can be cured by the establishment of the natural capacity for love.

The disposition to the emotional plague is general. There is no such thing as individuals completely free of the emotional plague on the one hand and emotional plague individuals on the other. Just as every individual, somewhere in the depth, has a tendency toward cancer, schizophrenia or alcoholism, so every individual, be it the most healthy and alive, has a tendency to irrational plague reactions in himself.

To distinguish the emotional plague from the genital character structure is easier than to distinguish it from the simple character neuroses. True, the emotional plague is a character neurosis or a biopathy in the strict sense of the word, but it is more than that, and it is this "more" which distinguishes it from the biopathy and the character neurosis: *The emotional plague is that human behavior which, on the basis of a biopathic character structure, makes itself felt in interpersonal, that is, social relationships and which becomes organized in corresponding institutions.* The sphere of the emotional plague is as large as that of the character biopathy. That is, wherever there are character biopathies, there is at least the possibility of a chronic effect or an acute epidemic outbreak of the emotional plague. In defining some typical fields in which this takes place we shall see immediately that it is precisely the most important sectors of life in which the emotional plague is active: mysticism in its most destructive form; passive and active striving for authority; moralism; biopathies of the autonomic life system; party politics; the familial plague which I termed "familitis"; sadistic methods of upbringing; masochistic toleration of such methods or criminal rebellion against them; gossip and defamation; authoritarian bureaucracy; imperialistic war ideology; everything which is subsumed under "racket"; criminal antisociality; pornography; usury; and race hatred.

We see that the realm of the emotional plague is about the same as that of all the social evils which any social freedom movement has fought against since time immemorial. It would not be incorrect to equate the realm of the emotional plague with that of "political reaction" or even with the principle of politics in general. In order to do this in a correct manner, one must apply the basic principle of all politics, to wit, greed for power and advantage, to the various spheres of life where one does not speak of politics in the ordinary sense of the word. A mother, for example, who uses the methods of politics in an attempt to estrange her child from her husband, would fall under this wider concept of political emotional plague; so would a career-minded scientist who attains a high social position not by factual achievement but by methods of intrigue, a position which in no way corresponds to his achievements.

We have already mentioned biological *sexual stasis* as the biophysical core which all forms of emotional plague have in common. As far as our experience goes, a genital character is incapable of using the methods of the emotional plague. This constitutes a great disadvantage in a social life which, to such a high degree, is dominated by the institutions of the emotional plague. There is a second common denominator of all forms of emotional plague: *The lack of the ability to experience natural orgastic gratification regularly leads to the development of secondary impulses, in particular, of sadistic impulses.* This is a clinical fact established beyond any doubt. It is not surprising, then, that the biopsychic energy which nourishes the emotional plague reactions has always the character of the energy of *secondary* drives. In full-blown cases, *sadism,* this specifically human drive, is never absent.

We understand now why *honesty* and *straightforwardness* are such rare human character traits; more than that, why such behavior, when it occasionally prevails, regularly evokes amazement and admiration. From the standpoint of "cultural" ideals, one would expect that honesty and straightforwardness would be everyday and matter-of-course attitudes. The fact that they are not, but, on the contrary, evoke amazement; that truthful and straightforward people are regarded as somehow queer; that, furthermore, to be honest and straightforward so often involves social danger to life; all this cannot be understood in any way on the basis of the governing cultural ideology, but only with a knowledge of the organized emotional plague. Only this knowledge will make understandable the fact that, century after century, the forces of any freedom movement, *truthfulness* and *objectivity,* failed to prevail. We must assume, then, that no freedom movement has any chance of success unless it opposes the organized emotional plague with truthfulness, and does it clearly and vigorously.

The fact that the nature of the emotional plague has remained unrecognized has been, up until now, its best safeguard. Consequently, the exact investigation of its nature and of the ways in which it works will tear down this protection. The bearers of the emotional plague, rightly, will interpret this as a fatal threat to their existence. The reaction of the bearers and spreaders of the plague to the factual presentations which are to follow will prove this inexorably. The reactions to come will make it possible, and mandatory, clearly to separate those who wish to help in the fight against the emotional plague from those others who wish to maintain its institutions. It has been shown again and again that the emotional plague—willy-nilly—discloses its *irrational* nature when one probes it. This cannot be otherwise, because the emotional plague cannot react but irrationally. It has to give way when confronted, clearly and uncompromisingly, with rational thinking and with the natural feeling for life. It is not at all necessary to attack it directly or to fight it. It will, automatically and inevitably, react with furor if one does no more than give a factual and truthful description of the natural living functions. There is nothing that the emotional plague hates more than precisely this.

## THE DIFFERENCES BETWEEN THE GENITAL CHARACTER, THE NEUROTIC CHARACTER, AND EMOTIONAL PLAGUE REACTIONS

### a. In thinking:

In the genital character, thinking takes its orientation from *objective facts and processes;* it differentiates between what is essential and non-essential or less essential; it attempts to detect and eliminate irrational, emotional disturbances; it is in its nature *functional,* not mechanistic and not mystical; judgment is the result of a thought process; rational thinking is accessible to *factual* arguments for it functions poorly without *factual* counterarguments.

In the neurotic character, true, the thinking also tries to take its orientation from objective processes and facts. Since, however, in the back of rational thinking, and interlaced with it, chronic sexual stasis is at work, it takes its orientation, at the same time, from the principle of *avoiding unpleasure.* That is, processes the thinking through of which would cause unpleasure or are at variance with the thought system, say, of a compulsion neurotic, such processes are avoided in various ways, or they are thought through in such a manner that the rational goal becomes unattainable. To exemplify: Everybody longs for peace. Since, however, the thinking takes place in largely neurotic character structures, since, consequently, there is at the same time *fear of freedom* and *fear of responsibility (pleasure anxiety),* peace and freedom are discussed in a formalistic, and not in a factual, manner; the simplest and most self-evident facts of life which obviously represent the natural foundations of peace and freedom are avoided as if intentionally; important connections are overlooked; thus, for example, the well-known facts that politics is ruinous and that humanity is sick in the psychiatric sense are in no way connected with the conscious demand for a usable self-governing social order. Thus, two more or less well-known and generally valid facts co-exist, side by side, without any connection. The reason for this is the following: A connecting of these facts would immediately call for *practical changes in everyday living.* These changes, the neurotic character is ready to *affirm ideologically* but he is *afraid of them practically;* his character armor does not allow of a change in his way of living which has become a rut; thus he will agree with the criticism of irrationality in society and science, but will change, in a practical way, neither himself nor society according to this criticism; consequently, he will not form a social center of necessary reform. More than that, it happens very often that the very character who agrees ideologically turns practically into a violent opponent if somebody else actually brings about a change. At this point, the boundaries between the neurotic character and the plague individual become blurred.

The individual afflicted with the emotional plague does not content himself with a passive attitude; he is distinguished from the neurotic character by a more or less life-destructive *social activity.* His thinking is completely blurred by irrational concepts and essentially determined by *irrational* emotions. True, as in the genital character, his thinking is fully in accord with his actions (as distinguished from the neurotic character, where thinking and acting are dissociated); but, in the emotional plague, the conclusion is always there ready-made *before* the thinking process; the thinking does not serve, as in the rational realm, to arrive at a correct conclusion; rather, it serves to confirm an already existing irrational conclusion and to rationalize it. This is generally called "prejudice"; what is overlooked is that this prejudice has social consequences of considerable magnitude, that it is very widespread and practically synonymous with what is called "inertia and tradition"; it is intolerant, that is, it does not tolerate the rational thinking which might do away with it; consequently, the thinking of the emotional plague is inaccessible to arguments; *it has its own technique within its own realm,* its own "logicality," as it were; for this reason, it gives the impression of rationality without being actually rational.

A strict authoritarian educator, for example, points, quite logically and correctly, to the existing unmanageableness of the children. In this *narrow* framework his conclusion seems to be correct. If, now, the rational thinking explains that this unmanageableness to which the irrational thinking points is itself a social *result* of precisely this irrational thinking in education, then one meets, typically, a block in thinking; it is precisely at this point that the irrational character of the plague thinking becomes evident.

Another example: Moralistic sexual repression creates the secondary drives, and the secondary drives make moralistic suppression necessary. Every conclusion here is in itself logical. If, now, one proposes to the one who advocates the necessity of repression the elimination of the secondary drives through the liberation of *natural* gratification, one has, it is true, broken through the thought system of the plague individual, but to that he reacts, in a typical manner, not with insight and correction, but with irrational arguments, with silence or even with hatred. It is *emotionally important to him that repression as well as secondary drives continue to exist.* As paradoxical as this may seem, the reason is simple: *He is afraid of the natural impulses.* This fear is the irrational motor power behind his whole system of thought, logical as it may be in itself; it is this fear which drives him to dangerous actions if one seriously endangers his social system.

### b. In acting:

In the genital character, motive, goal and action are in harmony; motives and goals have a rational, i.e., *social goal.* Motives and goals, on the basis of their primary *biological* nature, strive for an *improvement of the living conditions of one's self and of others;* it is what we call "social achievement."

In the neurotic character, the capacity for action is regularly reduced, because the motives are devoid of affect or are contradictory. Since the neurotic character usually has well repressed his irrationality, he has to fight it constantly. This, precisely, makes the reduction of his ability to act. He is afraid to let himself go in any activity because he never can be sure whether sadistic or other pathological impulses might not break through also. As a rule, he suffers under the insight into the fact that he is inhibited in his vital functioning, *without,* however, developing *envy of healthy individuals.* His attitude is: "I have had bad luck in life, and my children should have a better life." This attitude makes him a sympathetic though sterile spectator of progress. He does not impede progress.

In the individual afflicted with the emotional plague, things are different. Here, *the motive of an action is always an assumed one; the given motive is never the actual motive,* no matter whether the actual motive is conscious or unconscious. Nor are the given and real goal identical. In German fascism, for example, the alleged goal was that of the "preservation of a peaceful German nation"; the real goal—based on character structure—was the imperialist war, the subjugation of the world, and nothing but that. It is a basic characteristic of the plague-ridden individual that he believes, seriously and honestly, in the alleged goal and motive. I should like to emphasize the fact that one cannot understand the character structure of the plague-ridden individual if one does not take seriously the following facts: The plague-ridden individual acts under a *structural compulsion;* no matter how well-meaning he may be, *he cannot act but in the manner of the emotional plague;* acting in this manner is as much of his essence as the need for love or the truth is of the essence of the genital character; but the plague-ridden individual, protected by his subjective conviction, does not suffer under the insight into the harmfulness of his actions. A man may demand the custody of his child because he hates his wife who, say, was unfaithful to him; in doing so, he honestly believes to be acting "in the interest of the child"; he will be unable to correct this attitude when the child suffers under the separation from the mother and may even fall ill. The plague-ridden father will, secondarily, elaborate all kinds of rationalizations enabling him to maintain his conviction that he is acting "solely for the good of the child" when he keeps the child from the mother; he *cannot* be convinced that the *real* motive is that of a sadistic punishment for the mother. The plague-ridden individual—in contrast to the neurotic character—regularly develops an intense envy which goes with a deadly hatred for anything healthy. A character-neurotic spinster lives in resignation and does not interfere in the love life of other girls. A plague-ridden spinster, on the other hand, does not tolerate happiness in love in other girls; if she is an educator she will do everything in her power to *make the girls in her charge incapable* of experiencing happiness in love. This applies to all life situations. The plague character will, under all circumstances and by all means, try to change his environment in such a manner that *his* way of living and thinking is not interfered with. He experiences everything which contradicts his ways as provocation and consequently hates and fights it. This is particularly evident in ascetics. The ascetic attitude is basically the following. *"Others should not be any happier than I was; they should suffer the way I did."* This basic attitude, in every case, is so well camouflaged by an ideology or theory of life which is in itself quite logical that it takes a great deal of experience and thought to discover it. It must be said that European education, as recently as the early part of this century, followed this pattern.

*c. In sexuality:*

In the genital character, the sexual life is essentially determined by the basic natural laws of biological energy. To the genital character, joy in witnessing happiness in love in others is a matter of course, as is indifference toward perversions and repulsion toward pornography. The genital character is easily recognized by the good contact he has with healthy infants. To his structure, it is a matter of course that the interests of children and adolescents are largely *sexual* ones, and that the demands resulting from these biological facts should be fulfilled; this attitude is spontaneous, no matter whether there is, in addition, a corresponding knowledge. In the social life of today it is precisely such fathers and mothers—unless, by chance, they live in a favorable milieu which supports them—who are exposed to the great danger of being regarded and treated as criminals by the authoritarian institutions. They deserve the exact opposite, the maximum social protection. They form centers in society from which one day will come the rationally acting educators and physicians; the basis of their lives and their actions is the happiness in love which they experience. Yet today, parents who would let children live completely according to healthy, natural laws would be in danger of being dragged into court by any ascetic with influence, and of losing their children.

The neurotic character lives in sexual resignation or engages secretly in perverse activities. His orgastic impotence goes with longing for happiness in love. He is indifferent toward other people's happiness in love. He reacts with anxiety rather than with hatred when he comes in contact with the sexual problem. His armoring refers only to his own sexuality, not to that of others. His orgastic longing is often elaborated into cultural or religious ideals which do little harm or good to the health of the community. He usually is active in circles or groups with little social influence. Many of these groups have doubtless cultural value, but they cannot contribute anything to the problem of mass mental hygiene because the masses have a much more direct and immediate attitude toward the question of a natural love life than they have.

The basic attitude just described, of the sexually harmless neurotic character, may, given certain external conditions, take on the form of the emotional plague, at any time. What happens is usally this: the secondary drives which were held in check by the cultural and religious ideals, break through. *The sexuality of the plague-ridden individual is always sadistic and pornographic.* It is characterized by the *simultaneous existence of sexual lasciviousness* (because of incapacity for sexual gratification) and *sadistic moralism.* This fact is given in his *structure;* he could not change it even if he had insight and knowledge; on the basis of his structure, he cannot be any different than *pornographically lascivious* and *sadistically moralistic* at one and the same time.

This is the core of the character structure of the emotional plague. It develops violent hatred against any process which provokes orgastic longing and, with that, orgasm anxiety. *The demand for asceticism is directed not only against the self, but even more so, and in a sadistic manner, against the natural love life of other people.* Plague-ridden individuals have a strong tendency to form social circles. Such circles become centers of public opinion, which is characterized by a violent intolerance in questions of natural love life. These centers are everywhere and well known. They persecute severely any manifestation of natural love life under the guise of "culture" and "morals." In the course of time, they have developed a special *technique of defamation;* more about this later.

Clinical investigation leaves no doubt that to these circles of plague-ridden individuals, sexual gossip and defamation represent a kind of perverse sexual gratification. It is a matter of gaining sexual pleasure with exclusion of the natural genital function. Homosexuality, sexual intercourse with animals, and other perversions, are particularly often met with in these circles. The sadistic condemnation is directed against the NATURAL, and *not against the perverse,* sexuality of others. It is directed, furthermore, in a particularly violent manner, against the *natural* sexuality of *children* and *adolescents.* At the same time, it is as if blind toward any kind of perverse sexual activity. These people, who sit in secret court over the natural sexuality of others, as it were, have many human lives on their conscience.

## d. In work:

The genital character follows the development of a work process in an active manner. The work process is left to take *its own course*. The interest is essentially directed toward the work *process* itself; the result of the work comes about without any special effort, since it results spontaneously from the work process. *The product resulting from the course of the work process is an essential characteristic of biological joy in work.* These facts and considerations lead to a sharp criticism of all present methods of early upbringing in which the activity of the child is determined by an anticipated, ready-made work product. The anticipation of the product and the rigid determination of the work process chokes off the child's own imagination, that is, his *productivity.* Biological joy in work goes with the ability to develop *enthusiasm.* Compulsive moralism does not tolerate genuine enthusiasm, it tolerates only mystical ecstasy. A child which must build an *already given* house with *given* blocks in a *given* manner cannot utilize his imagination and therefore cannot develop any enthusiasm. It is not difficult to understand that this basic trait of authoritarian education owes its existence to the pleasure anxiety of the adults; it always strangles the child's joy in work. *The genital character guides the work achievement of others by his example, and not by dictating the product and the work methods.* This presupposes vegetative motility and the ability to let oneself go.

The neurotic character is more or less restricted in his work. His biological energy is essentially used up in the defense against perverse phantasies. The neurotic disturbance of work is due to the misuse of biological energy. For this reason, the work of the neurotic character is typically automatic, mechanical and devoid of joy. Since the neurotic character is incapable of genuine enthusiasm, he experiences children's capacity for enthusiasm as "improper"; just the same, he presumes, in a compulsion-neurotic manner, to determine the work of others.

The plague-ridden individual *hates* work, for he experiences it as a burden. He flees any responsibility and particularly any work which involves patient persistence. He may dream of writing an important book, of doing an extraordinary painting, of working a farm; but since he is incapable of working, he avoids the step-by-step organic development inherent in any work process. This makes him inclined to become an ideologist, mystic or politician, in other words, to engage in activities which require no patience and no organic development; he may equally well become a non-working vagrant as a dictator in this or that realm of life. He has erected in himself a ready-made picture of life woven of neurotic phantasies; since he himself is incapable of working, he wants to force others to work on the production of this pathological picture of life. What Americans call "boss" in the bad sense of the word is a product of this constellation. The genital character, who guides a collective work process, spontaneously sets an example: he works *more* than the others. The plague-ridden individual, on the other hand, always wants to work less than the others; the less his work capacity, the less, as a result, his self-confidence, the more he presumes to tell *others* how to work.

———

The above differentiation is of necessity schematic. In living reality, every genital character also has his character-neurotic inhibitions and his plague reactions; similarly, every plague-ridden individual has in himself the *possibilities* of the genital character. Orgone-therapeutic experience leaves no doubt that such individuals afflicted with the emotional plague as fall under the psychiatric concept of "moral insanity" are not only curable in principle, but are capable of developing extraordinary capacities as regards intellect, work and sexuality. This again emphasizes the fact that the concept of "emotional plague" does not imply any deprecation. In the course of almost 30 years of biopsychiatric work I have come to the conclusion that the tendency to fall victim to the emotional plague is a sign that the individual in question is endowed with particularly high quantities of biological energy. It is precisely *the high tension of his biological energy* which makes the individual fall victim to the emotional plague if, as the result of a rigid muscular and character armor, he cannot develop in a natural manner. The plague-ridden individual is a product of authoritarian compulsive education; he rebels against it, due to his greater capacities which remain unfulfilled, much more successfully than does the quiet and resigned neurotic character. He is distinguished from the genital character in that his *rebellion is aimless socially* and cannot bring about any rational changes in the direction of social betterment. He is distinguished from the neurotic character in that he *does not resign.*

The genital character masters his own emotional plague reactions in two ways: First, on the basis of his essentially rational character structure, he experiences his own plague reaction as alien and senseless. Second, he is rooted in rational processes to such an extent that he immediately senses the dangers to his life process as they might arise from his irrational tendencies. This enables him to control himself in a rational manner. The plague-ridden individual, on the other hand, derives so much secondary, sadistic pleasure from his behavior that he is inaccessible to any correction. The actions of the healthy individual derive, in an immediate manner, from the reservoir of biological energy. The actions of the plague-ridden individual, it is true, derive from the same reservoir, *but with each action the energies have to break through the characterological and the muscular armor; as a result of this, the best motives turn into antisocial and irrational actions. In passing through the character armor, the actions change their function: The impulse begins with a rational intention; the armoring makes a natural and organic development of the impulse impossible; this, the plague-ridden individual experiences as an intolerable inhibition; in order to express itself at all, the impulse first has to break through the armor; in this process, the original intention and the rational goal get lost.* The *result* of the action contains very little of the original, rational intention; it reflects the *destructiveness* which had to be mobilized for the breakthrough through the armor. *The brutality of the plague-ridden individual, then, corresponds to the failure to break the muscular and character armor.* A *dissolution* of the armor is impossible, because a plague action does neither provide the orgastic discharge of energy nor does it convey a rational self-confidence. In this manner, many contradictions in the structure of plague-ridden individuals can be understood. Such an individual may long for love and may find a woman whom he thinks he can love. When he proves incapable of love, he is driven to sadistic fury against himself or against the beloved woman, a fury which not infrequently ends in murder.

What characterizes the plague individual basically, then, is the *contradiction between intense longing for life and the inability to find a corresponding fulfilment in life,* resulting from the armor. The careful observer could notice that the political irrationalism in Europe was characterized precisely by this contradiction: the best intentions, with the logic of a compulsion, led to destructive results.

We shall now try to illustrate the above differentiations by way of everyday examples:

As the first example we take the *fight for the child* as it typically occurs in divorce cases. We have to expect one of three different reactions: the rational, the character-neurotically inhibited, and the plague reaction.

### a. Rational:

Father and mother fight for the healthy development of the child on rational grounds and with rational means. They may agree on principles in which case things are simple, or they may be of widely divergent opinions. In either case, they will, in the interest of the child, avoid the use of underhanded methods. They will talk frankly with the child and will let the child decide. They will not let themselves be influenced by their own personal interest in the possession of the child but will be guided by the inclination of the child. If one or the other marital partner is alcoholic or psychotic, the child will have to be made to understand this fact in a considerate manner as a misfortune which has to be borne. *The motive is that of avoiding damage to the child.* The attitude is determined by a relinquishing of personal interests.

## b. Character-neurotic:

The fight for the child is hemmed in by all kinds of irrelevant considerations such as fear of public opinion. It is determined not by the interest of the child but by adaptation to public opinion. Character-neurotic parents adjust to the current views in such things, such as the tenet that the child, under all circumstances, should remain with the mother, or they leave the decision to some authority such as a court. If one or the other marital partner is an alcoholic or is psychotic, the tendency is that of sacrifice, of hushing up the facts, with the result that the child as well as the other marital partner suffer and are endangered: *divorce is avoided.* The motive of this behavior is the motto: "Let's not make ourselves conspicuous." The attitude is determined by *resignation.*

## c. Emotional plague:

The interest of the child is regularly a *pretended,* and, as the result shows, an *unfulfilled* motive. *The true motive is revenge on the partner through robbing him or her of the pleasure in the child.* The fight for the child, therefore, makes use of the technique of defaming the partner, regardless of whether the partner is healthy or sick. The lack of any consideration of the child is expressed in the fact that the child's love for the other partner is not taken into account. In order to alienate the child from the partner, it is told that the partner is an alcoholic or psychotic, without there being any truth to such statements. The *result is damage to the child,* the *motive* is *destructive revenge* on the partner and domination over the child, but not love for the child.

This example allows of infinite variations, but in its basic traits it is typical and of general social significance. A rational jurisdiction would have to give primary consideration to such distinctions in passing judgment. It is safe to assume that divorces will increase considerably in numbers, and it is also safe to say that only the correctly trained psychiatrist and pedagogue can estimate the extent of damage done by such reactions of the emotional plague in divorces.

Let us take another example in which the emotional plague rages far and wide: the infidelity of a love partner.

### a. Rational:

In the case of threatening or actual "infidelity" of the love partner, the healthy individual reacts, in principle, in one of three ways: 1. with factual separation from the partner; 2. with competition and an attempt to regain the love partner; or, 3. with toleration, if the new relationship is not too serious and is of a transitory character. In this situation, the healthy individual does not take flight into neurosis; he does not make any demands of possession; and he shows anger only if what is happening takes on forms which are not decent.

### b. Character-neurotic:

The infidelity is either suffered masochistically, or the armor prevents its cognisance. There is severe fear of separation. Very often, there is flight into neurotic illness, into alcoholism or hysterical attacks, or resignation.

### c. Emotional plague reaction:

Infidelity, as a rule, is not the result of falling in love with another partner, but is motivated by weariness of the partner or revenge on the partner. On the part of the wronged partner, there are attempts of various kinds to hold him in the house, to break him down by hysterical attacks, to dominate him by scenes of the most abominable kind, or even to have him watched by detectives. Often, there is flight into alcoholism in order to facilitate the brutalization of the partner. The motive is not love for the partner, but lust of power and possession.

The tragedies of jealousy constitute a large sector of the activity of the emotional plague. There are at present neither medical or social nor legal views and measures that would take this vast and desperate realm of life into account.

We shall now consider a particularly impressive and typical mode of reaction of the emotional plague, a reaction which we call the SPECIFIC PLAGUE REACTION.

The specific plague reaction likes to make use of sexual, that is, moral, defamation. It functions in a way similar to the mechanism of projection in delusions of persecution: In this case, a perverse impulse which has broken through the armor is displaced to persons or objects of the outer world. What in reality is an inner impulse is misinterpreted as a threat from the outside. The same is true of sensations arising from orgonotic plasma currents: what to the healthy individual is part of his joyful experiencing of life becomes to the schizophrenic—as a result of his character armor—a mysterious machine which allegedly is used by some enemy to destroy the patient's body by means of electric currents. These delusional mechanisms of projection are well known in psychiatry. The mistake which psychiatry made was that of restricting such mechanisms of projection to psychotic patients. It overlooked the fact that precisely the same mechanism of projection is at large in social life in the form of the specific plague reaction in allegedly normal people. This is what we shall go into now.

The biopsychic mechanism is the following: Compulsive moralism in education and in life creates sexual lasciviousness. This has nothing in common with the natural need for love; it represents a true secondary impulse, like, say, sadism or masochism. Since aliveness in the natural experience of pleasure no longer exists, lasciviousness and sexual gossiping take its place, as a secondary, compulsive drive. Now, just as the schizophrenic projects his orgonotic currents and his perverse impulses to other people, and experiences them as a threat emanating from them, so does the plague-ridden individual project his own lasciviousness and perversity to other people. In contradistinction to the psychotic individual, he experiences his own impulses which he projects to other people not in a masochistic way as a threat. Rather, he uses gossip and defamation in a *sadistic* way, ascribing to others what he does not dare to take cognisance of in himself. This is true of natural genitality as well as of the secondary, perverse impulse. The way of living of the genitally healthy individual reminds the plague-ridden individual painfully of his own genital weakness and thus represents a threat to his neurotic equilibrium. All that remains for him to do is to drag into the dirt the other fellow's natural genitality, according to the principle of the sour grapes. Since, furthermore, he is not able completely to hide his lasciviousness behind the appearance of ethical moralism, he ascribes his lasciviousness to the victim of his gossiping. In every case of this kind of plague reaction, one will find that precisely those characteristics are being ascribed to the healthy individual against which the plague-ridden individual fights in himself in vain, or which, *with a bad conscience,* he is living out.

We shall now illustrate the specific plague reactions with a few examples from everyday life:

There is a type of "intellectual" who always talks of "cultural values." Such people keep referring to the classics without ever having understood or experienced the serious problems portrayed by, say, a Goethe or a Nietzsche. At the same time, they are cynical and consider themselves modern and liberal, untrammelled by convention. Incapable of a serious experience, they consider sexual love a kind of game about which one makes clever jokes, intimating how often one played the "game" the previous night, etc. The serious listener to such talk, who knows the abysmal sexual misery of the masses of people and the destructive role played by the lack of sexual seriousness, knows this lasciviousness to stem from sex hunger as it results from orgastic impotence.

Such "cultured" individuals are apt to consider sex-economy, which—against the greatest obstacles—seriously fights the emotional plague in the masses of people, as the product of a distorted mind. They keep talking of "cultural values" which have to be upheld, but they become furious when somebody translates this talk of the cultural values into social practice on a mass scale. Such an individual happened to meet a woman who intended to come to study with me. The subject of my work came up, and he warned her, saying he would not send his worst enemy to me, since, as he said, I was the "director of a brothel, without license." He immediately covered up this statement by saying that I was an excellent clinician. This defamation—which bears all the earmarks of the specific plague reaction—made, of course, the rounds. The woman came to study sex-economic pedagogy with me just the same and soon understood what we call the emotional plague.

In such situations, it is difficult to remain objective and correct. One cannot give in to one's understandable impulse to beat up such an individual, for one wishes to keep one's hands clean. To ignore such a happening means doing precisely what the plague-ridden individual counts on so that he can continue his social mischief. There remains the possibility of a libel suit. That would mean, however, fighting the emotional plague not *medically*, but by descending to its own level. One becomes inclined, then, to let matters take their course, at the risk that similar plague-ridden individuals take hold of the matter and that among them is some "scientific historian" who writes one down in history as a secret brothel keeper. The matter is important because the emotional plague has succeeded again and again in smashing honest and important achievements by such rumors. This makes the fight against the emotional plague a social necessity, for it is more destructive than thousands of guns. One only has to read in Lange's GESCHICHTE DES MATERIALISMUS what defamations were suffered by De la Mettrie, the 17th century pioneer in natural science. He had not only correctly comprehended the essential connections between perception and physiological stimulus, but had even correctly described the connection between the mind-body problem and the biological sexual process. That was too much for the Philistines whose number is ever so much greater than that of honest and courageous searchers. They began to spread the rumor that De la Mettrie could develop such concepts only because he was a "libertine." In this manner has come down to us the rumor that he died from eating a pie with which he gorged himself in the typical manner of the voluptuary. Not only is this nonsense, medically speaking. It is a typical example of plague-ridden rumor-mongering, which, taken over by human organisms incapable of pleasure, comes down to posterity, defiling a decent name without any rhyme or reason. It is easy to see what a catastrophic role such plague reactions play in social life.

I shall cite another example, one in which the projection mechanism of the emotional plague, in the form of a defamation, is even more clearly evident. Back in Norway, I heard that a rumor was going around to the effect that I had developed schizophrenia and had spent some time in a mental institution. When I came to the United States in 1939, I found that this rumor had become widespread in this country, even more so than in Europe, where my work was better known. It soon became evident that the rumor emanated from the same European source, a person who had since moved to America.[1]

The situation did not lack a certain irony: This person, shortly after my break with the Psychoanalytic Association, had suffered a nervous breakdown and had to spend some weeks in a mental institution. The accident of the nervous breakdown apparently gave the later rumor-monger quite a shock. At that time, he found himself in a difficult conflict: On the one hand, he realized the correctness of my scientific development; on the other hand, he was incapable of breaking with his organization which had come into sharp conflict with my development. As is apt to happen in such cases, he grasped the opportunity of diverting attention from himself to me, who at that time was in the center of dangerous and widespread polemics. He was convinced that I was hopelessly lost, and the temptation to give me an additional push was too great. His reaction was a projection according to the specific pattern of the emotional plague. *I had never been psychotic or in a mental institution.* Rather, I have carried the heaviest burden to this day without disturbances of my capacity for work and for love.

After all, a mental disease is not in itself a disgrace. Like any decent psychiatrist, I have deep sympathy for mental patients and often even admiration for their conflicts. A mental patient is much more serious, much closer to living functioning, than a Babbitt or a socially dangerous plague-ridden individual. This

---

1 One of our prominent physicians returned from Oslo to the U.S.A. in 1939. He spent a few days in Zürich where he told a former psychiatric colleague that he had been working with me. Much surprised, he said: "But So-and-So said Reich had become schizophrenic." "So-and-So" was the person in question. Soon after his return to the States, he learned from an acquaintance that his analyst had told him the same thing: "So-and-So [again the same person] told me Reich was schizophrenic." This rumor-monger died a few years later from heart failure. I had known for a long time that he suffered from impotence.

defamation was intended to ruin me and my work. It led to some dangerous and difficult situations. For example, in many students I had at that time the additional task of convincing them that I was *not* psychotic. In certain phases of orgone therapy, a specific mechanism of the emotional plague makes its appearance in a typical manner: As soon as the patient or student comes in contact with his plasmatic currents, he develops severe orgasm anxiety. In this phase, the orgone therapist is considered a "dirty, sexual swine" or as "crazy." I emphasize the fact that this reaction occurs in *all* cases. Now, most of the students had heard of the rumor in question. The theory of sex-economy is in many ways so revolutionary that it is very easy to call it "crazy." It must be said that, as a result of this rumor, complicated situations became such as to be a danger to life. Such consequences of a plague reaction should be made impossible by all available legal means. I owe it only to my clinical experience that I was able to master the dangers resulting from this rumor.

When, a few years later, it was talked about that my scientific work was incompatible with the diagnosis of schizophrenia, our rumor-monger altered his statement in an almost humorous manner. Now he said that I had "recovered" from my schizophrenic disease.

The specific reactions of the emotional plague are seen with particular frequency in political life. In recent history, we have seen again and again how imperialistic dictatorships, with every new act of aggression, ascribe to their victim the very intention which they had themselves and which they proceeded to put into action. Thus, Poland was accused of secretly planning to attack the German Reich, that one had to anticipate such an action and thus was justified in attacking Poland, etc.

If we go back only a few decades in the history of politics we find the famous Dreyfus case: High members of the French General Staff had sold plans to the Germans; in order to cover themselves, they accused Dreyfus, an innocent and decent captain, of their very crime, and succeeded in having him banned to a far island. Without the courageous action of Zola, this specific plague reaction would not even have been uncovered. If politics were not governed to such a far-reaching extent by the laws of the emotional plague, it would be a matter of course that such catastrophes could not happen at all. But since the emotional plague governs the formation of public opinion to a very great extent, it succeeds again and again in presenting its misdeeds as a regrettable miscarriage of justice, only to be able to continue its mischief.

If one takes the trouble of really studying the working of the emotional plague in high politics, one is hard put to it to believe in history. Is it possible, one must ask oneself, that the clericalism of a political dictator, or a love affair of a king, should be able to influence the weal and woe of several generations, of millions of people? Does irrationalism in social life really go that far? Is it really possible that millions of adult, industrious people do not know this, or even refuse to acknowledge it?

These questions seem peculiar only because the effects of the emotional plague are too fantastic to be felt really to exist. Human reasoning apparently refuses to admit that such nonsensicality should be prevailing. It is precisely the gigantic illogicality of such social conditions which safeguard their continued existence. I would like to ask the reader to take this contradiction between the *immensity* and the *incredibility* of the emotional plague as seriously as it deserves to be taken. I am deeply convinced that not one social evil of any dimension can be effaced from the earth as long as public consciousness refuses to accept the fact that this nonsensicality actually exists and that it is actually so gigantic that it is *not* seen. Compared with the immensity of the social nonsense which is constantly nourished by the well-rooted emotional plague, the basic social functions which govern the life process, *love, work, and knowledge,* appear dwarfish; more than that, they appear socially ridiculous. This is not difficult to see:

We know from extensive medical experience that the problem of adolescent sexuality, unsolved as it is, has a much more far-reaching effect on social life and moral ideologies than say, a tariff law. Let us imagine a parliamentarian, who happened to be a physician, suggesting to his government an extensive presentation and parliamentary discussion of the problem of puberty. Let us imagine, further, that this parliamentarian, after his suggestion was turned down, would use the method of filibuster. This illustration shows clearly the basic contradiction between everyday human life and the form of administration which governs it. If we consider the matter calmly and factually, we find that there would really be nothing extraordinary in a parliamentary discussion of the problem of puberty. Everyone, including every parliamentarian, has gone through the hell of sexual frustration in puberty. Nothing in life can compare in severity and significance with this conflict. It is a problem of general social interest. A rational solution of the puberty problem would, at one stroke, eliminate a number of social evils, such as adolescent criminality, the misery attending divorces, the misery governing early upbringing, etc. Thus, we will have to consider the demand of our hypothetical parliamentarian as completely rational and useful. But at the same time we will feel ourselves shrink from it. Something in us recoils from a public, parliamentary discussion of the puberty problem. This "something" is precisely the intention and the effect of the social emotional plague which strives constantly to preserve itself and its institutions. It has divided social life into a private and an official life. Private life is excluded from the public stage. Official life is asexual toward the outside, and pornographic or perverse inside. It would immediately be identical with the private life, and would correctly represent everyday life in large social forms if this chasm did not exist. This unification of life as it is lived and of social institutions would be simple and uncomplicated. But then that sector in the social structure would automatically disappear which not only does not contribute anything to the continuation of social life but which, periodically, and again and again, brings it to the verge of disaster. This sector is what is called "high politics," in all its aspects.

The maintenance of the chasm between the actual life of a social organism and its official façade is a violently defended intention of the emotional plague. This is why the emotional plague regularly becomes destructive when this chasm is approached in a factual and rational manner. Again and again, it was representatives of high politics who proceeded against a spreading of the sex-economic realization of the connection between the biological organism of the animal, man, and its state. This procedure, in its *mildest* form, is somewhat like this: "These 'sex philosophers' are immoral sores of the body social which continue to break open from time to time. Unfortunately, it is true that the animal, man, has a sexuality; it is a deplorable fact. For the rest, sexuality is not everything in life. There are other, more important questions, such as economics and politics. Sex-economy exaggerates. We would be much better off without it."

This argument is regularly met in the individual treatment of a biopathy or the training of a student. It is an unequivocal fact that this argument stems from orgasm anxiety and is made in an attempt to avoid having the resignation disturbed. Confronted with this same argument in a public meeting, say, one on mental hygiene, one cannot disarm the representative of cultural and other "values" by pointing to his personal armoring and pleasure anxiety. The sex-economist who did that would find that the meeting was *against him*, for its members have these character traits, and the irrational argument stemming from them, in common with the adversary. This is the point in the dispute at which many a physician or teacher has suffered shipwreck. But there is an irrefutable, purely logical argument which, according to our experience, is successful:

We agree with the adversary: It is perfectly true that sexuality is not everything in life. We can even add the further fact that in healthy individuals sexuality is not a subject for talk and not in the center of thinking. Why, then, we must ask, does sexuality— in spite of these facts—assume the central spot in the life and the thinking of people? Let us illustrate by an example:

It goes without saying that the circulation of the steam in a factory is the prerequisite of its functioning. Yet, the workers in this factory never give a thought to the circulation of the steam; they are completely concentrated on the manufacture of their product. The steam energy is indeed not "everything"; there are other, more important interests, such as the making of machines, etc. But let us assume that suddenly some valves in the circulation system get stuck: the circulation of the energy ceases, the machines stop, and with that, the work. Now, the workers' attention becomes centered exclusively on the disturbance of energy circulation, and on how it could be remedied. But what if some workers were to argue as follows: "This silly heat theory exaggerates the role of the steam. Yes, it is true that the steam is necessary, but, by golly, that is not everything. Don't you see that we have other interests, that there are economic factors to be considered?" In this case, these "wise guys" would simply be laughed at and one would first try to eliminate the disturbance in steam circulation before one would "think of other things."

In such a situation is the sexual problem in our society. The flow of biological energy, of sexual energy, is disturbed in the overwhelming majority of people. This is the reason why the biosocial mechanism of society does not function properly or does not function at all. This is why there is irrational politics, irresponsibility of the masses of people, biopathies, murder and manslaughter, in brief, the emotional plague. If all people were able to fulfil their natural sexual needs without disturbance, there would be no talk about the sexual problem. Then one would be justified in saying that "there are other interests."

The tremendous effort of sex-economy consists precisely in trying to help these so-called *"other"* things *get their proper due.* That today everything revolves around sexuality is the surest indication of a severe disturbance in the flow of sexual energy in man, and with that in his biosocial functioning. Sex-economy strives to unlock the valves of the biological energy flow so that, as a result, "other" important things, such as clear thinking, natural decency, and joyful work, can function, so that, in other words, sexuality, in its prevailing pornographic form, ceases to comprise *all* thinking as it does today.

The disturbance of energy flow, as just described, acts deep down at the basis of biosocial functioning and thus governs all functions of man. I doubt that the basically biological character of this disturbance has been comprehended even by some orgone therapists in its full measure and depth. Let us study this depth, and the relationship of orgonomy to other natural sciences, by way of the following example:

Let us compare the natural sciences which leave out of consideration the basic biological disturbance which we just described to a group of railroad construction engineers: These engineers write thousands of books, all of them most exact, about the size and material of doors and windows, seats, etc.; about the chemical constitution of the steel and wood, the strength of the brakes; about speeds, arrangement of stations, etc. Let us assume that, in a typical manner, they regularly leave out *one* definite thing: they leave out the steam energy and its functioning. The natural sciences do not know the functional exploration of living functioning. They can be compared, therefore, to these engineers. The orgonomist cannot do his work unless he comprehends fully that he is the *engineer of the life apparatus*. It is not of our doing that, as engineers of the life apparatus, we have to deal first of all with biosexual energy. Nor is there any reason why this fact should make us feel inferior. On the contrary: we have every reason to be proud of our hard work.

One will ask how it was possible that the raging of such a plague could be overlooked so thoroughly and for such a long time. The point is that this obscurity is part of the essence of the emotional plague. The impossibility of seeing it and seeing through it is the intention and success of the plague. As I have said before, the immensity of the pandemic was too obvious to be remarkable (Hitler: "The bigger the lie, the more readily is it believed"). Before the development of orgonomy, there was no scientific method for the discovery and understanding of the emotional plague. Politics not only appeared to have its own kind of reason; not only did nobody have an inkling of the irrational character of the political plague; the plague even had at its disposal the most important social means of preventing a recognition of its nature.

In every case of treating a biopathy or of changing the character structure of a physician or teacher we run into the emotional plague in the form of characterological resistance reactions. In this way, we learn to know it clinically. Clinical experience fully justifies our contention that there is no human being which the emotional plague has left undamaged.

Another way in which we become acquainted with the emotional plague is the reaction to the scientific discoveries of orgonomy. The bearers of the emotional plague may not be at all affected directly by the effects of our scientific work; they may be quite unacquainted with it; yet, they have sensed the disclosure of the emotional plague as it took place in the studies of the character-analysts and later orgone therapists and felt it to be a threat. To this, they reacted with the means of defamation and the specific plague reaction, long before any of us were aware of the fact that we were entering upon the hardest struggle in which physicians and teachers had ever engaged. By well-disguised and rationalized actions, the plague knew how to prevent its unmasking. It behaved like a criminal in dinner dress whose mask is torn from his face. For more than a decade, it was successful; it almost succeeded in securing its continued existence for centuries more. It would have succeeded if it had not made its appearance, in an all too disastrous and often revealing manner, in the form of dictatorships and mass infections. It stirred up a war of undreamed-of proportions, adding it to chronic, everyday murder. It tried to hide behind the "interests of the state," behind "New Orders," and the "demands of the state or race." For years, a psychically sick world gave it credence. But it betrayed itself too thoroughly. It has come in conflict with the natural feeling for life in all people; for there is no family or profession which it left untouched. That which the orgone therapist had learned to comprehend and to master in his study suddenly converged into *one* with the manifestations of the world catastrophe. The basic traits were the same on the large scale as on the small one. In this manner, the emotional plague itself came to the aid of natural science, of a few psychiatrists and educators. The world has begun to ask about the nature of the emotional plague and expects an answer. It is being given to our best knowledge. Every conscientious person will discover the emotional plague in himself and thus will begin to understand what it is that again and again brings the world to the verge of disaster. The "New Order," as always, has to begin in one's own house.

The disclosure of these hidden activities and mechanisms of a distorted life has two aims: First, the fulfilment of a duty toward society; if, in the case of a fire, the water supply fails and there is someone who knows the location of the trouble, it is his duty to name it. Second, the future of sex-economy and orgone bio-physics has to be protected against the emotional plague. One is almost inclined to feel grateful to those who, in 1930 in Austria, in 1932 and 1933 in Germany, in 1933 in Denmark, in 1934 in Luzern, in 1934 and 1935 in Denmark and Sweden, in 1937 and 1938 in Norway and in 1947 in the U. S. A., ganged up on honest but guileless work on the human structure; grateful for having done away with such guilelessness and having opened one's eyes to a socially dangerous, though pathological, system of defamation and persecution. If a burglar goes too far and becomes careless, he risks being caught and put out of commission. About 10 years ago, the bearers and spreaders of the emotional plague still felt secure. They were sure of their victory and, in fact, it looked for years as if they were going to succeed. Only great perseverance, deep roots in natural-scientific work, and independence of public opinion, prevented their success. The emotional plague has never rested until it had annihilated great achievements, the fruits of human industry and search for truth I do not think that it has succeeded this time, or that it will succeed. It is the first time that the emotional plague has met not merely with decent sentiments but with the necessary knowledge of life processes, processes which, to an increasing degree, prove their superior strength. It was the strength and the consistency of orgonomic natural science which made it possible for me to recover from the heavy and dangerous blows from the emotional plague. If that was possible, then the greatest difficulty seems overcome.

With regard to my person and my work, I would like to ask the reader to consider a simple fact: neurotic psychoanalysts call me schizophrenic; fascist Communists fight me as a Trotskyite; sexually lascivious persons accused me of keeping a brothel; the

German secret police pursued me as a Bolshevik, the American secret police as a Nazi spy; domineering mothers wanted me to be known as a seducer of children; charlatans in psychiatry called me a charlatan; future saviors of the world called me a new Jesus or Lenin. All this may have been flattering or not. In addition, as I have shown, I am engaged in other work which takes up all available time and strength: the work on the irrational human structure and on the study of the cosmic life energy discovered many years ago; in brief, my work in orgonomy.

Great writers and poets have described and fought the emotional plague ever since it has been raging. However, these great literary achievements *have remained, on the whole, without social effects.* They were neither organized nor have social administrations made them the basis for life-furthering institutions. True, monuments were erected for these masters of literature, but it looks all too often as if the emotional plague had succeeded in building a gigantic museum in which all achievements were locked up, hidden by false admiration; achievements which, each by itself, had been sufficient to build a reasonable world if they had been taken seriously in a practical manner. Thus, I am far from being the first who tried to comprehend and fight the emotional plague. I only believe myself to be the first worker in natural science who, by the discovery of the orgone, provided a solid scientific basis on which the emotional plague can be *understood* and *mastered.*

Today, five, eight, ten and fourteen years after different unexpected and incomprehensible catastrophes, my standpoint is the following: *Just as the bacteriologist sees his lifework in the elimination of infectious diseases, so is it the task of the medical orgonomist to disclose the nature of the emotional plague and to fight it as a ubiquitous disease.* The world will become accustomed to this new field of medical work. One will learn to comprehend the emotional plague in oneself and outside one, and will appeal to scientific centers instead of the police, the district attorney or the party leader. The police and the district attorneys too, and even saviors, have an interest in mastering the emotional plague in themselves and outside of themselves. For the police and the district attorney deal with biopathic criminality, and the savior with the helplessness and the mass biopathies of humanity. We consider it a crucial criterion whether somebody in his dealings with us uses the means of defamation and persecution, or whether he uses the means of scientific discussion. This shows who is plague-ridden and who is not.

I believe the time has come when the helplessness in the face of the emotional plague begins to pass. Up until now, one experienced its attacks as one experiences the falling of a tree or the falling of a stone from a roof: such things, one says, happen; either one is lucky and does not get hit, or one is unlucky and gets killed or maimed. Now we know that the tree does not fall by accident and the stone does not fall harmlessly. We know that in either case some disturbed human, keeping himself hidden, causes the falling of the tree or the stone. From that, everything else follows by itself.

If, then, some physician causes a suit to be brought against some orgonomist because of this or that "illegal activity"; if a politician reports an orgonomist to the police because of "income tax fraud," or "seduction of children," or "espionage," or "Trotskyism"; if we hear rumors that this or that orgonomist is psychotic, that he seduces his patients, that he keeps a brothel, etc., then we know that we are dealing with the emotional plague and not with scientific discussion. The Orgone Institute, with its training requirements, and the demands of our daily work are a guarantee to the community that it is precisely we who wage a vigorous fight against these basic traits of the emotional plague.

We cannot believe in a satisfactory human existence as long as biology, psychiatry and pedagogy do not come to grips with the universal emotional plague and fight it as ruthlessly as one fights plague-transmitting rats. Extensive, painstaking and conscientious clinical investigation makes unequivocally clear the fact that *one thing alone, the re-establishment of the natural love life of children, adolescents and adults can eliminate from the world the character neuroses, and with the character neuroses the emotional plague in its various forms.*

CHAPTER XIII

# A NOTE ON THE BASIC CONFLICT
# BETWEEN NEED AND OUTER WORLD*

In order to be able to evaluate the theoretical significance of our clinical presentations we have to consider some questions of the theory of instincts. Clinical experience provided ample proof for the correctness of Freud's assumption of a fundamental dualism in the psychic apparatus, but it also showed some contradictions in it. In the present clinical presentation, the problem of the relationships between instinct and outer world cannot be dealt with extensively. A few words must be said about it, both to give the present work a theoretical conclusion and as a counterweight against the over-biologization of analytic psychology.

In Freud's theory of the instincts there are a series of pairs of antithetical instincts and, generally, the assumption of antithetical tendencies in the psychic apparatus. With the formulation of psychic tendencies which, though antithetical, nevertheless belong together, Freud, for the first time, although unconsciously, laid the foundation for a future functional psychology. Originally, the instinct for self-preservation (hunger) was contrasted to the sexual instinct (eros). Later, the destructive instinct, the death instinct, came to be considered the counterpart of sexuality. Originally, analytic psychology started from the antithesis between *ego* and *outer world*; to this corresponded the antithesis between *ego libido* and *object libido*. The antithesis between *sexuality* and *anxiety* was not thought of as the basic antithesis of the psychic apparatus; it played, nevertheless, a fundamental role in the explanation of neurotic anxiety. According to the original concept, libido, when barred from motility and consciousness, is converted into anxiety. Later, and I believe, quite unjustifiedly,

---

* (1948): The discovery of the organismic orgone energy will force a re-evaluation of our concepts of the "instincts"; they are concrete PHYSICAL ENERGY functions.

Freud gave up this close connection between sexuality and anxiety.[1] It can be shown that these various antitheses do not co-exist in a haphazard manner; rather, they derive from each other according to definite laws. It is a matter of comprehending which is the basic antithesis and which influences bring about the development of the further antitheses.

Every analysis which goes deep enough shows that the basis of all reactions is not the antithesis love and hatred, nor that of eros and death instinct, but the antithesis of *ego* ("person"; id = pleasure ego) and *outer world*. From the biopsychic unit of the personality derives at first only one striving: that of eliminating inner tensions, be they in the sphere of hunger or that of sexuality. Either is impossible without contact with the outer world. Consequently, the *first* striving of *any* living organism will be a striving for contact with the outer world. Psychoanalysis assumes that hunger and libidinal need are antithetical and yet at the beginning interlaced since it is the libidinal stimulation of the mouth zone, the pleasure in sucking, which induces food intake. This concept leads to surprising consequences if one applies to these questions the concepts of the biologist Hartmann concerning the function of surface tension in the organs. Assuming the correctness of Hartmann's theory which in certain aspects is confirmed by the findings of Kraus and Zondek, psychic energy must derive from simple physiological and mechanical surface tensions which are formed in the various tissues, particularly the vegetative system and the blood and lymph system. The disturbance of the physiochemical equilibrium produced by these tensions, then, would be the motor power behind action and, in the last analysis, also, behind thinking. These disturbances of the osmotic equilibrium of the organ tissues are of two kinds: one is a shrinking of the tissues due to loss of tissue fluid, the other an expansion of the tissues due to an increase in fluid content. In either case there is unpleasure. In the first case, however, the unpleasurable sensation corresponds to a decrease in surface tension which can be eliminated only by the taking up of new substances. In the second case, on the other hand, the unpleasure corresponds to a real *tension*; this can be eliminated only by a *relaxation*, that is, an

---

[1] *Cf.* Freud, "Hemmung, Symptom und Angst," Ges. Schr., Bd. XI.

*elimination* of substances. Only the latter case provides actual pleasure; in the first case it is only a matter of the elimination of unpleasure.

In either case there is an "instinct"; in the first we recognize hunger and thirst, in the second the prototype of the orgastic discharge which is characteristic of all sexual tensions. A protozoon must move plasma from the center to the periphery, that is, increase the tension at the periphery when it wants to take up food, that is, to eliminate a negative pressure in the center. In our language: it must, with the aid of a libidinal mechanism, approach the outer world in order to eliminate its "negative pressure," that is, hunger. Growth, copulation and cell division are determined by the libidinal function of peripheral tension with consecutive relaxation, in other words, decrease in surface tension. That is, the sexual energy is always in the service of the gratification of the hunger need, while, conversely, the taking up of nourishment introduces the substances which finally, by way of a physiochemical process, lead to libidinal tensions. Food intake is the basis of existence and of the libidinal functions; the latter, in turn, are the basis of productive achievement, beginning with the most primitive one, locomotion. These biophysiological facts are fully confirmed in the higher organization of the psychic apparatus: hunger cannot be sublimated, while the sexual energy is alterable, and productive. This is based on the fact that in the case of hunger there is no production of pleasure, but only the elimination of a negative condition; in the case of the sexual need, there is a discharge, that is, a production in its simplest form. In addition, the relaxation provides pleasure which —according to a law as yet not understood—makes the organism repeat the action; this repetition is probably an essential aspect of the problem of memory. Hunger, then, is a sign that an energy *loss* has taken place; the gratification of the hunger need does not produce an energy which would manifest itself as achievement (expenditure of energy); it is merely the elimination of a lack. As obscure as this fact is, the empirical psychoanalytic thesis that achievement in work is a process of libidinal energy, that, further, disturbances of working ability are closely connected with disturbances in the libido economy, seems to be based on this difference of the two basic biological needs.

But to return to the oppositeness of the drives. They are not originally part of the biopsychic unit, but one opposite part is represented by the outer world. Is this in conflict with Freud's assumption of an *inner* oppositeness of the drives? Obviously not. The question is only whether the inner antithesis, the inner dualism, is a biologically given fact or whether it develops secondarily, as a result of the conflict with the outer world; further, whether the first conflict within the personality is one between drives or something else. Let us examine ambivalence.

"Ambivalence" in the sense of co-existing reactions of love and hatred is not a biological but a socially conditioned fact. In the anlage there is only the ability of the biopsychic apparatus to react to the outer world in a manner which may—but must not necessarily—become chronic and which we term ambivalence. Only in a superficial layer does this phenomenon mean an oscillation between hatred and love. In a deeper layer, which corresponds to an earlier stage of development, such signs of ambivalence as hesitation and indecision are to be understood as signs of a libidinal striving which urges for expression but which again and again is inhibited by fear of punishment. Very often, in the compulsive character always, the love impulse is replaced by hatred which, in the depth, continues to strive for the unattainable love goal and which is also inhibited by anxiety. Thus, ambivalence means three different things, according to its genesis and the depth at which it functions:

1. "I love you, but I am afraid of being punished for it" (*Love—fear*).

2. "I hate you because I am not allowed to love you, but I am afraid of expressing the hatred" (*Hatred—fear*).

3. "I don't know whether I love you or hate you" (*Love—hatred*).

Thus, we arrive at the following picture of the genesis of the psychic contradictions:

First we have the antithesis ego—outer world which we find later as the antithesis *narcissism—object libido*. This is the basis of the first antithesis *within* the person in the form of the antithesis between *libido* (movement toward the outer world) and *anxiety* which represents the first and basic narcissistic flight from the unpleasure of the outer world back into the ego. The sending out and retracting of pseudopodia in the protozoon is much more than a mere analogy for the sending out and retracting of "libido." Unpleasure created by the outer world leads to a retraction of the libido or anxious flight toward the inside (narcissistic flight); the unpleasurable tension created by the ungratified needs, on the other hand, leads to a stretching out toward the world. If the outer world provided nothing but pleasure and gratification there would be no anxiety. Since, however, it provides unpleasure and danger, the striving of the object libido is complemented by its counterpart, the tendency to narcissistic flight. The most primitive expression of this narcissistic flight is anxiety. Libidinous approach to the world and narcissistic flight from it are only the expression of a very primitive function which exists in all living organisms without exception. In the protozoon, it is present in the form of two opposite directions of plasma current, one from the center to the periphery, the other from the periphery to the center.[2] The pallor in fright, the trembling in an anxiety state correspond to a flight of the cathexes from the body periphery to the center, caused by the contraction of the peripheral vessels and dilatation of the central vessels (stasis anxiety). The turgor, the color and warmth of the peripheral tissues, the skin, in sexual excitation are the exact opposite of the anxiety state and correspond, psychically as well as physiologically, to a movement of the energy in the direction from the center to the body periphery and, with that, toward the world. The erection of the penis and the becoming moist of the vagina are nothing but the expression of this direction of the energy in a state of sexual excitation; the shrinking of the penis and the becoming dry of the vagina, conversely, are nothing but the expression of the opposite direction of the cathexes and the body fluids from the periphery to the center.

---

[2] According to Weber, sensations of unpleasure go with a centripetal, sensations of pleasure with a centrifugal movement of the body fluids. *Cf.* also Kraus, Fr., Syzygiologie. Allgemeine und spezielle Pathologie der Person, 1926.

The first antithesis between *sexual excitation* and *anxiety* is only the intrapsychic reflection of the basic antithesis between individual and outer world which then becomes the psychic reality of the inner conflict, "I wish—I am afraid." Anxiety, then, is always the first expression of an inner tension, no matter whether this is caused by a frustration of gratification from the outside or a flight of the energy cathexes to the center of the organism. In the former case we are dealing with stasis anxiety ("actual anxiety"), in the latter case with "real anxiety," which also leads to stasis and with that to anxiety. That is, both forms of anxiety (stasis anxiety and real anxiety) rest on one and the same basic phenomenon: central stasis of energy. The difference is that stasis anxiety is the immediate expression of the stasis while real anxiety, to begin with, means only the expectation of a danger; it becomes affective anxiety secondarily when the flight of cathexes to the center produces a stasis in the central vegetative apparatus. The original flight reaction of "crawling-back-into-the-self" later takes the form of a phylogenetically younger form of flight which consists in increasing the distance from the source of danger; it depends on the development of a locomotor system (muscular flight).

In addition to the flight into the own body center and the muscular flight there is, on a higher plane of biological organization, another meaningful reaction: the elimination of the source of danger. This can take no other form than that of a *destructive impulse*.[3] Its basis is the avoidance of the stasis or anxiety which develops with narcissistic flight; it is, fundamentally, nothing but a special mode of avoiding or eliminating tension. On this level of development, the striving toward the world may be of two kinds: either for the satisfaction of a need (libido) or the avoidance of an anxiety state by destruction of the source of danger

---

[3] One might see a destructive tendency in the processes of gratifying hunger, in the destruction and incorporation of the food. In that case, the destructive impulse would be a *primary* biological tendency. However, one has to distinguish between destruction for the sake of destruction and destruction for the purpose of stilling hunger. Only the former can be considered an instinctive drive as such, while the latter constitutes only a means to an end. In the former case, destruction is *subjectively* desired, in the latter case it is only an objective fact. The motive behind the action is hunger, not destruction.

(destruction). On the basis of the first antithesis of libido and anxiety there arises another, that between libido ("love") and destruction ("hatred"). Every frustration of an instinctual gratification may call into play either the first counterpart of the libido, anxiety, or, for the purpose of avoiding the anxiety, the genetically younger impulse, the destructive impulse. There are two character forms which correspond to these two modes of reaction: the hysterical character takes flight from the danger, the compulsive character wants to destroy the source of danger. The masochistic character lacks the genital object libido as well as the direct destructive impulse for the elimination of the source of danger. For this reason, he must try to relieve his inner tension by an indirect approach, by a disguised demand on the object for love, for some kind of relief from libidinal tension. Understandably enough, these attempts are always doomed to failure.

The function of the second pair of antithetical impulses—libido and destruction—undergoes a new change as a result of the fact that the outer world denies not only libidinal gratification but also the gratification of the destructive impulse. As a result of threatened punishment, every destructive impulse becomes anxiety-laden, which again increases the tendency to narcissistic flight. There develops a fourth antithesis, that between *destruction* and *anxiety*. Though this is entirely at the surface of the personality, Adler's individual psychology has never gone beyond it. The process of the formation of new antithetical strivings, as they result from the conflicts between previous strivings and the outer world, continues. On the one hand, every frustration of a libidinal striving brings forth destructive impulses; these can easily turn into sadism, which combines in itself both the destructive and the libidinal striving. On the other hand, the destructive impulses are strengthened by the great tendency to anxiety and the attempts to relieve anxiety-creating tensions in a destructive manner. Since, however, each of these newly developing strivings provokes the punitive attitude of the outer world, there develops a vicious circle, beginning with the first anxiety-creating frustration of a libidinal impulse. The inhibition of the destructive impulses by the threatening outer world not only increases anxiety and makes the discharge of the libido even more difficult than before; in addition, it creates a new antithesis. The destructive impulses toward the world are more or less turned toward the self, thus adding the counterparts of *self-destruction* to the destructive impulse and *masochism* to sadism.

The guilt feeling in this connection is a late production, the result of a conflict between love and hatred toward the same object. Dynamically, it corresponds to the intensity of the inhibited aggression, which is the same as the intensity of the inhibiting anxiety.

This derivation of a total picture of the psychic processes from clinical experience shows the following: 1. Masochism is a very late product of development. It is rarely seen before the third or fourth year of life; for this reason alone, it cannot be the expression of a primary biological impulse. 2. All those phenomena from which one might deduce the existence of a death instinct are shown to be signs and results of a *narcissistic* (not muscular) flight from the world: Self-damaging impulses are a result of destruction turned back on the self; physical deterioration as a result of chronic neurotic processes are shown to be due to the chronic disturbance of the sexual economy, the chronic effect of unrelieved inner tensions which, as we know, have a physiological basis; it is the result of chronic psychic suffering which has an objective basis but which is not subjectively desired; conscious longing for death, for non-existence ("Nirvana") occurs only under the conditions of genital frustration and hopelessness; it is nothing but the ultimate expression of resignation, the flight from a reality which has become exclusively unpleasurable, into nothingness; this nothingness, due to the primacy of the libido, is thought of in terms of *another kind of libidinal gratification,* such as being in mother's womb, or being taken care of and protected by mother. Every retraction of the libido from the outer world into the ego, that is, every phenomenon of narcissistic regression, was adduced as proof for the existence of the death instinct. In reality, they are nothing but reactions to actual frustrations of the gratification of hunger or libidinal needs by the

outer world. If this reaction is fully developed even in the absence
of actual frustration from the outer world, analysis shows that
it was *early infantile* frustrations of the libido which necessitated
a flight from the world into the ego and created a psychic structure which, later on, makes a person incapable of making use
of the pleasure possibilities which the world may present. It
is precisely melancholia, so often cited as proof for the existence
of the death instinct, which shows that the suicidal impulses are
secondary. They are a superstructure first, on an orality which
had been frustrated and, as a result of a completely inhibited
genital function, had become a fixation point, and second, on a
destructive impulse which, inhibited and turned back on the self,
can find no other way of expression than that of self-destruction.
If a person destroys himself, then, he does so not because he has
a biological urge to do so, not because he "wants to," but because reality has created inner tensions which have become
intolerable and can be relieved only by self-destruction. Just as
the outer world became an exclusively unpleasurable external
reality, so did the instinctual apparatus become an exclusively
unpleasurable internal reality. Since, however, the ultimate motive power of life is tension with the prospect of relaxation, that
is, pleasure, an organism which is deprived of these possibilities
both internally and externally will wish to cease living. Self-
destruction becomes the last and only possibility of relaxation.
Thus we can say that even in the will to die the pleasure-unpleas-
ure principle expresses itself.

Every other concept neglects basic clinical findings, avoids the
problem of the real structure of our world which leads of necessity
to a criticism of our social order, and gives up the best oppor-
tunities for therapeutic help. This can consist only in helping the
patient analytically to overcome his fear of the punishments from
the outer world and to relieve his tensions in the only way which
is biologically and sex-economically sound, that of orgastic gratification.

The clinical findings in masochism make the assumption of a
primary need for punishment superfluous. If it does not apply in
masochism it could hardly be found in any other form of disease.

The suffering is real, objective, and not subjectively desired; self-degradation is a mechanism of protection against genital castration; self-damaging acts are the anticipation of milder punishments as a protection against the punishment which is really feared; the phantasies of being beaten are the only remaining possibilities of relaxation without guilt. The original genetic formula of the neurosis is still correct: the neurosis develops from a conflict between sexual drive and fear of actual punishment at the hands of an authoritarian society. Adherence to this formula leads to different conclusions than does the adherence to a death instinct. If the suffering is caused by society we must ask why that is so, what interest society has in inflicting it. According to Freud's formula, frustration comes from the outer world. This simple fact has been obliterated to a considerable degree by the hypothesis of the death instinct. This is shown, for example, in the following formulation of Benedek's: "If we accept the dualistic theory of the instincts only in the sense of the old theory of the instincts, we find a gap. Then the question remains unanswered why mechanisms have developed in the human organism which constitute an antithesis to sexuality." Thus, the hypothesis of the death instinct makes one forget completely that the "inner mechanisms" which constitute an antithesis to sexuality are moral inhibitions which represent the prohibitions imposed by the outer world, by society. The death instinct, then, is supposed to explain, biologically, facts which, if one continues to adhere to the old theory, derive from the structure of present-day society. It remains to be shown that the "unmastered destructive impulses" to which human suffering is ascribed are not of a biological nature but are socially conditioned; that it is the inhibition of sexuality by authoritarian education which makes aggression a power beyond mastery, because inhibited sexual energy turns into destructive energy. Those aspects of our cultural life which look like self-destruction, finally, are not the manifestation of any "impulses to self-destruction," but the expression of very real destructive intentions on the part of an authoritarian society interested in the suppression of sexuality.

# PART THREE

# FROM PSYCHOANALYSIS TO ORGONE BIOPHYSICS

## Chapter XIV

# PSYCHIC CONTACT AND VEGETATIVE CURRENT

### PREFACE

This monograph is an expansion of a paper read at the 13th International Psychoanalytic Congress in Lucerne, August, 1934. It continues the discussion of the character-analytic problems outlined in my book, CHARAKTERANALYSE, published in 1933. It deals essentially with two problems which were not discussed there: *psychic contactlessness* and the mechanisms of *substitute contact;* and the *antithetical unity of the vegetative and psychic manifestations of affect life.* As far as the latter problem is concerned, it continues my articles, "Der Urgegensatz des vegetativen Lebens" and "Die vegetative Urform des Libido-Angst-Gegensatzes" (*Zeitschr.f.polit.Psychol.u.Sexualökonomie,* 1934).

This monograph presents again only a small, though clinically well substantiated advance into the obscure problems of the relationships between psyche and soma. The application of the technique of character-analysis will enable anyone to check on these findings, once he has overcome the initial technical difficulties.

A discussion of the literature concerning the problem of "totality" and the unity of psychic and somatic functions was purposely avoided. Sex-economy approaches the problem from a customarily neglected manifestation, *the orgasm,* and applies the method of functionalism. A critical discussion of the literature, therefore, would be premature. It would presuppose a certain completion of my own concepts as well as a definite point of view on the orgasm problem on the part of the other authors. Both are as yet lacking.

The clinical refutation of Freud's theory of the death instinct has remained valid. More deep-reaching analyses of the so-called striving for the Nirvana have confirmed my view that this theory attempted an explanation of certain facts which cannot yet be given, and that, furthermore, this attempt was misleading.

Perhaps this essay will, better than previous ones, provide to the psychoanalysts with a functional orientation and to the young sex-economists and character-analysts some theoretical clarity and some practical help in the application of character-analytic technique. The discovery of contactlessness and fear of contact has given a new impetus to the character-analytic concept and technique. It may be that these presentations may soon prove incomplete or partially incorrect. This would only prove that one can keep pace with the development of a new concept only by living practice. Those who seriously strive to learn the character-analytic technique will not find it difficult to recognize and practically utilize the connections between psychic contact and vegetative excitability which are here presented for the first time. These connections will not only help to take our psychotherapeutic work out of the mystical atmosphere of present-day psychotherapy but will also make possible results which hitherto were unattainable. At the same time, I must warn against too great a therapeutic enthusiasm. The superiority of character-analysis can no longer be doubted. On the other hand, the terminal stages of character-analytic therapy, in particular the reactivation of orgastic contact anxiety and its elimination, are not yet sufficiently studied. Also, the orgasm theory is often grossly misunderstood, even among its friends. The most common misunderstanding is due to the ignorance of the uninhibited involuntariness of the orgastic surrender which is often confused with *pre*-orgastic excitation. It must be said that successful termination of a character-analysis, without clarity in the orgasm problem, can be due only to chance.

With the reading of the paper which forms the basis of this essay at the last Psychoanalytic Congress my membership in the International Psychoanalytic Association came to an end. Its leadership no longer wished to identify itself with my concepts.

*February, 1935.*                                            W. R.

## 1. THE STARTING-POINT: CONFLICT BETWEEN INSTINCT AND OUTER WORLD

I will have to recall first the *older* psychoanalytic views which form the starting-point of my own work. Without a knowledge of this starting-point, an understanding of the results of character-analytic investigation is impossible.

The earliest psychoanalytic concepts derived from the conflict between *instinct* and *outer world*. The complete obfuscation of this basic concept by present-day theories does not alter the fact that it is correct, that it is unmistakably tangible to every clinician in every case, and that it is the most fruitful formulation of all analytic psychology. In the light of this concept, the psychic process is the result of a conflict between instinctual demand and external instinctual frustration; from this conflict develops, only secondarily, an inner conflict between wish and self-denial. This self-denial is the core of what is called "inner morality." It is important to keep in mind what basic theoretical concepts derive from this formula about the psychic conflict. If one inquires into the origin of instinctual frustration, one goes beyond the confines of psychology; one enters the field of sociology and deals with problems basically different from those of psychology. The question as to why society demands the suppression of the instincts can no longer be answered psychologically. It is *social,* more strictly, economic interests which cause this phenomenon.[1] Political psychology—the reproach of my opponents that I mix politics with science notwithstanding—begins precisely with this strictly scientific question.

When an adolescent learns that the suppression of his natural sexual strivings is due not to biological factors, say, a death instinct, but, rather, to definite interests of present-day society; that, further, parents and teachers are only unconscious executive organs of this social power, then he will not consider this merely a highly interesting scientific thesis, but he will begin to comprehend his misery, will deny its divine origin and begin to rebel against his parents and the powers whom they represent. Perhaps

[1] *Cf.* my book, DER EINBRUCH DER SEXUALMORAL.

for the first time, he will begin to use his critical faculties and to think about things. This is one of the many consequences which comprise what I have called sex politics.

It is the social, that is, political practice which results from the realization of the *social* origin of sexual repression. At the 13th Congress, Bernfeld expressed the view that adolescent sexual intercourse was due to poor educational conditions. Such a concept will only confirm the adolescent's neurotic guilt feelings; in addition, it will only confuse the issue of puberty and will impede any positive sex-economic aid to adolescents. The question of puberty belongs entirely in the framework of the connections between vegetative excitation and psychic behavior, in spite of all the "objective scientific" ignoring of the fact that adolescent development is crucially determined by the social inhibition of adolescent sex life. For whether or not a sex-economic regulation of the vegetative energies is possible depends on the structure which society forms in the adolescent.

As we know, the ego has to mediate between such social influences which later become internalized as morality or inner instinct inhibition on the one hand, and biological needs on the other. If we continue the study of the psychic manifestations of the biological needs, the id phenomena, we arrive at problems of physiology and biology which are no more accessible to our psychological method of investigation than are the sociological problems. I see myself forced to recognize the limitations of the psychological method; my opponents, on the other hand, psychologize sociology as well as biology. After this, the reader may be surprised that my subject is precisely the investigation of the development of vegetative excitations from the character, that is, from psychic formations. He may ask whether I am not violating my own principle. We shall defer the answer to this question until later.

## 2. SOME TECHNICAL PREMISES

The connections between psychic apparatus and vegetative excitation cannot be understood unless one frees oneself, first of all, from a source of error inherent in our theoretical methods.

In our work, theory and practice are inseparable. *An erroneous theoretical position must create an incorrect technique, and an incorrect technique must lead to erroneous theoretical concepts.* If one looks for the sources from which the theory of the death instinct stemmed one finds, in addition to social reasons—which I discussed elsewhere—mainly technical reasons. Many participants of the Vienna Seminar for Psychoanalytic Therapy will remember how difficult was the theoretical and practical mastery of the problem of *latent negative transference.*

While the negative transference had been formulated theoretically by Freud long ago, it was not until the years between 1923 and 1930 that we learned to comprehend it practically. The clinical basis on which Freud constructed his theory of the death instinct was the so-called "negative therapeutic reaction." This term means that many patients react to our interpretation work not by getting better but, on the contrary, by an intensification of their neurotic reactions. Freud then assumed that this was the result of an unconscious guilt feeling or, as it came to be called, of a "need for punishment" which forces the patient to resist the analytic work and to retain his neurotic suffering. I confess that, during the first few years after the publication of DAS ICH UND DAS ES, I was of the same opinion and that only gradually did I begin to doubt the correctness of this formulation. The secret of the negative therapeutic reaction gradually revealed itself in the technical reports in the Seminar. They showed that the negative tendencies in the patients which corresponded to their repressed hatred were insufficiently, if at all, analyzed; that the analysts operated almost exclusively with positive manifestations of transference; that even the most experienced analysts were no exception in this; and that, most importantly, manifestations of latent, disguised and repressed hatred were usually mistaken for signs of positive transference. I did not arrive at a correct formulation of this fact until shortly before the meeting of the Scandinavian psychoanalysts in Oslo in 1934. Our analytic work liberates psychic energies which urge for a discharge. If one analyzes the transferences predominantly, exclusively, or from the very beginning as *positive* transferences, without *first* thoroughly uncovering the negative tendencies, the following will happen: The liberated love demands urge for gratification and meet frustration in the analysis, as well as the inner inhibitions formed by the repressed hate impulses toward the love object. In brief, one may believe to have "liberated" love impulses but will find that the patient continues to be incapable of loving.

Frustrated love turns into hatred. Unconscious hate impulses act like a magnet on this artificially produced hatred; the two combine; this secondary hatred becomes also unconscious and, since it has no discharge, *it turns into self-destructive impulses.* The need for punishment, then, which we find in our patients, is not the cause but a *result* of the neurotic conflict; and *the negative therapeutic reaction resulted from the fact that there was no adequate technique for dealing with the latent negative transference.* This is proved by the fact that a negative therapeutic reaction does not occur if one follows two rules: The first rule is that of crystallizing out, first of all, the secret negative attitude of the patient and of making it conscious; to secure discharge for all liberated aggression; to treat any masochistic tendency not as the expression of a primary instinct for self-destruction but as a masked aggression directed against objects in the outer world. The second rule is to leave positive manifestations of love alone until they either turn into hatred, that is, disappointment reactions, or until they finally become concentrated in ideas of genital incest. At this point an objection must be mentioned which was raised by Freud when I presented my early concepts of character-analytic technique, and which has since been repeated again and again by most of my colleagues. The objection is this: One should not make any selection, one should analyze everything in the order in which it comes up. The answer to this question was given in my book, CHARAKTERANALYSE and need not be repeated here. The objection leads, however, to a fundamental clarification of the theory underlying character-analytic technique. This I shall briefly summarize here.

It is the task of our technique to make the unconscious conscious. This is called interpretation work. It is determined by the *topical* standpoint. In this interpretation work, we have to take into consideration the fact that resistances are interpolated between the unconscious psychic material and our interpretations; these resistances must be eliminated if the interpretation is to have a therapeutic effect. This is the *dynamic* view of the psychic process. Experiences in control analyses and in the technical seminar make it clear that, while both these views are theoretically known to the analysts, they usually proceed according to the topical viewpoint alone. This is expressed in pure form in Stekel's and Rank's concept of analytic technique. We have to admit, however, that all of us more or less in the past neglected the dynamic view in our practical work, simply because we did not know how to handle it.

Character-analytic work adds to the topical and the dynamic the *structural* and *economic* point of view. To me at least, this inclusion of the totality of our concepts of the psychic process in practical work has had even more far-reaching consequences in practice than the earlier shift from direct interpretation of unconscious contents to resistance technique. If one includes the structural and economic viewpoints, the concept that one should analyze what happens to come to the surface becomes untenable.

The material presented even during one session is manifold; it derives from different psychic layers as well as from different stages of development. Sex-economic considerations force us to stick to a strictly prescribed path which begins with the dissolution of the pregenital and negative attitudes and ends with the concentration of all the liberated psychic energy at the genital apparatus. The establishment of orgastic potency is the most important goal of therapy. Also economically determined is the fact that the repressed affects are to be found mostly in the various forms of behavior; they must be crystallized out by consistent analysis of the behavior and again be connected with the infantile ideas.

*Character-analysis, then, proceeds according to a definite plan which is determined by the structure of the individual case.* Correctly carried out character-analyses, in spite of all the infinite variation in contents, conflicts and structure, present the following typical phases:

a) Character-analytic loosening of the armor;

b) Breaking down of the character armor, that is, definite destruction of the neurotic equilibrium;

c) Breaking through of deeply repressed and strongly affect-charged material, with reactivation of the infantile hysteria;

d) Working through of the liberated material without resistance; crystallizing out of the libido from pregenital fixations;

e) Reactivation of infantile genital anxiety (stasis neurosis) and of genitality;

f) Appearance of orgasm anxiety and establishment of orgastic potency which is the prerequisite of full functioning.

Although today the establishment of genitality already seems a matter of course to many analysts, orgastic potency is still unknown and unrecognized. Until 1923 the only recognized goals of therapy were "condemnation of the instincts" and sublimation. Impotence and frigidity were not considered the specific symptoms of the neurosis but were considered one symptom among many others, symptoms which might be present or absent. True, one knew that there is an orgasm but the contention was made that there were any number of severe neuroses with "completely undisturbed orgasm." The neuroses were considered the expression of a sexual disturbance in general, while sex-economic findings show that neuroses are not possible without a disturbance of genitality and that their cure is not possible without the elimination of this disturbance. Freud, Sachs, Nunberg, Deutsch, Alexander and most other analysts refused to accept my concept of the psycho-economic and therapeutic significance of genitality. Freud's INTRODUCTORY LECTURES ON PSYCHOANALYSIS, published as late as 1933, do not even mention the problem of the genital orgasm; nor does Nunberg's NEUROSENLEHRE. Thus the question as to the source of the energy of the neurosis remained unanswered. The inclusion of the function of the orgasm in the theory of the neuroses was always considered an inconvenience and was resented. True, its study had originated not in psychoanalysis but in physiology.[1] Ferenczi's attempts at a theory of genitality consisted only in psychologizing physiological and biological phenomena. The orgasm is not a psychic phenomenon.

---

[1] *Cf.* Reich, "Zur Triebenergetik." *Zeitschr. f. Sexualwissenschaft,* 1923.

On the contrary, it is a phenomenon which comes about only by the reduction of all psychic activity to the basic vegetative function, that is, precisely by the elimination of psychic activity. Nevertheless, it is the crucial problem of psychic economy. Its inclusion in psychology not only made possible a concrete comprehension of the quantitative factor in psychic functioning and the establishment of the connection between psychic and vegetative functioning; more than that, it led, of necessity, to important changes in the psychoanalytic concept of the neurotic process. Previously, the fact that modern man has an Oedipus complex was considered an explanation of his neurotic illness. Today, this thesis, while not given up, is of relative importance: The child-parent conflict becomes pathogenic only as a result of a disturbed sexual economy on the part of the child; in this way, it conditions the later inability to regulate the libido economy and derives its energy precisely from what it helped to condition, namely, from stasis of genital sexual energy.[2] With this realization, the accent shifted from the experiential content to the economy of vegetative energy.

It became less important whether, early in the analysis, one obtained much or little material, whether one learned much or little about the patient's past. The decisive question came to be whether one obtained, in a correct fashion, those experiences which represented *concentrations of vegetative energy.*

Many analysts who have come into contact with sex-economy have not seen the development of this divergence in the concept of the neurosis and consequently do not comprehend the central significance of the orgasm problem. If one takes into consideration the fact that only with the character-analytic technique is it possible to penetrate to the physiological phenomena of the orgastic disturbance and its psychic representations, and the further fact that this technique is refuted by some, and not mastered by others, then one can readily understand why analysts are surprised at the finding that masochists are essentially characterized by a

---

[2] *Cf.* my presentation of the interrelationships of psychoneurosis and actual neurosis in DIE FUNKTION DES ORGASMUS, 1927.—*Translator's note: Cf.* also THE FUNCTION OF THE ORGASM, 1942, 1948.

specific kind of fear of the orgastic sensation. A person who has not gone through a character-analysis is unable to criticize its findings, simply because he lacks the sense organ for it. He will understand it intellectually, at best, but the core of the orgasm theory will remain incomprehensible to him. I have had the occasion of analyzing trained analysts with considerable experience who came to me with a good deal of scepticism or with the conviction of "knowing it all anyhow." Regularly, they had to convince themselves that what they experienced in the character-analysis could not have been known to them before, simply because it could be brought to the surface only by a definite technique; this is especially true of the genuine orgastic sensations which make their appearance for the first time with the involuntary contractions of the genital musculature.

I shall confine myself to this brief summary. The inclusion of structure and of libido economy into the analytic work has altered and complicated not only the whole picture and way of working but even the basic concepts of technique to a considerable degree. The technical problems are more complex, but this is compensated for by a greater security and better and more enduring results wherever a character-analytic unfolding of the case succeeds. It must be admitted that it does not as yet succeed in all cases.

As a result of the changes in technique and in many basic concepts of the dynamics of psychic functioning, those analysts who have not closely followed the development over the past 12 years no longer understand my technical and theoretical concepts. The gap, I fear, has become difficult to bridge, even where it is asserted that one shares my views.

In this connection, I wish to clarify a misunderstanding which recurs whenever I present my concepts. The analysts then usually divide into two groups. One of them contends that all these things have been known all along, that they are banal and nothing new, while the other group declares that my technique no longer has anything to do with psychoanalysis, that it is erroneous and misleading. How is this possible? It is not difficult to understand if we consider the way in which my scientific findings developed. My character-analytic technique developed out of Freud's resistance technique; more than that, it represents its most consistent continuation. For this reason, my technique must be in basic agreement with Freud's technique. Because of this, the first group believes it uses exactly the same technique as I. On the basis of a great many after-analyses, I can assure the reader that nothing is farther from the truth. To state this is made necessary by my responsibility toward the work. On the other hand, there is not only agreement but there are also far-reaching and fundamental differences. The inclusion of new points of view, in particular that of orgastic potency as the therapeutic goal, has altered the technique to such an extent that the second group no longer recognize the analytic technique in it. This explanation is unequivocal and in accord with the history of all sciences: new findings, concepts and methods never develop out of nothing; they are always based on the firm foundation of hard work on the part of other searchers.

### 3. THE CHANGE OF FUNCTION OF THE IMPULSE

It will be shown that the theoretical conclusions at which I arrived are made possible and provable only by using the character-analytic technique, and not by the simple resistance technique or even the obsolete technique of direct interpretation. It is a basic principle of character-analytic technique to approach the repressed material always by analyzing the defense against it and never by direct analysis of the instinct.

This principle was misinterpreted by my critics to the effect that to me character and defense are identical, that, consequently, I restricted the meaning of character unjustifiedly. If that were so, I would have to correct my statements. What I really said, however, was that *the main character trait, during analysis, becomes the chief resistance, just as in infancy it was formed for this purpose.* That, in addition, it has many other functions, particularly sex-economic functions, that it serves the maintenance of the relationships with the outer world as well as the maintenance of psychic equilibrium, all this was described extensively in my book, CHARAKTERANALYSE. This criticism, then, does not seem to be objectively motivated.

The most important theoretical question in this context, then, is the question as to the structure, function and genesis of the ego from which the defense stems; for our therapeutic work will be efficient to the extent to which we understand the ego defense. If our therapeutic abilities are to be extended it is no longer by a better understanding of the id but of the ego.[1] Here, the problem of character-analysis coincides with the problem which has occupied psychoanalytic thought for some fourteen years: *how does the ego function?* We all remember how impressed we were when Freud told us: Thus far we have studied and understood only the

---

[1] *Footnote, 1945:* This formulation was one-sided and therefore incorrect. The investigation of the armoring of the ego was only the first indispensable step. Only after the theoretical and practical comprehension of the armoring had succeeded was the way open into the vast realm of the biological energy, a way which finally resulted in the discovery of the organismic and the cosmic orgone energy. What psychoanalytic theory calls "id" is in reality the physical orgone function in the biosystem. The term "id" expresses, in a metaphysical manner, the fact that there is in the biosystem a "something" the functions of which are determined *outside* of the individual. *This "something," the "id," is a physical reality: the cosmic orgone energy.* The living "orgonotic system," the "bio-apparatus," represents nothing but a special state of concentrated orgone energy. In a recent review, a psychoanalyst described the "orgone" as "identical with Freud's id." This is as correct as the contention, say, that the "entelechy" of Aristotle or Driesch is identical with the "orgone." It is true, indeed, that the terms "id," "entelechy," "élan vital" and "orgone" describe "the same thing." But one makes things all too easy for oneself with such analogies. *"Orgone" is a visible, measurable and applicable energy of a cosmic nature.* Such concepts as "id," "entelechy" or "élan vital," on the other hand, are only the expression of *inklings* of the existence of such an energy. Are the "electromagnetic waves" of Maxwell "the same" as the "electromagnetic waves" of Hertz? Undoubtedly they are. But with the latter one can send messages across the oceans while with the former one cannot.

Such "correct" equations without a mention of the *practical* differences serve the function of verbalizing away great discoveries in natural science. They are as unscientific as the sociologist who, in a recent review, referred to the orgone as a "hypothesis." With hypotheses, with such things as the "id" or "entelechy," one cannot charge blood corpuscles or destroy cancer tumors; with orgone energy, one can.

The discussions of psychological problems, as presented here in the text, are important and correct *in the framework of depth psychology*. Orgone biophysics transcends this framework. With the progress of our knowledge of the orgone functions of the organism, these depth-psychological problems lose in significance. The solution of the psychological problem lies outside of the realm of psychology. A block of the orgonotic pulsation, say, in the throat, makes the most complicated problems of oral sadism understandable in a simple manner. In retrospect, we understand how hard was the struggle of the serious psychoanalyst with biophysical problems and why he could not find a real approach to them. Operating with the drives in depth psychology is as difficult as drinking water from a glass which one sees in a mirror.

repressed, but we know far too little about the origin of the repression and about the structure of the ego defense. It is rather surprising that one knew so little about the ego, that it seemed so much more inaccessible than the id. Nevertheless, it is a fact, and there must be reasons for it. They lie not only in difficulties of *psychological* understanding.

True, in THE EGO AND THE ID Freud asked the question as to the origin of the energy of the ego instinct, and at that time, in 1922, this was something quite new. Freud answered the question with his theory of the death instinct. He arrived at it as the result of the difficulties which the ego creates in resisting the elimination of repressions and in resisting the cure. According to this theory, these difficulties derive from the unconscious guilt feeling, or, in the last analysis, from a primary masochism, that is, a will to suffer. But the theory of the death instinct answered neither the question as to the structure of the ego defense and the repression of libidinal impulses nor the other question, *What is the ego instinct?*

Let us recall the lack of clarity with regard to the ego instincts which has always been present in analytic theory. Originally, hunger, in contrast to sexuality, was considered the ego instinct in the service of self-preservation. This formulation was in conflict with the other formulation that the ego instincts are *antagonists* of sexuality. Furthermore, sex-economic considerations showed that hunger cannot be considered an instinct in the strict sense of the word because, unlike sexuality, it is not the expression of an excess in energy but, on the contrary, of a sinking of the energy level in the organism. In addition, hunger had long since been thought of as belonging to the id and not the ego, in the structural sense. All of which means that hunger could not be what constitutes the energy of the ego instinct.

Schilder had tried to contrast the instincts of grasping and taking hold of to sexuality. This concept also was untenable because these impulses undoubtedly are part of the function of the muscular apparatus and, with that, of vegetative functioning. Freud's final attempt of replacing the mysterious ego instincts by the death instinct as the antagonist of sexuality merely meant replacing the antagonism between ego and id by an antagonism between two tendencies in the id itself. With that, the problem became more complicated than before.

Character-analytic work on the ego defense provided an answer which seems so self-evident that one must ask oneself how it could have been overlooked in spite of the fact that analytic theory pointed to it in many ways.

We have to take our orientation again from the basic conflict, that between drive and outer world. The drive, directed toward the objects of the outer world, is opposed by the prohibitions of the outer world (D, W, schema I). The question arises: Where does the prohibition of the outer world derive the energy for its function? The answer is that only the content of the prohibition derives from the outer world, while the energy, the cathexis, of the prohibition, derives from the energy reservoir of the individual itself. The pressure of the outer world brings about a split, a dissociation of a unitary striving in the person; thus it becomes possible that one drive turns against another or even that one and the same drive is split up into two tendencies, one of which continues to strive toward the world while the other turns against the self. This turning against the self of a drive has been described by Freud in his "Triebe und Triebschicksale." The new problem begins, however, with the process of *inner dissociation* and *antithesis*. For example: When a little boy masturbates with incest phantasies, his self-love and his object-love form a unity; the striving toward the mother and the self-love are in the same direction, they do not contradict each other. Prohibition of masturbation on the part of the mother frustrates the object-libidinal tendency and threatens the narcissistic integrity by the punishment of castration. But as soon as the external frustration becomes active, the narcissistic striving for self-preservation forms an antithesis to the object-libidinal masturbation striving (schema II and III). A variation of this is the antithesis between the tender attachment to the mother, the fear of loss of love on the one hand and the sensual sexual striving on the other; originally, they had also formed a unity. The dissociation of a unitary striving, then, is followed by the opposition of one part of the dissociated striv-

I. *Basic conflict* between drive (D)
and outer world (W)

II. *Dissociation* of the unitary striving
under the influence of the outer world

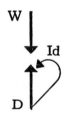

III. *Antithesis* of the dissociated strivings
Id = the Id in the function of the ego
instinct (defense, change of function)

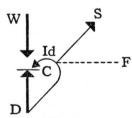

IV. *Drive (D) in double function* (Id = defense;
S = substitute contact).
F = place where change of function takes place
C = structural contactlessness
Defense (Id) and actual outer world situation
become a unity (inner morality, social ideology)

*Diagram: Change of function of the drive, inner
dissociation and antithesis*

ing by the other. It is clear now that the prohibition from the outer world can exert its influence only with the help of this energy which has become *antithetical.*

I shall amplify this schematic presentation with a practical example of a patient who was characterized by an exaggerated tendency to help others, a lack of aggression, a tendency to lean on others and an essentially passive behavior. All the traits of his passive-feminine character were concentrated in a certain obtrusive attitude which served the purpose of constantly establishing and maintaining contact with other people. It was not difficult to see that the instinctual force which maintained these attitudes was his passive-anal homosexuality. That is, the ego utilized an id striving for the maintenance of object relationships. This was the *object-libidinal,* or id function, of his anality.

In the analysis, the character of the patient proved a powerful resistance. From the character-analytic point of view, it would have been a mistake to interpret his behavior as the expression of unconscious anal-homosexual strivings, although, "in itself," this would have been correct. The economic and structural point of view dictated a different procedure. If it is correct that the main character trait becomes the main character resistance during the treatment, then the banal fact that the patient lives out anal-passive-feminine object strivings becomes unimportant compared with the question, *Where is the defense energy?* After some time, it was found that the same anal-passive-homosexual attitude which maintained the outer world relationships also fulfilled the defense function of the ego. That is, one and the same striving was split up and served, either alternatingly or simultaneously, two opposite functions: one time as object striving, the other time as defensive ego drive. Careful check-up in other cases showed that this *change of function,* this simultaneous functioning in the service of the id and in the service of the defending ego is a universal phenomenon. Before drawing the theoretical conclusion we shall mention a few clinical illustrations with which every analyst is familiar. The sexual coquetry of hysterics shows this dual function clearly. On the one hand, it is the expression of repressed genital desires, that is, directed toward the world;

on the other hand, it is also a defense against genitality, the expression of apprehensiveness in the approach to the objects, as if to find out from where the genital danger may be threatening. Only this explains the fact that women with a hysterical character have extensive sexual experiences in spite of intense genital anxiety. The same is true of the sadistic attitude of the woman with a compulsive character: her aggression toward the love object satisfies her sadistic object relationship and at the same time it wards off her real vaginal coitus desires.

*The ego instincts, then, are nothing but the totality of the vegetative demands in their defense function.* The ego instinct is an id instinct turned either against itself or against another instinct. The whole psychic process seems to be characterized by the splitting up and antithesis of unitary tendencies. All this would be of only academic interest if it did not have certain consequences.

First, a theoretical consequence: If our concept of the structure of the ego and the defense function is correct, then the systems "Ego" and "Id" appear merely as different *functions* of the psychic apparatus[2] and not as separate realms. At an earlier time, we had to answer the similar question as to the form in which infantile historical experience is preserved in present-day actuality. Clinical experience showed that it was by no means completely submerged but active in the form of character attitudes; and that it is from these that the content of infantile experience can be crystallized out. We see something similar in the psychic system: The repressed and the repressing are not two disparate, topically separated realms or forces; rather, they are a functional unity with simultaneous antithesis. The topical concept of the psychic apparatus is no more than an auxiliary concept, and Freud was right in refusing to relegate the system "Unconscious" to a lower part of the nervous system. The perception on the part of the ego, for example, is no less a function of the vegetative system than is an instinct.

Second, the technical consequence: Experience shows that we do not liberate the energy of the repressed instinct, or only insufficiently, if we begin by interpreting its id function. In such a

---

[2] *Footnote, 1945:* "Biopsychic apparatus," "human orgonotic system."

case, the patient may develop a good intellectual understanding and perhaps a conviction of the theoretical correctness of the analytic work; the real goal, however, the liberation of the instincts from repression, is far from reached, and there is very little change in structure. It is an entirely different thing if we make it our principle first to destroy the defense function of *the same* instinct. Ample clinical experience shows that only in this way do the vegetative sources of the personality begin to flow again. The inescapable conclusion is that in reality we do *not* eliminate the repression if we work with id interpretations. We do it almost regularly if we isolate the repressed instinct from the character defense formation not as repressed but, to begin with, as the *repressing* agent. To return to our patient: He remained affectively untouched as long as he did not clearly understand that his submissive attitude was not love, not gratefulness, not cooperation, nor homosexuality, but that it was, above all, a defense against something else. This something else was envy, inhibited aggression, destructive tendencies, etc.

Another patient exhibited jerky, unharmonious movements of which he was unaware; it was a kind of tic.[3] If I had interpreted to him the libidinal motives of these movements, say, their masturbatory significance, the result certainly would not have been the same. I pointed out first that it was a matter of embarrassed movements, of a defense against the painful perception of his appearance, that his vanity made it difficult for him to recognize certain bodily characteristics. My interpretation of this defense resulted in great excitation, an aggravation of the tic and the embarrassment, and, to my great surprise, violent convulsions of the abdominal musculature. These convulsions revealed themselves as a defense against fantasied blows against his "pregnant" abdomen. They were interpreted not as a mother identification, but as defense against aggressive impulses against an object. This immediately resulted in jerky leg movements, then violent pelvic movements with masturbation and orgasm. To

---

[3] *Footnote, 1945:* At that time, in 1933, I did not know yet that such spontaneous movements in the patients represented split-off parts of the orgasm reflex. I did not understand the biophysical function of these movements but only their "psychic meaning." This is still the case with most, if not all, psychoanalysts today.

interpret the tic-like movement as a masturbation substitute was entirely superfluous; he experienced the connection in an immediate and unmistakable manner. This result would have been made impossible by the slightest deviation from the rule that attitudes must consistently be treated as defenses.

The reader will ask what is the essential difference in the case of id interpretation and that of resistance interpretation, respectively. It is this: With a correct analysis of the defense functions and avoidance of any interpretation of their id functions, states of vegetative excitation and tension make their appearance which had previously been unknown to the patient. In the case of id interpretations, these states do not occur, or if they do, they occur by accident and in an unpredictable manner. The patient just mentioned, for example, experienced sensations that had been unknown to him since a phase of strong repression during puberty: hot flushes, severe oppression in the cardiac region and sensations in the pit of the stomach such as are experienced on a roller coaster or in an elevator. In other cases such sensations occur together with sensations of floating or falling.

The more important symptoms of vegetative excitation are the following: sensation of oppression in the cardiac region; sensation of tension in the musculature; sensations of vegetative current and pleasurable sensations such as are experienced after a gratifying sexual act; sensation of tension in the head; sensations of heat and cold; gooseflesh; itching, particularly in urethra and at the perineum; increased flow of saliva, or dry mouth; sensations of choking; the feeling of not being able to get one's breath; vertigo; nausea; a "pulling sensation" in the genital (as in falling); sensations in the pit of the stomach (as on roller coaster or in elevator); involuntary jerks of the musculature; pleasurable sensations with the contraction of groups of smooth muscles, etc.

Before attempting a theoretical orientation in the wealth of these phenomena, we have to return to the starting-point, the structure of the character armor, for, as we have seen, it is this armor from which we liberate the vegetative energy with our character-analytic technique.

### 4. THE INTELLECT AS DEFENSE FUNCTION

A clinical example will show again how precisely character attitudes both preserve and ward off infantile situations. According to the common view, the function of the human intellect is exclusively objective and directed toward reality; ethics and philosophy, in particular, regard intellectual activity one that comprehends reality "incorruptibly," and which is absolutely antithetical to the affect. This view overlooks two things: first, the intellectual function is itself a vegetative activity, and second, the intellectual function may have an affect charge no less intensive than that of any purely affective reaction. Character-analytic work, furthermore, reveals a specific defensive function of the intellect. Intellectual activity has often such a structure and direction that it impresses one as an extremely clever apparatus precisely for the *avoidance* of facts, as an activity which really *detracts* from reality. The intellect, then, can work in both of the basic directions of the psychic apparatus, toward the world and away from it; it can work in the same direction as a vivid affect, and it may be in opposition to it. That is, there is no mechanistic, absolutely antithetical relationship between intellect and affect but, again, a functional relationship.

Up until now, it has appeared extremely difficult to derive the intellectual function from the vegetative function. Certain character-analytic experiences, however, open an avenue of approach also to this problem. This will be shown in the case of a patient who presented the affective genesis of an artful, cunning intellectual function in a particularly interesting manner.

In this patient, character-analysis had unmasked and eliminated his politeness and seeming surrender as a defense against his violent aggression. After this, he began to develop the following kind of defense: In an extremely intelligent manner, he tried to divine every one of his unconscious mechanisms; in fact, he succeeded in destroying almost every affect situation by guessing it beforehand. It was as if, secretly, he used his intellect to look into every corner in order not to be surprised by anything. It became increasingly clear that his intellect was in the service of avoiding anxiety, that the motive of his intellectual activity was an apprehensive anticipation. For example, he always, most cleverly, was able to find out what I was thinking about him, or he deduced it by putting things together, or from the course of the analysis; he also knew how to anticipate what was going to happen at any given time. This behavior was by no means regarded as welcome cooperation; on the contrary, it was treated as an extremely clever manoeuvre of avoidance. The next task was that of making this weapon useless to the patient; this could be done only by consistent analysis of its function and extreme reserve in other interpretations. For a while, the patient continued his intellectual approach, but soon he became insecure and uncomfortable, and finally he began to protest violently, saying that I refused to understand him, that his intellectual help showed his cooperation, etc. Now I intensified my interpretation of his intellectual activity, pointing out that it was a defense against surprise. I also told him that his behavior seemed like that of a *wily fox*. One day, after a short period of excitation, his defensive behavior broke down in the following manner: At first, he again expressed his exasperation over my no longer understanding him. Then his attention shifted gradually to a scene from his third year of life which he had mentioned once before in passing, without any details or affect.

He had injured his left arm in a fall and had to be operated on. His father carried him along the street to the hospital. Now, with violent crying, he remembered the following details: They passed a shop window in which there were stuffed animals. Of these, he remembered two distinctly: *a fox* and a reindeer with large antlers. During this hour, he did not remember what happened between this observation and the operation. Later, however, he saw himself lying on the operating table, with arms bound, shoulders tense in expectation. He seemed to smell chloroform, and suddenly he remembered the *chloroform mask*. When they were about to put it over his face, he had thought: "But this is a fox face that I'm going to have!" A fox's head and a chloroform mask have, in fact, a very similar shape. Foxes, he knew as a child, are caught in traps with teeth that catch the animal's leg and "break its bones." On the way to the hospital, then, the boy had used all his intellectual powers to find a way out of the threatening disaster; it was perhaps at this time that his intellect first entered the service of defense against a threatening danger. The danger which the analysis represented was also warded off in a cunning, "foxy" manner. The patient remembered definitely how, after much effort to think of a way out, he had finally concluded: "It's useless, it's absolutely useless. I'm caught." It became clear now what was the basis of one of his great weaknesses: He was slyly cautious to such a degree that, for example, he could neither form positive political opinions nor, because of his fear, proceed to any kind of action. His whole life, he had been a fox in the trap; by being a wily fox, he had neutralized the infantile fear of being a fox in the trap.

### 5. THE INTERLACING OF THE DEFENSIVE FORCES

It would be erroneous to assume that the loosening or elimination of a single defense could liberate libidinal functioning or could even make it possible for the patient to associate freely. True, it happens frequently that after the elimination of one layer of the defense apparatus liberated affects with corresponding infantile experiential material pour forth. One would ruin every chance for a *complete* dissolution of the armor if, during such a phase, one were to do more than to connect with the actual transference situation only those parts of the flowing material which have directly to do with it. One will find that the gap in the armor soon closes up again and that the armor continues to function as if nothing had happened. These small breakthroughs after the elimination of individual layers of the armor should not be confused with the final *breakdown* of the armor. This distinction is based on a specific structure of the armored psychic apparatus which one might call the *interlacing of the defensive forces* and which may be described as follows:

If, for example, one has unmasked an over-polite attitude which forms the top layer, as a defense function, that which was warded off makes its appearance, say, aggression. It would be wrong at this point to tell the patient that he is living out his infantile aggression, even if this aggression appears in an unmistakable manner. This aggression is not only the expression of an infantile relationship toward the world, but at the same time itself a defense against something which is more deep-lying, against, say, passive-anal impulses. If one succeeds in eliminating this defense layer also, it may happen that what appears is not the expected passivity, but contactlessness, in the form of indifference toward the analyst, etc. This contactlessness is unequivocally a defense, say, against an anticipated disappointment. If one succeeds, by dissolving the contactlessness, in bringing the fear of disappointment to the surface, it may have all the appearances of a deep infantile fear of losing the love object; but at the same time it is the defense against deep aggressive impulses towards the love object which once withdrew its love. This example could be varied, complicated or simplified indefinitely, according to the type concerned. For example, the *deeper* layer of aggression which now appears could be itself the expression of *original* destructive tendencies but it could, at the same time, serve the function of warding off intensive oral-narcissistic demands. In that case, it would again have to be interpreted character-analytically as a defense and not as a vegetative instinctual demand. *The layers of the armor, then, are interlaced: every warded-off impulse also serves the function of warding off a more deeply repressed impulse.* Thus, to stay with our example, only the analysis of the oral-narcissistic love demands as a defense against genuine, original oral or genital love impulses would bring about the breakthrough of vegetative excitation. Not until one has worked one's way through the diverse defense functions does the final breakthrough succeed. This work requires infinite patience and the absolute knowledge that finally original instinctual impulses will break through which no longer have a defense function. When this point is reached, the patient usually has already reactivated his genitality. The interlacing of the defense functions, however, still needs intense detailed clinical study.

In this connection we will have to discuss the standpoint of Kaiser[1] who believes that he can do without interpretation alto-

[1] "Probleme der Technik." *Internat. Zeitschr. f. Psychoan.*, 1934.

gether. One misunderstanding, to begin with, is that Kaiser restricts the concept of interpretation to the making conscious of the repressed, while in my book, CHARAKTERANALYSE, the term is used as meaning any kind of analytic communication. Kaiser's restriction of the meaning of the term "interpretation" may even have its advantages; in this case, the making of a superficial analytical connection or the making objective of a character trait would not be an interpretation in the strict sense. But even with this restriction of the term, if Kaiser says that consistent resistance analysis not only makes any interpretation superfluous but a mistake, I could agree with him only on the ground of theoretical principles. In saying so, he forgets that my formulation of the "interpretation at the end" is practically necessary as long as character-analytic technique is not perfected to such a degree that we no longer have any difficulty at all in finding our way in the maze of defenses. His contention, then, is correct only for the ideal case of character-analytic work. I must admit that I am still far from that ideal and that I still find the dissolution of the defense formation difficult work, particularly with regard to contactlessness and the interlacing of defenses. What makes character-analytic work so difficult is a consideration which Kaiser overlooks, the sex-economic consideration; this makes it necessary to work in such a fashion that the maximum amount of sexual excitation becomes concentrated on the genital and thus appears as *orgasm anxiety*.

### 6. CONTACTLESSNESS

The early character-analytic concept of the character armor was this: it forms the sum total of all repressing defense forces; it can be dissolved by an analysis of the modes of behavior. Later it was shown that this concept of the character armor was incomplete; more, that it seemed to have overlooked the most important fact. Gradually it became clear that although a thorough dissolution of the modes of behavior led to deep-reaching breakthroughs of vegetative energy, nevertheless, it was incomplete in a way difficult to define. One had the feeling that the patient did not relinquish some outposts of his "narcissistic position" and knew how to hide them from himself and the analyst in a very clever fashion. Since the analysis of the active defense forces and of the characterological reaction formation seemed complete, and since, on the other hand, the existence of this poorly defined remainder could not be doubted, one was confronted with a difficult problem. The theoretical concept of the armor was correct: a sum total of repressed impulses, directed toward the outer world, was opposed by a sum total of defense forces which maintained the repression; the two formed, in the character of the patient, a *functional unity*. Where, then, did one have to look for the unknown remainder, since both the repressed and the repressing forces were comprehended?

The explanation that one and the same impulse is directed toward the world and at the same time, in a defense function, against the ego, while contributing to the knowledge of the ego structure, did not solve the riddle. A clinical illustration will show that the hidden remainder of the armor is to be found in the phenomenon of *psychic contactlessness*.

In the patient mentioned earlier, analysis revealed, behind his reactive passive-feminine attitude, a marked lack of contact with the world; he was not interested in it and not influenced by it. The patient himself had no immediate awareness of this; on the contrary, his passive-feminine tendency to lean on others deceived him about it and gave him the feeling that he had especially intensive relations with the outer world. This seemed a difficult contradiction. On the one hand, there was his libidinal stickiness, his readiness to be of help and of service, that is, seemingly intensive object relationships, and on the other hand there was doubtless a contactlessness. The situation became clear when we understood, from the patient's history, that his attachment and readiness to help had assumed not only the function of warding off his repressed aggressive impulses but also that of compensating for his lack of contact with the world. We must distinguish, therefore,

First, the repressed impulses;

Second, the repressing defense forces; and

Third, a layer of the psychic structure between the two, the contactlessness.

The latter appears, at first glance, not as a dynamic force, but as a rigid, static formation, as a wall in the psychic organism, as *the result of the conflict between two opposite libidinal currents.* This structure is most easily comprehended from its history.

In going over earlier clinical experiences after the discovery of this contactlessness in this patient, I found it to be as general a phenomenon of the neurosis as the change of function in impulses. I shall first give the theoretical concept of contactlessness and then present its history by way of another clinical illustration. When libidinal tendencies toward the outer world are inhibited by a prohibition coming from this outer world, an equilibrium between the instinctual and the inhibiting force may be established. This is seemingly a static condition. It may be that the basis of the fixation of impulses on earlier developmental stages as well as of psychic inhibition in general is precisely this dynamic condition. It might also be described in the following way: When an impulse meets an inhibition it may, as we said before, split up. Part of it turns against the self (reaction formation), and part of it remains in the original direction toward the outer world. But now the dynamic situation has been altered by the dissociation and antithesis. At the point where the two tendencies—that directed toward the self and that directed toward the outer world—split, there must be a condition of paralysis or rigidity as the result of two opposing forces. This is by no means merely an auxiliary hypothetical concept. Once one has comprehended the essence of this process and lets the patients describe their feelings in detail, one will find that they experience this inhibition very vividly, in spite of any object relationship which may be present. I shall mention a few of the most common clinical manifestations of this dynamic-structural condition.

The most frequent is a feeling of *inner loneliness* in spite of frequently ample social and objective relationships. In other patients we find a feeling of *"inner deadness."* This is undoubtedly the basis of compulsion-neurotic and schizoid depersonalization;

in schizophrenics, this condition is immediately represented in the form of sensations of splitting. When patients feel themselves to be strange, unrelated and lacking interest, it is because of this conflict between an object-libidinal tendency and the tendency to flee back into the self. The split and the ambivalence are the direct expression of this; the lack of interest is a result of the equilibrium between the two opposing forces. The concept of the contactlessness as a static thing, a wall, therefore, is not correct. It is not a passive attitude but a dynamic interplay between opposing forces. The same is true of the affect-block in compulsion neurotics, and of catatonic rigidity. These few examples must suffice here.

After the breakdown of the armor, we see in our patients an *alternation* of vegetative streaming and affective block. The reestablishment of vegetative streaming being the most important therapeutic goal, the transition from the streaming condition to the frozen condition is one of the most important therapeutic and theoretical problems. Similar conditions of affective blocking are known under conditions of war and among political prisoners. Here, rage impulses are inhibited by brutal external power. Since a constant oscillation between one and the other direction gradually becomes intolerable, a dulling takes place; this, however, is not a passive condition, nor a final freezing of a dynamic condition, but, as we already said, the result of an opposition of forces. That this is so is proved by the fact that this condition of dulling—as a result of external conditions or of our character-analytic efforts—can be dissolved again into its constituent parts. To the extent to which the dulling gives way, there appear sexual and aggressive impulses as well as anxiety, that is, centripetal flight. This confirms again the sex-economic concept of sexuality and anxiety as two opposite directions of vegetative streaming.

In our patients, we find the repressed impulses, the repressing force and the interposed contactlessness existing side by side and acting at the same time. Analysis, however, reveals a definite sequence of historical development. This will be shown in the following example.

This patient suffered intensely from his feeling of inner deadness, in contradistinction to the patient mentioned earlier who had no perception of this condition. In his external behavior, he was exaggeratedly polite and reserved and somewhat dignified; people with free vegetative motility felt him to be rigid and unalive. He himself had no more intense secret wish than that of being able to "feel the world," of being able to "stream." The character-analytic liberation of his affects from his behavior resulted in a complete reactivation of those infantile situations in which he had acquired his contactlessness as well as his longing for aliveness. One of his outstanding neurotic symptoms was a most intense fear of object loss; he reacted with strong depression if, on kissing a woman, he did not immediately have an erection. Analysis revealed that there was, in addition to his strong longing for an alive object relationship, a strong *tendency to retreat,* to give up the object at the slightest provocation. This tendency was due to his fear of his own hatred toward the very object toward which he wanted to let himself "stream." It is important to note that he suffered from penis anesthesia, that is, a lack of *vegetative contact.* Such conditions are most outspoken in compulsive characters. Their formula of the "new life" which they constantly have to begin, the feeling that they should be able to be "different," that is, alive and productive instead of rigid and unalive, is only the expression of the last remnants of vegetative motility and usually the strongest incentive to get well. To return to our case: when the penis anesthesia was eliminated, the feeling of contactlessness also disappeared, only to reappear immediately when the genital disturbance recurred. This connection between psychic contactlessness and physiological anesthesia on the one hand, and psychic contact and vegetative excitability on the other, had its basis in the patient's early history. Briefly, this was the following:

The patient had had strong genital wishes for his mother. His first attempts at a genital approach were rebuffed. It is important to point out that the mother did not prohibit any non-genital contact, such as lying beside her, embracing her, etc.; more than that, she encouraged these contacts. As a result of the genital frustration, he developed a strong aggressive-sadistic attitude toward the mother; this also had to be repressed for fear of punishment. Now he was in a severe conflict. On the one hand, there was his tender love for his mother and the striving for physical contact with her. On the other hand, there was his hatred for her, and the fear of this hatred as well as the fear of his genital striving, and the fear of losing the love object. Later on, every time he approached a woman, the genital striving, which was more or less repressed, was replaced by the sadistic impulses, and this forced him to retreat. As a child, in order to achieve the repression, he had had to kill the sensations in his penis. How this is possible is as yet an unsolved problem. Probably, the aggressive impulse inhibits the sexual one and vice versa. The fact is that genital anesthesia in the presence of erective potency is the *immediate* expression and the most important sign of the loss of the ability for contact. Probably, this is not merely a psychic process but a disturbance of the electrophysiological function at the penis surface. On a deeper level, the feeling of "being dead" meant the same to the patient as having no penis or not feeling his penis. This had a rational basis in the actual loss of sensation in the penis. This is what gave rise to his depressions.[1]

We see, then, that his contactlessness with the world had developed at the time when his natural genital striving had come in conflict with his hatred toward the object and the resulting tendency to retreat. We can say without hesitation that this process is a general one: Whenever natural impulses toward objects are frustrated, the result is not only anxiety, as an expression of the withdrawal into the self, but also contactlessness. This is true in the child after the first intense phase of genital repression as well as in the adolescent who, for external reasons or because of inner

---

[1] *Footnote, 1945:* As time went on, the clinical manifestation of "contactlessness" came to be the guiding line in the search for orgone-biophysical disturbances. Contactlessness is based on a block in the motility of the body orgone (anorgonia). In the case of penis anesthesia, the skin lacks an orgonotic charge, the orgone energy field is shrunk; touching the penis results only in tactile sensations but not in pleasure sensations. Since only a *change* in the energy level results in pleasure, it goes without saying that a block in plasmatic motility results in contactlessness. In 1942, the demonstration of the orgone energy field succeeded by way of lumination of a filament. *Cf.* also "The bio-electric function of pleasure and anxiety," THE FUNCTION OF THE ORGASM, 1942, p. 326ff, 1948, p. 289ff.

inability, cannot find his way to the object. It is equally the case in marriages of long standing when a dulling in the genital relationship occurs and the way to other sexual gratification is barred by repression. In all these cases we see the picture of psychic dulling, characterized by resignation, lack of interest, feelings of loneliness and a serious impairment of practical functioning.

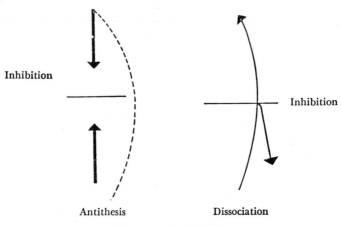

Inhibition

Inhibition

Antithesis                    Dissociation

*Schema of the inhibition*

In trying to comprehend the dynamics of the character, we must make a further correction in our concept of the psychic apparatus. We said that, between the repressed and the repressing (defense forces), there is interposed a layer of contactlessness, and that the latter corresponds to an inhibition which results from the antithesis of two impulses or the splitting up (dissociation) of one and the same impulse.

In formulating this definition, we overlooked the fact that the neurotic psychic apparatus does not consist of *one* repressed and *one* repressing impulse but of an infinite number of impulses which are in part antithetical, in part dissociated. The *interlacing* of the defense forces shows, furthermore, that an impulse in the depth of the armor may fulfil a defense function at the surface, and makes it likely that all psychic tendencies are dissociated into impulses "toward the world" and "away from the world" and at the same time antithetical. In brief, we have the picture of a complicated *structure of the armor* in which the repressed and repressing are by no means neatly separated but are interlaced in a complex and seemingly disorderly manner. It is only the character-analytic work which brings order in the picture, an order which corresponds to the history of the structure. This structural concept is incompatible with a topical concept. The repressed and the repressing form a functional unit, say, that of a characterological inhibition. If one considers the infinite multitude of such unifications of different tendencies and of such dissociations of unitary tendencies it is obvious that the process cannot be understood by any kind of mechanistic or systematic thinking but only by functional and structural thinking. Character development is a process of progressive development, dissociation and antithesis of simple vegetative functions, of forces acting in different directions as in the following schema:

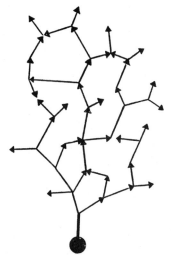

*Schema of the structure of the armor*

Consequently, contactlessness is not a layer interposed between two layers of opposite forces, but an expression of the *concentration* of antitheses and dissociations. What impresses us in a character-analysis as a compact formation is nothing but such a concentration of opposing forces in the character. We have already pointed out how important it is to begin at "the right end" if one wishes to dissolve such a character formation.

For example, the character trait of reserve may become a compact character resistance during treatment in the form of a stubborn, apprehensive silence. In a character-analysis, one would not think of trying to overcome such a silence by urging, persuading or threatening the patient. This silence is mostly the result of an *inability* to give verbal expression to inner impulses. Urging and persuading the patient only increase the stubbornness because such measures do not eliminate the patient's inability to express himself; on the contrary, they accentuate it. For in reality the patient would like to talk and express himself but is somehow inhibited; he finds himself confronted with the task of expressing himself and fails for that very reason. He does not know that he is incapable of expressing himself; usually he believes himself that he does *not want to*. His secret hope is that the analyst will understand him in spite of the fact that he cannot express himself. This wish "to be understood" is usually combined with a defense against any help, and the defense takes the form of stubbornness. This makes the work difficult but not impossible. Instead of urging the patient or even using the famous "silent treatment," one assures the patient that one understands his inhibition and that, for the time being, one does not expect him to express himself. With that, one relieves him of the pressure of the "task" and takes away his reason for his stubbornness. If one succeeds in simply and accurately *describing* his attitudes, without trying immediately to change them, one finds regularly that the patient feels himself immediately "understood." With that, he will have certain feelings which at first he will fight by accentuating the silence but which will create a certain unrest. This unrest is the first sign of a movement out of his rigid condition. After a few days, or at most weeks, of patient description of his attitudes, he will gradually begin to talk. In most cases, the character attitude of silence is based on a spasm of the throat musculature of which the patient is unaware and which keeps down excitations as soon as they begin to appear.

In order to eliminate the contactlessness, it is by no means sufficient to reconstruct the history of its development or to find the constituent repressed and repressing impulses. Rather, as with every character attitude, the patient must learn to view it objectively before it can be analytically dissolved. The most important measure to bring this about is an exact description of the behavior. Others are: constantly showing the patients the difference between the ideals they set for themselves and the emptiness of their actual living; constant demonstration of the lack of real interest as it shows itself in conflicts and failures in work; demonstration of the lack of real inner experience in spite of a seemingly intense love life. All this gradually makes the patient experience his contactlessness in a painful way. Usually, this is possible fully only when a certain amount of sexual energies have already been liberated and have increased the patient's demands for living contact with reality. The contactlessness becomes intolerable when he has begun to experience the first, although weak, sensations of orgastic streaming in the body and particularly in the genital. General psychic contactlessness is only the general reflection of orgasm anxiety, that is, *fear of orgastic contact;* correspondingly, it disappears automatically and completely when the ability for orgastic contact has been established.

Our knowledge of the psychophysical mechanisms which mediate between a condition of experiencing things and people fully and the condition of inner emptiness is still incomplete. This is true particularly with regard to the question of how it is possible that a withdrawal of sexual interest or the inhibition of an outward impulse is experienced in an immediate manner as a "going cold," "freezing up," or "dying off." Our earlier explanation of this phenomenon as an "inhibition" resulting from the action of two opposing forces is correct but incomplete. To say that libido is being withdrawn means nothing; one cannot put words in the place of dynamic comprehension. In brief, we do not yet know.[2] However, we learn much about this phenomenon if we make the patient relive the *transition* from the alive to the dead condition as vividly as possible, and if we pay the closest

[2] *Cf.* preceding footnote, p. 289.

attention to the swings from one condition into the other during treatment. If one does so, one observes very peculiar reactions. One patient, for example, experienced the transition by having to repeat mechanically, "It's no good, it's no good at all," etc. The meaning of this was: "It is no good to try, to make sacrifices, to try to get love, because I'm not being understood anyhow." Small children have a most tragic experience: Not being able to express their wishes and needs in words, they appeal to the adult in some form for understanding; the adults, as they are, are quite unable to feel what is going on in the child; the child tries and tries to make himself understood, in vain; finally it gives up the struggle for understanding and resigns: "It's no good." The transition from full living experiencing to inner deadness is usually caused by severe disappointments in love. However, this still does not explain the mechanism of this inner freezing up.

Very often one finds that this condition of being frozen is motivated and maintained by a fear of contact with things, experiences and people; the core of this fear is the fear of orgastic contact. This fear usually is acquired in connection with infantile masturbation. There can be no doubt: *The core of the fear of genuine, immediate psychic contact with people and the world in general is the fear of orgastic contact.* The elimination of this orgasm anxiety is the most important as well as the most difficult task of character-analysis. One sees again and again that patients, no matter how completely they were released from their infantile fixations, immediately relapse into their old neurotic condition when they are confronted with the task of establishing orgastic genital contact. This is not possible without elimination of orgasm anxiety. This phase, more or less sharply circumscribed, occurs in every correctly carried out character-analysis. It is characterized by the following manifestations: superficiality of analytic communications, dreams and phantasies of falling, increased reserve, avoidance of the subject of genital desires, increased ideas of bodily disintegration (which have to be distinguished from castration ideas), relapse into earlier symptoms, flight from sexual and other relationships with the world, reactivation of infantile modes of reaction, recurrence of the sensation of emptiness, etc.

In this phase, a most exact analysis of the attitudes and sensations during masturbation and the sexual act is necessary. One then finds that the patients inhibit the increase in excitation in one way or another. For example, they do not admit the increase of excitation; they disrupt the excitation by rapid, jerky movements; they tighten the pelvic musculature without being aware of it; often, they hold still at the approach of the orgastic sensations instead of allowing the excitation to increase in a spontaneous rhythm. The elimination of the orgastic inhibition is most difficult when none of the signs just mentioned is present and the excitation simply dies off.

A striking, yet regularly overlooked, attitude in the sexual act is the following: With full preorgastic contact, there is a spontaneous vegetative impulse for friction movements; in the presence of orgasm anxiety and psychic contactlessness, this impulse is regularly absent. The soft, spontaneous friction rhythm induced by contact sensations is then replaced by a forced, voluntary, more or less violent friction in an attempt to overcome the contactlessness and bring about a discharge in spite of the inhibition. For this reason, it is impossible to uncover and eliminate the genital contact fear as long as this mode of friction is not dissolved as a defense against the orgastic sensations. The patients usually put up a strong fight against giving up this mode of friction and against giving themselves over to the vegetative mode of friction. They avoid being overwhelmed by the orgastic experience.

Generally speaking, then, a correct and successful character-analysis is characterized by three phenomena:

1. Thorough breakdown of the armor;

2. full development of the fear of orgastic contact; and

3. complete overcoming of the orgastic inhibition and the establishment of completely uninhibited, involuntary movement at the moment of the acme.

The rapid and complete change in general behavior in the sense of free-flowing vegetative motility amply compensates for the effort involved in a correct concentration of the excitation in the orgasm anxiety and its overcoming.

## 7. SUBSTITUTE CONTACT

The more extensive the suppression of vegetative motility in the child, the more difficult will it be for the adolescent to develop the relationships to the world which correspond to the age of adolescence, relationships to love objects, to work, and to reality in general; the more readily will the adolescent sink back into a condition of contactless resignation and unnatural substitute contacts. Most of what is officially called the "characteristics of puberty" is shown by character-analysis to be the artificial effect of the supression of natural love life. This is true of the daydreaming as well as the inferiority feelings. The latter are not merely the expression of too highly pitched ideals and imagined inferiority but correspond to a concrete contradiction in the structure: The inferiority feeling is the inner perception of the gap between actual achievement, sexual and social, on the one hand, and the latent abilities and possibilities which are paralyzed by the inhibition of vegetative motility on the other. Most people are actually much less potent than they see themselves in their daydreams and at the same time endowed with far greater capabilities than they express in action. This grotesque contradiction in the structure of modern man is a result of the destructive social regulation of sexuality to which he is subjected. To eliminate this contradiction will be one of the most important tasks of a new social order, for the productive power, "working power," depends above all on actual achievement being equal to the latent capacity for achievement, and this means the re-establishment of vegetative motility.

This condition becomes psychically intolerable and socially damaging. The psychic apparatus protests against it and attempts to handle it in various ways. We shall not discuss here the neurotic symptoms as they result from sexual stasis. What we are interested in here are the character functions which are newly formed in this struggle. Once the immediate vegetative contact with the world has been more or less destroyed, so that the remainder is not sufficient to maintain the relationships with the outer world, then substitute functions develop, that is, attempts to establish a *substitute contact*. A few clinical illustrations will show what has to be considered substitute contact in contradistinction to immediate vegetative contact. The difficulty lies in the fact that the substitute contact also is based on vegetative energy. Nevertheless, the differences are far more important than this common factor. The behavior of the passive-feminine character, for example, is based on anal excitations, but this represents a substitute contact which has replaced the natural contact which was made impossible by frustration. The young man, in growing up, should, say, fight against the domination and authority of his father, should become independent and should develop his own capacities. But he does not have at his disposal the aggression which is necessary for this because it is repressed. In order to keep it in repression he develops his passive-feminine modes of behavior; now, instead of mastering the world with sublimated aggression, he tries to secure his existence by neurotic adaptation although this involves the greatest personal sacrifices. The sadistic attitude of the compulsive woman toward the man has not only the function of warding off her genitality but also that of compensating for the resulting libidinal contactlessness and of maintaining the contact with the original love object, although in a different form. Similarly, the artificial and exaggerated affectionateness between spouses represents a substitute contact because of the lack of a genuine sexual relationship. The neurotically aggressive behavior of querulous people is not only a defense against passive-feminine tendencies toward the man or of natural genital tendencies toward the woman but, in addition, an attempt to remain in contact with the world in spite of the lack of immediate vegetative contact. Masochistic behavior is not only the expression of a defense against sadistic aggression, but also a substitute for direct expression of love of which the masochistic character is incapable.

Once one has grasped the difference between the manifestations of free-flowing, immediate vegetative contact and those of secondary, artificial contact relationships, the latter are easy to see in everyday life. The following are a few examples of ungenuine behavior: loud, obtrusive laughter; forced, rigid handclasp; never-changing, lukewarm friendliness; narcissistic display of superficial knowledge; stereotyped, meaningless portrayal of surprise or delight; rigid sticking to certain views, plans or goals; obtrusive modesty in behavior; grandiose gestures when talking; childlike wooing of people's favor; sexual boasting; prancing with sexual charms; indiscriminate coquetry; sex-economically unhealthy promiscuous sexuality; exaggeratedly dignified behavior; affected, pathetic or exaggeratedly refined talk; dictatorial or patronizing behavior; exaggerated hail-fellow-well-met behavior; rigid conversational way of talking; rowdy or lascivious behavior; sexual giggling and smutty talk; Don Juan behavior; embarrassment. Similarly, accompanying movements often express, in addition to narcissistic tendencies, a substitute contact: shaking one's hair into place in a striking manner, stroking one's forehead frequently in a typical manner, looking suggestively into the other person's eyes in talking, forced swaying of the hips, forced athletic gait, etc.

Generally speaking one can say that wherever an attitude stands out from the total personality, as if isolated or in conflict with it, one is dealing with a substitute function which hides a more or less deep-reaching contactlessness. Character-analytic experience suggests that character traits which are popularly considered "bad," "unpleasant" or "disturbing" are usually identical with neurotic behavior, and the same is true of attitudes which rule the life of so-called "better people" who consider form more important than content. Conversely, most of what is popularly called "simple," "natural," "sympathetic," "attractive," etc., is identical with the unneurotic behavior of the genital character. ("Neurotic" here means a condition which results from the repression of an impulse and which continues to exist as the result of a counter-cathexis which consumes energy.)

One is again and again deeply impressed by the double life which people are forced to live. Their exterior attitude, which differs according to their social position, is an artificial formation which is in constant conflict with the true, vegetatively determined nature of the person and often covers it up only insufficiently. The most imposing policeman, the most refined and reserved scientist, the elegant, unapproachable lady from the social register, the "dutiful" official functioning like a machine— all of them reveal themselves as basically harmless individuals with the simplest longings, anxieties and hatreds. To point this out is all the more important in view of the incredible respect for these characterological masks on the part of the "common man."

Character-analytically speaking, the difference between natural sexual rhythm and trumped-up sex appeal, between natural and artificial dignity, between genuine and artificial shame, between vegetative muscular rhythm and swaying of hips and pulling back of shoulders, between fidelity due to sexual gratification and fidelity out of fear and guilt feeling, etc.—is the same as the difference between a structure capable of development and a conservative structure, between a life that is truly alive and a life of empty substitutes. Here we find an access to the psychic-structural basis of ideologies and social practice.

In the ideology of all authoritarian social organizations, vegetative life is contrasted as primitive, animal-like, to the "cultural," highly differentiated substitute life. In reality, this life, since it is divorced from the vegetative and therefore not its continuation, but a substitute for it, is unproductive, a matter of rigid forms and formulae, unfruitful like a dried-out plant. The vegetative life, on the other hand, because it lacks the chronic rigidities and immobilizations of energy, has infinite possibilities of development. It is not the substitute formations which created culture, but all progress derived from the remnants of immediate vegetative contact with the world. It is easy to see, then, what enormous forces wait for development when it will be possible to liberate the human structures from their substitute functions and to give back to them the immediateness of their relation with nature and society. This could not take the form of a new religion, say, of a new kind of Yoga movement in which people would "practice the function of immediate contact." No, such a change in structure would presuppose a change in the social order which is incomprehensible to followers of mystical practices.

Since man, as the only living being, is denied the realization of his natural demands and since, in the last analysis, the basis of the necessity of living in social relationships is of a vegetative nature, the substitute contact which he establishes is only a compromise between the will to life and the socially conditioned fear of life. Unlike the immediate vegetative contact, the substitute contact has a structure like the neurotic symptom: it is a substitute function for something else, it serves a defense purpose, it absorbs energy, and is an attempt to harmonize conflicting forces. As in the symptom, the result of the achievement is out of all proportion to the energy expended. The substitute contact, then, is one of the many manifestations of a disturbed social and personal sex-economy. Since the function of substitute contact has remained unknown and since its manifestations have taken on the form of tradition, they have come to be considered naturally given and unalterable. Nevertheless, as social phenomena and as elements of human structure these manifestations of substitute contact form a historical structure; that is, they have developed in a definite manner and are alterable. When riding on a poor train one hesitates to leave it before another, better one is available which will take one to one's destination; one will develop not only a peculiar inertia but also illusions about the train. Similarly, it is quite clear that the idea of an orderly sex-economy must become as much general consciousness as is now the idea of the unalterability of a disordered sex-economy; only then will the forces be liberated which will suffice to replace one way of living by another.

If the life of people today is a substitute life, if their work is an unwelcome duty, their love a substitute love and their hatred a substitute hatred; if character-analytic dissolution of the character armor destroys these substitute functions; if this human structure, which functions primarily reactively, is the result and the indispensable basis of the present social order, then, the reader will ask: What takes the place of this kind of psychic functioning after a successful character-analysis? What is the relationship between social achievement and sexuality then? These are difficult questions involving a great deal of responsibility. The character-analytic formulation of the "neurotic character" and the "genital character" has already provided some of the answers. However, the exploration of the functioning of the healthy individual is only in its beginnings; furthermore, it meets the strongest resistance on the part of a world based on a moralistic and authoritarian order. This order, with all its institutions and ethical norms, is strictly at variance with a psychic structure which is characterized not by moralistic regulation but by sex-economic self-regulation, whose work does not stem from duty but from objective interest, whose vegetative sources are in free-flowing contact with the world. One of the most difficult theoretical and practical tasks will be the application of the knowledge gained in the character-analytic alteration of individual structure to the alteration of structure on a mass basis by collective education.

## 8. THE PSYCHIC REPRESENTATION OF THE ORGANIC

### a) The idea of "bursting"

The fact that biophysiological states are reflected or represented in psychic modes of behavior fits entirely in the framework of our knowledge concerning psychophysical relationships. There is, however, a peculiar fact which is as yet quite obscure: that language as well as the perception of other's behavior renders the respective physiological state unconsciously, not only figuratively, but in an *immediate* manner. For example: Analytic experience shows that if somebody is called "inaccessible" and "hard," he is also muscularly hypertonic. If many patients feel themselves to be "slimy" or "dirty," analysis shows that their character contains largely anal elements. If the genital character is termed "free," "flowing," "immediate," "relaxed" and "natural," this corresponds entirely to the biophysical structure of his vegetative apparatus. If somebody is "false," "un-genuine," analysis shows a prevalence of substitute contacts and an almost complete absence of free-flowing genital libido. This peculiar connection between the perception of the vegetative state and its linguistic formulation would deserve detailed study; we shall study only one aspect of it here.

Patients feel the character-analytic attack on their armor as a threat to the self. Thus the analytic situation regularly becomes connected with the fear of bodily harm (castration anxiety); the victory of the character-analysis comes to be dreaded as a bodily catastrophe. Intellectually, the patient wishes for the success of the threatening attack, for the breaking down of his psychic rigidity. That is, he wishes for something of which he is, at the same time, intensely afraid. Not only is the breakdown of the character armor feared as a catastrophe; there is, in addition, the fear of losing hold on everything. Thus, the simultaneous wish for and dread of the same thing becomes a typical resistance. What is meant here is not the attitude of the ego toward an impulse but that toward the help expected from the analyst. As long as the character armor is not broken down, the patient is incapable of freely associating as well as of experiencing himself in an alive manner. Thus he expects of the analyst that he will do everything for him, in some magical manner; he assumes a passive attitude which, however, has an entirely active content. That is, the patient mobilizes his *masochistic* tendencies and utilizes them in the service of his resistance. The psychic content of his resistance is the following: "You don't help me, you don't understand me, you don't love me; I shall force you to help me with my stubbornness and my secret reproaches to you." In reality, however, the patient wards off any influence of the analysis. Such situations finally found their explanation in a peculiar situation: *The destruction of the armor, the penetration into the patient's unconscious secrets, is unconsciously felt to be a process of being pricked open or being made to burst.* It is easy to understand that in this connection the passive-feminine phantasy of being pierced fully develops, in male as well as in female patients. Particularly in male patients, there is the following variation of this unconscious phantasy. Lacking genital self-confidence, the patient feels himself impotent. He then forms the phantasy that the analyst lends him his potency, his ability for achievement, in the last analysis, his penis. Underlying this phantasy is occasionally the idea that the analyst, while the patient has intercourse with a woman, penetrates with his penis into the anus of the patient, thus filling and strengthening his own penis and making him potent. This unconscious phantasy explains the identification with the analyst and the reproachful demand to be helped; at the same time it explains the resistance against accepting this help because its unconscious meaning is that of an injury, of being pricked open.

As we know, the masochistic tendency is based on the fact that the patient cannot bring about a physiological relaxation by himself because he experiences the increase in pleasurable excitation as the danger of bursting. Since, however, for natural reasons, he desires this situation intensely, he develops the attitude of expecting and demanding from somebody else that he help him to obtain release; since this release, at the same time, means being made to burst, it is also dreaded and warded off. This state of affairs one does not discover until the first orgastic sensations at the genital appear. Up until that time, it remains hidden; and it remains totally incomprehensible to those psychoanalysts who have not acquired the technique of establishing the capacity for orgastic excitation.

These clinical findings lead us to an important question. The sensation of melting away or of disintegrating is undoubtedly an immediate expression of the excitations occurring in the muscular and vascular systems during the orgasm. Ejaculation as such is analogous to the process which we can bring about by the pricking of a tautly filled bladder. This process is dreaded by patients with orgasm anxiety. The question, then, is, how is it possible that a physiological function finds such an immediate representation in psychic behavior? Frankly, I do not know. But the clarification of this question will mean a great step ahead in our understanding of the interrelationships between physiological and psychological functions. For the time being, it remains obscure.[1] But this clinical observation leads us to another very important question: How is the idea of death represented psychically?

[1] *Footnote, 1945:* Three years later, this assumption was confirmed: The bio-electrical experiments concerning pleasure and anxiety showed that *the intensity of the sensation is functionally identical with the quantity of bio-energetic excitation.*

## b) On the idea of death

The question of the psychic representation of biophysiological processes meets at certain points with the question as to the existence of a will to die. This is a field not only most inaccessible but also most dangerous because here, more than anywhere else, premature speculation bars the way to concrete fact-finding. The theory of the death instinct is, as we said, an attempt to explain with a metaphysical formula manifestations which, with the present state of our knowledge and method, cannot yet be explained. Like any other metaphysical concept, the theory of the death instinct must contain some rational core; but it is difficult to detect because its mystification gets us bogged down in erroneous assumptions. The theory of primary masochism contends that the will to suffer and die is biologically given in the so-called Nirvana principle. The sex-economic investigation of pleasure-creating and pleasure-inhibiting mechanisms, on the other hand, led to the orgasm theory. I shall summarize here the preliminary findings as presented in "The masochistic character."[2]

1. Masochism, which is erroneously thought of as a striving for unpleasure, beyond the pleasure principle, is a *secondary* neurotic formation; it can be analytically dissolved into its component parts and is therefore not a primary biological fact. Rado, in his "new" theory of the neuroses, reduces all anxiety to a "breakthrough of primary masochism." This shows not only a misunderstanding of the libido theory but the same mistake which Adler had made previously: that of stopping with an explanation where the question really begins. The question is: *How can the living organism wish to experience unpleasure or annihilation?*

2. The seeming striving for unpleasure is due to the fact that an original striving for pleasure met with a definite kind of frustration. The patient, in his strivings for pleasure, keeps coming up against the fixed situation of frustration; it *looks as if* he were striving for this situation, while actually he strives for a *pleasurable* goal hidden behind it. *The suffering of the masochist, then,*

---

[2] Cf. *supra*, p. 208ff.

*is objectively given and not subjectively desired;* this distinction is of primary importance.

3. The masochist suffers from a specific disturbance of the pleasure mechanism which is revealed only by the character-analytic dissolution of the psychic armor. It is this: As a result of muscular spasms, the patient experiences the increase of his orgastic sensations beyond a certain measure as unpleasurable and as a danger of "dissolving." The orgastic discharge is felt to be a bursting, disintegrating or melting away in the physical sense and is for this reason warded off. The phantasy of being beaten has the function of obtaining the relaxation which is longed for and at the same time dreaded, of obtaining it without guilt because it is brought about by somebody else who then is responsible for it. This can be found in every case of erogenous masochism. The bringing about of a lesser danger to avoid a greater one is only an intermediate mechanism.

4. If outer and inner reality, as a result of an external inhibition of the striving for pleasure, has become an exclusively unpleasurable situation, then the organism still follows the pleasure-unpleasure-principle even when it destroys itself. Suicide in melancholia, for example, is only the last possible means of release from painful tension.

The clinical investigation of masochism, then, led to formulations which are not at variance with the pleasure-unpleasure-principle or our general knowledge of psychic functioning. But there remained a number of unsolved questions, particularly that of the fear of death and of the idea of death. Character-analysis shows that the "death instinct" is a result of biopsychic inhibition and that there is no such thing as a primary masochism. More, it seems unjustified to speak of masochism as a special impulse which strives for unpleasure. However, other complications entered the questions.

In my search for facts which would make the "Nirvana principle" understandable, I found in my patients a striving for dissolution, for unconsciousness, for non-existence; psychic material, in other words, which seemed to confirm the existence of a genuine and original striving for death. I was always ready to revise my position in the question of the death instinct and to agree with my opponents if clinical material should warrant this.

But my assiduous search for clinical material which would prove the death instinct theory was in vain. Precisely where I began to waver in my strict refutation of the theory I would find a new incontrovertible argument *against* it. To begin with, it was striking to see that this intensive striving for dissolution, etc., appeared in most cases at the end of the treatment, that is, at a time when the patients had to overcome their orgasm anxiety. This was, of course, confusing. Further, this striving rarely appeared in masochists but particularly often in patients who manifested few masochistic mechanisms but had developed the genital mechanisms to a high degree. This increased the confusion. For why should in these patients, who were just on the point of getting well, who had hardly any masochistic mechanisms, who also did not show any negative therapeutic reaction, that is, an "unconscious need for punishment," why should, just in these patients, the "mute" death instinct express itself so strongly?

In going through older theoretical concepts I came across a passage in my book, DIE FUNKTION DES ORGASMUS, which showed me that as early as 1926 I had pointed out a clinical fact which now found its satisfactory explanation. I had mentioned there the peculiar fact that orgasm anxiety appears so often under the mask of fear of death, and that in many neurotic individuals the idea of full sexual gratification is associated with the idea of dying.

A typical clinical illustration will show the fact which has been generally overlooked here. It is necessary to point out again that a check on these clinical phenomena is impossible without the application of the technique of character-analysis which fully liberates the vegetative excitations. A patient with hysterical character developed, toward the conclusion of her treatment, some time after the breakdown of her armor, intense genital anxiety. In her phantasies, the sexual act was an injury to her vagina; she developed the idea that a very big penis penetrated into her much too small vagina and made it burst. These phantasies were based on apprehensions dating from earliest childhood, in connection with sexual play. To the extent to which her genital anxiety was dissolved she began to have orgastic sensations in the genital and the thighs, sensations which heretofore had been unknown to her. She described them as "streaming," "flushes," "sweet-like feelings," and finally as an exquisite pleasurable sensation of *melting*. Nevertheless, an undefinable remnant of genital anxiety remained. One day she started having phantasies about a physician wanting to perform a painful operation on her, and in this connection she remembered the violent fear of physicians she had had at the age of 2 or 3. It was clearly a matter of an anxiety-laden genital striving toward the analyst, warded off by means of the infantile fear of a genital operation. So far, there was nothing unusual in the situation. But now she began to have *pleasurable* phantasies about a painful genital operation. She said, "That's wonderful, one just dissolves, one dies, one finally has peace." She fantasied, in an almost ecstatic manner, the sensations one has under general anesthesia. The feelings one had with it, she said, were those of losing oneself, of "becoming one with the world," of hearing sounds "and yet not hearing them," of withdrawing into the self and dissolving. Now, one could hardly wish for a better description of the "death instinct." Further analysis, however, revealed the true function of this strange behavior. Gradually, the phantasies became more concrete and revealed distinctly two different series, a pleasurable and an unpleasurable one. The content of the unpleasurable phantasies was a prerequisite for the realization of the pleasurable ones. What seemed to be one unpleasurable experience, masochistically striven for, consisted actually of two parts. The anxiety-laden phantasy by itself was: "The physician takes 'something' away at my genital." The hidden pleasurable phantasy was: "In its stead, he gives me a better genital, a male one." In order to make this understandable, the fact must be mentioned that she had a brother two years her senior whom she greatly envied for his genital. She had the idea that a girl could not obtain as much pleasure as a boy; for this reason she wanted to get rid of her genital and get a male one instead. What she was striving for, in reality, was the most intense orgastic pleasure possible; for this, she believed, a male genital was necessary. *The orgastic sensation itself, however, she experienced in the same feelings in which she expressed her striving for death.* Orgasm as well as death were represented by dissolution, losing oneself, melting away; thus, the same thing could be the object of intense striving as well as of intense fear. This association of the ideas of the orgasm and of dying is a general phenomenon. *The striving for non-existence, for the Nirvana, for death, then, is identical with the striving for orgastic release,* that is, the most important manifestation of life. There can be no idea of death which derives from the actual dying of the organism, for an idea can only render what has already been experienced, and nobody has experienced his own death. The ideas of death and dying as we see them in analysis are of two kinds. Either they are ideas of severe injury or destruction of the psychophysical organism; in this case they are accompanied by severe anxiety and are grouped around the idea of genital castration. Or they are ideas of full orgastic gratification and pleasure in the form of bodily dissolution, melting away, etc.; in this case they are basically ideas with a sexual goal. Under specific circumstances, as in the masochist, the orgastic sensation itself is experienced with anxiety; then one finds, extremely rarely, no matter how paradoxical this may sound to the death instinct theorist, a wish for the Nirvana. That is, it is precisely the masochists in whom the ideas of death are little developed, as is stasis anxiety.

Only now, about 12 years after the beginning of the severe differences between the metaphysical death instinct theory and the clinical orgasm theory, the essential point begins to become clear: These two antithetical views had their starting point in the patient's negative therapeutic reaction to direct symptom interpretation. Both tended to go in a biophysiological direction. The former ended in the assumption of an absolute wish for suffering and death, the latter opened an avenue of approach to character-analytic, physiological and psychophysiological problems. It may well be that the difficult struggle for the correct comprehension of the underlying facts will one day be terminated by discoveries concerning the life process *per se.* This much is already certain: what the death instinct theory tried to present as a dissolution of life is precisely what orgasm research, to an increasing extent, begins to comprehend as the very essence of living matter.[3] This dispute, being, as it is, basically a biological one, will not be settled in the realm of psychology. It is certain that it is not a dispute about trifles and that much depends on its outcome, that it is a matter of a decisive question in natural science. It is the question as to the essence and the function of the striving for relaxation inherent in everything living, something which heretofore was subsumed under the vague concept of the "Nirvana principle."[4]

## 9. PLEASURE, ANXIETY, ANGER AND MUSCULAR ARMOR

In character-analytic work, we meet the function of the armor also in the form of chronically fixed *muscular* attitudes. The identity of these functions can be understood only from one principle: the *armoring of the periphery of the biopsychic system.*

Sex-economy approaches these questions from the side of the psychic function of the armor, from the therapeutic task of making the patient regain his vegetative motility. Besides the two basic affects of sexuality and anxiety, we have a third, *anger* or *hatred*. Here, too, we must assume that everyday language reflects a reality when it speaks of "boiling inside" as long as the affect of anger or hatred is not discharged. The assumption of these three basic affects covers, in principle, the realm of the affects: all more complicated affective reactions can be derived from them. It remains to be shown how and to what extent anger can be derived from definite fates met by the two other affects.

Sexuality and anxiety, we found, can be comprehended as two opposite directions of excitation. What, then, is the functional relationship of hatred to the two other basic affects?

Let us proceed from the clinical phenomena of the character

---

[3] One could think here, for example, of the fusion of two gametes. The deeper connection with the orgastic sensations of fusion can only be vaguely guessed at.

[4] *Footnote, 1945:* The decisive significance of the sex-economic concept concerning the ideas of "bursting," "dying," "dissolution," etc., did not become clear until the years of 1936 to 1940 when, on the basis of this hypothesis, the bions and the biological energy in the atmosphere were discovered. Today we know that the neurotic fear of bursting is the expression of an *inhibited* orgonotic expansion of the biosystem.

armor. This concept arose from the study of the dynamic and economic function of the character. In the course of the conflicts between libidinal need and fear of punishment, the ego takes on a definite form. In order to achieve the libidinal restrictions as required by present-day society and in order to master the resulting stasis of energy, it must undergo a change. The ego, the exposed part of the personality, under the continued influence of the conflict betwen libidinal need and threatening outer world, acquires a certain rigidity, a chronic, automatically functioning mode of reaction, that which is called "character." It is as if the affective personality put on an armor, a rigid shell on which the knocks from the outer world as well as the inner demands rebound. This armor makes the individual less sensitive to unpleasure but it also reduces his libidinal and aggressive motility, and, with that, his capacity for pleasure and achievement. The ego becomes more rigid, less mobile; the extent of the armoring determines the extent of the capacity to regulate the energy economy. The measure of this capacity is orgastic potency because it is the immediate expression of vegetative motility. The character armor consumes energy, for it is maintained by the continued consumption of vegetative energies which otherwise, under conditions of motor inhibitions, would create anxiety. The consumption of vegetative energy, then, is one of the functions of the character armor.

The character-analytic dissolution of the armor regularly reveals bound-up aggression. But how does this oft-mentioned binding of aggression or anxiety take place, concretely? If the analysis succeeds in freeing the aggression which is bound in the armor, anxiety makes its appearance. That is, anxiety can be "converted" into aggression, and aggression into anxiety. Are we dealing here with a relationship analogous to that of sexual excitation and anxiety? This is not an easy question to answer.

To begin with, clinical observation reveals a number of peculiar facts. Inhibition of aggression and psychic armoring go hand in hand with an increased tonus, even a rigidity, of the musculature. Affect-blocked patients lie on the couch stiff as a board, without any motion. It is difficult to eliminate this muscular tension. If one lets the patient relax consciously, the muscular tension is replaced by restlessness. In other cases patients carry out various unconscious movements, and when these are stopped, anxious sensations immediately make their appearance. It is observations like these that made Ferenczi, with a good intuition, develop his "active technique." He realized that the inhibition of chronic muscular reactions increased the tension. While this is correct, it is not merely a matter of a quantitative change in excitation. Rather, it is a matter of a functional identity of character armor and muscular hypertension. *Every increase of muscular tonus in the direction of rigidity indicates that a vegetative excitation, anxiety or sexuality, has become bound up.* Many patients succeed in eliminating or at least alleviating genital sensations or anxious sensations by motor unrest. One is reminded here of the great role played by motor unrest in children as a discharge of energy.

One finds very often that the state of muscular tension is different *before* the solution of an acute repression and *afterwards*. When patients are in an acute resistance, that is, when they try to keep an idea or an impulse from consciousness, they often feel a tension, say, in the head, the thighs or the buttocks. After having overcome the resistance, they suddenly feel relaxed. One patient said in such a situation, "I feel as if I had had sexual gratification."

We know that every recollection of a repressed ideational content goes with a psychic relief, which, as we also know, does not yet mean cure. Whence this relief? We used to say that it is a matter of a discharge of psychic energy which previously was bound. Psychic tension and relief cannot be without a somatic representation, for tension and relaxation are biophysical processes. Heretofore, we have transferred these concepts to the psychic realm. This was correct, except that it is not a matter of "transferring" the physiological concept to the psychic realm, not a matter of an analogy, but that of a true identity, the identity of psychic and somatic function.

Every neurotic is muscularly dystonic, and every cure is directly reflected in a change of muscular habitus. This is most readily observable in the compulsive character. His muscular rigidity is expressed in awkwardness, unrhythmical movements, particularly in the sexual act, a lack of mimetic expression, a typical rigidity of the facial musculature which often gives a mask-like impression. There is, typically, a deep line between nostril and corner of the mouth, and a certain rigid expression in the eyes resulting from a rigidity of the lid muscles. The musculature of the buttocks is always tense.

While the typical compulsive character develops a general muscular rigidity, we find in other patients a rigidity in certain regions combined with a flaccidity (hypotonus) in other regions. This is particularly frequent in passive-feminine characters. The complete rigidity in the catatonic stupor corresponds to a complete psychic armoring. This is ordinarily explained by disturbances of extrapyramidal innervations. That nerve tracts are involved in changes of muscular tonus goes without saying, but it should be equally clear that such innervations are only the expression of a general disturbance of function. To believe that finding the innervation or its path explains anything is naive.

The psychic rigidity of post-encephalitics is by no means an "expression" or a result of their muscular rigidity; rather, muscular rigidity and psychic rigidity together are the sign of a disturbance in the vegetative motility of the total biological system. The question remains open whether the disturbance of extrapyramidal innervation is not itself the result of a primary factor which makes itself felt not at the end organs, but at the vegetative apparatus itself. Mechanistic neurology explains, say, a spasm of the anal sphincter from the continued excitation of the corresponding nerves. Here, the difference between a mechanistic-anatomical and a functional view is easily demonstrated: sex-economy thinks of the nerves only as the transmitters of general vegetative excitation.

The spasm of the anal sphincter, which leads to a number of severe intestinal conditions, results from an infantile fear of defecation. The explanation that it is due to the pleasure connected with holding back the feces is incomplete, to say the least. The muscular holding back of the feces is the prototype of repression in general and is its initial step in the anal sphere. In the oral and genital sphere, repression is muscularly represented as a tightening of the mouth, a spasm in the throat and chest, and in a chronic tension in the pelvic musculature.

The liberation of the vegetative excitation from its fixation in the tensions of the musculature of the head, neck, throat, etc., is the indispensable prerequisite of dissolving oral fixations in general. Neither the recollection of oral experiences nor the discussion of genital anxiety can take its place. Without it, one may obtain the memories but not the corresponding excitations. These are usually well hidden. They easily escape attention because they are hidden in unobtrusive modes of behavior which seem to be quite natural to the person in question. The mechanisms of the pathological displacements and fixations of the vegetative energies may be hidden in such phenomena as the following: a weak voice which hardly sounds at all, a lack of movement of the mouth in talking, a slightly mask-like facial expression, a slight indication of the facial expression of a suckling infant, an unobtrusive wrinkling of the forehead, drooping eyelids, a tension in the scalp, a latent hypersensitivity of the larynx, a hasty, jerky way of talking, seemingly incidental sounds or movements in talking, a certain way of holding the head to one side, of shaking it, etc. One will find that the fear of genital contact does not make its appearance as long as these symptoms in the head and neck regions have not been uncovered and eliminated. Genital anxiety, in most cases, is displaced from below upwards and is bound in the hypertonus of the musculature of the neck. For example, in the case of a young girl, the fear of an operation at the genital was expressed in an attitude of her head which, after having become aware of it, she described as follows: "I'm lying here as if my head were nailed down." She looked, in fact, as if her head were held down by an invisible force which made it impossible for her to move.

One will rightly ask whether these concepts are not at variance with another concept, and point out that the increase in muscular tonus is a sexual-parasympathetic function and the decrease in muscular tonus and muscular paralysis an anxious sympathetic function. How is it possible, then, one will ask, that, say, the anxious holding back of the feces in the child goes with a muscular *contraction*? For a long time, I was unable to solve this contradiction. But, as is always the case with such difficulties in the exploration of connections, it was precisely the objection which led to increased insight.

To begin with, one had to realize that the process of muscular tension in sexual excitation and that in anxiety could not be the same thing. In the expectation of a danger, the musculature is tense, as if ready for action; think, for example, of a deer ready to run away. In fright, the musculature is suddenly depleted of energy ("paralyzed with fright"). The fact that in fright a sudden diarrhea may occur as a result of sudden paralysis of the anal sphincter fits our concept of the connection between anxiety and sympathetic function. Thus one can distinguish a sympathetic anxiety diarrhea in fright from a parasympathetic diarrhea in sexual excitation. The former is due to a paralysis of the sphincter (sympathetic function), the latter to increased peristalsis (parasympathetic function). In sexual excitation, the musculature is under tonus, that is, ready for motor action, for contraction and relaxation. In anxious expectation, on the other hand, the tension of the musculature becomes lasting if it is not followed by motor activity. This is replaced by paralysis if the fright reaction follows, or by the reaction of motor flight. But also, neither of these reactions may occur. Then, we have a condition which, in contradistinction to the paralysis with fright, one might call rigidity with fright ("scared stiff"). In paralysis with fright, the musculature becomes flaccid, depleted of energy while the vasomotor system, conversely, is in full excitation: palpitation, sweating and pallor. In the rigidity with fright, on the other hand, the peripheral musculature is rigid, the sensation of anxiety hardly present if at all; one is "seemingly calm"; but in reality one is incapable of moving, incapable of motor flight as well as of vegetative flight into the self.

These facts show the following: *Muscular rigidity can take the place of the vegetative anxiety reaction,* in other words, the same excitation which in the case of fright paralysis retreats to the center of the organism forms, in the case of fright rigidity, *a peripheral muscular armor of the organism*.[1] Muscular tension which is lasting and is not resolved in motor activity absorbs energies which otherwise would appear as anxiety; that is, the tension prevents the anxiety. In this process we recognize the prototype of the well-known binding of anxiety through aggression, which aggression, when itself inhibited, leads to *affect-block*.

These clinical findings are of the greatest importance for the theory of the affects. Now we understand the connection between each of the following:

Character armor and muscular armor;

Loosening of the muscular armor and reappearance of anxiety;

Binding of anxiety and establishment of muscular rigidity;

Muscular tension and libidinal inhibition;

Development of libidinal motility and muscular loosening.

Before drawing a theoretical conclusion, we shall adduce further clinical facts concerning the connection between muscle tonus and sexual tension. When during character-analysis, as a result of the dissolution of the character rigidities, the muscle tensions begin to give way, one or the other of three reactions occurs: anxiety, destruction or a libidinal impulse. The libidinal impulse is a flowing of excitation and body fluids to the periphery, anxiety a flowing to the center of the organism. The destructive excitation also corresponds to an excitation in the direction of the periphery, but only to the musculature of the extremities. As we have seen, all three basic excitations can be released from the muscular armor. The inevitable conclusion is the following: *Chronic muscular hypertension represents an inhibition of every kind of excitation, of pleasure, anxiety and hatred alike*. It is as if the inhibition of the vital functions (libido, anxiety, destruction) took place by way of the formation of a muscular armor around the center of the biological person. If character formation has such close connections with the tonus of the musculature, we are safe in assuming a functional identity of neurotic

---

[1] It remains to be seen whether the biological armorings, say, of turtles, develop in a similar manner.

character and muscular dystonus. We shall adduce further facts which confirm this assumption, as well as others which might possibly restrict the validity of the concept of the functional identity of character armor and muscular armor.

Purely from the point of view of appearance, sexual charm goes with a relaxed musculature and free-flowing psychic activity. The rhythm of the motions, the *alternation* of muscular tension and relaxation, combines with modulation in speech and general musicality; in such people one also has the feeling of immediate psychic contact. The charm of children who have not yet effected any severe repressions, particularly in the anal sphere, has the same basis. Rigid, awkward and unrhythmical people impress us as also psychically stiff, wooden and immobile; there is little modulation in their speech and they are not musical. Many of them never "thaw out" and are able "to let go a little" only under conditions of intimate acquaintanceship. The trained observer will, in such a case, immediately notice a change in the muscular behavior. Psychic and somatic rigidity, then, are not mutual expressions of one another, but form a unitary function. Strongly armored people impress one as unerotic as well as lacking anxiety. Depending on the depth of such armoring, the rigidity may be combined with varying degrees of *inner* excitation.

In melancholic or depressed patients, speech and facial expression are stiff, as if every motion required the overcoming of a resistance. In a manic condition, on the other hand, the impulses seem to suddenly flood the whole personality. In the catatonic stupor, psychic and muscular rigidity are completely identical, just as a dissolution of the condition brings back psychic as well as muscular motility.

Here, we may gain some insight into the nature of laughing (joyful facial expression) and grief (depressive expression). With laughter, the facial musculature contracts, with depression, it becomes flaccid. This is in harmony with the fact that muscular contraction (clonus of the diaphragm, "belly-shaking laugh") is parasympathetic, libidinous, while muscular flaccidity is sympathetic, anti-libidinous.

The question arises whether in the "genital characters" who do not suffer from chronic stasis of energy, there is or can be a muscular armoring. If so, this would constitute an objection to my thesis of the functional identity of character armor and muscular armor. For the genital character, too, has formed a "character." Examination of such characters shows that here, too, an armoring can take place, that the ability to avoid unpleasure and anxiety by the formation of a peripheral armor is present. In such cases, total attitude and facial expression also become more tense. Then, sexual excitability and capacity for sexual pleasure are reduced, sometimes working capacity also. What happens is merely that free-flowing, gratifying work is replaced by mechanical, pleasure-less performance. For this reason, a happy sexual life is the best structural basis for productive achievement. The difference is this: in the case of neurotic armoring, the muscular rigidity is chronic and automatic, while the genital character has his armor at his disposal; he can put it in operation or out of operation at will. What matters here, from the point of view of sex-economy, is not the fact *that* biopsychic energy becomes bound but *in which form* this takes place, whether the availability of energy is reduced or not. It cannot be the goal of mental hygiene to prevent the ability to form an armor; the goal can only be that of guaranteeing the maximum vegetative motility, in other words, the formation of an armor which is mobile. This is a task which is incompatible with any of the existing educational and moral institutions.

The following example will demonstrate the functional relationship between character attitude, muscular tension and vegetative excitation. The most striking thing about this patient was that everything he presented was superficial; he himself felt it to be nothing more than "chattering" even when he talked about the most serious things. It soon became clear that this superficiality would become the central character resistance, for it made it possible for him to nullify any affective impulse. It turned out that "chattering" and "superficiality" corresponded to an identification with his stepmother who had these same characteristics. This identification contained his passive-feminine attitude toward the father; his chattering was an attempt to win, placate and entertain his homosexual object, to "stroke" it like a dangerous beast, as it were. But it also served as a substitute contact, for, as the analysis showed later, the patient had no contact with his father. This contactlessness hid the repression of violent aggression toward his father. The chattering, then, meant three different things: Passive-feminine wooing (vegetative function), defense against aggressive impulses (armor function), and a compensation of the contactlessness. The psychic content of the superficiality was something as follows: "I must win over my father, must please and entertain him; but I feel empty with it, I don't care about him, for in reality I hate him; that I cannot show, and basically I don't have any contact with him." The patient's awkwardness and muscular rigidity was no less striking than the psychic behavior just described. He would lie on the couch stiff as a board, without moving at all. It was clear that any analytic endeavor was hopeless without an attempt to break through this muscular armoring. In spite of the fact that the patient gave an impression of apprehensiveness, he denied feeling any anxiety. He had severe conditions of depersonalization and felt himself to be unalive. At this stage, his infantile experiences were not important in themselves or in connection with his neurotic symptoms, but only in their connection with this armoring. The task was that of breaking through this armor and of crystallizing out of it the infantile history as well as the suppressed vegetative excitations.

To begin with, the superficiality revealed itself as a "fear of depth" or fear of falling. For a long time, the patient had suffered from intense fear of falling, of drowning, of dropping into an abyss, of falling into the water from a boat, a fear of sleigh-riding, etc. It soon became clear that these fears were based on the fear of the typical sensations in the diaphragmatic region which are experienced on a roller coaster or in a suddenly descending elevator. As I have shown in my book, Die Funktion des Orgasmus, the fear of orgastic excitation is often expressed as a fear of falling. It was not surprising, therefore, to find that this patient suffered from a severe orgastic disturbance precisely of this kind. The superficiality, then, was not merely a passive attitude but served a well-defined function. It was an *active* attitude, a defense against the "fear of the depth," and the fear of vegetative excitation. One had to assume that there was a connection between these two warded-off conditions, that the *fear of falling* was identical with the *fear of vegetative excitation*. What, then, was this connection?

The patient remembered that as a child, when on the swing, he would make himself rigid as soon as he felt the sensations in the diaphragmatic region. From this period dated his muscular habitus which was characterized by lack of rhythm and coordination and by awkwardness. It may be of interest to musical theorists that he seemed to be completely unmusical. This lack of musicality, however, also had its definite history. In connection with his contactlessness and muscular armor, the analysis revealed the fact that this defect was also due to a defense against vegetative excitation. He remembered that his mother, when he was a small child, used to sing sentimental songs to him. This used to excite him tremendously, causing conditions of tension and motor unrest. When, as a result of frustration, he repressed his libidinal attachment to his mother, his musicality suffered the same fate. Not only because musical experiences were an integral part of the relationship with his mother but also because he could not stand the vegetative excitations aroused by the music. This was connected with the excitation experienced with infantile masturbation which had caused severe anxiety.

In dreams, the patients' resistance against the uncovering of unconscious material is often represented as the fear of, say, going down into a basement or of falling into an abyss. About this connection, there can be no doubt, but it is not immediately understandable. Why should the unconscious be associated with the depth and the fear of the unconscious with the fear of falling? The riddle solved itself in the following manner: The unconscious is the reservoir of repressed vegetative excitations, that is, of excitations which are barred from discharge. The healthy individual perceives them as sexual excitation and gratification; people with inhibited vegetative motility experience them as unpleasurable sensations of anxiety or oppression in the solar plexus region. These sensations are very similar to those experienced in fright or with the sudden descent in an elevator or on a roller coaster, or the sensations in the genital region experienced when one stands above a precipice and looks down. In such a situation, there appears, together with the idea of falling down, a sensation of contraction in the genital. That is, at the mere idea of the danger the organism behaves as if the danger were actually present, and withdraws into itself. Since, in fright, the excitations and body fluids are withdrawn to the center of the organism; since, further, in the case of actual falling, this process takes place as the automatic reaction of the organism, it becomes clear that *the idea of depth and of falling must be identical with the sensation of central excitation in the organism.* This makes us understand the otherwise incomprehensible fact that so many people experience riding on a swing or roller coaster with a mixture of pleasure and anxiety. According to the sex-economic concept, anxiety and pleasure are nothing but the same vegetative excitation flowing in opposite directions. To return to our patient: His fear of the unconscious was indeed objectively identical with the fear of the depth. Now, his superficiality becomes sex-economically understandable as an active attitude for the avoidance of the vegetative excitations of anxiety as well as of pleasure, the latter being experienced with anxiety and therefore unpleasurably.

There remains the question as to the connection between muscular rigidity and characterological superficiality and contactlessness. One can say that the muscular armor fulfils the same function in the physiological behavior as does contactlessness and superficiality in the characterological and psychic behavior. Since the sex-economic concept of the basic relationship between physiological and psychic apparatus is not merely one of mutual interdependence but one of functional identity with simultaneous antithesis, the further question arises whether muscular rigidity is not functionally identical with the character armor, with contactlessness, affect-block, etc. The *antithetical* relationship is clear; the physiological behavior determines the psychic behavior and vice versa. But this is much less important for an understanding of psychosomatic relationships than is their functional identity.

I shall present another clinical example to show how the vegetative energy can be liberated from the psychic and muscular armor. This patient was characterized by his intense phallic-narcissistic defense against his passive-homosexual impulses. This central psychic conflict was represented in his appearance as follows: He was somatically rigid and aggressive in a compensatory way. It was very difficult to make him aware of this conflict because he fought tremendously against the breakthrough and the realization of his anal-homosexual tendencies. When the breakthrough finally succeeded, the patient, to my surprise, developed a vegetative shock. One day he came to the hour with a stiff neck, violent headache, dilated pupils, patchy redness and pallor of the skin, and severe oppression. When he moved his head, the pressure in it became less, when he held it still it became worse. Nausea and vertigo completed the picture of sympatheticotonia. The patient soon recovered from this condition. It provided a drastic confirmation of my concepts of the relationships between character, sexual stasis and vegetative excitation. The problem of schizophrenia seems to lie here. The connections between the vegetative and the characterological, so striking in the psychoses, may one day find their clarification along these concepts. What is new in these concepts is not that there is a connection between psychic apparatus and vegetative system, nor that they have a mutual functional relationship. What is new is this:

1. That the basic function of psychic life is of a sex-economic nature;

2. That the excitations of sexuality and anxiety are identical excitations with opposite direction; that they represent the basic antithesis in vegetative life which allows of no further derivation than a physical one;

3. That character formation results from a binding of bio-energy;

4. That character armor and muscular armor are functionally identical;

5. That the bio-energy can be re-mobilized from the character armor and muscular armor with a definite technique, and, for the time being, only with this technique.

I should like to emphasize that the theory developed out of character-analytic clinical observation is only the beginning of an extensive comprehension of functional psychosomatic relationships, that the problems are incomparably more difficult and complex than what is covered by the results to date. However, it has been possible to make some fundamental formulations which will further our knowledge of psychophysical relationships. The attempt to apply the functionalistic method of investigation was successful and is justified by the results. It is in sharp contradistinction to the attempts of arriving at a usable knowledge of psychosomatic relationships by way of metaphysical-idealistic or mechanistic-causal-materialistic methods. This is not the place to present the fundamental epistemiological objections to the methods just mentioned. The sex-economic concept differs from the recent "organismal" concepts of psychophysical relationships by the functional approach and the concentration of the problem in the function of the orgasm.

## 10. THE TWO GREAT LEAPS IN NATURAL DEVELOPMENT[1]

Thus far, we have formed a concept of the connection between psychic and somatic, a concept based on ample clinical experience. On the basis of this concept we may venture to formulate a hypothesis for further work in this field, as long as we are willing to give it up if it should prove unfruitful or misleading.

In natural development we find two great and sudden leaps which in turn give rise to other, *gradual* processes. The first is that from the inorganic into the organic, into vegetative life. The second leap is that from organic-vegetative development into that of the psychic apparatus, in particular, into consciousness with its central ability of *self-perception*. The organic, in growing out of the inorganic, and the psychic, in growing out of the vegetative, both retain, in their function and process, the

---

[1] *Footnote, 1945: Cf.* my orgone-biophysical publications in the *International Journal of Sex-economy and Orgone-Research,* 1942-1945.

laws operating in their matrix. In the organic realm, we find the same basic physical and chemical laws as in the inorganic; in the psychic, we find the same basic reactions of tension and relaxation, stasis and discharge of energy, excitability, etc., as in the vegetative. The functional phenomenon which we found in character formation and which we described as dissociation and antithesis apparently governs also the more comprehensive developments from inorganic to organic and from organic-vegetative to psychic. In the organism, the organic assumes a position antithetical to the inorganic, and the psychic to the vegetative.[1] They are unitary and yet at the same time antithetical.

In the ability of the psychic apparatus to develop consciousness and self-perception, the most peculiar and most obscure functions of conscious psychic life, we see the *immediate* expression of this antithesis; in the phenomenon of depersonalization the function of self-perception appears in a pathologically distorted form. A more thorough study of depersonalization and related phenomena by way of the functional method will probably contribute to a solution of the problem of consciousness.

I must ask the reader to take these suggestions for what they are: rough sketches in a very obscure field to which the right access still remains to be found. True, they differ fundamentally from previous views of the interrelation between the psychic and the somatic. On the other hand, they cannot claim to be taken seriously until they succeed in solving those problems which thus far have remained inaccessible to older views (such as the mechanistic-materialistic or the idealistic) and which, from all appearances, will remain inaccessible to them. These basic questions of life are still entirely obscure. This imposes two demands on us: first, to be extremely cautious in formulating new views; and second, on the other hand, to break with all views which fail to lead us ahead even one step and which present only premature attempts to anticipate the solution of problems which are as yet not possible. The path before functional psychology is uncertain

---

[1] These statements are inexact. However, it would be premature to make, at this time, binding statements concerning the relationship of the "psychic" to the vegetative and of consciousness to both of the former.

and full of stumbling-blocks; only recently has sex-economy found a basis in some fundamental formulations, and it still awaits experimental orgasm research. One thing, however, is certain: If natural science once succeeds in really solving the problem of psychosomatic interrelations, that is, in solving them in such a manner that it results in practical human endeavor instead of merely in armchair theories, that achievement will mean the death-knell of all transcendental mysticism, of the "absolute objective spirit" and of all those ideologies which are subsumed under mysticism in the stricter and wider sense. Human vegetative life is only a part of the general process of nature. In his vegetative current, man experiences a bit of nature. Its real comprehension will leave no room for psychic formations which owe their life-destructive existence only to our sketchy knowledge of their sources, which prevent the productive unfolding of vegetative energy, thus causing suffering and disease, and which, on top of everything, in order to justify their existence, are presented as fate-given and unalterable. Man, moved by obscure "oceanic" feelings, dreams instead of mastering his existence, and perishes from dreams. But this dreaming is only an inkling of the future productivity of his vegetative life. Perhaps, science will one day succeed in making humanity's dream of happiness a reality. Then, the question, forever unanswerable, as to the meaning of life, will be replaced by the fulfilment of life.

## Chapter XV

# THE EXPRESSIVE LANGUAGE OF THE LIVING IN ORGONE THERAPY

## 1. THE FUNCTION OF EMOTION

The concept of "orgone therapy" comprises all medical and pedagogical techniques operating with the "biological" energy, the orgone. True, the cosmic orgone energy was not discovered until 1939, but, long before this discovery the established goal of character-analysis was the liberation of "psychic energy," as it was then called, from the character armor and muscular armor, and the establishment of orgastic potency. The reader who is familiar with orgone biophysics knows the development of character-analysis (from 1926 to 1934) into "vegetotherapy" (from 1935 on). It was not sensationalism which caused such diverse terms to be coined within one and the same branch of science. Rather, a consistent application of a natural-scientific energy concept in the field of psychic processes led, of necessity, to new terms for new techniques in the successive stages of development.

The fact that it was sex-economically oriented psychiatry which provided the access to the cosmic energy must be regarded as a great triumph for *orgonomic functionalism*. Although the orgone energy is a strictly physical form of energy, there are good reasons why it was discovered by a psychiatrist and not a physicist. The logic of this discovery within the realm of biopsychiatry is shown in its development, as presented in THE DISCOVERY OF THE ORGONE, vol. 1: THE FUNCTION OF THE ORGASM.

When, in 1935, the orgasm reflex was discovered, the accent in character-analytic work shifted to the *somatic* realm. The term "vegetotherapy" represented the fact that now my therapeutic technique influenced the character neurosis in the *physio-*

*logical* realm. We spoke of "character-analytic vegetotherapy," indicating the simultaneous work on the psychic and somatic apparatus. This term had its disadvantages, which, at that time, could not be helped. For one thing, it was too long. It contained the term, "vegetative," which sounded correct in German but reminded one of "vegetables" in English. Finally, it still represented a division of the organism into a psychic and a somatic part, which was in contradiction with our unitary concept of the organism.

These conceptual difficulties were ended by the discovery of the orgone. *The cosmic orgone energy functions in the living organism as specific biological energy.* As such, it governs the total organism and expresses itself in the emotions as well as the purely biophysical organ movements. Thus psychiatry, for the first time and with its own means, had found roots in objective natural-scientific processes. This statement calls for some amplification:

Up to the discovery of the orgone, psychiatry always had to turn to inorganic physics in its attempts to give an *objective* and *quantitative* basis to its psychological contentions. Neither mechanical brain lesions nor the chemicophysical processes in the organism, nor the obsolete concepts of the cerebral localisation of sensations and ideas ever succeeded in satisfactorily explaining emotional processes. In contradistinction, orgone biophysics, from the very beginning, was concerned with the central problem of all psychiatry, the *emotions.* Literally, "emotion" means "moving out," "protruding." It is not only permissible but necessary to take the word "emotion" literally in speaking of sensations and movements. Microscopic observation of amebae subjected to slight electric stimuli renders the meaning of the term "emotion" in an unmistakable manner. *Basically, emotion is an expressive plasmatic motion.* Pleasurable stimuli cause an "emotion" of the protoplasm from the center towards the periphery. Conversely, unpleasurable stimuli cause an "emotion"—or rather, "remotion"—from the periphery to the center of the organism. These two basic directions of biophysical plasma current correspond to the two basic affects of the psychic apparatus, pleasure and anxiety.

As the experiments at the oscillograph have shown, the physical plasma motion and the corresponding sensation are functionally identical. They are indivisible; one is not conceivable without the other. But, as we know, they are not only functionally identical, but at the same time antithetical, for a biophysical plasma excitation results in a sensation, and a sensation is expressed in a plasmatic motion. These facts, today, provide a sound fundament of orgone biophysics.

No matter whether we release the emotions from the character armor by way of "character-analysis," or from the muscular armor by way of "vegetotherapy," in either case we cause plasmatic excitations and motions. What moves is essentially the orgone energy with which the body fluids are charged. *The mobilization of the plasmatic currents and emotions, then, is identical with the mobilization of orgone energy in the organism.* It is clearly evidenced by vasomotor changes. In every case, whether we produce memories, dissolve defense mechanisms or muscular spasms, we work on the orgone energy of the organism. The difference lies merely in the efficacy of the various methods; a memory will not produce affect outbreaks like the dissolution of, say, a diaphragmatic block.

All this will explain why the term "orgone therapy" includes character-analysis and vegetotherapy.[1] The common goal is the mobilization of the patient's plasmatic currents. In other words, we cannot split up a living organism into character attitudes, muscles and plasma functions if we take our *unitary* concept of the organism seriously, in a practical way.

In orgone therapy, we work on the biological depth, the plasma system, the "biological core" of the organism. The reader will realize that this is a decisive step. We have left the realm of psychology, including "depth psychology," and have even gone beyond the physiology of the nerves and muscles into the realm of the protoplasmatic functions. These steps are to be taken very seriously; they have far-reaching practical and theoretical consequences, for they change our biopsychiatric techniques basi-

---

[1] The purely physiological orgone therapy by means of the orgone accumulator is discussed in THE DISCOVERY OF THE ORGONE, vol. 2: THE CANCER BIOPATHY.

cally. We no longer work merely on individual conflicts and special armorings but on the *living function* itself. As we gradually learn to understand and influence this function, the purely psychological and physiological functions are influenced automatically. Schematic specializing is thus excluded.

## 2. PLASMATIC EXPRESSIVE MOVEMENTS AND EMOTIONAL EXPRESSION

It is difficult to give a strict functional definition of "the living." The concepts of traditional psychology and depth psychology are bound up with *word* formations. The living, however, functions beyond all verbal ideas and concepts. Verbal language is a biological form of expression on a high level of development. It is by no means an indispensable attribute of the living, for the living functions long before there is a verbal language. Depth psychology, therefore, operates with a function of recent origin. Many animals express themselves by sounds. But the living functions beyond and before any sound formation as a form of expression.

The process of word formation itself shows the way in which the living "expresses itself." The term "expression," apparently on the basis of organ sensations, describes precisely the language of the living: *The living expresses itself in movements, in "expressive movements."* The expressive movement is an inherent characteristic of the protoplasm. It distinguishes the living strictly from the non-living systems. The term means, literally, that something in the living system "presses itself out" and, consequently, "moves." This can mean nothing but the movement of the protoplasm, that is, expansion and contraction. The literal meaning of "emotion" is "moving out," which is the same as "expressive movement." The physical process of plasmatic emotion or expressive movement always goes with an immediately understandable *meaning* which we call the *emotional expression*. The movement of the plasm, then, has an expression in the sense of an emotion, and the emotion or the expression of an organism is bound to movement. The latter part of this sentence will require some qualification, for we know from orgone therapy that many people present an expression which is caused by immobility and rigidity.

All this is not a play with words. It is clear that language, in the process of word formation, depends on the perception of inner movements and organ sensations, and that the words which describe emotional states render, in an *immediate* way, the corresponding expressive movements of living matter.

Even though language reflects the state of plasmatic emotion in an immediate way, it cannot itself reach this state. The living not only functions before and beyond word language; more than that, it has *its own specific forms of expression which cannot be put into words at all*. Every musical individual knows the state of emotion created by great music; yet, it is impossible to put this emotion into words. Music is wordless. Nevertheless, it is an expression of movement and creates in the listener the expression of being "moved." The wordlessness of music is generally considered either a sign of mystical spirituality or of deepest emotion incapable of being expressed in words. The natural-scientific interpretation is that musical expression comes from the very depths of the living. What is described as the "spirituality" of great music, then, is an appropriate description of the simple fact that seriousness of feeling is identical with contact with the living *beyond the confine of words*.

Thus far, science has had nothing decisive to say about the nature of musical emotional expression. Doubtless, the artist speaks to us in the form of wordless expressive movements from the depth of the living function; but what he expresses in music or painting he could no more put into words than can we. More, he guards against attempts to translate the expressive language of art into word language; he is much concerned about the purity of his expressive language. He thus confirms the orgone-biophysical contention that the living, beyond any word language and independent of it, has its own expressive language. Let us illustrate from everyday experience in orgone therapy.

The patients come to the orgone therapist full of problems. To the experienced eye, these problems are directly visible in their expressive movements and the emotional expression of their bodies. If one lets the patient talk at random, one will find that the talking *leads away* from the problems, that it *obscures* them in one way or another. In order to arrive at a true evaluation, one has to ask the patient *not* to talk for a while. This measure proves highly fruitful. For as soon as the patient ceases to talk, the bodily expression of emotion becomes clearly manifest. After a few minutes of silence, one usually comprehends the outstanding character trait, or, more correctly, the plasmatic emotional expression. While the patient, during his talking, seemed to smile in a friendly manner, now, in silence, the smile turns into an empty grin the mask-like character of which will soon become obvious even to the patient. While the patient, talking, seemed to talk about his life with a restrained seriousness, now, in silence, an expression of, say, repressed anger will appear in chin and neck.

These examples may suffice to show that *word language very often also functions as a defense:* the word language obscures the expressive language of the biological core. In many cases this goes so far that the words no longer express anything and the word language is no longer anything but a meaningless activity of the respective muscles. Long experience has convinced me that in many psychoanalyses of years' duration, the treatment became the victim of this pathological kind of word language. This clinical experience can—and must—be applied to the social scene: innumerable speeches, publications and political debates do not have as their function the disclosing of vital questions of life but of drowning them in verbiage.

Orgone therapy is distinguished from all other modes of influencing the organism by the fact that the patient is asked to express himself *biologically* while word language is eliminated to a far-reaching degree. This leads the patient to a depth from which he constantly tries to flee. Thus one learns, in the course of orgone therapy, to understand the language of the living and to influence it. The primary expressive language of the living protoplasm is not present in "pure" form; if the patient's mode of expression were "purely" biological, he would have no reason for seeking the help of the orgone therapist. We must first penetrate through layers of pathological, unnatural modes of expression before arriving at the *genuine* biological mode of expression. After all, human biopathy is nothing but the sum total of all distortions of the natural modes of expression of the living organism. By disclosing the pathological forms of expression we learn to know human biopathy in a depth which is inaccessible to the therapeutic techniques working with word language. Unfortunately, *the biopathy, with its distorted expression of life, is outside the realm of language and concepts.*

Orgone-therapeutic work on the biopathy, therefore, takes place essentially outside the realm of word language. Of course, we also use the spoken word; but the words do not refer to the ideational concepts of everyday, but to *organ sensations.* It would be perfectly useless, for example, to try to make the patient understand his condition in terms of, say, physiology. We cannot say to him, "Your masseter muscles are in a state of chronic contraction, that is why your chin does not move in talking, why your voice is monotonous, why you cannot cry; you have to swallow constantly in order to suppress an impulse to cry." True, the patient would understand such statements intellectually, but that would not change his condition.

We work on a biologically deeper level of understanding. It is not very important, anyhow, just what *individual* muscles are contracted. It would be useless, for example, to press on the masseter muscles; the only reaction would be ordinary pain. *We work with the expressive language.* Only when we have *felt* the facial *expression* of the patient are we also in a position to understand it. To "understand" it means here, quite strictly, to know which emotion is "expressed" in it. In that, it makes no difference whether the emotion is actively mobile or whether it is held back, immobile. We have to inquire as to what is the difference between a mobile and a held-back emotion.

In "feeling" the emotional expression of a patient we operate with primary biological functions. If, in a flock of birds, one becomes restless and, "sensing danger," flies off, the whole flock will do so, irrespective of whether or not the other birds have noticed the cause of the restlessness. The panic reaction among animals is based on an involuntary reproduction of the emotional expression of anxiety. It is not difficult to cause people on the street to stop and scan the sky if one acts as if one were observing something very interesting in the sky. These examples may suffice.

The emotional expression of the patient produces in our organism an involuntary *imitation*. Imitating, we feel and understand the expression in ourselves and with that in the patient. Since every motion has an expression and thus discloses the emotional state of the protoplasm, the language of expression becomes an essential means of communication with the patient's emotions. As already stated, the word language *disturbs* the language of expression. By "character attitude" we mean the total *expression* of an organism. This is literally identical with the total *impression* which the organism makes on us.

The emotional expression may greatly vary, in its details, from individual to individual. There are no two individuals with exactly the same speech, the same respiratory block or the same gait. Nevertheless, some general types can be easily distinguished. In depth psychology, we distinguish the "neurotic" and the "genital" character, on the basis of the type of muscular and character armor. We call a character neurotic when the organism is governed by a rigid armor which the individual cannot alter or eliminate. We speak of a genital character when the emotional reactions are not inhibited by rigid automatisms, when, in other words, the individual is capable of reacting biologically, according to the situation in which he finds himself. These two basic character types can be equally sharply distinguished in the realm of biological functioning:

Once one has learned to understand the language of biological expression, the kind of armor and the extent of its rigidity are not difficult to evaluate. The total expression of the armored individual is that of "holding back." This expression has to be taken literally: *the organism expresses the fact that it is holding back.* The shoulders are pulled back, the thorax pulled up, the chin is held rigid, respiration is shallow, the lower back is arched, the pelvis is retracted and "dead," the legs are stretched out stiffly or lack expression; these are some of the main attitudes of total holding back. Schematically, it can be represented as follows:

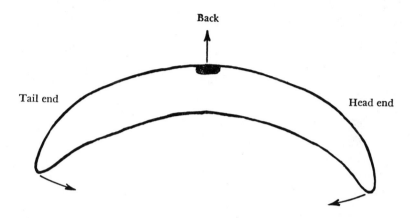

*The basic biophysical attitude of the* unarmored *organism*

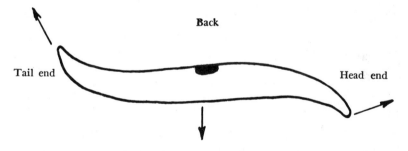

*The basic biophysical attitude of the* armored *organism: "holding back"*

This basic bodily attitude is most clearly expressed in the "arc de cercle" of hysteria and the "opisthotonus" of stuporous catatonia. One can readily see that this basic attitude of the armored organism is not a voluntary manifestation but is autonomous. The armored individual does not himself feel the armor as such. If one tries to describe it to him in words he usually does not know what one is talking about. What he feels is not the armoring itself but only the distortion of his perceptions of life: he feels himself uninterested, rigid, empty, or he complains about nervous unrest, palpitations, constipation, insomnia, nausea, etc. If the armoring is of long standing and has also influenced the tissues of the organs, the patient will come to us with peptic ulcer, rheumatism, arthritis, cancer or angina pectoris. This brief enumeration may suffice here, since the clinical facts have been presented elsewhere. What we are concerned with here is to penetrate to *the functions of the biological depth* and to deduce from them the functioning of the living.

The armored individual is incapable of dissolving his armor. He is also incapable of expressing the primitive biological emotions. He knows the sensation of tickling but not that of orgonotic pleasure. He cannot emit a pleasurable sigh or imitate it. If he tries, he will produce a groan, a repressed roar or an impulse to vomit. He is incapable of letting out an angry yell or convincingly imitating a fist hitting the couch in anger. He is incapable of full expiration: the movements of his diaphragm (as Xrays readily show) are very limited. If asked to move the pelvis forward, he is incapable of doing so, and often even of understanding what one asks of him; he may even execute the opposite motion, that of retracting the pelvis, a motion which expresses holding back. The tension of the peripheral muscle and nervous system is shown in an exaggerated sensitivity to pressure. It is impossible to touch certain parts of an armored organism without producing intense symptoms of anxiety and nervousness. What is commonly called "nervousness" is the result of this hypersensitivity of highly tensed muscles.

The total holding back results in the incapacity for the plasmatic pulsation in the sexual act, that is, orgastic impotence. This in turn results in a stasis of sexual energy, and from this follows all that which is comprised by the term "biopathy."

The central task of orgone therapy is the destruction of the armor, in other words, the reestablishment of plasma mobility. In the armored individual, the function of pulsation is more or less restricted in all organs. The task of orgone therapy is that of reestablishing the full capacity of pulsation. This is done, biophysically, by dissolving the attitude of holding back. Ideally, the result of orgone therapy is the appearance of the *orgasm reflex*. As we know, this reflex, next to respiration, is the most important motor manifestation in the animal kingdom. At the moment of the orgasm, the organism "gives itself over" completely to its organ sensations and involuntary pulsations. Therefore, the motion of the orgasm reflex inevitably contains the expression of "giving." It would, of course, be useless to preach the patient "to give," because he is incapable of doing so. If he were not, he would not need our help. Nor do we let him practise the attitude of "giving," for no such voluntary technical measure could possibly bring about the *in*voluntary attitude of giving. *The living functions autonomously, beyond the realms of language, intellect or volition.* It functions according to certain natural laws which we will have to examine. As we shall soon see, the orgasm reflex, with its expression of giving, is the key to an understanding of *basic* natural processes which go far beyond the individual and even the living itself. The reader who is to follow this presentation with understanding will have to be prepared for a serious excursion in the realm of cosmic energy. He will fail to achieve understanding and will be disappointed if he has not freed himself completely from the concept of sexuality as portrayed by the night club.

We have already sufficiently studied the functions of the orgasm in the realms of psychology and physiology to concentrate our attention here exclusively on the basic natural phenomenon, "orgasm." Peculiarly enough, *in the orgasm the organism constantly tries to bring together the embryologically important mouth and anus.* Its form is the following:

Back

Front

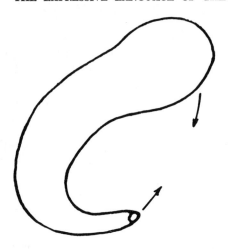

*The emotional expression of the orgasm reflex*

As we said, the attitude of the orgasm reflex is that of "giving." The organism gives itself over to its plasmatic excitations and sensations of streaming; also, it gives itself over completely to the partner in the sexual embrace, without any kind of reserve, holding back or armoring. All biological activity is reduced to the basic function of plasmatic pulsation. In man, all thinking and phantasy activity cease.

The emotional expression of giving is clear. *What is not clear is the function of the orgastic convulsion.* It consists in alternating contractions and expansions of the total body plasma. *What function has the approximation of the two ends of the torso in the orgastic convulsion?* At first glance, it does not seem to convey any "meaning." The expression of this movement seems incomprehensible. If we are correct in stating that every organismic movement has an *understandable* expression, this does not seem to apply in the case of the orgastic convulsion. We are unable to find in the orgasm a comprehensible expression which could be translated into word language.

Instead of engaging in natural-philosophical speculations about this problem, we must give the natural-scientific answer that, while the orgastic convulsion seems incomprehensible, it still must have a hidden expression. For, like any other movement of the living, it is a pure *expressive* movement and, consequently, must also show an emotional expression.

In due course, we shall arrive at an astounding but conclusive answer to this basic question of the living function. But before finding this answer we must collect and correctly interpret a great number of biological manifestations. The answer lies beyond the individual biological organism and yet is in no way mystical, metaphysical or spiritualistic. It answers the riddle as to the *concrete* manner in which the animal and the plant are connected with the cosmic orgone energy. Thus it also answers the question as to why orgastic longing is not only the deepest longing but why it is, characteristically, a *cosmic longing*. True, that the organism is a bit of cosmos is generally known but what has remained unknown so far is *how*. Let us return to orgone-therapeutic experience:

The task of orgone therapy is that of enabling the human organism to give up the automatism of holding back and, instead, to "give." As long as the two embryonic ends of the torso bend backwards instead of forwards, towards each other, the organism is incapable of giving itself to any experience, be it work or pleasure. Since it is the muscular armoring which prevents any kind of giving, of surrender, and which causes biopathic restriction of living functioning, this muscular armor has to be dissolved. Only this will achieve our therapeutic goal; neither psychoanalysis, suggestion, praying or gymnastics will. Nor do we inform the patient concerning the therapeutic goal; we know from experience that he will inevitably develop the total orgasm reflex if we succeed in dissolving the muscular armor. In the course of every treatment we see that *the basic function of the muscular armor is that of preventing the orgasm reflex from taking place.*

The numerous manifestations of the muscular armor and the corresponding character armor have been described elsewhere. Here, I would like to introduce a new point of view which makes the character and muscular armor comprehensible on the level of the most primitive life functions. It is based on observations over some ten years, so that I can take full responsibility for their significance in biophysics.

### 3. THE SEGMENTAL ARRANGEMENT OF THE ARMOR

In psychiatry, it has been known for decades that the somatic disturbances of hysteria do not correspond to the anatomy and physiology of muscles, nerves and blood vessels but to emotionally significant organs. Pathological blushing, for example, is usually restricted to face and neck, although the blood vessels run essentially lengthwise. Similarly, sensory disturbances in hysteria do not correspond to a certain nerve path, but to emotionally significant regions of the body.

In dissolving the muscular armor, we meet the same phenomenon: the individual muscular blocks do not correspond to an individual muscle or nerve. If, now, one looks for some rule which these blocks must inevitably follow, one finds that the muscular armor has a *segmental* arrangement.

Segmental function is a much more primitive mode of living functioning than that found in highly developed animals. It is most clearly seen in worms. In the higher vertebrates, only the segmental structure of the spine which corresponds to the segments of the spinal cord and the spinal nerves, and the segmental arrangement of the autonomic ganglia, indicate the origin of the vertebrates from segmentally functioning primitive organisms.

I am trying to give here a rough sketch—it can be no more than that—of the segmental structure of the muscular armor. This description is based on many years' observation of armor reactions.

Since the body of the patient is held back and since the goal of orgone therapy is that of reestablishing the plasmatic currents in the pelvis, it is necessary to start the dissolution of the armor in the regions farthest away from the pelvis. Thus, the work begins with the facial expression. At the head, at least two segmental armorings can be clearly distinguished: one including forehead, eyes and the cheekbone region, the other including lips, chin and throat. A segmental structure of the armor means that it functions in front, at the sides and in the back, that is, like a *ring*.

Let us call the first armor ring the *ocular*, the second the *oral* ring. In the ocular armor segment we find a contraction and immobilization of all or most muscles of the eyeball, the lids, the forehead, the tear glands, etc. This is expressed in immobility of the forehead and the eyelids, empty expression of the eyes or protruding eyeballs, a masklike expression or immobility on both sides of the nose. The eyes look out as from behind a rigid mask. The patient is unable to open his eyes wide, as if imitating fright. In schizophrenics, as a result of contracted eyeball muscles, the expression of the eyes is empty or as if staring into the distance. Many patients have been unable to cry for many years. In others the eyes represent a narrow slit. The forehead is without expression, as if "flattened out." Very often, there is myopia, astigmatism or other visual disturbances.

The dissolution of the ocular segment of the armor takes place by one's having the patient open his eyes wide, as if in fright; with that, forehead and eyelids are mobilized and express emotions. This usually includes the upper parts of the cheeks, particularly if one has the patient make grimaces. The pulling up of the cheeks usually results in a "grin" which has the character of a spiteful provocation.

The segmental character of this muscle group is shown in the fact that every emotional action in this region also influences other parts, while the oral segment remains uninfluenced. The opening wide of the eyes as in fright will, for example, mobilize the forehead or bring about a grin in the upper parts of the cheeks, but it will not provoke, say, the biting impulses which are held back in the rigid chin.

*Armor segments, then, comprise those organs and muscle groups which are in functional contact with each other, which can induce each other to participate in expressive movement.* The next-following segment is that which remains unaffected by the expressive movements of the neighboring region.

The segmental structure of the armoring is always *transverse* to the torso, never along it. The only remarkable exception to this are the arms and legs. They clearly function coupled with the corresponding segments of the torso, that is, the arms with the segment comprising the shoulders and the legs with the segment comprising the pelvis. We shall keep this exception in mind; its explanation will be found in a definite biophysical context.

The second or oral armor segment comprises the musculature of the chin, the throat and the occipital musculature, including the annular muscle of the mouth. They form a functional unit, for dissolution of the chin armoring results in clonisms in the lips and the corresponding emotions of crying or the desire to suck. Similarly, production of the gag reflex may mobilize the total oral segment.

The emotional expressions of crying, angry biting, of yelling, sucking and grimacing of every kind are dependent on the free mobility of the ocular segment. For example, it will be found difficult to mobilize an impulse to cry by mobilizing the gag reflex if one has not previously mobilized the ocular segment. And even after the dissolution of the two uppermost segments it may still be difficult to liberate the crying impulse as long as the third and fourth segment, in neck and thorax, are still in a state of spastic contraction. This difficulty in the liberation of emotions discloses an extremely important biophysiological fact:

1. The armorings are segmental, in rings at right angles to the spine.

2. The plasmatic streamings and emotional excitations which we produce are along the body axis.

*The inhibition of the emotional language of expression, then, works at right angles to the direction of the orgonotic streaming.*

Since the orgonotic streamings can unite in the orgasm reflex only when they can pass freely *along* the total organism, and since, furthermore, the armorings are in segments at right angles to the movement of the currents, it is clear that the orgasm reflex cannot establish itself until after the dissolution of all the segmental armor rings. This is why the feeling of the unity of all body sensations does not make its appearance until the first orgastic convulsions occur. They herald the breakdown of the muscular armor. The orgonotic streamings which break through with each new dissolution of an armor ring are a great help in the work of dissolving the armor. For the liberated energy, which tries spontaneously to stream longitudinally, meets the still existing transverse contractions; this conveys to the patient the unmistakable feeling of a "block," a feeling which was very weak or entirely absent as long as there were no free plasmatic streamings.

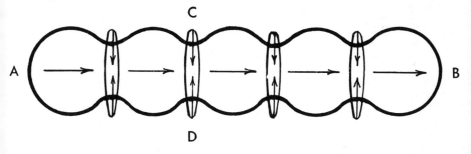

*The direction of orgonotic streaming is transverse to the armor rings*

The reader will realize that these processes are a matter of primary functions of the plasma system, processes not only beyond any word language, but representing *basic* processes of the life apparatus. It is a matter of phylogenetically primordial functions. *The segmental structure of the muscular armor represents the worm in man.*

The movements of the worm are based on waves of excitation running from the tail end to the front end. The waves of excitation progress continually from segment to segment until they reach the front end. At the tail end, one wave motion after the other develops with locomotion. The segments alternate rhythmically and regularly between contraction and expansion. In worms and caterpillars, locomotion is inextricably connected with this plasmatic wave-like motion. Since it can be nothing else, we must conclude that *it is the biological energy itself which moves in this wave-like manner.* This contention is confirmed by the observation of the inner movements of bions. The wave-like movement of the body orgone is slow and corresponds, in its tempo and expression, entirely to the emotional excitations of the pleasure function which we experience subjectively as wave-like.

In the armored human organism, the orgone energy is bound up in the chronic muscular spasms. After the loosening of the armor ring, the body orgone does not immediately begin to stream freely. What appears at first is clonisms, together with prickling and crawling sensations. This indicates that the armoring is loosened and that energy becomes free. Genuine sensations of waves of plasmatic excitation do not appear until a number of armor segments have been dissolved, such as blocks in the musculature of the eyes, mouth, neck and diaphragm. Then we can clearly see *wave-like* contractions in the loosened parts of the body, moving up towards the head and down toward the genital. Very often, the organism reacts to these first streamings and convulsions with renewed armoring. Spasms of the deep throat musculature, reverse peristalsis of the esophagus, diaphragmatic tics and other phenomena clearly show the struggle going on between streaming impulse and armor block. Since more energy was liberated than the patient is able to discharge, and since there are still numerous spasms which prevent plasmatic streaming, acute anxiety develops. These manifestations confirm the orgone-biophysical concept of the antithesis of pleasure and anxiety (*cf.* THE DISCOVERY OF THE ORGONE, vol. 1). Here, however, I have to stress a phenomenon which has as yet not been described clearly enough:

As soon as the first armor blocks are dissolved we find that, with the orgonotic streamings and sensations, the expression of "giving" develops more and more. However, still existing armorings prevent its full development. Then, it is as if the organism were trying to overcome the remaining armor blocks *by force.* In this process, the rudimentary expression of "giving" turns into one of *hatred.* This process is typical and deserves close attention.

When, for example, the armoring of the mouth region is suffi-ciently dissolved to stimulate an impulse to cry, while at the same time the armoring in the throat and the chest remain in full force, we see the lower part of the face begin to give in to the crying without being able to let it come through. The crying expression may change into a hateful grin. It is an expres-sion of desperation, of utter frustration. This is an illustration of the following general fact: AS SOON AS THE EXPRESSION OF GIVING MEETS ARMOR BLOCKS, SO THAT IT CANNOT FREELY DEVELOP, IT CHANGES INTO DESTRUCTIVE RAGE.

The armoring of the *third* segment is found mainly in the deep neck musculature, the platysma and the sternocleidomastoid muscles. One only has to imitate the attitude of holding back anger or crying to understand the emotional function of the armoring of the neck. The spastic contraction of the neck seg-ment also includes the tongue. This is easy to understand ana-tomically, since the muscles of the tongue insert mainly on the cervical bone system. Thus we find spasms in the musculature of the tongue in a functional connection with the depression of the Adam's apple and the contraction of the deep and superficial neck musculature. The movements of the Adam's apple show clearly how an anger or crying impulse, without the patient's being aware of it, is literally "swallowed down." This mechanism of suppressing emotions is very difficult to handle therapeutically. One cannot get with one's hands at the larynx muscles as one can with the superficial neck muscles. The best means of interrupting this "swallowing" of emotions is the elicitation of the *gag reflex*. With this reflex, the wave of excitation in the esophagus runs counter to that occurring in the "swallowing" of rage or crying. If the gag reflex develops fully or the patient even reaches the point of actually vomiting, the emotions which are held back by neck armoring are liberated.

Here, we realize again the significance of the longitudinal course of the excitation: The gagging reflex goes with an expan-sion of the diaphragm, that is, elevation of the diaphragm and expiration. Work on the neck armoring brings with it a loosening of the fourth and fifth armor segments. It follows that we cannot dissolve one armor segment after the other, cleanly separated one from another, in a mechanical manner. Rather, we work on a unitary life system the total plasma function of which is hindered by transverse armor rings. However, loosening of one armor segment leads, as a result of the motion produced, to the mobilization of armor rings above or below. For this reason, it is also impossible to give a mechanical description of the process of dissolving the muscular armor.

I am turning now to the *fourth* or chest segment. Although, again, the armor functions of this segment can be subdivided, it is better to treat the chest as a whole. The chest armoring is expressed in a chronic attitude of inspiration, shallow breathing and immobility of the thorax. As we know, the attitude of inspiration is the most important means of suppressing *any* kind of emotion. The armoring of the chest is particularly important not only because it is a main part of the total armoring of the organism but also because here the biopathic disease symptoms assume a particularly dangerous character.

The muscles that take part in the armoring of the chest are the intercostal muscles, the large chest muscles (pectoral muscles), the shoulder muscles (deltoid muscles) and the muscles on and between the shoulder blades. The expression of the chest armoring is essentially that of "self-control" and "restraint." The shoulders, which are pulled back, literally express "holding back." Together with the neck armoring, the chest armoring expresses suppressed "spite" and "stiff-neckedness" (again to be taken literally). In the absence of an armor, the expressive movement of the fourth segment is that of "free-flowing feeling." In the presence of an armor, the expression is that of "immobility" or "being unmoved."

The chronic expansion of the thorax goes with a tendency to increased blood pressure, palpitations and anxiety, in severe cases of long standing also to enlargement of the heart. Various kinds of heart disease result either directly from the chronic expansion or indirectly as a result of the anxiety syndrome. Pulmonary emphysema is an immediate result of the chronic expansion of the thorax. Presumably, we have to look here also for the disposition to pneumonia and tuberculosis.

The emotions arising from the chest segment are essentially those of "raving rage" and "heart-breaking crying," of "sobbing" and "intolerable longing." These natural emotions are alien to the armored individual. His rage is "cold"; crying he considers "unmanly," "childish" or "unseemly"; longing he considers "soft," indicating a "lack of character."

It is from the plasmatic emotions of the chest that most emotional expressive movements of the arms and hands originate. These limbs are, biophysically speaking, extensions of the chest segment. In the artist who is capable of freely developing his longings, the emotion of the chest is directly extended into identical emotions and expressive movements of the arms and hands. This is true for the violinist and pianist as well as the painter. In the dancer, the main expressive movements derive from the total organism.

Armoring of the chest results in "awkwardness" of the arms and is largely responsible for the expression of "hardness" and "inaccessibility." The total armoring of the head, neck and chest segments gives the organism in the patriarchal cultural milieu—particularly in Asiatics of the "higher castes"—an atmosphere of "distinction." To this correspond the ideas of "stalwart character," "inaccessibility," "distance," "superiority" and "restraint." Militarism everywhere makes use of the expression embodied in the armoring of head, neck and chest. It goes without saying that these attitudes are based on the armoring, and not vice versa.

In certain patients we meet a syndrome stemming from the armoring of the chest which produces a particularly complicated system of difficulties. These patients complain, typically, of a "knot" in the chest. It seems to be a matter of a spasm in the esophagus similar to the globus hystericus in the pharynx. It is difficult to say whether the trachea is also involved, but it seems likely. This "knot," as becomes evident during its dissolution, contains the emotions of angry yelling or anxiety. To dissolve this "knot," it is often necessary to press down the chest and have the patient yell at the same time. The inhibition of the

chest organs usually extends to an inhibition of those arm movements which express "reaching-for-something" or "embracing."
It should be noted that these patients are not paralyzed, mechanically; they are capable of moving their arms very well. *But
as soon as the movement of the arms becomes associated with
the expression of longing or desiring, the inhibition sets in.* In
severe cases, the hands, and even more so the fingertips, lose
their orgonotic charge, become cold and clammy, and sometimes
quite painful. It is likely that Raynaud's gangrene is based on
this specific anorgonia. In many cases it is simply an impulse to
choke someone which is armored off in the shoulder blades and
the hands and which is responsible for the constriction in the
fingertips.

The lives of such patients are characterized by a general lack
of initiative and by work disturbances based on the inability to
use their hands freely. In women, the chest armoring is often
expressed in a lack of sensitivity in the nipples. Disturbances in
sexual gratification, and disgust of nursing are an immediate
result of this armoring.

Between the shoulder blades, in the region of the trapezius
muscles, one finds two painful muscle bundles the armoring of
which gives the impression of suppressed spite which, together
with the pulled-back shoulders, is best expressed in the words,
"I won't."

In the armored chest, the intercostal muscles show an exaggerated sensitivity to tickling stimuli. That this is not simply
"an aversion to being tickled" but a biopathic overexcitability is
shown in the fact that it disappears with the dissolution of the
chest armor. In a certain case, the character attitude of inaccessibility had essentially the function of the expression, "Don't touch
me, I'm ticklish."

I have, of course, no idea of ridiculing these character attitudes.
We do not impute the banality of so many "dignified" attitudes
but find them in their biological expression, whether we want
to or not. A general may be a "dignified" person; we do not
want to magnify or minimize him. But we are entitled to regard
him as an animal which is armored in a certain way. I would

not object if some scientist were to reduce my scientific curiosity to the biological function of a puppy sniffing at everything. I would be glad to be compared, biologically, to an alive, friendly puppy, for I do not have the ambition to distinguish myself from the animal.

The fact must be emphasized that the establishment of orgastic potency is out of the question without the previous dissolution of the chest armor and without liberating the emotions of raving rage, of longing and genuine crying. The function of giving surrender is most closely linked to the plasmatic motility of the chest and neck segments. Even if it were possible to mobilize the pelvic segment by itself, the head, instead of falling backwards, would inevitably move forward, in a defensive movement, as soon as the slightest sensation of pleasure was felt in the pelvis.

The armoring of the chest, as explained elsewhere, is a central part of the muscular armor as a whole. It was developed at the time of critical conflicts in the life of the child, probably long before the pelvic armor. It is easy to understand, therefore, that the traumatic memories of mistreatments of all kind, of frustrations in love and of disappointments in parents, appear in the course of dissolving the chest armor. The eliciting of memories is not important in orgone therapy; they help little if they appear without the corresponding emotion. The emotion in the expressive movements is ample for an understanding of the misery suffered by the patient, and finally the memories come up by themselves if one works correctly. It remains a riddle that unconscious memory functions can depend on the processes of plasmatic excitation, that memories are preserved, so to speak, in the plasmatic readiness for action.

Let us now turn to the fifth, the *diaphragmatic* segment. This segment, which comprises the diaphragm and the organs under it, is independent of the chest segment in its functioning. This is shown in the fact that the diaphragmatic block may persist even though the chest has become mobile and rage and crying have broken through. Xray fluoroscopy readily demonstrates the immobility of the diaphragm. True, with forced breathing one will find that the diaphragm moves better than before the dissolution of the chest armor. The block, however, consists in the fact that there is *no spontaneous diaphragmatic pulsation*. There are, then, two stages in the process of dissolving the diaphragmatic block:

In dissolving the chest armor, the patient was made to force his breathing voluntarily. In this process, of course, the diaphragm is also mobilized, but its movement is not spontaneous. As soon as the breathing is no longer being forced, the movement of the diaphragm ceases, and with that the respiratory movements of the chest. In order to take the second step, that of bringing about *spontaneous* pulsation of the diaphragm, we must get the emotional expression of the diaphragmatic armoring. This demonstrates again that one cannot reactivate any emotional functions by mechanical means. Only the biological *expressive motion* can dissolve the armor ring.

The fifth armor segment is a contraction ring over the epigastrium, the lower end of the sternum, along the lower ribs to the posterior insertions of the diaphragm, that is, to the tenth, eleventh and twelfth thoracic vertebrae. It comprises essentially the diaphragm, the stomach, the solar plexus, pancreas, liver, and two always plainly evident muscle bundles alongside the lower thoracic vertebrae.

This armor ring is expressed in a lordosis of the spine. As a rule, it is possible to put one's hand between the hollow back of the patient and the couch. The anterior costal margin sticks out in a rigid manner. The patient is more or less incapable of bending his spine forward. The fluoroscopic screen shows the immobility of the diaphragm under ordinary conditions and a very limited mobility with forced breathing. If one asks the patient to breathe, he will always breathe *in;* expiration as a *spontaneous* action is foreign to him. If one asks him to breathe out, he has to make much of an effort. If he succeeds, in a measure, to breathe out, the body automatically assumes some such attitude as opposes the breathing out. For example, the head is shoved forward, or the oral armor ring becomes more sharply contracted; the shoulder blades are pulled back or the arms are brought stiffly to the sides of the body; the pelvic musculature is contracted and the lower back arched more strongly.

The diaphragmatic block is the central armoring mechanism in this region. For this reason, the dissolution of this block is a central therapeutic task.

One asks oneself why precisely the dissolution of the armoring in the diaphragmatic segment is so particularly difficult. The bodily expression says clearly—though the patient is unaware of this—that the organism refuses to let the diaphragm swing freely. If the work on the upper segments was done correctly, the dissolution of the diaphragmatic block will sooner or later succeed. For example, forced breathing in the chest segment or repeated eliciting of the gag reflex will push the organism in the direction of the orgastic contraction; the same is true of irritation of the shoulder muscles by pinching.

Theoretically speaking, the reasons for this strong resistance against the full pulsation of the diaphragm are clear enough: the organism defends itself against the sensations of pleasure or anxiety which inevitably appear with diaphragmatic movement. But we should not forget for a moment that this is a rationalistic, psychologistic and finalistic statement. It implies that the organism "thinks" rationally, in somewhat the following manner: "This bothersome physician asks me to let the diaphragm swing. If I give in, I am going to have the sensations of anxiety and pleasure which I experienced at the time when my parents punished me for my pleasure sensations. I have reconciled myself to the situation as it is, and so I'm not going to give in."

But the living does not think rationalistically, does not do or not do things "in order to . . ." It functions according to the primary plasmatic emotions the function of which is the gratification of biological tensions and needs. One would inevitably go astray were one to translate the language of the living *immediately* into the word language of consciousness. To emphasize this is important because that rationalistic thinking which has given rise to mechanistic civilization has extinguished the understanding of the *basically different* language of the living function.

I shall illustrate these new phenomena as they appeared in a particularly clear clinical case: A patient who had an extraordinary intellectual understanding of orgone therapy and who had already achieved a great deal of dissolution of his upper armoring, was confronted with the task of breaking through the diaphragmatic armor. The therapeutic situation was quite clear. In the spoken word and in the conscious effort to master the armorings, there was an unequivocal YES. But, every time a small breech had been achieved in the armoring of the diaphragm, the patient's body, from the diaphragm down, began to jerk *sidewise*. It was only after considerable attempts to understand this that the expression of this became clear: The lower part of the body, in its sidewise movement, expressed a resolute NO. One only has to move one's right hand from side to side, as in saying, "No, no," in order to grasp this expression.

One might put on this the psychologistic, or rather mystical, interpretation that the plasma, beyond the word language, says NO to a thing which "the cortex" and the word language affirms. Such an interpretation of the process would be erroneous and would not bring us one step closer to an understanding of the living and its expressive language. The abdomen and the pelvis of the patient did not "consider" the task demanded of the organism; they did not "decide" not to give in. The interpretation is a different one, one which corresponds better to the expressive language of the living:

The plasmatic movements of a worm, as we said, are *longitudinal,* along the body axis. When the body of the worm, as a result of the orgonotic waves of excitation, moves ahead, we have the "impression" that the worm acts "conscious" of its aim, "volitionally." The emotional expression of the worm can be translated in words of our language which connote "volition" or "affirmation." If, now, we pinch the worm around the middle of its body, thus interrupting the orgonotic excitation as by an armor block, the unitary forward movement ceases, and with it the emotional expression of "volition" or "affirmation." It is replaced by a different kind of motion, say, a bending from *side to side* of the hind part of the body while the front part is pulled in. The immediate impression conveyed by this sidewise movement is one of pain or a violent, "No—don't do that—I don't want it." Let us not forget that we are dealing here with an *impression,* that is, an interpretation which we *experience immediately* while observing the worm. We would act exactly alike if somebody were to grab our torso with huge pincers; we would inevitably pull in head and shoulders and would fight, sidewise, with pelvis and legs.

This interpretation, of course, does not mean that we have joined the subjectivists who claim that we "perceive nothing but our sensations" and that there is no reality corresponding to these sensations. Since everything living is functionally identical, the reactions of the worm to the pinching are identical with our own reactions in the same situation; the pain and the defense are the same reactions. It is this functional identity of man and worm which enables us to be "impressed" by the expression of the writhing worm in the correct, *objectively true* sense. The expression of the worm is what we experience through identification. But we do not experience immediately the pain of the worm and its objection; rather, we perceive an emotional expression which is the same as ours would be in the same painful situation. From this it follows that *we comprehend the expressive motions and the emotional expressions of another living organism on the basis of the identity of our own emotions with those of all that is living.*

We comprehend the language of the living *immediately* on the basis of the functional identity of the biological emotions. *After* having understood it in this biological language of expression, we also put it in "words," translate it into the word language of consciousness. But the "NO, NO" of word language has no more to do with the language of expression of the living than has the word "cat" with the real cat we see before us. The word "cat" and the specific orgonotic plasma system we see before us have in reality nothing to do with each other. It is merely, as the many terms applicable to the phenomenon "cat" show, one of the loose, exchangeable terms which are applied to real phenomena, motions, emotions, etc.

All this sounds like natural philosophy. The layman is averse to natural philosophy and will be inclined to put this book aside because, he may say, it is "not based on hard reality." This thought is erroneous. I shall have to show how important it is to think *correctly* and to use concepts and words correctly. It will be shown that a whole world of mechanistically thinking biologists, physicists, bacteriologists, etc., in the past 10 years, while the functions of the living were being discovered, actually believed that what was moving there on the street was the word "cat" and not a complicated living organism.

To return to the NO-NO of our patient. The answer to the riddle is this: *When a plasmatic current cannot run along the body because transverse blocks make it impossible, a transverse movement develops which secondarily, in word language, means* NO. This NO of word language corresponds to the NO in the expressive language of the living. It is not by accident that NO is expressed by a sidewise movement of the head and YES by nodding. The NO-NO which our patient expressed by the sidewise movements of his pelvis did not disappear until the diaphragmatic block was dissolved. On the other hand, it made its reappearance every time when this block recurred.

These facts are of eminent significance for an understanding of the body language. Our patient was generally negativistic; his characterological basic attitude was also "NO." He suffered severely from it, he fought against this character attitude, but to no avail. In spite of his conscious and intellectual attempts to say YES, to be positive, his character constantly expressed NO. This characterological NO was not difficult to understand, functionally as well as historically. Like so many children, his severely compulsive mother had given him enemas. Like other children, he suffered this with horror and inner rage. In order to subdue his rage, in order to be able to submit to the torture at all, he "restrained himself," pulling up his pelvic floor, holding his breath, and generally developing the bodily attitude of NO-NO. When the living in him wanted to cry out, NO-NO against this assault, and could not, he acquired an irreparable scar for the rest of his life: the expression of his life system, toward everything and everybody, became a NO-NO. Although this characterological NO-NO was a severe symptom, it was, at the same time, also the expression of a vigorous protest which originally had been rational and justified. But this originally rational protest had assumed the form of a chronic armor and was thus rigid and directed against everything.

As I have shown elsewhere, a traumatic infantile experience can have a present-day effect *only if it is anchored in a rigid* armor. The originally rational NO-NO, in the course of years, turned into a neurotic, irrational NO-NO. This was due to the armoring which, as we saw, expressed a NO-NO. The expression, NO-NO, decreased when, during therapy, the armor was dissolved. With that, the historical assault by the mother also lost its pathogenic significance.

Depth-psychologically, it is correct to say that in this case the affect of defense, of yelling, NO-NO, was "suppressed." In the biological depth, however, it was not a matter of a suppressed NO-NO, *but of the inability of the organism to say* YES. A positive, giving attitude in life is possible only when the organism functions as a total unit, only when the plasmatic excitations with the corresponding emotions can freely pass all organs and tissues. As soon as, however, one single armor block inhibits this function, the expression of giving is disturbed. Then we have infants who cannot give themselves fully to their play, adolescents who fail in school, adults who function like an automobile with the emergency brake on. The observer then has the "impression" of laziness, spite or incapability. The individual with the block experiences himself as "failing in spite of all his efforts." Translated into our expressive language of the living, this means: *The organism always begins, biologically correctly, with achievement, that is, with streaming and giving. During the passage of the orgonotic excitations through the organism, however, the functioning becomes inhibited, and thus the expression of "joyous achievement" turns into an automatic "NO, I don't want to."* This means that the organism is not responsible for its non-achievement.

This process has general significance. I chose my clinical examples intentionally from those that have general significance, for the restrictions of human functioning as described will make it possible for us better to understand a number of unfortunate social phenomena which cannot be understood without their *biophysical* background.

Let us, after this long but inevitable digression, return to the fifth armor segment. In the upper segments, we had no great difficulty in discerning the emotional expression. The inhibition of the eye muscles, for example, expresses "empty" or "sad" eyes; a rigid chin may express "suppressed anger"; the "knot in the chest" will dissolve into crying or yelling. Here, in the upper four segments, we understand the emotional expressions *immediately*. and the body language is easily translated into word language. With the diaphragmatic segment, things are more difficult. When this segment is loosened, we are *no longer able to translate the expressive language into word language.* The expression which then comes about leads us into as yet uncomprehended depths of the living function. We meet here the problem as to the concrete manner in which the animal, man, is connected with the primitive animal kingdom and with the cosmic functions of the orgone.

The armor in the diaphragmatic segment can be loosened if the patient repeatedly elicits the gag reflex, without, however, at the same time interrupting his expiration. This measure is successful, however, only if all the armorings in the four upper segments have been previously dissolved so that the orgonotic streamings in the regions of head, neck and chest function freely.

As soon as the diaphragm swings freely, that is, as soon as there is full spontaneous respiration, the torso tends to fold up with each expiration. That is, the upper part of the body tends toward the pelvis, while the upper abdomen recedes. This is the picture of the *orgasm reflex* as it presents itself to us for the first time, although it is still disturbed because the pelvis is not yet loosened. The bending forward of the torso, while the head falls back, immediately expresses "giving, surrender." This is not difficult to understand. What is difficult to understand, however, are the forward convulsions. *The expression of the convulsions in the orgasm reflex is at first incomprehensible. It cannot be translated into word language.* We must assume some basic difference between the expressive movements found thus far and the expression of the total body which appears when the diaphragmatic block is dissolved.

I must ask the reader for a good deal of patience here; the final result will be worth it. I may say that for more than ten years I had to exercise a great deal of patience in order to reach the finding I will have to describe. During these years, I was again and again on the point of giving up the attempt to understand the orgasm reflex, because it seemed so senseless to try to make this basic biological reflex comprehensible. But I stuck to it because I could not admit that, while the living has an immediately understandable expressive language in all other realms, it should express "Nothing" in the orgasm reflex. This seemed too contradictory, too "senseless." I kept telling myself that it was I myself who had stated that the living simply functions, that it has no "meaning"; that perhaps the meaninglessness of the orgastic convulsions simply demonstrated this. The attitude of giving surrender, however, which ushers in the orgasm reflex, is full of expression and meaning. The orgastic convulsions themselves are doubtless full of expression. I had to conclude that natural science had not yet learned to comprehend this general expression of the living. In brief, "an expressive movement without an emotional expression" seemed an absurdity.

What provided access to the problem was the process of vomiting which often sets in when the diaphragmatic armoring is loosened. Just as there is an inability to cry so is there an inability to vomit. This inability is easy to understand, orgone-biophysically. The "knot" in the chest, the "swallowing" and the contraction of the eye muscles prevents crying. In the same way, the diaphragmatic block, together with the armor rings above, prevents the peristaltic movement of the body energy upwards, from stomach to mouth. In many cases of diaphragmatic block there is, together with the inability to vomit, more or less constant nausea. There can be no doubt that the so-called "nervous" stomach disorders are the direct result of the armoring in this region. Vomiting is a biological expressive movement the function of which achieves exactly what it "expresses": convulsive expulsion of body contents. It is based on a peristaltic movement of stomach and esophagus in the opposite direction of its normal function, that is, toward the mouth (antiperistalsis). The gag reflex dissolves the armoring of the diaphragmatic segment quickly and radically. Vomiting is accompanied by a convulsion of the body, a rapid folding in the epigastrium, with a *forward* jerk of head as well as pelvis. In the colic of infants, vomiting is accompanied by diarrhea. Energetically speaking, *strong waves of excitation run from the middle of the body upwards and downwards, toward mouth and anus.* The corresponding expression is so elementary that its deep biological nature cannot be doubted; it is only a matter of also understanding it.

The total movement of the body in vomiting is purely physiologically—though not emotionally—the same as in the orgasm reflex. This is confirmed clinically: the dissolution of the diaphragmatic block inevitably ushers in the first convulsions of the body which subsequently develop into the total orgasm reflex. These convulsions go with deep expiration and a wave of excitation from the diaphragmatic region to the head on the one hand and the genitals on the other.

As we know, the loosening of the upper armor segments is indispensable for the establishment of the total body convulsion. In moving toward the pelvis, the wave of orgonotic excitation typically meets a block in the middle of the abdomen. What happens is either that the abdomen contracts rapidly, or that the pelvis is retracted and held in this position.

The contraction in the middle of the abdomen represents the *sixth* armor ring. The spasm of the large abdominal muscles (Rectus abdominis) goes with a spastic contraction of the lateral muscles (Transversus abdominis) which run from the lower ribs to the upper margin of the pelvis. They can be easily palpated as hard, painful cords. In the back, this segment is represented by the lower sections of the muscles running along the spine (Latissimus dorsi), sacrospinalis, etc. These muscles also can be felt as hard, painful cords. The dissolution of the sixth segment is easier than that of all others. After its dissolution, the way is open to that of the *seventh* or pelvic segment.

The armor of the pelvis comprises in most cases practically all the muscles of the pelvis. The pelvis is retracted and sticks out in the back. The abdominal muscle above the symphysis is painful, as are the adductors of the thigh, the superficial as well as the deep. The anal sphincter is contracted and the anus pulled up. The gluteal muscles are painful. The pelvis is "dead" and expressionless. This expressionlessness is the emotional expression of asexuality. Emotionally, there is no perception of sensations or excitations; the pathological symptoms, on the other hand, are very numerous:

There is constipation, lumbago, various kinds of growth in the rectum, inflammation of the ovaries, polyps of the uterus, benign and malignant tumors, irritability of the bladder, vaginal anesthesia, anesthesia of the penis surface with irritation of the urethra. There is frequently leukorrhea with the development of protozoa from the vaginal epithelium ("Trichomonas vaginalis"). In the man, anorgonia of the pelvis results in erective impotence or premature ejaculation; in the woman, we find complete vaginal anesthesia or spasm of the vaginal muscles (vaginismus).

There is a specific *pelvic anxiety* and a specific *pelvic rage.* Just like the armoring of the shoulders, the pelvic armor also contains the emotions of anxiety and rage. Orgastic impotence creates *secondary* impulses to achieve sexual gratification by force. Thus, while the impulses of the sexual act begin according to the biological pleasure principle, what happens is this: *the pleasure sensations turn inevitably into rage impulses because the armor does not permit the development of involuntary movements,* of convulsions, in this segment. Thus there develops a painful feeling of "having to get through" which cannot be called anything but sadistic. Like anywhere else in the realm of the living, in the pelvis also *inhibited pleasure turns into rage, and inhibited rage into muscular spasms.* This is easily demonstrated clinically: no matter how far the dissolution of the pelvic armor has progressed, no matter how mobile the pelvis has become, there will be *no pleasure sensations in the pelvis as long as the anger has not been released from the pelvic muscles.*

Just as in other armor segments, there is a "beating" or "piercing" by means of violent forward movements of the pelvis. The corresponding expression is unmistakable. Aside from the expression of anger, there is also one of contempt: contempt of the pelvis and all its organs, contempt of the sexual act and, in particular, of the sexual partner. I say on the basis of ample clinical experience that only in few cases in our civilization is the sexual act based on love. The intervening rage, hatred, sadistic emotions and contempt are part and parcel of the love life of modern man. I am not referring to the clear-cut cases where the sexual act is based on mercenary motives; I am referring to the majority of people in all social strata. On this is based what has become a scientific axiom: "Omne animal post coitum triste" ("Every animal is sad after the sexual act"). Man only has committed the error of ascribing his own disappointment to the animal also. The rage and contempt connected with the sexual act is vividly expressed in the common "cusswords" applied to it.

#### 4. THE EMOTIONAL EXPRESSION OF THE ORGASM REFLEX, AND SEXUAL SUPERIMPOSITION

As we have seen, the pelvic armor has an expression easily translatable into word language, and the emotions released from it speak a clear language. This is true, however, only of the emotions of the armor. It is not true of the expressive movements which regularly appear *after* the dissolution of the anxiety and the rage. These movements consist in gentle forward movements of the pelvis which clearly express desire. It is reminiscent of the rhythmical movements of the tail end of insects, such as bees or wasps, a movement which is particularly clearly seen during the sexual act of such insects as dragonflies or butterflies. The basic form of this movement is the following:

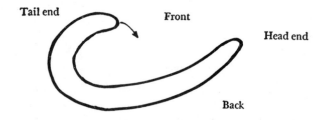

It continues the expression of giving surrender. Subjective perception tells us that his attitude is accompanied by *longing*. The question is: longing for what? and surrender to what?

Word language expresses the goal of the longing and the function of the surrender as follows: As the organism develops the orgasm reflex, the longing for "gratification" makes its unmistakable appearance. The goal is clearly that of the sexual act. In the sexual act one "surrenders" to the pleasure sensation; one "gives oneself" to the partner.

Word language seems to describe this natural phenomenon unequivocally. But it merely *seems* to. Since word language is only a translation of the expressive language of the living, we do not know whether the words "sexual act" and "gratification" really express the function of the orgasm reflex. In addition, the expression of the orgastic *convulsions* cannot be translated into word language. Let us go a step further in doubting the ability of word language to comprehend natural phenomena *immediately*. Our next question will baffle the reader. But after some consideration, he will have to admit that words often obscure processes rather than explain them. The question is the following:

*What is the reason for the extraordinary significance of the genital drive?* Nobody doubts its elemental power; nobody can avoid it. The whole living world is subject to it. Copulation and the biological functions connected with it form the very basic function of the living which guarantees its continued existence. Copulation is a basic function of the "germ plasm" in the sense of Weissman which is immortal in the strict sense of the word. The species man has simply denied this powerful natural force, but by no means abolished it. We know the terrible tragedies created by this.

The existence of the living is due to the *superimposition* of two orgonotic systems of different sex. We must admit that we have no answer to the simplest of all questions: *What is the origin of this superimposition of two living organisms of different sex? What is its significance and "meaning"? Why is the continued*

*existence of living nature bound up with this form of movement
instead of any other?*

The most common form of this movement of sexual superimposition is the following:

Sexual superimposition goes together with orgonotic lumination of the body cells, with penetration and fusion of two orgonotic energy systems into one functional unity. At the acme of the excitation (= lumination) the two orgone systems, which have become *one,* discharge their energy in clonic convulsions. In this process, highly charged substances (the sperm cells) are discharged which in turn continue the function of superimposition, penetration and fusion.

Word language cannot explain anything here. Its concepts of the process of sexual superimposition derive from the organ sensations which give rise to the superimposition, which accompany and follow it. "Longing," "urge," "copulation," "gratification," etc., are merely pictures of a natural process. In order to understand this natural process we have to find other primary natural processes which have a more general significance than the sexual superimposition of the organisms and which certainly are deeper than the organ sensations to which the concepts of word language correspond.

That the orgasm reflex follows natural laws is beyond any doubt. In every successful treatment, it regularly appears when the segmental armorings which prevented it are completely dissolved. Nor is there any doubt that the sexual superimposition follows natural laws. It occurs inevitably when the orgasm reflex functions freely and if there are no social obstacles which prevent it.

We shall have to collect a great number of natural phenomena before we understand the expressive language of the living in the orgasm reflex and in the superimposition. The failure of word language here points to a natural function *beyond* the realm of the living. Not, of course, in the sense of the supernatural mystics, but in the sense of a *functional connection between living and non-living nature*.

We must assume that word language can describe only such manifestations of life which can be expressed in terms of organ sensations and the corresponding expressions, such as anger, pleasure, anxiety, annoyance, grief, surrender, etc. The organ sensations and expressive movements, however, are nothing ultimate. At a certain point, the natural law of the non-living substance must of necessity penetrate the living and express itself in it. This cannot be otherwise if the living derives from the non-living and returns to it. While the organ sensations, which correspond specifically to the living, can be translated into word language, those expressive movements of the living which do not specifically belong to the living but which derive from the realm of the non-living, *cannot be put into word language.* Since the living derives from the non-living, and since non-living matter derives from cosmic energy, we must conclude that there are *cosmic energy functions in the living*. The non-translatable expressive movements of the orgasm reflex in the sexual superimposition could, therefore, represent the cosmic orgone function.

I know how far-reaching this working hypothesis is, but it is inevitable. It is a clinical fact that orgastic longing, that is, the longing for superimposition, always goes hand in hand with cosmic longing and cosmic sensations. The mystical ideas of so many religions, the belief in a hereafter and in a transmigration of souls, all derive from cosmic longing; and cosmic longing is functionally anchored in the expressive movements of the orgasm reflex. *In the orgasm, the living is nothing but a bit of pulsating nature.* After all, the ideas of man, of animal in general as "a bit of nature" are widespread and commonly known. But it is easier to use a phrase than to comprehend scientifically wherein this functional identity of the living and of nature consists *concretely*. It is simple to state that the principle of a locomotive is basically identical with that of a primitive wheel-barrow; but it is necessary to state how the principle of the locomotive, in the course of thousands of years, has developed from that of the wheel-barrow.

We find that the problem of the expressive language of the living poses difficult questions. Let us further look for the common features which connect the more highly developed with the lower forms of life.

The technique of orgone therapy has shown us that *in the animal, man, there still functions a worm*. The segmental structure of the armor rings can mean nothing else. The dissolution of this segmental armoring liberates expressive movements and plasmatic currents which are independent of the anatomy of muscles and nerves. They correspond much more closely to the peristaltic movements of an intestine, of a worm or a protozoon.

One still frequently meets the concept that man—in spite of his development from phylogenetically older forms—represents a living being of a *new* kind, without connection with the forms from which he stems. In the segments of the spine and the ganglia, the segmental character, and with that, the worm character of the biological system is clearly expressed. This system, however, is segmental not only morphologically, that is, in its rigid form. The orgone functions and the armor rings also represent *functional* segments. They are not—as one might say of the vertebrae—remnants of a dead past in a new living present. Rather, they represent the most active and important functional apparatus of the present, the core of all biological functions of the animal, man. From the segmental functions derive the biologically important organ sensations and the emotions, pleasure, anxiety and rage. Also, *expansion* and *contraction*, as functions of pleasure and anxiety, are present from the ameba to man. One carries one's head high with pleasure and pulls it in in anxiety, just as does the worm. If the ameba and the worm continue to function in man as a basic part of his emotional functioning, then it is correct to try to connect the basic biological reflex of orgastic superimposition with the simplest plasmatic functions in order to understand it.

As we said, the dissolution of the diaphragmatic block leads inevitably to the first orgastic convulsions. We also said that the limbs represent only continuations of the chest and pelvic segment. *The largest and most important ganglion apparatus is located in the middle of the torso, close to the back.*

Everybody has seen a cat being lifted by being held by the skin of the back. The body of the cat seems doubled up, the head brought close to the pelvis, head and legs hang down limply, somewhat like this:

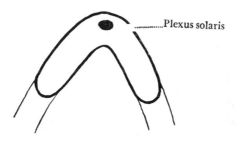

We can conceive of any other animal, including man, in this position. As always when the body assumes a certain attitude, there is an expression. It is not easy to recognize the expression of this attitude immediately. After some observation, we have the picture of a jelly-fish with tentacles.

Biophysics will have to learn to read *forms of movement from bodily forms,* and *expressions from forms of movements.* More will have to be said about this later. At this point, the similarity with the jelly-fish must suffice. We can go further in this analogy. The central nervous apparatus in the jelly-fish is located in the middle of the back, like the solar plexus in the vertebrates. When the jelly-fish moves, the ends of the body move towards each other and away from each other, in rhythmical alternation. We come to the following assumption:

*The expressive movements in the orgasm reflex are functionally identical with those of a living and swimming jelly-fish.* In either case, the ends of the body, that is, of the torso, move towards each other, as if they tended to touch each other. When they are close, we have contraction; when they are as far apart as possible we have expansion or relaxation of the orgonotic system. It is a very primitive form of *biological pulsation.* If this pulsation is accelerated, so that it assumes *clonic* form, we have the expressive movement of the orgastic convulsion before us.

The expulsion of the spawn in fishes and of the semen in higher animals is bound up with this plasmatic convulsion of the total body. The orgastic convulsion is accompanied by high excitation which we experience as the pleasure of the "acme." The expressive movement of the orgasm reflex, then, represents a most important, present-day mobilization of a biological form of movement which goes way back to the jelly-fish. The following drawing shows the bell shape and the jelly-fish-like form of movement:

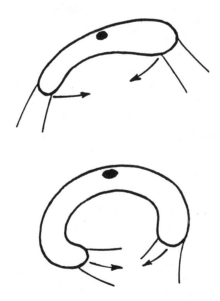

On closer consideration, the functional identity of the j movement and orgastic convulsion seems less strange. Whe consider that in the segmental structure of the armor rings a of the emotional functions we met the worm in man, it is no particularly surprising that in the total body convulsion the jelly-fish function is expressed. We have to realize that it is not a matter of dead, archaic remnants from a phylogenetic past, but of *present-day*, bio-energetically highly significant functions in the highly developed organism. The most primitive and the most highly developed plasmatic functions exist alongside each other. The development of complicated functions in the organism, of "higher" functions as we call them, does not change the existence or function of the "jelly-fish in man." It is precisely this jelly-fish in man which represents his unity with the lower animal world. Just as Darwin's theory derived man's origin from the lower vertebrates from his morphology, so does orgone physics reduce the *emotional* functions of man even much further, to the forms of movement of molluscs and protozoa.

What is called "nature in man," then, can be taken out of the realm of mystic and poetic phantasy and can be translated in the concrete language of natural science. It is not a matter of metaphors or analogies, nor of sentimental perceptions, but of concrete, visible and manageable processes of the living.

CHAPTER XVI

# THE SCHIZOPHRENIC SPLIT*

## 1. THE "DEVIL" IN THE SCHIZOPHRENIC PROCESS

The idea of the "DEVIL" is a true expression of the *distortion* of nature in man. There is no other human experience which would lend itself as well as the *schizophrenic* experience to the study of the "DEVIL." The schizophrenic world in its purest form is a mixture of mysticism and human emotional inferno, of penetrating though distorted vision, of God and Devil, perverse sex and murderous morals, sanity to the highest degree of genius and insanity to its deepest depth, welded into a single horrible experience. I have in mind here the schizophrenic process which in classical psychiatry is called "dementia paranoides" or "praecox" and not the so-called "catatonic stupor" or the "hebephrenic process." Whereas the catatonic is typically characterized by total withdrawal from reality and total muscular armoring; whereas the hebephrenic process consists mainly in a slow torpid deterioration of biophysical functioning, the initial phases of paranoid schizophrenia, especially in puberty, are characterized by bizarre ideas, mystical experiences, ideas of persecution and hallucinations, loss of the power of rational association, loss of the factual meaning of words, and, basically, by a slow disintegration of organismal, i.e., unitary functioning.

I shall limit myself to those processes in the schizophrenic which have a bearing on our main line of thought: the "Devil" as the representative of perverted nature in man. This comprises: the realm of the secondary, perverse and antisocial drives which are rarely manifested in well-armored neurotics; the realm of primary biophysical sensations, plasmatic streamings and experi-

---

* Conceived, 1940-1948. Written in English by the author, August-September, 1948.

ences derived from contact with cosmic functions, experiences which are almost completely blocked off in the so-called normal human being; and finally, it comprises the ideas of persecution as experienced by a sick though most sensitive biosystem.

The schizophrenic world mingles into one experience what is kept painstakingly separated in the homo normalis. The "well-adjusted" homo normalis is composed of exactly the same type of experiences as the schizophrenic. Depth psychiatry leaves no doubt about this. Homo normalis differs from the schizophrenic only in that these functions are differently arranged. He is a well-adjusted, "socially minded" merchant or clerk during the day; he is orderly on the surface. He lives out his secondary, perverse drives when he leaves home and office to visit some faraway city, in occasional orgies of sadism or promiscuity. This is his "middle layer" existence, cleanly and sharply separated from the superficial veneer. He believes in the existence of a personal supernatural power and its opposite, the Devil and hell, in a third group of experiences which is again cleanly and sharply delineated from the two others. These three basic groups do not mingle with one another. Homo normalis does not believe in God when he does some tricky business, a fact which is reprimanded as "sinful" by the priests in Sunday sermons. Homo normalis does not believe in the Devil when he promotes some cause of science; he has no perversions when he is the supporter of his family; and he forgets his wife and children when he lets the Devil go free in a brothel.

There are psychiatrists who deny the truth of these facts. There are other psychiatrists who do not deny them, but who say that "this is as it should be," that this type of clean separation of the devilish inferno from the social veneer is only to the good and that it makes for security in social functioning. But the true believer in the true Jesus might object to this. He might say that the realm of the Devil should be extinguished and not be shut off *here* only to be opened up *there*. To this, another ethical mind might object that true virtue is shown not by the absence of vice but by resisting the temptations of the Devil.

I do not wish to participate in this argument. I believe that, again *within* this framework of thinking and living, each side may point to some truth. We want to stay outside this vicious circle in order to understand the Devil as he appears in the daily life and in the world of the schizophrenic.

The fact is that the schizophrenic is, on the average, much more honest than homo normalis, if one accepts directness of expression as an indication of honesty. Every good psychiatrist knows that the schizophrenic is embarrassingly honest. He is also what is commonly called "deep," i.e., in contact with happenings. The schizoid person looks through hypocrisy and does not hide it. He has an excellent grasp of emotional realities in sharp contradistinction to homo normalis. I am stressing these schizophrenic characteristics in order to make it comprehensible why homo normalis hates the schizoid mind so much.

The objective validity of this superiority of schizoid judgment manifests itself quite practically. When we wish to obtain the truth about social facts, we study Ibsen or Nietzsche, both of whom went "crazy," and not the writings of some well-adjusted diplomat or the resolutions of the communist party congresses. We find the wavy character and blueness of orgone energy in Van Gogh's marvelous paintings, and not in any of his well-adjusted contemporaries. We find the essential characteristics of the genital character in Gauguin's pictures and not in any pictures of homo normalis. Both Van Gogh and Gauguin ended as psychotics. And when we wish to learn something about human emotions and deep human experiences, we resort as biopsychiatrists to the schizophrenic and not to homo normalis. This is so because the schizophrenic tells us frankly what he thinks and how he feels, whereas homo normalis tells us nothing at all and keeps us digging for years before he feels ready to show his inner structure. Therefore, my statement seems quite correct that the schizophrenic is more honest than homo normalis.

This seems to be a sad state of affairs. It should be the other way around. If homo normalis is actually as normal as he claims to be; if he claims that self-realization and truth are the greatest goals of good individual and social living, then he should be much more able and willing to reveal himself to himself and his doctor than the "crazy man." There must be something basically wrong with the structure of homo normalis if truth is so hard to get out of him. To declare, as the well-adjusted psychoanalysts do, that this is as it should be because otherwise it would be impossible for him to withstand the impact of all his emotions, would amount to complete resignation regarding the improvement of the human lot. We cannot base improvement of conditions on broader knowledge of man's soul and simultaneously defend his reluctance to reveal himself. Either—or: Either we keep on broadening the scope of our knowledge of man, then we must condemn the general evasive attitude of homo normalis, *or* we defend this attitude and we must give up the task of understanding the mind of man. There is no other alternative.

In order to understand homo normalis and his opposite, the schizoid character, we must again put ourselves outside the framework of thinking of both. Homo normalis blocks off entirely the perception of basic orgonotic functioning by means of rigid armoring; in the schizophrenic, on the other hand, the armoring practically breaks down and thus the biosystem is flooded with deep experiences from the biophysical core with which it cannot cope. Therefore, it is understandable that armored homo normalis develops anxiety when he feels threatened by the findings of orgonomy, whereas the schizoid character understands them instantly and easily, and feels drawn toward them. For the same reason, the mystic, who is structurally close to the schizoid character, usually comprehends orgonomic facts, although only as in a mirror, whereas the rigid mechanist looks upon all scientific dealings in the realm of the emotions with arrogant disdain and calls them "unscientific."

I suggest we study the relevant details of these important human functions by means of a concrete case of paranoid schizophrenia. This will convey a picture of the Devil's realm much better than any merely theoretical abstraction of psychiatric clinical experience.

The experimental world of the schizophrenic is boundless and rich in variations to such an extent that we must limit our theme to those details which have a bearing on our main subject:

How does the schizophrenic experience his biophysical core? Why does his ego break down in such a typical manner?

I am going to present the case history of a paranoid schizophrenic. The clinical psychiatrist will understand that I have to disguise the case to be presented here in such a manner that her identity cannot be established while at the same time the typical disease mechanisms nevertheless emerge clearly.

It was the first case of schizophrenia I had ever treated experimentally with orgone therapy. I approached this case with some general theoretical assumptions which were derived from my previous experiences with schizophrenics, such as the following:

1. The psychoanalytic arrangement of mental functions according to the three great realms of the Ego, the Superego and the Id has to be sharply distinguished from the *biophysical* arrangement of the functions of the total organism according to the functional realms of BIO-ENERGETIC CORE (PLASMA SYSTEM), PERIPHERY (SKIN SURFACE), and ORGONE ENERGY FIELD beyond the body surface. These two theoretical structures describe different realms of nature in a different manner. Neither is applicable in the other realm of organismic functioning. There is only *one* meeting point of the two theoretical schemata, i.e., the "ID" of psychoanalytic theory, where the realm of psychology ends and that of biophysics *beyond* psychology begins.

2. The most effective therapeutic approach to any emotional (= biophysical) disease is, if at all possible or indicated, the *withdrawal of bio-energy from the biopathic symptoms.* In order to destroy psychoneurotic or psychotic symptoms it is unnecessary and even harmful to delve into all details of the countless pathological ramifications; instead, opening up the core of the biosystem and establishing a balanced energy economy will automatically make the symptoms disappear, since, seen energetically, they are results of a disorderly energy metabolism in the biosystem.

3. Great danger arises in neurotics as well as in psychotics when the armor begins to dissolve. Utmost caution and medical skill are required to guide this process. Therefore, the practice of medical orgone therapy is restricted to well-trained physicians.

We know our responsibilities better than anyone else and we do not have to be reminded of them by people who know little about orgonomy.

I knew well beforehand that the patient could or even would break down when her armoring dissolved completely. But the chance that she would stand the procedure was great enough to warrant the experiment. The patient had been in mental institutions several times over long periods of years. The diagnosis was "schizophrenia" and, according to the reports, the patient was in the process of deterioration. The eventual final breakdown was inevitable; therefore, the risk taken in this case was not too great and the outlook was promising enough to satisfy the conscience of the experimenting physician.

The patient, a 32-year-old Irish girl, had been brought to me by her relatives who had heard about my new medical approach to the biopathies. I informed them of the great danger of precipitating a breakdown. They were ready to take the risk and to sign an affidavit to this effect. I also warned them of the risk of a sudden outbreak of destructiveness. Since I was well acquainted with the manifestations preceding a destructive attack, I felt sure that I would sense the danger in time. Therefore, I undertook the experiment outside the institution under the strict condition that a nurse or a relative should always be around the patient and that at the first sign of unrest and destructiveness the patient should be committed to the institution. A further condition was that the patient, who at the time was free under parole, should see the parole physician regularly and that all arrangements should be made with the institution, where the patient had been before, for instant commitment in case of a breakdown. I also kept in touch with the psychiatrist in charge of the case at the institution by mail, and secured his cooperation.

Such precautions are indispensable if one wants to treat a schizophrenic outside an institution. One would prefer to rely on an institution which conducts experimental orgone therapy within its walls. But, unfortunately, mental institutions—with very few exceptions—are not inclined to bother with new, hopeful medical attempts in the treatment of schizophrenia. Shock therapy is too readily available to dull schizophrenic activities, and there are too many psychotics to be taken care of by too few physicians. There is no time for extensive and deep-reaching scientific investigation. I understand this attitude though I cannot condone it. A few cases of schizophrenia, well understood instead of "shocked," would, in the long run, save society countless millions of dollars. It seems too much to expect such foresight. It is known that mental institutions are, in reality, jails for psychotics, with little medical care, scarce funds, and, in most of them, no research at all. Moreover, some medical administrators are reluctant to consider any serious attempt to improve the condition of these patients. Sometimes they even meet such medical endeavors with great hostility.

This short description of the *social* situation may suffice to explain my precautions and my willingness to take the risk. I knew the danger well, but the possible future reward seemed great enough. I was not disappointed later:

The patient who had taken refuge in a mental institution for many years and who was already deteriorating at the time I accepted her for the experiment has remained out of the institution for more than six years since the treatment. She resumed her profession; the process of deterioration was stopped. The patient became social in many ways.

It cannot be predicted whether this situation will last. I hope it will. The scientific and medical reward was great: *Orgone therapy can be applied successfully in certain cases of schizophrenia where all other methods fail.* The result justified the risk. Furthermore, orgonomic theory was confirmed in some of its basic assumptions and was adjusted in others. Many entirely new facts about basic functioning in the biosystem of man were secured and for the first time in the history of medicine and psychiatry, some central questions as to the nature of paranoid mechanisms in schizophrenia were answered.

I shall describe the therapeutic experiment as it developed over a period of three months from treatment to treatment. I took notes carefully on the most essential details immediately after each session, and I kept a special record of the general line of development in order to find, if possible, some consistency or law in this development. The case itself offers nothing new in manifestations or symptomatology of the schizophrenic psychosis. What is new, however, is the response to orgone-therapeutic measures. It revealed some hitherto unknown connections between known schizoid functions and it brought to light some new functions in the depth of the biosystem which are of the greatest importance for the understanding of human biology in general.

### The outer appearance of the patient:

The first impression was not that of a schizophrenic. She spoke about her symptoms and experiences in a coherent, orderly manner. One felt great embarrassment in the background of her behavior; she spoke in an artificially eager manner. She seemed very intelligent, gave penetrating answers to most difficult questions; she knew the psychiatric language in an unusually clear way. She said that she had longed to meet a psychiatrist who would understand her inner emotions, but the psychiatrists always thought she was "crazy." Her eyes had the typical faraway, slightly veiled look of the schizophrenic character. At times she became confused but regained her clarity easily. As the conversation proceeded, one could clearly discern certain subjects which she tried to evade. When asked whether she knew of any queer or unusual experiences, her eyes became "dark" and she said: "I am in contact with some powerful forces but they are not here now."

The subject was clearly charged with emotion and we did not delve into it any further. It became clear, furthermore, that she "dissimulated" and disguised her situation. She declared herself willing to undergo the experiment of orgone therapy. She had read the literature and thought that I was right.

### 1st session:

I restricted the work to an orientation on her armoring and character defenses. Her mannerisms were stronger than they had been during the initial meeting. She understood the principle of orgone therapy excellently. She had known for years that most people were armored and therefore did not understand the inner life of the schizophrenic "who feels and knows everything." I tried to find out more about the "forces," but she refused to talk about them. The forces had, she said, nothing whatsoever to do with her own inner urges. She had excellent contact with the issues of the discussion.

She seemed *not to breathe at all*. On physical examination her chest appeared soft, *not rigid* as in cases of compulsion neurosis. This softness and mobility of the chest were found later in other initial schizophrenics. It should be further investigated whether and to what extent the lack of armoring in the chest is or is not a characteristic of the schizophrenic biopathy.[1]

The softness of her chest would have appeared normal if it had not been accompanied *by lack of respiration*. Respiration was so shallow that it seemed altogether absent. When I asked the patient to inhale and exhale audibly, she refused; it was later shown that she was *unable* to do it. She seemed to stop the respiration somewhere in the cervical segments.

She became increasingly restless, looked anxiously at the walls and along the ceiling. "There are some shadows," she said. Suddenly she made the sign of a cross over her chest with her hands. "I am dedicated; the forces come to me; I can call them and make them come; the forces love me. . . ."

I asked her whether the forces had ever incited her to commit murder. She would have to answer this question very soon, I said. For if the experiment was to be conducted safely, we had to know everything about the forces. I asked her whether she would promise to tell me immediately when the forces wanted her to do dangerous things to herself or to other people. She would tell me immediately, she said; she said this with very deep sincerity. She told me that sometimes the forces told her to commit murder. Once she had suddenly felt as if she *had to* push a woman off a station platform.

She had scarcely finished this sentence when she became quite absent-minded; she did not listen to my questions and

---

[1] This assumption gained some support by examinations of schizophrenics by Dr. Elsworth Baker at the Marlboro State Hospital in New Jersey.

appeared completely dissociated. She was murmuring incoherently and unintelligibly. I could only discern the words: ". . . The forces betrayed . . . what did I say. . . ."

I knew from her relatives that she hated her mother bitterly and that at the same time she was strongly dependent on her. The ideas of "murder," "menstruation," and "mother" were closely linked together. The urge to murder was also somehow connected with the experience of the "forces" or betraying the "forces."

The patient recuperated after a while and regained her composure.

### 2nd through 5th sessions:

During the following four therapeutic sessions, I tried cautiously to approach her dysfunction of respiration. The problem was not, as in the armored neurotic, to break down the armoring of the chest. *There seemed to be no armor.* The problem was how to make her draw in and expel air through the larynx. She began to struggle severely whenever I tried to bring about full respiration. I had the impression that the function of respiration was not stopped by any immobility due to armoring, but *was inhibited as if by a strong, conscious effort.* There was also the other impression that her organism suffered severely from this effort but that she did not feel the effort.

She responded to every attempt on my part to induce respiration with severe irritation. The typical armored neurotic would have appeared untouched or he would have smiled maliciously at my efforts. Not so our schizophrenic. She tried to cooperate intelligently but became panicky whenever I came close to succeeding. Anxiety overwhelmed her, fear of the "forces"; she felt them coming close and being all around her, on the walls, under the sofa, etc. She told me now that it was this same anxiety which drove her to me as a physician in whom she could have confidence. She had understood from my books that I would know what she was talking about.

I gave up any further attempts to make her breathe whenever the anxiety set in. She was told that this was one of her major pathological disturbances, that we would have to overcome it;

that she would have to help me to do so; and that overcoming this disturbance would relieve her to a great extent. She promised to help me; she felt sure that I was right. She had known it for a long time.

I was able to form the following opinion of the situation:

Our patient did not shut off or was not able to shut off completely the sensation of plasmatic currents as does the rigidly armored neurotic. She felt the orgonotic streamings in her body "very close by," and she fought them by not permitting the passage of air to and from the lungs. Whether she had ever actually and fully experienced the body streamings, I could not tell and she did not know. She had only experienced the "oncoming" of "forces" but she *did not feel the forces as her own.* She was terror-stricken when she felt the forces; at the same time she felt "dedicated to them," dedicated to "a mission." She was reluctant to say what kind of mission it was.

It is an essential rule in working with schizophrenics (and also with non-psychotics, for that matter) to give the patient the full understanding that one takes his complaints seriously, that one does *not* think them queer or "crazy" or "antisocial" or "immoral." One gets nowhere if the patient does not have or does not develop *absolute* confidence in his physician which allows him to feel that he is trusted basically and that his words and feelings are understood, however peculiar they may appear to the layman. One must show *genuine* understanding to the schizophrenic even if he threatens to kill the physician. This is an absolutely necessary requirement which makes orgone-therapeutic treatment of psychotics inaccessible to the physician who is not perfectly equipped emotionally to do the job. The further report will corroborate this statement.

### 6th session:

After about half an hour of careful and painstaking work on her cervical armoring, the first outburst of hate occurred. This first outburst was accompanied by quiet crying; at the same time she developed severe anxiety, tremor in her lips, shoulders and also partially in her chest.

In such situations, where different kinds of emotions are mingled into one, it is necessary to separate the emotions from one another. This can be done by promoting the most superficial emotion, the one which fights off the deeper emotion, and by "pushing back" the latter. Accordingly, I encouraged her crying which blocked the rage, and after some tearful release of sorrow I let her develop her rage by encouraging her to hit the couch. *This is a dangerous procedure if the patient, especially the schizophrenic, is not in perfect contact with the physician.* In order to secure this contact, one must explain to the patient that he must stop his rage action instantly when asked to do so. It is the task of the physician to decide when the point in emotional release is reached where the patient is in danger of getting out of control. Only very skilled orgone therapists can accomplish this task. Therefore, I warn physicians who have not been trained in the technique of medical orgone therapy, and trained orgone therapists who do not have the necessary experience, against tackling schizophrenics. One cannot proceed in such cases without releasing the rage and one cannot release the rage without much experience previously gained in less emotional situations.

Toward the end of the sixth session, the patient had released enough emotion to relax. She uttered astonishment that such relief was possible and expressed her thanks with tears in her eyes. She realized now for the first time that her idea that "people looked at her" was of a delusionary nature (the rational element in the persecutory idea will be elaborated later). Her communications flowed freely. She had fought against the "influences" of the "forces" as far back as she could remember. She realized that she held on to reality only with great effort; she had felt as though she were hanging over an abyss most of the time, especially during puberty. She always became confused when her fear of the "forces" met with her love for them. She confessed that it was in such moments of confusion that *murderous impulses* would surge up in her.

This seemed the proper moment to tell her fully about my worries concerning a possible uncontrolled breakthrough of destructiveness. She understood immediately what I meant. She agreed and assured me with a quite unschizophrenic look that she had had this worry herself for a long time. I told her then that I knew well from experience that most schizophrenics in the initial phases of the disease have the same worry as to whether they would be able to fight off the upsurge of murderous destructiveness. She also agreed that there was no other way of safeguarding herself against committing murder than the security of an institution. She realized quite on her own that it was in such emotional situations that she sought the safety of an institution. She felt safer inside, she said, because there life made no demands on her, demands she was unable to fulfill. She knew she would not commit murder when in the institution; but she also knew that life in the institution was bad for her. She felt that slow but sure deterioration was inevitable because life within the walls of the institution made her dull or furious, according to the special situation she met. She understood the inmates fully and felt sympathy for them; at the same time she felt horror toward their kind of existence. In her lucid phases, she looked through the glib and superficial attitudes of so many psychiatrists toward the psychotic, their lack of understanding, the brutality of many of the procedures, the injustices so often committed, etc.; she had, in short, excellent insight when the "forces" were absent or were present "without making too strong demands on her."

As the therapeutic process progressed, one single question gained an overall importance:

DO THE "FORCES" WHICH HAUNT HER AND WHICH SHE LOVES DEVOTEDLY REPRESENT HER BODY SENSATIONS OF STREAMINGS OF PLEASURE?

IF THIS IS THE CASE, WHY IS SHE AFRAID OF THEM? (IT IS CLEAR SHE IS *devoted* TO THEM.) WHAT KIND OF MECHANISM IN HER BODY BLOCKS THE STREAMINGS OF PLEASURE? HOW DO THE BLOCKED-OFF PLASMATIC STREAMINGS TURN INTO "EVIL" FORCES? WHAT IS THE CONNECTION BETWEEN THIS BLOCK AND THE SCHIZOPHRENIC PROCESS?

I began to direct my attention toward the functions which possibly would answer these questions. My impression was that the blocking mechanism was somehow connected with her cervical segment, especially with the peculiar respiratory disturbance: *No respiration in the presence of a soft chest.*

*7th session:*

During the 7th session it became obvious that the partial breakthrough of rage that I had kept under control during the previous treatment had increased her physiological need for full respiration. This could be seen in her even more desperate attempts *to prevent* the air from passing fully through her throat, larynx and trachea. I encouraged her to exhale fully and helped by softly pressing down on her chest. She gave in to expiration suddenly but went into a state of trance immediately afterwards. She did not respond to my calling her; her eyes were turned toward a corner of the ceiling in a staring manner; she seemed to be hallucinated. Her legs trembled severely and she had fascicular convulsions in the muscles of her shoulders for about 30 minutes.

I succeeded in bringing her out of her trance by pinching her hard enough to make her aware of the sensation of pain. Slowly she began to return to full consciousness. She was obviously confused; she tried to convince herself that she was awake by knocking at things. She grasped my hands, began to cry out and said: "I want to come back, oh, I want to come back . . ." This lasted another ten minutes. Then she said: "I am not quite back yet . . . where are you? . . . With the Lord . . . I asked him whether I should give in to the Devil . . . that you are the Devil . . ." In answer to my question, she said that she did not "see things" any more but had "some contact" (with the forces). She had felt the tremor in her legs and shoulders, she also had heard my voice and yet she "felt far, far away." It was the first time that she could not "come back" quickly. "It lasted so long this time . . . Where are you? . . . Please let me hold your hands . . . I want to feel sure that I am here . . ."

Holding my hands, she looked around the room suspiciously, along the walls and at the ceiling. She felt exhausted and remained for more than an hour after the treatment to compose herself again.

I told her to come back next day for further treatment, and to call me or to have me called as soon as she felt the need to talk to me.

*8th session:*

After the experience of the previous day, she had felt very tired and had gone to bed as soon as she got home. She felt calm and safe now, her eyes were clear. I decided not to proceed further in breaking down her armor but only to bring her back to where she had been the previous day.

It is an important rule in disarmoring people to proceed slowly, step by step, and not to advance further into the biophysical depth unless one knows *exactly* what is going on and unless the patient has become *accustomed* to the situation which has already been reached. This is valid for all types of medical orgone therapy; it is especially necessary in the treatment of schizoid characters. If one neglects this strict rule, one will lose sight of the total process and will endanger the patient. Patients who feel better after partial breakthroughs often implore the physician to proceed faster, to let them come more often, etc. This should not be granted. When a certain breakthrough has been accomplished, the organism must be given time to organize and to assimilate the emotions which have broken through. The position from which we proceed further must first be firmly established. A certain amount of ill-being due to the remainder of the armoring is necessary in order to proceed further in the proper manner. One has to guard especially against the mystical, religious-like expectation on the part of the patient that now he has been "freed," "redeemed," "liberated." It is true that the first few breakthroughs of the solid armor are accompanied by feelings of great relief. This often disguises the true situation in the depth of the biophysical structure. Therefore, the rule should be to be cautious as long as the basic orgastic pleasure anxiety does not appear in an unequivocal manner. As long as this deep terror of spontaneous plasmatic contraction is not at the surface and has not been overcome, great caution is indicated.

In this 8th session, the patient was very cooperative. She had less anxiety, permitted the clonisms to occur much more easily and willingly; but it was clear that she still watched anxiously every bit of what was going on, that she was "on guard" not to lose hold of herself, and that she had to fight hard not to run away again into a state of trance.

One should never proceed without great care as long as the basic distrust has not come forth which is to be expected in every single case. The schizophrenic is far franker than the neurotic in showing this typical distrust. In neurotics, one must dig up the distrust from under the veneer of friendliness and politeness. Our patient asked me point blank: "Can I trust you? Oh, if I only could trust you . . ." [looking at me with great fear in her eyes]: *"Are you a German spy?"*

It was soon after the FBI had mistaken orgone research for German (or Russian?) spy activity and had taken me into custody (as an "enemy alien") at the entry of the U. S. A. into World War II. The fact that I was soon released unconditionally after a hearing did not matter much to the patient. What mattered was the fact that I had been suspected of subversive activities, and this, of course, was in harmony with the general attitude of neurotics as well as psychotics to distrust everything, especially their own inner feelings. Our patient wanted to be able to trust me because, as she said plainly, she needed my help in her fight against the "forces." I assured her that I was not a German or, for that matter, any other type of spy and never had been. Thereupon she said that everybody thinks only in terms of his own nature or character structure and that hence the FBI could not think of anything but spy activity when they could not understand what I was doing. I had to agree with this statement and I found my liking of the schizoid mind again justified. Schizophrenics are able in their lucid periods to see through individual and social matters as intelligently as no other character type. Later we shall see that this lucidity of intelligence in the schizophrenic is one of the major dangers which threaten his existence in present-day society.

The patient was scheduled for a parole visit the following day at the State Hospital. I told her not to hide anything, but I also told her to be prepared that the parole physician would not be able to understand everything she would explain to him. We had the good luck to deal with a psychiatrist who was not of the type of the brutal shock therapy surgeon. The patient left this session quiet and completely orderly.

*Summary after the 8th session:*

1. The patient came with a remainder of a sharp sense of reality to which she held on desperately in order not to break down completely.

2. The patient sought my help because she felt that I understood the "forces" and had "contact" with them.

3. She felt herself as something better than the rest of the world because of her contact with the "forces." Her criticism of the world of homo normalis was correct, nearly perfect and rational in accordance with her contact with the "forces," whatever they represented.

4. Her armoring differed from the armoring in a simple neurotic biopathy in that it was not complete and only superficially constructed. Her chest was mobile, but she did not breathe fully. Because of the weakness of her armoring, she felt as though she were hanging only by a thread above an abyss. "Beyond" were the "forces" which were *"devilish"* and *"attractive"* at the same time.

5. The melting sensations of orgonotic streamings in her body had a close connection with her idea of "forces," but these sensations were projected upon walls and ceilings. Her schizophrenic fear of breaking down was somehow dependent on her contact with the "forces."

6. The perception of the inner "forces" at the walls and the ceiling constituted the main riddle. The word "projection" obviously did not explain anything.

### 2. THE "FORCES"

The patient knew the "forces" well. She described them in detail. Some of the characteristics of the forces were the same as those ascribed to an omnipotent Being = *God;* others were those of the Devil, evil, cunning, sly and maliciously tempting. The first group of characteristics made the patient feel safe and protected and therefore "devoted" to the "forces"; in regard to the second group of characteristics the patient behaved as if she had to be protected against the "forces," their evil intentions and temptations, such as murder. This ambiguity in the nature of the "forces" became quite clear as the work proceeded.

My assumption at that stage of the work was the following: If the "forces" represent the "GOOD" and the "EVIL" in one and the same emotional formation, then it was necessary to assume that the split-up into two diametrically opposite kinds of experiences was due to TWO DIAMETRICALLY OPPOSITE SITUATIONS IN HER CHARACTER STRUCTURE which were mutually exclusive and incompatible. That is, the schizophrenic split of the personality had to be ascribed to this incompatibility; each of the two opposite emotional structures would alternately take hold of the organismic functioning. In contradistinction to the schizophrenic structure, the structure of homo normalis keeps one or the other of the contradictory structures continually in a state of repression. Thus, in homo normalis, the split of the personality is hidden. The common functioning principle of both GOD as well as the DEVIL is the *basic biophysical functioning of the organism*, the *"biological core"* whose most significant manifestation is the plasmatic current and its subjective perception as a melting sensation of love, as anxiety or hate. All this had to be confirmed by further developments in this case.

### 9th session:

The patient came to the 9th session full of joy and perfectly coordinated. She had visited the parole psychiatrist the day before. He had told her that he knew me to be "brilliant." She had explained to him my method of therapy as one of "letting off steam." The institutional psychiatrist had encouraged her to go on with the therapy. His attitude must have meant a support of her own hopes, since she had doubted my honesty previously ("Are you a German spy?").

Her respiration was *physiologically* nearly complete that day;

her eyes were clear and not "veiled" as usual. She reported that she had had the urge to satisfy herself genitally. The inexperienced physician would have triumphed about the "success." But I knew that great danger was just ahead of us:

A sick organism can take a slight increase in energy functioning easily and enjoys this well-being very much, more than the healthy organism does because of the great difference between the usual state of tension and the slight release of tension after a partial disarmoring. But the bio-energetic system continues to increase its energy level unless periodic releases of energy take place. And the only way of *full* release of built-up bio-energy is, as we well know, that of full orgastic convulsions during the natural process of mating. The problem of mental hygiene would not be as tough as it is if nature had not made the total orgastic convulsion entirely dependent on the absence of chronic body armoring. We are, as natural scientists and physicians, not responsible for this situation; we have only found and described it.

The patient herself was well aware of the danger ahead, far better than a simple neurotic would be. She told me that the "forces" had not been around lately, but they "could and would surely come back, malicious as they are."

She asked me whether I would abandon her if the "forces" came back. She wanted to know what exactly was the mechanism of orgone-therapeutic cure. Her questions were very intelligent and to the point. She inquired as to whether she would have to resign from her present "superior" position in the world, and whether she could become a useful member of society.

These questions appear peculiar to one who does not know what this case revealed in such an unequivocal manner:

The schizoid character has a far better contact with and insight into the functions of nature and society than homo normalis. This imbues him with a rational feeling of superiority to the average homo normalis who lacks such insight. It is logical, then, that in order to become a "useful member of society," i.e., a "homo normalis," she would have to lose some of her insights and with them her superiority.

Such feelings of superiority contain a great deal of rational truth. The schizoid character is, on the average, really superior to the average homo normalis in intelligence just as is the "criminal character." But this intelligence is impractical because of the deep-seated split. It is unable to perform lasting, rational biological activities as in the case of what is called "genius."

I took this opportunity to brace her against future dangers. I told her that she had experienced only a first relief, but that she would become frightened to a dangerous degree when her forces emerged fully from the depth. She understood and promised to keep close contact with me during the coming procedures.

The events which I am going to describe now would appear utterly incredible to anyone who did not try to understand this case (and any other, for that matter) from the beginning in terms of the natural functions of "*bio-energy*" and its blocking in the "*biopathies.*" These events would appear to him just as other examples of "crazy reactions," "unintelligible," "dangerous," "antisocial," as good reasons for commitment of the patient to a lunatic asylum. I fully agree that what was to come *was* dangerous, antisocial, a good reason for commitment; but I cannot agree that it was unintelligible or that it was any more "crazy" than the deeds, or rather misdeeds, of our dictators or warmakers who are not committed to institutions, but, on the contrary, are worshipped and honored by masses of homines normales. Therefore, I cannot become excited about the far lesser "craziness" in the schizophrenic. To put it bluntly, if worse comes to worst, he kills himself or he threatens to kill somebody else, but he never drives millions of innocent people from their homes for the "honor of the fatherland"; he does not demand at the point of a gun that millions be sacrificed for his impotent political ideas.

Therefore, let us be reasonable; let us abandon our false righteousness. There must be a potent reason why the schizophrenic is treated so cruelly and the cruel homo normalis is honored so crazily all over this planet.

*10th session:*

The attitude just described saved this particular case. It could,

I firmly believe, save thousands of lives which are rotting away innocently in obsolete mental institutions due to the typical evasiveness of homo normalis and his cruelty as applied in irresponsible, universal and indiscriminate "shock therapy."

The patient had felt perfectly at ease during the day. But when she undressed, I saw the figure of *a cross* cut into the skin of her chest at the sternum, about 6 cm. long and 4 cm. across. She had done it the previous evening "quite without any conscious motive." She *"just had to"* do it. She felt now highly "pent up." "I must let off some steam or I am going to burst."

It was immediately obvious (to the well-trained orgone therapist) that her cervical segment was severely contracted, pale, and immobile. Severe rage was visible in her face which appeared nearly blue, cyanotic. It took about ten minutes to release this severe cervical block. I succeeded by letting her gag, until the gag reflex operated well, and by forced respiration. As soon as the block in the throat gave way, she began to cry silently. Repeated encouragement to cry *loudly* met with no success. We find this phenomenon very often in neurotic biopathies: the emotion of crying is too strong to be let out fully at once. Usually there is severe rage held down by the emotion of crying. If the patient let go in crying fully and freely, he would feel that he had to commit murder.

Such armoring usually results from cruel punishment for quite innocent behavior in childhood. The mother hated the father; she wanted to murder him, to get rid of him; he was too strong for that and the mother was too weak to do anything about it. So she punished the 3 or 4 year old child for making noise or for dancing in the street or for some other quite innocent activity. The natural reaction on the part of the child is quite justified rage against such cruelty; but the child is afraid to show the rage and wants to cry instead; but crying, too, is "forbidden"; "a good boy and a good girl don't cry, they don't show their emotions." This is the type of much vaunted "education" of small children in the 20th century of culture and civilization at the beginning of the great "atomic age" . . . which "will either make humanity soar to heaven or go to hell . . . depending

on . . ." . . . *What?* ON WHETHER THE HUMAN RACE WILL OR
WILL NOT SUCCEED IN ERADICATING SUCH CRIMINAL BEHAVIOR ON
THE PART OF SICK MOTHERS AND FATHERS TO THE LAST VESTIGE;
ON WHETHER OUR PHYSICIANS AND EDUCATORS AND JOURNALISTS
WILL OR WILL NOT MUSTER THE COURAGE TO TACKLE THIS SU-
PREMELY IMPORTANT PROBLEM AND WILL FINALLY SUCCEED IN NOT
SUPPORTING IT, IN OVERCOMING THEIR ACADEMIC EVASIVENESS,
ALOOFNESS AND "OBJECTIVITY."

Our patient had suffered several decades of cruel monstrosi-
ties on the part of her nagging mother. She had developed the
impulse to choke her mother in order to defend herself. Such
impulses are very strong and cannot be fought off in any other
way than by armoring against the welling-up of the murderous
hate in the throat.

Quite spontaneously, the patient asked me *whether I would
permit her to choke my throat.* I confess that I felt, not embarrassed, but a bit frightened; however, I told her to go ahead
and do it. The patient put her hands *very cautiously* around my
throat and exerted a slight pressure; then her face cleared up and
she sank back exhausted. Her respiration was full now. She trembled severely in her whole body with every exhalation. The
streamings and sensations seemed strong, to judge from the way
she stretched her right leg in order to avert the full force of the
emotions. From time to time, her body would become quite rigid
in a position of opisthotonus and then relax again. Her face became
alternately red with crying or blue with anger. This process lasted
for about 30 minutes. I knew well that now her psychotic ideas
would emerge with full force. When a certain degree of emotional
upheaval was reached, I asked her quietly to try to stop the reaction. She responded instantly with full cooperation and began
slowly to calm down. I had held her hand in my palm all through
the breakthrough.

In 22 years of psychiatric work with psychotics and so-called
psychopaths, I had acquired a certain skill in handling such
emotional situations. I claim that all psychiatrists should be skilled
enough to handle them. But I also claim that nowadays few
psychiatrists are equipped to do so and, therefore, I would most

emphatically advise *against* repeating my experiment unless the proper skill has been acquired. I do not wish to be made responsible for a disaster that might happen in some psychiatrist's office because of his lack of training.

If we are to understand the schizophrenic world, we must never judge it from the standpoint of homo normalis; the sanity of the latter has itself come under sharp scrutiny. We must try instead to understand it when the schizophrenic expresses *rational* functions in a *distorted* manner. Therefore, it is necessary to judge him from BEYOND this "orderly" world of ours; *we must judge him from his own standpoint*. This is not easy. But if one penetrates the distortions, a wide vista opens up on a vast realm of human experience, rich in truth and beauty. It is the realm from which all the great deeds of genius emerge.

To continue with the patient:

I asked her what was the meaning of the cross on her chest. I did not scold her nor did I threaten to commit her. This would not have achieved anything.

She rose, her whole body trembling, and held on to her throat. Then she said: "I don't want to be Jewish" (she was *not* of Jewish origin). Since every schizophrenic of whatever faith could have said this, I did not try to convince her that she was not Jewish but, on the contrary, I took her words seriously: "Why not?" I asked. "The Jews crucified Jesus," she said. Thereupon she asked for a knife to cut a large cross into her *belly*.

The situation was not clear at once. After a while it became clear that she was trying hard to go into the state of trance, but apparently did not succeed. After a while, she said: "I tried to get in touch with them [the 'forces'] again . . . but . . . I cannot . . ." She began to cry. I asked her why. "Perhaps there are three reasons: 1. I fought them too strongly. 2. I did not make the cross deep enough. 3. They reject me because I am Jewish."

The exact connection between her biophysical status and these psychotic ideas was still not clear. It was possible that the system of delusions no longer worked as well as before; that she felt guilt toward the "forces" to whom her life was dedicated, and that, accordingly, she tried hard to make a self-sacrifice in order to regain the benevolence of the "forces." Such mechanisms are well known from so-called "normal" religious behavior. Here, too, the loss of contact with "God" will lead to greater sacrifice in order to regain His benevolence.

Did she identify herself with Jesus Christ?

She calmed down after a while and went home safely. Why did I not commit her to the institution after what had happened? I asked this question myself. The answer was this: I knew from long experience with such emotional situations that any threat would only have increased the danger, and that, on the other hand, only perfectly genuine confidence in her, which she felt, would save the situation. Somehow I had great confidence in her. But the risk was great, too, of course. The danger of suicide was present but that of destructiveness toward somebody else was not present. Clinically, she seemed close to a major change in her structure as indicated by her inability to get in contact with the "forces." This was an important gain to be further developed.

### 11th session:

She came back in good humor with bright eyes, but slightly manic. She spoke much and with great wit. Therapeutically, not much progress can be made when the patient feels too well. One has to dig up another piece of conflict and to increase the energy level sufficiently to proceed further. This is done by full respiration.

As soon as the patient started to yield to deeper respiration she developed strong psychotic emotions again. She began to look around the room in her typical paranoid fashion. She became anxious and began to quiver all over her body. Her eyes changed: appearing empty at first, they later sharply observed the red-hot coil of the electric heater. This went on for quite a while. She fought off anxiety and then she said:

"A funny thought I had . . . THAT THIS HEAT AND THE SUN ARE ALSO FORCES; that they [the 'real forces'] could think that I could prefer this *other* force [from the heater and the sun]."

I was flabbergasted. What deep thought, and how close to the truth! I assure the reader that at that time she knew nothing of the orgone phenomena and that I had not told her anything about them. The truth she touched upon by her remark was this:

If it was true that her "forces" were distorted perceptions of her own bio-energy; if it is further true that organismic energy and sun energy are basically the same, then she had made a truly scientific statement, and a great one at that. Was her organism trying to regain health by turning away from the delusion about a reality to the reality proper? She obviously was fighting hard to widen the scope of her sense of reality. Replacement of the "forces" by *other, natural* forces seemed a logical step in this direction. Somehow the delusional "forces" had lost some power over her as expressed in the following statement: "I also thought they could befuck themselves . . . Oh, what did I say . . ." Great anxiety overcame her instantly after having said this as though she had called for the Devil.

I ventured the following work hypothesis:

The respiration had increased her bio-energy level. She had come closer to the natural forces, the "melting" sensations, within herself. If this was correct, the *delusion* of "forces" from "Beyond" had lost some of its energy and thus had weakened. *She came closer to reality by coming closer to the real forces of life, the orgonotic sensations, within herself.* This was a major finding about the schizophrenic delusion: The delusion of "forces from beyond" is not merely a psychotic construction without a basis in reality; rather, it describes a deeply felt reality, although in a *distorted* manner. The further progress had to prove or disprove this assumption. It later proved it correct. Basically, this amounts to the fact that in their delusions the psychotics tell us important things about deep functions of nature. We must only learn to understand their language.

She had come very close to the meaning of her delusion without sinking fully into it. The function which was responsible for this success was her improved respiration. Strong clonisms developed during the rest of this session which she tolerated much better and with less anxiety. But her eyes became veiled whenever the orgonotic sensations became too strong for her.

I felt that she wanted to tell me something but that she did not trust me fully. I asked her whether my guess was right that she was in conflict over the "forces" and me; that she was *for* and at the same time *against* the "forces," and *for* as well as *against* me. She was afraid of the "forces" when she affirmed me too much, when she applied for my help against the "forces." She understood this instantly and perfectly well. In fact, she had had this thought herself.

The clonisms continued while we talked. She felt dizzy and I asked her to stop the reactions of her organism. She did. In the end she told me quite spontaneously that she *had become seriously ill for the first time when the "forces" had told her to poison the whole family with gas.* She had in fact turned on the gas one evening but had turned it off again. Soon after she told me this, she began to murmur unintelligibly. It sounded like a mystical ritual to placate evil ghosts. She did not leave the room for about an hour. She stood rigidly on one spot and did not move. One had the impression of a cataleptic posture. She did not answer my repeated questions why she did not leave. Finally she said: "I cannot step over this spot."

During this session, the prospects of her therapy had become clear:

1. The more and better contact she made with her plasmatic, bio-energetic streaming sensations, the less the fear of the "forces" would be. This would also prove my contention that the *"forces" in schizophrenia are distorted perceptions of the basic orgonotic organ sensations.*

2. This contact with her body sensations would help to establish some degree of orgastic satisfaction, and this in turn would eliminate the energy stasis which operated at the core of her delusions.

3. The undistorted experiencing of her body sensations would enable her to identify the true nature of the "forces" and would thus slowly destroy the delusion.

Before this could be accomplished, the patient would have to pass through a series of dangerous situations. Delusions and catatonic reactions were to be expected with each breakthrough of strong orgonotic streamings in her body. She would perceive these sensations with terror; she would block them off by bodily rigidity, and the blocked-off plasmatic currents would be transformed into *destructive* impulses. Therefore, the "secondary" impulses which derive from the blocking of the original, basic emotions would have to be handled carefully and would have to be "let out" slowly, step by step. This danger would become especially great when the first spontaneous orgastic contractions of her organism began to occur.

### 12th session:

We had come very close to hopeful changes and with them to great dangers too. She came to this session with strong anxiety and excitement. She asked innumerable questions and fought hard and long against any attempt to dissolve her blocking in the throat which was particularly strong that day. Her respiration was very shallow and her face was quite pale and bluish.

*She wanted a knife.* I told her that I would give her a knife if she told me first what she needed it for. "I want to cut your stomach wide open . . ." While saying this, she pointed to *her own* stomach. I asked her why she wanted to cut open her stomach and mine. "It hurts here . . . you did not release enough steam yesterday . . ." Did she feel strong tension there? "Yes . . . yes . . . it's awful . . . also in the throat . . ."

I suddenly understood with perfect clarity why and in what emotional situations murders are committed by schizophrenics and schizoid types of "criminals": When the tension in the organs, especially in the diaphragmatic region and in the throat become unbearably strong, the urge appears to cut one's own stomach or throat. The Japanese habit of hara-kiri, disguised as it is by ideological rationalization, is an extreme expression of such a bio-energetic situation. The murder occurs when the impulse is directed away from oneself toward somebody else. Just as a child easily develops a contraction in its own throat when it has the impulse to choke its mother's or father's throat, *so does the schizoid murderer cut somebody else's throat when his own choking sensation becomes unbearable.*

I succeeded in forcing the patient to take several breaths and to exhale fully three or four times. Then a spasm of the glottis occurred. Her face became blue, her whole body trembled, but finally the spasm gave way and autonomic movements of her chest and legs set in. She fought desperately against these movements, apparently without success. The close connection between the autonomic movements and the development of her delusion became quite clear now:

She turned her eyeballs upward and said in a desperate tone of voice: "Do you think I cannot make contact with them ['the forces'] any more? . . . Did you really do that to me? . . ."

*She had lost contact with the "forces" through the contact which her self-perception had made with her own autonomic body functions.*

I answered: "I am not concerned with your 'forces.' I know nothing about them. I am only concerned with bringing you into contact with your own body." If I had fought her idea of "forces" or had uttered personal opinions about them she would have reacted antagonistically since she felt devoted to them. My policy, therefore, was to leave the "forces" untouched and to work solely on the blocks in her organism which created the delusion of "forces."

She said after a while: "I want to go to Bellevue [a psychiatric institution in New York] to search for the 'forces' . . . I must find them somewhere . . . They wanted me to be superior, better, not a brute . . ."

Here, in one neat grouping, we had together before us the whole system of ideologies of homo normalis directed against natural body functions. The "forces" in the psychosis had a double function: One was that of representing the primary body functions, especially the orgonotic, biosexual streaming sensations; the other represented the contempt of the body, the being "superior" to such "earthly" and "base" things as bodily urges. The delusion had thus brought into ONE two diametrically opposed functions of homo normalis. But seen from "beyond," from outside the world of homo normalis, this unity made good sense: It represented the *functional unity of superior goodness, of being godlike, and the basic natural bodily streamings.* This functional unity was projected in the form of the delusion of persecuting "forces." Now, when the contact with her body sensations was made for the first time, she split this unity up into the idea of "moral superiority" as against the "brutishness of the bodily urges."

These connections and interactions are rarely seen so clearly in simple neurotic biopathies. Here the "Devil" is well separated from "God" and is kept apart safely and continuously.

The patient trembled severely all through this process. Alternately, she gave in partially to the body sensations and movements, and then stiffened up again. The struggle was tremendous. Her face became spotty as in shock. Her eyes were alternately clear and veiled. "I do not want to be an average human being." I asked her exactly what did she mean. "A human being with brutal emotions." I explained to her the difference between primary and secondary, antisocial drives and how the former turned into the latter. She understood it well. Then she gave in fully and relaxed. The severe tension in the abdominal muscles disappeared. She felt relieved and rested quietly.

We have seen how the sweet, "melting" organ sensations, the most longed-for experience in the organism, are dreaded and fought off as "brutal flesh" in the sense of homo normalis and as evil "forces" or the "devil" in the psychosis.

I would like to stress this structural function of the armored human animal most emphatically. To the biopsychiatrist with long experience in orgone therapy, this dichotomy and ambivalence towards one's own organism appears as the crux of the misery of the human animal. It is the core of all human functions which are *deviations* from the natural law of living matter. It is the core of criminal behavior, psychotic processes, neurotic deadness, irrational thinking, of the general basic split into the world of GOD and the world of the DEVIL in human intellectual existence. What is called GOD turns into the DEVIL by exactly these distortions of living functions, i.e., by the "denial of God." In the schizophrenic, these natural functions as well as their distortions appear in quite an undisguised manner. One has only to learn to read the schizophrenic language.

The "High" represents the "Low" and vice versa. The instincts became "low" because of the split in the structure. The originally "high," the "godlike," became unattainable and returns only as the "Devil." "God" is right there within homo normalis, but he changed God into the Devil; God became unreachable and has to be sought for—in vain. What a tragedy! Since nobody else but the human animal himself has created his philosophies of life and his religions, it must be true that whatever dichotomies appear in ideologies and thinking stem from this structural split with its insoluble contradictions.

The painful dilemma between God and Devil dissolves without pain or terror when one sees it from *beyond* the framework of mechanistic-mystical thinking, from the standpoint of *natural, biophysical* human functioning. This has been clearly demonstrated. But it needs further elaboration. We shall now return to the patient for further instruction.

I had had the impression during the last few sessions that the patient, as she emerged from the delusion, was facing one of the following two developments: She would either fall into stupor due to sudden complete armoring against the plasmatic currents; or she would become neurotic before reaching a satisfactory degree of health. The real process followed *both* lines of reasoning, but in quite an unexpected manner.

### 13th session:

She was reluctant to come that day. She only wanted to talk. The day before, after the treatment, everything was "unreal, as if a wall had been erected around all things and people . . . there were no emotions at all . . . How is it that in such a state I feel everything clearly and yet as though through a thin wall?"

I explained to her that she had discharged a great amount of energy; that, therefore, her worst symptoms were temporarily gone; but that also her inner contactlessness was laid bare. She understood perfectly well that the lack of real contact in a certain layer of her structure made her feel things and people "as if through a wall." "Yes," she said, "I could not move freely; all movements are so slow; I could not raise my legs or walk faster than I did . . ."

Such disturbances cannot be understood unless one knows of the anorgonotic attacks which so often follow extreme emotional upheavals, in simple neurotic biopathies, also. It seems as if the organism were not used to strong emotions and as if it became partially immobilized.

Her orgasm reflex was fuller and stronger that day. Her face was strongly flushed, with no cyanosis intervening; the clonisms occurred freely and were not met with much anxiety.

After a while she said: "Your eyes look like those of the Greeks . . . Have you some connection with the Greek Gods? . . . Oh, you look like Jesus . . ."

I answered nothing and let her go on talking. "Oh, I must think so much . . . there are so many emotions, contradictions . . . What is a split personality?"

I explained to her that one feels as if split into two, and that one really is split when one feels exactly what is going on around one and yet feels walled in, too. She understood. Toward the end she became anxious; sudden convulsions in the total body occurred several times. She asked me what was meant by the term "energy stasis." And then, continuing instantly, she asked why I was interested in her "forces."

I had the impression that *her organism began to connect the "forces" with the perception of her streamings*. It appeared as if her splendid intellect were helping to unite the delusion and the understanding of the delusion into one. This was in the direction of our efforts to overcome the split which *separated her organ sensations from her self-perception*. Seemingly unrelated was her question: "I often look at blond Christian girls . . . I envy them . . ." "But you are a blond Christian girl yourself," I said. "Oh, no, I am a dark Jewess . . ."

*14th session:*

She had felt well during the three days since the last treatment. The "forces" had not been there; she had not longed for them. She had gone to a movie with a girl friend; she had been to a museum and had taken a bicycle trip.

She looked well that day, but she was reluctant to yield to deep respiration; she tensed up her chest and shut off her respiration again. I could not understand this reaction. After much talking she said: "I had the same feeling in the movie toward a girl friend which I had had before I went to the hospital the first time . . . I don't like you today . . ."

She armored strongly in the musculature of her thighs, especially in the deep adductor muscles. This type of armoring is well known to the experienced orgone therapist as a sign of strong but fought-off genital excitations. "The pressure on these muscles releases *nasty feelings* . . . perverse feelings . . ."

She had obviously developed some homosexual ideas against strong, natural genital impulses. She gave in partially to the sensations that day and continued to feel clear and happy.

Her relative, who had brought her to me originally, phoned and said that she was greatly improved. I knew, however, that the greatest danger was just ahead of us exactly because of this great improvement. Her organism, unaccustomed as it was to functioning on a high energy level, was not yet ready to take too much well-being and pleasure. Accordingly, I warned against too great optimism. My warning proved correct, as we shall soon see.

*15th session:*

The well-trained and experienced orgone therapist becomes very cautious in handling the process of therapy just when great improvements develop too suddenly. As long as the *basic orgasm anxiety* has not appeared and has not been lived through, there is great danger of complete regression, or worse, of suicide in some severe cases. It was the first time that this danger had to be faced in a case of schizophrenia. Therefore, all necessary precautions were taken.

The patient came with clear, happy eyes and apparently perfectly sane and healthy to this session. She asked me for advice about a diaphragm and other matters of mental hygiene. But she fought hard against full respiration; she blocked in her throat and around her mouth. Slowly a scornful smile developed in her face; she understood what had happened. She yielded again and went very far in admitting the tremor in her body; but her face became bluish-spotty as in shock. Her eyes turned upward again; she gave the impression of a beginning strong withdrawal. She had quite obviously experienced some very strong orgonotic sensations in her body. I asked her at this point whether she gained contact with her "forces." "Yes, nearly . . . ," was her answer. Now it also seemed clear to her that the *"forces" were identical with the orgonotic streaming sensations in her body.*

After the session she remained in the room for a very long time. I let her come at the end of my work day in order to give her more time if necessary. From my adjoining study I suddenly heard peculiar noises. When I reentered the room, the pillows and the mattress were strewn all over the floor, the heater was turned over with the heat on, the leg of one chair was put on an ashtray.

"The 'forces' told me to do this . . ." she said calmly. I told her not to worry, but next time to tell me when the "forces" induced her to do such things. After all, these were my possessions and not those of the "forces." She said "Yes," in a dull and faraway manner.

### 16th session:

Her action the previous day had pointed to very severe hate impulses against me. According to the old rule of character-analysis, taken over into orgone therapy, one must not proceed unless the hateful attitudes have been cleared up first. Therefore, I did not proceed further physically, but worked merely psychologically by means of character-analysis. I told her that she had felt neglected by me. Had she phantasied about living in my house? She had. Now she took revenge in a petty manner because she was very sensitive. She had received no love at all from her mother, only nagging all her life long. She had withdrawn into a phantasy life and there the "forces" had come in. She listened to my explanation with disdain in her face. I told her that she would have to overcome this attitude before I could proceed further. Otherwise I would have to send her away.

After a while she gave up her disdainful expression and yielded. But her attitude was full of meaning and typical for such situations. It occurs regularly that the patient despises the therapist when the orgonotic streamings break through; this happens in all cases, including neurotics; it is quite a typical reaction. It corresponds to the hate and disdain shown by impotent, armored individuals toward healthy people and genital sexuality; usually, antisemitic ideas occur at this point, in the Jew as well as in the non-Jew. The disdain usually centers around the idea that the therapist, who deals with natural genitality, *must* be a "sexual swine."

She accepted my explanations, but declared that she did not want to give up her "forces."

The whole situation seemed perfectly clear: Her natural genitality threatened to overwhelm her and to demand gratification. Her organism could not stand the strong excitations. Together with the weakening of the schizophrenic split her impulsiveness from which the split had once grown began to increase. Therefore, the next task was:

a. *to open the energetic valve of the organism:* SELF-SATISFAC-TION;

b. *to brace her against breakdown* by thorough working-through of her hate against me;

c. *to prevent,* if possible, *any attempt on her part to escape from the perception of her high-pitched organ sensations into delusions.*

### 3. THE REMOTE SCHIZOPHRENIC EXPRESSION IN THE EYES

It is well known that one can diagnose the presence of schizophrenia by careful observation of the expression in the eyes. Schizoid characters and fully developed schizophrenics have a typical *faraway* look of remoteness. It seems as if the psychotic looked right through you with an absent-minded but deep look into far distances. This look is not there all the time. But when emotions well up or when serious subjects are touched upon in conversations, the eyes *"go off,"* as it were.

One can see the same expression in some truly great scientists and artists, for instance in Galileo and Beethoven. One could venture the assumption that the great creator in science or art is deeply engrossed in his inner creative forces; that he is and feels removed from petty, everyday noise in order to follow his creativeness more fully and ably. Homo normalis does not understand this remoteness and is apt to call it "crazy." He calls psychotic what is foreign to him, what threatens his mediocrity. The psychotic is also deeply engrossed in his inner life forces; he listens to them just as the man of genius does; the difference, however, is great: The genius produces out of this contact with his forces great, lasting accomplishments; the schizophrenic becomes enmeshed in them because he is *split* and afraid of them, and not united with his bio-energy as is the creative human structure. But the expression of the *eyes* is deep in both cases, and not flat, empty, sadistic or dull as in neurotic characters who have no contact with their bio-energy at all.

I knew this symptom well since I had worked in the psychiatric hospital in Vienna some 20 years before I met this case. But I knew nothing about its function in connection with the mechanism of delusion and disorientation. Our patient showed this peculiar symptom in an especially clear manner. When the "forces" came close, her eyes would become veiled, the expression would become one of looking into the far distance, and, in addition, the eyeballs would turn sharply upward when the "melting" organ sensations became very strong. I decided to concentrate my attention on this symptom, and, if possible, to remove it, since it seemed to be the main mechanism by means of which she "went off."

*17th session:*

Entering the room she asked: "Can I become a nurse again? My record is very bad . . ." She had never been a nurse. I answered that I did not know. At present she would have to find out why she turned her eyeballs upward whenever the "forces" took hold of her. In orgone therapy one talks little; one lets the patient take on exactly the special attitude which he tries to avoid. Accordingly, I let her turn her eyeballs upward. She did it hesitatingly; but when she had reached a certain position with her eyeballs, she became afraid and said: "This is the place where I usually go off . . . I know it now . . ." I urged her to try it again. She tried, but became afraid. She said: "Our agreement was that we should not touch the 'forces' . . . I don't want to give them up . . ."

I did not urge her any more that day. But *one* thought stuck in my mind and did not budge: *Is it possible that the schizophrenic attack or process is locally anchored just as are other disease symptoms such as anorexia or a headache or cardiac anxiety? Is it the base of the brain, the region of the crossing of the optic nerve?* Would it be reasonable to assume that schizophrenia is a true "brain disease," induced by some specific type of emotional upheaval, with a *local contraction of special parts of the brain due to severe anxiety?* Many symptoms in schizophrenia seemed to confirm the validity of this assumption: The typically schizophrenic look in the eyes, the degenerative processes in the brain found in old schizophrenics (they would be *secondary* structural changes in tissues due to misuse just as calcification of blood vessels is due to chronic, anxious contraction of the vascular system); the report of so many schizophrenics that they felt as if veiled or "flattened" on the forehead at the outbreak of the disease. It seemed important to pursue this chain of thoughts.

### 18th session:

The patient came back feeling quite well. We worked on the expression of her eyes. I urged her to try again to "go off" and to make contact with the "forces" by turning her eyeballs upward, and to reproduce by will the empty, faraway look. She cooperated readily, but whenever she came close to a certain position and expression of her eyeballs she became anxious and stopped. We seemed to be following the right line. Suddenly and without any apparent reason, she said: "You are suggesting all that happens to me."

There was only one possible interpretation of this utterance: The deliberate turning of the eyeballs provoked her schizophrenic mechanism. Since I had urged her to do it, I was logically the one who was suggesting all that happened to her. This idea of being influenced by me emerged from a purely biophysical attitude. This bodily attitude obviously provoked the "beyond" in her self-perception and thus produced the idea of being influenced. This mechanism could possibly apply to many—if not all—cases of ideas of persecution.

I ventured the preliminary assumption *that the "going off" in the eyes was due to a local contraction of the nerve system at the base of the brain.* According to this assumption, this contraction had the same function as all other biopathic contractions: *to prevent too strong bodily streamings and sensations.* I had thus reached a first firm foundation for the orgonomic understanding of the schizophrenic process.

### 4. THE BREAKTHROUGH OF THE DEPERSONALIZATION AND FIRST UNDERSTANDING OF THE SCHIZOPHRENIC SPLIT

We must keep well in mind that this orgone-therapeutic experiment in a schizophrenic case was not done on a psychological basis. On the contrary: All psychological manifestations of the schizophrenic process had to be understood in terms of deep *biophysical processes which underlie and determine the functions of the mind.* Our assumption is that the realm of the psychic is much narrower than the realm of biophysical functioning; that the psychological functions are merely functions of self-perception or the perception of objective, biophysical plasma functions. Thus, a schizophrenic will fall into a state of disorientation when his self-perception is overwhelmed by strong sensations of orgonotic plasma streamings; the healthy genital character will feel well, happy and highly coordinated under the impact of orgonotic streaming.

Our approach to schizophrenia is a *biophysical,* and not a psychological one. We try to comprehend the psychological disturbances on the basis of the *plasmatic* dysfunctions; and we try to understand the *cosmic* phantasies of the schizophrenic in terms of the functions of a truly *cosmic* orgone energy which governs his organism, although he perceives his body energy in a psychotically distorted manner. Furthermore, we do not believe that the psychological interpretation of schizophrenic ideas can go beyond the meaning of words and historical events. It *cannot,* by any means, reach the purely physical and biophysical processes since they function *beyond* the realm of ideas and words. This constitutes what is rightly called the "depth" of the schizophrenic world, in contradistinction to the superficial world of the neurotic.

*Schizophrenia is not a psychological disease;* it is a *biophysical* disease which also involves the psychic apparatus. In order to understand this process the knowledge of the functions of orgone energy are quite indispensable. The core of the problem is the disruption of the unitary, total orgone functioning and the subjective perception of this disruption. Certain schizophrenic symptoms such as disorientation, the experience of "world collapse," loss of the power of association, the loss of the meaning of words, the withdrawal of interests, etc., are secondary reactions to a shattering of *basically organismic, biological* functions. Other symptoms such as the faraway look, the trance, automatisms, flexibilitas cerea, catalepsy, slowdown of reaction, etc., are direct expressions of the biophysical disturbance and *have nothing to do with psychology.* The withdrawal of libido from the world is a *result* and not the cause of the disease. The general deterioration of the organism in later phases of the process is due to chronic shrinking of the vital apparatus as in the cancer biopathy, though different in origin and function. The shrinking carcinomatous organism is not in conflict with social institutions, due to its resignation. The shrinking schizophrenic organism is full of conflicts with the social pattern to which it reacts with a specific split.

If we did not keep distinct these methods of approach, we would not obtain any practical results. We would become confused ourselves, as to the nature and functions of schizophrenia. It is necessary to give a résumé of these facts *before* continuing the study of our case. It will become quite apparent from the facts themselves that what is commonly called the "schizophrenic process" is a mixture of objective *biophysical* processes and the psychological perception of and reaction to these processes; last but not least, a *third* element is involved which could not possibly be known before the discovery of the atmospheric orgone energy.

What is to follow now will appear utterly incredible. Therefore, I wish to assure the reader that I had not the faintest idea of the existence of such mechanisms. But since the treatment of this case the facts to be described have been found in several other cases of schizophrenia. Clinically, as well as orgone-biophysically, there can no longer be any doubt as to the reality of these facts:

The patient came to the *19th session* very calm and coordinated, but slightly absent-minded. She spoke very slowly as if against some great obstacle; she said that she was very much depressed. She had been shopping the day before, for the first time in many months; she had bought many things, had enjoyed them as never before, had shown them to her friends and had slept well. The following morning, however, she was overcome by great emptiness and tiredness. There was a "nothingness" in her; and she had felt the need to sit quietly in some corner "and not to move at all." "Every movement was such a great effort." She wanted to be by herself. She gave the impression of an oncoming catatonia with immobility and perseverance.

"Everything was very far away . . . I watched myself as if I were outside of myself; I felt clearly double: a body here and a soul there . . . [saying this she pointed outward toward the wall] . . . *I know well that I am one person . . . but I am outside myself . . . perhaps there where the 'forces' are . . ."*

She searched with her eyes anxiously along the walls. Then, suddenly, she asked: "*What is the aurora borealis?* [very slowly as if with great effort] I heard about it once; there are patterns and wavy pathways in the sky . . . (she looked again searchingly along the walls of the room, as if strongly absent) . . . I hear you, I see you, but somehow far away . . . at a very great distance . . . I know very well that I am trembling now, I feel it . . . but it is not me, it is something else . . . [after a long pause] . . . I would like to get rid of this body; it is not me; *I want to be there where the 'forces' are . . ."*

I was deeply moved in a quite unprofessional manner when I witnessed her experience of the schizophrenic split and depersonalization in such an unequivocal manner. It was the first time in my long psychiatric career that such a thing had happened so clearly before my eyes. I explained to her that she was experiencing the split which had been in her since childhood. "Is it what they call the 'split personality'?" she asked. She had not connected her own words with what I had just explained. "All those girls [in the mental institution] spoke about it . . . is it that?"

These patients apparently experience the split in the organism quite clearly but can neither grasp it nor describe it intellectually. While she continued speaking, she trembled severely all over her body; she kept her chest high in an inspiratory position fighting hard against exhaling fully. Thorough exploration on my part made it quite clear that she did not perceive the holding of her breath *at all; her chest seemed excluded from self-perception.* Her eyes were heavily veiled, her forehead was bluish, her cheeks and eyelids spotty. "My brain is like empty . . . It was never so strong before . . ." I asked her whether this type of attack was known to her from earlier experience. She answered in the affirmative. I explained to her that this attack was not stronger than before but only more clearly in the foreground of her self-perception.

She repeated: "What is it with the aurora borealis? . . . I would prefer to be soul only, my body to be not . . ." Thereupon her speech began to deteriorate.

This was clearly one of the most important sessions in her treatment, and, I must add, one of the most instructive happenings in my whole medical experience. Let us pause for a while and try to understand what had happened. To the disinterested institutional psychiatrist, who sees such things happen many times every day, it means "just nothing"; only another of those "crazy things going on in the lunatic." To us, this experience of a living organism is full of meaning and deep secrets. I shall try to connect these phenomena with what we know from orgone-biophysical functioning of the organism. As far as I know, neither psychology nor chemistry nor classical physics could offer any plausible interpretation.

*Why did she mention the aurora borealis in connection with her depersonalization?* What did it mean when she said that she found "herself," her "soul," "there where" her "forces" used to be? What was meant by "THERE"?

We are reminded here of such experiences as are reported by great spiritualists and mystics such as Swedenborg. To do away with these things with a smile or the feeling of superiority of an ignoramus does not get us anywhere. We must adhere to the logical conclusion, from which there is no escape, *that a living organism cannot experience anything without there being some kind of reality behind it. To investigate the mystical experience on a scientific basis does not imply that one believes in the existence of supernatural forces.* What we want, is to comprehend what is going on in a living organism when it speaks of the "beyond" or of the "spirits" or of the "soul being outside the body." It is hopeless to try to overcome superstition without understanding what it is and how it functions. After all, mysticism and superstition govern the minds of the vast majority of the human race, ruining their lives. To ignore it as "fake," as the ignorant and therefore arrogant mechanist is wont to do, will not accomplish anything. We must seriously try to understand the mystical experience *without becoming mystics ourselves.*

*The patient had projected a part of her organism toward the walls of the room, and had observed herself from the walls.* If we want to describe exactly what had happened, we must say *that her self-perception had appeared where her "forces" usually used to appear: at the walls of the room.* Therefore, the conclusion is warranted that the "forces" represented a certain function of her own organism. *But why at the walls?*

Hearing voices from and seeing things at the walls is a common schizophrenic experience. At the bottom of it, there must be a certain basic function which is responsible for this typical experience. The projection of a certain function outward is obviously responsible for the feeling of being split into two. At the same time, the chronic split in the personality, or, in other words, the lack of ONENESS in the organism, is the background from which the acute splitting emerges. The psychoanalytic explanation of the projection mechanism in terms of repressed drives which are ascribed to other people or things outside oneself, only relates the content of the projected idea to an *inner* entity, but it *does not explain the function of projection itself,* regardless of the projected idea. These projected ideas vary with the patients; *the mechanism of projection is the same in all cases.* Therefore, the mechanism of projection is far more important than its content. It is important to know that the persecutor in the paranoic delusion is the loved homosexual object; but why does one human being project his homosexual desire whereas the other represses it only and forms it into some type of symptom? The content is the same in both cases. The essential thing, therefore, is the *difference*, that is, the *mechanism of projection, the ability to project*. This, however, has never been understood.

Let us take the expressions of our patient seriously. Let us believe what she says word for word. Afterwards, we can decide what has been distorted and what is actually true. The most amazing thing is the statement that the perception is "there where the 'forces' used to be." It is *as if the perceptions were located at some distance outside the skin surface of the organism.* It is obvious that there must exist a severe disturbance of the inner ability of self-perception *before* "feeling oneself outside" is at all possible. This inner disturbance is, as we found earlier, the splitting-off of self-perception from the objective biophysical process which ought to be perceived. In the healthy organism, they are united into one single experience. In the armored neurotic individual the biophysical organ sensations do not develop at all; the plasmatic streamings are greatly reduced and accordingly *below* the threshold of self-perception ("deadness"). *In the schizophrenic*, on the other hand, *the plasmatic currents remain strong and unimpaired, but their subjective perception is impaired and split off;* the function of perception is neither repressed nor united with the streaming; the function of self-perception appears as if "homeless," in the experience of the schizophrenic. Since the subjective perception is not related *experientially* to the objective plasmatic streamings, it seems understandable that the *schizophrenic searches for a reason for these experiences which he does not feel as his own.*

This situation may account for the *confusion* which so often overcomes the schizophrenic when the split between excitation and perception becomes acute. He perceives something which is not his own; there must be a reason for the experience, which he cannot find; people do not understand him; the physician says "it's crazy"; this only adds to the confusion; anxiety and unrest are the logical outcome of this confusion. The schizophrenic hears himself speak, but since his self-perception is split off from the biological process to which it belongs, he sounds strange and far away to himself; the words lose their contact with the things they are to connote, as Freud has so aptly described; this is the beginning of the disorganization of speech. It was quite clear in our patient that her speech began to deteriorate whenever the perception of the self "at the walls" was at its peak.

To drive the basic schizophrenic split to its peak in an acute experience of sensory delusion such as "being outside oneself," requires a certain bodily function. In our patient, it was the severe blocking of the respiration against strongly forthcoming plasmatic sensations which constituted the *immediate* cause of the projection. HER HEAD WAS QUITE UNMISTAKABLY IN A STATE OF SHOCK BECAUSE OF LACK OF OXYGEN DUE TO BLOCKED RESPIRATION.

In this connection I may mention an experience I had once myself some 28 years ago during a general anesthesia. I had gone into it with the firm determination to observe the onset of the loss of consciousness. I managed to remember quite a bit of the experience after I woke up. The most impressive part of it was the feeling that the voices of the people in the operating room receded farther and farther away, became more and more unreal; furthermore, I felt as if my perceiving ego were receding into some far distance. The depersonalization due to the central effect of the drug was experienced in this form: "I perceive that I still perceive . . . I perceive that I perceive that I perceive . . . I still perceive that I still perceive that I still perceive, etc. . . ." endlessly. At the same time, I felt my ego receding, as it were, into some far, *outer* distance, in the same way as one experiences hearing voices in the far distance while the body is seen asleep in the bed.

The complete loss of self-perception is preceded by an experience very similar to that described by our patient. Thus, it loses much of its mystery.

*"Projection" is factually the process of recession of the ability to perceive, its detachment from the organismic functions to be perceived or usually perceived.* Its result is the delusion of sensory impression "from outside the organism."

This detachment of the function of self-perception from the organismic functions cannot be experienced in some cases in any other way than as the experience of "the soul leaving the body" or "the soul being *outside* the body." Since the perception has only a weak contact and finally no contact at all with the bio-energetic functions which it reflects subjectively, one experiences in a very typical manner "self-estrangement," or "oneself being removed far, far away." Accordingly, the processes of projection, trance, depersonalization, hallucination, etc., have as their basis a *concrete* split in the bio-energetic system.

The split between the *bodily excitation* and the *psychic perception of this excitation* removes the body sensation into the far distance, as it were. It does not make much difference whether the organ excitation or its perception is experienced as receding. In any case, the blocking occurs *between excitation and perception:*

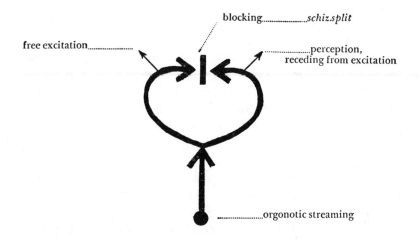

blocking..................*schiz.split*

free excitation.....................

.................perception, receding from excitation

.................orgonotic streaming

**Schizophrenic split, due to blocking of perception of excitation; *excitation is perceived as "strange," "foreign" or "removed"***

and not, as in the "cold" compulsion neurotic, between energy source and its motility:

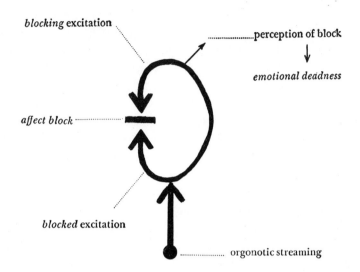

*Compulsion neurotic affect block, due to blocking of bio-energy by total armoring. Excitation is not perceived at all:* deadness; *self-perception is full, but "unalive," "dead," or "empty"*

In the compulsion neurotic, the flow of energy is actually reduced or is bound in a complete armor as soon as it increases. In the schizophrenic, the energy flow is *not* reduced; there is no blocking of the energy production itself, but only lack of perception of the high-pitched excitation. This lack of perception is undoubtedly linked up with a definite blocking in the region of the base of the brain, especially in the optical nerve as expressed in the typical schizophrenic look. I believe, therefore, that it is *correct* to search for the somatic lesion somewhere in the brain. It is, however, utterly misleading to believe that one can remove a schizophrenic process by a frontal lobotomy. Schizophrenia as well as cancer are *general* biopathic processes, with local symptoms due to disturbed functioning in the organs. To mistake the local disturbance in the brain for the schizophrenic process would be just as bad as to mistake the *local* cancer tumor for the total cancer process. Both mistakes run counter to the medical tasks.

I told the patient everything I understood about her illness. She cooperated in a magnificent manner, although her speech was severely disturbed and considerably slowed down most of the time.

The function of SELF-PERCEPTION appeared severely disturbed, depending on how strongly the split between excitation and perception of excitation developed. The dissociation and the production of senseless words increased when the split increased. The normal function of speech and association returned when the split disappeared and the patient began to feel her bodily streamings as her own again. This permitted the conclusion that the *function of self-perception as a whole depended on the contact between objective excitation and the subjective feeling of the excitation.*

The closer this contact, the stronger self-perception functioned. This observation was of the greatest importance theoretically; it was now possible to draw a hypothetical conclusion in a more general way.

## 5. THE INTERDEPENDENCE OF CONSCIOUSNESS AND SELF-PERCEPTION

The following is a first orgonomic attempt to approach the problem of consciousness and self-perception. It does not attempt to solve this greatest riddle in nature; however, it seems to survey the problem of self-awareness in a rather promising manner: *Consciousness is a function of self-perception in general and vice versa.* If self-perception is complete, consciousness also is clear and complete. When the function of self-perception deteriorates, the function of consciousness in general also deteriorates, and with it all its functions such as speech, association, orientation, etc. If self-perception itself is not disturbed, but only reflects a *rigid* organism, as in the affect-blocked neurotic, the functions of consciousness and intellect, too, will be rigid and mechanical. When self-perception reflects dull organismic functioning, then consciousness and intellect, too, will be dull. When self-perception reflects a removed, faint organ excitation, consciousness will develop ideas of being "beyond" or of "foreign and strange forces." This is why the schizophrenic phenomena lend themselves so well—better than any other type of biopathy—to an understanding of the most difficult and most obscure problem of all natural science, the ability of living matter to perceive itself and, in higher developed species, to be "conscious" of itself.

Although self-perception constitutes self-awareness; and although the *kind* of self-perception determines the *type* of consciousness, these two functions of the mind are not identical. Consciousness appears as a higher function, developed in the organism much later than self-perception. Its degree of clarity and oneness depends, to judge from observations in schizophrenic processes, not so much on the strength or intensity of self-perception as on the more or less complete *integration of the innumerable elements of self-perception into one single experience of the* SELF. We can see how in the schizophrenic breakdown this unity falls apart, and how, together with it, the functions of consciousness disintegrate. Usually, the disintegration of self-perception *precedes* the disintegration of the functions of consciousness. *Disorientation and confusion* are the first reactions to one's own perceptional discoordination. Thought association and coordinated speech which depends on it are the next functions of consciousness in the human animal which fall apart when the disintegration of self-perception has gone far enough. Even the *type* of discoordination of consciousness reflects the type of disintegration in self-perception.

In paranoid schizophrenia, where self-perception is severely disturbed, association and speech are also disjointed. In the catatonic stupor where the organism is acutely and severely contracted and immobilized, complete mutism, i.e., absence of speech and emotional reaction are the rule. In the hebephrenic disease picture, where a slow deterioration and dulling of all biophysical processes are in slow progress, perception and consciousness are also, as a rule, dulled, severely slowed down and increasingly less effective.

Thus, we must conclude that the mental functions of self-perception and consciousness are directly related to, and correspond to, certain bio-energetic states of the organism, in kind as well as in degree. This permits, accordingly, the conclusion that *schizophrenia is a truly biophysical, and not "merely" a mental disease*. The basis of the mental dysfunctions was sought heretofore in chemical or mechanical lesions of the brain and its appendices. Our functional approach permits a different understanding of these interrelations:

The mental dysfunctions express the schizophrenic process of disintegration of the biophysical system in an amazingly immediate manner. The dysfunctions of self-perception and of consciousness are directly related to dysfunctions of the emotional functions; however, the emotional functions are functions of orgonotic plasma motility, and NOT of structural or chemical conditions. *Emotions are bio-energetic, plasmatic, and not mental or chemical or mechanical functions*. We must arrange the bio-energetic, the mental and the structural functions with the emotional functions as the common functioning principle, in the following manner:

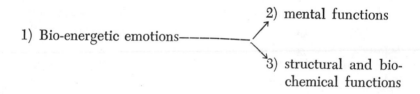

No other arrangement is possible. To put 3) in place of 1) would mean to bog down in the mechanistic ways of thinking of classical psychiatry which led nowhere. To put 2) in place of 1) would mean to derive the emotional disturbances from confusion and to put the functions of the mind *before* the functions of the protoplasm. It would not work and would lead only into metaphysics.

Let us try to understand the functional relation between self-perception and biophysical emotion (= plasma-motion):

In my book, THE CANCER BIOPATHY, I have tried to draw a rough picture of the small child's development in the following manner:

The movements of a newborn baby are not yet coordinated

into ONE whole function and, accordingly, there is no "purpose" or "meaning" in the movements. True, pleasure and anxiety reactions are already clearly formed; but we do not find as yet any coordinated movements which would indicate the existence of total consciousness and self-awareness. We must assume that in the newborn child self-perception already exists and functions fully, but *not in a coordinated, unitary manner.* The hands move for themselves and the eyes, which to begin with are not yet centered on objects, move for themselves too. The legs show only meaningless and purposeless motions, without any connection with the movements of other organs. During the first few months of life, the coordination of the independent and separate movements slowly develops. We must assume that some kind of functional CONTACT is progressively established between the many organs; and with the more numerous contacts the oneness begins to develop. We are probably not too far from the truth if we also concede a development and coordination of the functions of different perceptions. Accordingly, on the basis of the dependence of self-perception on plasmatic motion, self-perception in the uterine and post-uterine existence would be only a dim one and split up into many separate experiences of the self in accordance with the separateness of the plasmatic organ movements. With the growing coordination of the movements, their perceptions also are coordinated one by one with each other until, gradually, the point is reached where the organism moves in a coordinated fashion as a *whole* and, therefore, the many different perceptions of the self are united into ONE total perception of the moving self. Not until then, we must further conclude, can we speak of a fully developed consciousness. "Purpose" and "meaning" of biological activity seem to arise as secondary functions, closely linked up with this process of coordination. It also seems dependent on its tempo of development. It proceeds much faster in the animal than in man. The reason for this difference is entirely unknown. In the human child, the faculty of speech does not develop until the bodily movements and the corresponding self-perception have reached a certain oneness and, with it, purpose and meaning.

It should be noted carefully that purpose and meaning are derived here from the function of coordination, and not vice versa. *"Purpose" and "Meaning" are, therefore, secondary functions, entirely dependent on the degree of coordination of the single organ movements.*

We must further assume, if we follow logically, step by step, the different levels of coordination and the corresponding functions of the organism that RATIONALITY or activity which is purposeful and meaningful in regard to the environment and one's own bio-energetic situation, now also appears as a function of emotional and perceptual coordination. It is obvious that no rational activity is possible so long as the organism is not functioning as a whole in well-coordinated fashion. We see it clearly in the schizophrenic disintegration, which is the reversal of the original process of bio-energetic coordination, that rationality, purposefulness, meaningfulness, speech, association and other higher functions of the organism disintegrate to the same extent to which their emotional, *bio-energetic* foundation disintegrates.

It is understandable now why the schizophrenic dissociation is so regularly found to be rooted in prenatal and immediate postnatal development: Every severe disturbance which took place during the process of organismic coordination constitutes a weak spot in the personality where later, under certain emotional conditions, the schizophrenic discoordination will be most likely to set in.

What is called in psychoanalysis "fixation in early childhood," is in fact nothing but this ever-present weakness in the structure of functional coordination. The schizophrenic does *not* "regress to childhood." "Regression" is merely a psychological term describing the *actual,* present-day effectiveness of certain historical events. Childhood experiences could, however, not be effective 20 or 30 years later, had they not *actually damaged the process of coordination of the biosystem.* It is this *actual lesion in the emotional structure,* and not the long past experience in childhood, which constitutes the dynamic disease factor. The schizophrenic does not "go back to mother's womb." What he actually does is to become a victim of *exactly the same split in coordination of his organism which he suffered when he was in the dead-*

*ened mother's womb;* and he has maintained the split throughout his lifetime. We are dealing here with *actual, present-day functions of the organism,* AND NOT WITH HISTORICAL EVENTS. The U. S. A. does not function the way it does because of the historical event of the Declaration of Independence, but solely because this historical event has become a living, *present-day* reality in the lives of Americans. The historical Declaration of Independence is effective today only to the extent to which is was actually anchored in the emotional structure of American citizens, and not an iota more or less than that. It is because psychiatry did not go beyond merely historical thinking and exploration, that it bogged down therapeutically. A memory *can,* but does not necessarily, mobilize the actual emotions in the present-day organism.

Orgone-therapeutic medicine does not attack memories but the *present-day biophysical anchoring* of the historical experiences; thus it works with high-pitched realities, and not with shadows of memories from the past. A memory may or may not develop in this process of emotional upheaval. It is of no therapeutic importance whether it does or not. *The factor which changes the human structure from "sick" to "healthy" is the emotional, bioenergetic coordination of the organism.* The orgasm reflex is merely the most prominent indication that the coordination has actually succeeded. Respiration, breaking of muscular blocks, resolution of rigid character armor are nothing but tools in this process of reintegration of the organism. They are, most unfortunately, often mistaken for a therapeutic end in itself, even by some close workers in our fields. To mistake mere tools of medical endeavors for the end itself is the result of bad thinking due to lack of coordinated knowledge of the organism, i.e., a narrow judgment which does not fit the breadth and the depth of human emotional diseases.

With such a narrow approach to human organisms, one will never penetrate to the *basic* bio-energetic concepts of orgonomy. One will be only a healer or a businessman in human misery at best, but not a scientific medical worker. I would like to warn especially against any attempts to master schizophrenic biopathies if one has not mastered the *deep* biophysical interrelations between emotions and plasmatic activities, perceptions and the functions of consciousness. These functional interrelations were hitherto completely hidden and unknown. We are only beginning to understand them; the riddles are still numerous. Therefore, utter caution in forming an opinion is essential. In the course of our development we face the danger of doing away with basic problems of natural functioning by using terms loosely. One can already hear people saying that orgone therapy is nothing but "work with the hands on the muscles" or "letting the patient breathe"; or that man suffers from "tensions." The tendency of the average human animal to escape from simple though basic realities by way of verbalization of alive functions is tremendous and among the most damaging attitudes in life. It is not a matter of "muscles" or of "breathing" or "tension," but it is a matter of understanding *in which ways cosmic orgone energy came to form plasmatic moving substance, and in which ways cosmic orgonomic functions are present and active in the human animal,* in his emotions, in his thinking, in his irrationalism, in his innermost experience of himself. Schizophrenic dissociation is *only one,* though a very characteristic, example of the interrelations between emotional processes in living matter and the orgone energy field (or the ether) around it. *This* is what matters, and not a muscular tension. It seems to be in the nature of things that the living just functions, and is satisfied with mere functioning; reflecting about its own existence and ways and whys of being is an age-old activity of the human animal; but whether it is just as much a necessity of life as mere living seems very doubtful. In any case, the institution of statehood has reduced all human interests to the questions of mere existence. And somehow the human animal accepts this viewpoint *en masse* and as a matter of course.

To know one's standpoint of judgment is essential to any sound conclusion. What I am trying to convey here, is the great depth of the functions we encounter in the schizophrenic. I mean *depth* and not complication. The functions which appear in the schizophrenic, if only one learns to read them accurately, are COSMIC FUNCTIONS, that is, functions of the cosmic orgone energy within the organism in undisguised form. Not a single symptom in schizophrenia makes sense if one does not understand that the sharp borderlines which separate homo normalis from the cosmic orgone ocean have broken down in the schizophrenic; accordingly, some of his symptoms are due to the intellectual realization of this breakdown; *others are direct manifestations of the merger between organismic and cosmic (atmospheric) orgone energy.*

I am referring here to functions which bind together man and his cosmic origin into ONE. In schizophrenia as well as in true religion and in true art and science, the awareness of these deep functions is great and overwhelming. The schizophrenic is distinguished from the great artist, scientist or founder of religions in that his organism is not equipped or is too split up to accept and to carry the great experience of this identity of functions inside and outside the organism. It happens that, after a period of great productivity, an artist or a "KNOWER" breaks down psychotically. It was too much to carry; homo normalis, who has lost his first sense, has made life too hard and unbearable for such individuals. The final breakdown in such great men as Van Gogh, Gauguin, Nietzsche, Doeblin, Ibsen and many others is the work of homo normalis. Mystical deviations such as those of Swedenborg, Lodge, Eddington, Driesch, etc., are due to the lack of *physical* comprehension of cosmic and organismic orgone energy functions. And this lack of knowledge is again due to the mechanical armor of homo normalis. But to go back to our patient:

*20th session:*

A new problem arose: *What exactly is the bodily mechanism which underlies the schizophrenic split between organ excitation and perception of excitation?* The events pointed sharply to the peculiar disturbance of respiration: *A severely restricted volume of respiration in connection with a mechanically soft chest.* In the well-armored neurotic, the chest itself is usually quite rigid; thus no strong emotions are developed. In the schizophrenic, on the other hand, the chest is soft, the emotions are fully developed, but *they are not fully perceived;* most probably the inhibition of the motion of the chest structure constituted the mechanism which split the perception off from the excitation.

This had to be corroborated clinically. The further course of events confirmed this assumption.

The immobility in her chest and throat was especially severe that day. No air at all seemed to pass in or out through the larynx. At the same time the patient was softer in her chest and neck musculature than ever before. She said: "I am very emotional to-day . . ." Any attempt to induce passage of air through the throat met with no success. There was no trembling, but only severe aversion against respiration. There were no "forces" around that day.

The patient asked me whether she could go to the bathroom. I began to worry when she stayed there very long. After quite some time the patient came back. Her upper abdomen showed a *cut in the skin about 10 cm. long* across the region of the solar plexus beneath the sternum. She said: "It is here where I feel the strongest emotions . . ."

I told her that such actions would not eliminate the pressure; she agreed. To become excited and anxious about such actions would not help. It would only induce the patient to do *worse* things. If one has good control over the case one will accept such actions as a special mode of self-expression. This requires, of course, the absolute confidence of the patient in the physician and vice versa, a confidence established firmly by working through the distrust and by complete frankness.

*21st session:*

The patient came to this session in good humor and, to my greatest astonishment, breathing fully. But she had added three cuts across the one of the day before. She explained: "I had to do it on behalf of the 'forces'; otherwise, they could have become worried because of the incompleteness of the cut. . . . It has to be a *cross*. . . . I am afraid that they [the 'forces'] will not condone the interval of 24 hours between the first cut and the addition of the crosses. . . ."

It was quite obvious that she had cut herself in an attempt to release bio-energetically her terrific emotional tension in the dia-phragmatic region. This is called "crazy" in the schizophrenic. It is called "national custom of hara-kiri" when a Japanese general does the same thing with the consequence of death. Basically, they are of the same nature; they have the function, in the schizophrenic as well as in the general, of eliminating the unbearable emotional tension in the upper abdomen.

I had the impression that day that psychotic delusions were present but that they were very weak. She told me that the "forces" had not been around all day. She had felt her emotional excitation fully. The contact between excitation and perception seemed reestablished; this had obviously made perception of the streamings as *outer* "forces" more difficult. She was still afraid of the "forces"; she did not trust the situation, as it were; the previous request on the part of the "forces" to "sacrifice herself" could now be understood as inner urges to release the terrific emotional strain by "opening the tight bladder" with a knife. This only confirmed what orgone-biophysical research had brought to light in other biopathies such as masochism: strong emotions correspond to an expansion of the plasma system. Under the condition of some constriction of organs, the feeling of "bursting" appears, together with the *inability* to "*let off steam.*" In such situations self-injury, suicide, actual smashing-up of the body structure occur. Bio-energetically speaking, an unbearably tight bladder has been pricked open.

The improvement did not last long. I may say that I had never before experienced the *incapacity for full healthy functioning* in a biopathic organism as clearly as in this case. *The biopathic structure is used to the biopathic functioning; it is incapable of "taking" or managing strong natural emotions fully and of directing them.* It became clearer than ever before that there are two sharply delineated groups of human animals: the ones *without* and the ones *with* an armor. What appears easy and self-evident to the unarmored individual is utterly incomprehensible and impossible to manage in the armored individual, and vice versa. A certain way of life requires a certain character structure; this is valid for both realms. *Our patient was unable to stand healthy functioning.* We can understand better now how useless, in the face of this inability to function healthily, the usual measures of mental hygiene appear. To impose healthy conditions of living on armored organisms is like asking a lame man to dance. The measures of rational mental hygiene are all right; *they require, however, thorough disarmoring of the human animal on a mass scale and, first of all, prevention of biopathic armoring in the newborn babies.* The breadth and depth of this task is obvious.

### 22nd session:

Her reactions, especially her speech, were severely slowed down. Every single word was repeated several times. She could not formulate words. Her face was frozen; she could not move her facial muscles; she knew the answers to my questions but could not formulate them; she was slightly confused; her skin was pale and spotty-white and bluish; she felt entirely empty.

She said slowly: "I *could* move if I made a very great effort. . . . Why is every effort so difficult? . . . What is happening to me? I had such states before, but I never felt them so clearly."

I told her that her full respiration the other day had made the appearance of the "forces" impossible. She rose and wanted to leave, but fell back on the couch.

I moved her facial muscles passively, raised her eyelids, moved the skin of her forehead. It helped a little, but the catatonic attack went on. She had apparently reacted to the strong emotions of the day before with an anorgonotic attack, with immobility; but her intelligence was clear; she knew what was going on. In the end, she still felt "empty," but less "faraway." "If I become healthy, and if I commit murder, I shall be convicted. Today the boys were electrocuted. . . ." (Some execution had actually taken place that day.)

Her cataleptic attack during the session was due to a breakthrough of a certain deep blocking. The medical orgone therapist knows well that each pathological layer has to appear from the depth. This does not interfere with the life outside. She had worked well in the office that day and was orderly.

She remained in the room after I had left. When I returned ten minutes later, I found her coiled together, with her head between her pulled-up legs, her hands at her knees. SHE COULD NOT

MOVE. "I prayed to God that you would come in and free me from this position. . . . I suddenly could not move at all. . . ."

I helped her to get up and she began slowly to move again. She said: "I thought that the 'forces' might have done that to me, but I don't know. . . ." Thereafter, her head began to tremble; after a while she recovered fully and left, reassuring me that she felt better.

### 23rd session:

The misconception prevails in certain circles that the essential thing in orgone therapy is the establishment of orgastic potency and nothing but that. It is true, of course, that this is and remains the main goal of our technique. But the manner in which this goal is reached is quite decisive with regard to the firmness and durability of the success. *It is essentially the slow and thorough overcoming of the emotional blocks in the organism and of the anxieties connected with each single block which secures lasting results.* Our schizophrenic patient was very close to the goal of therapy; but the disease mechanisms which were interpolated were the most essential obstacles to be overcome if the eventual success was to be a lasting one. It is easy in certain cases to achieve release of pent-up energy. But if the main blocks remain unresolved, relapse with worse effects than the disease before will result. Therefore, we obey the rule of proceeding slowly and of carefully working through each single layer of blocking. These biophysical blocks, which impede the free flow of bodily energy, constitute exactly the "disposition" to various kinds of symptomatic diseases.

I knew that our patient carried strong inclinations to catatonic stupor within herself. These tendencies would have to develop fully; they would have to come to the surface and would have to be overcome. The greatest danger was still *ahead* of us. One must not brag about success too early.

The patient had suffered a slight catatonic attack during the previous session. She came back happy and looking very well: she told me that she had had a very good time since the last session. She could move her facial muscles, but was unable to move the skin of her forehead, as in "astonishment" or "frowning."

She related quite spontaneously that she felt impelled to make a lot of grimaces when she felt strongly emotional; but she was not able to make any grimaces at all when she felt "estranged." "I have learned hard not to show any emotions in my face . . . I don't like women who show emotions; *I want them to be like nice, slender statues. . . .*"

These few sentences, although spoken calmly, contained much emotional dynamite. Her head and neck musculature was severely blocked and rigid. Therefore, grimacing partially relieved her from the feeling of tension and immobility. Strong depersonalization and splitting wiped out the ability to grimace. We understand now why catatonics and advanced schizophrenics grimace: it is a desperate attempt to release the deadness and immobility which overcome their organism in the state of stupor. They test themselves to see whether they still feel anything at all.

I did not understand immediately what the ideal "slender statues" meant. I was soon to learn about it the hard way.

She spoke much about "dying" that day. The idea of "dying" is well known to orgone therapists. It usually comes up when the patient is close to orgastic release of bio-energy; it is connected with severe fear of letting go fully. The anxiety will persist as long as the main blocks in the organism, usually in the pelvis, are not dissolved. Her head was *visibly* disturbed in a most severe manner. Therefore, I feared a premature breakthrough of total body convulsions. The outcome would inevitably have been a total breakdown because of the remaining blocking in her forehead. "The emotions are hurting me lately in my belly," she said. "Here . . ." and she pointed to the upper abdomen. "My left arm also lives and acts on its own. . . . I do not feel it as *my* arm. . . ."

Whenever a neurotic or psychotic symptom increases in strength, it indicates that the emotion contained in the local region has become urgent and tends to break through. The detachment of her left arm could possibly be the expression of strong impulses to touch her genitals. Her idea of "nice, slender statues" could, in this connection, have no other meaning than that of being a "statue without genitals," something "godlike."

In order to prepare her for her genital breakthrough, I concentrated on her immobilized forehead and eyes. I let her move the skin of her forehead, roll her eyes in all directions, express anger and fear, curiosity and watchfulness. THIS IS NOT MANIPULATION AND HAS NOTHING WHATSOEVER TO DO WITH ANY KIND OF MANIPULATION. We do not "manipulate" mechanically; *we induce emotions* in the patients *by letting them imitate willfully this or that emotional expression.*

She objected very strongly to showing the expression of anxiety in her eyes. This objection is usually much more intense in schizophrenics than it is in neurotics. The reason, based on several cases of schizophrenia, is the following: Raising the eyelids, opening the eyelids wide and showing anxiety releases a sensation of severe terror with the feeling of oncoming disaster. Sometimes panic sets in. Some such patients have the feeling that they are dying, "going off," and that they will be unable to "come back again." It is essential to be very careful at this point.

I worked very cautiously on her expressions in the forehead, stopping her whenever she showed too strong anxiety. After some time, she could move her forehead more easily and she felt freer. Her self-perception of the total organism was still severely disturbed; to let her total pre-orgastic contractions break through would have been dangerous and inadvisable. She was sensitive to touch, pressure, cold and heat, *but at times she did not feel the quivering.* After the therapeutic session, she asked many intelligent questions about herself, but her speech was considerably slowed down; she spoke as if against some great counter force.

It was during the experiment with this schizophrenic that the following idea came up for the first time: *The organ sensation or "orgonotic sensation" is a true* SIXTH SENSE. Besides the abilities to see, hear, smell, taste, touch, there existed unmistakably in healthy individuals a *sense of organ functions,* an ORGONOTIC SENSE, as it were, which was completely lacking or was disturbed in biopathies. The compulsion neurotic has lost this sixth sense completely. The schizophrenic has displaced this sense and has transformed it into certain patterns of his delusional system, such as "forces," "the Devil," "voices," "electric currents," "worms in the brain or in the intestines," etc.

Since the orgonotic sensations and organ perceptions seem to constitute a great part of what is called the EGO or the SELF, it appears clear now why a splitting and dissociation of perception and speech usually go hand in hand with the dissociation and displacement of these organ sensations.

We must also assume that the severity and the outcome of a disease depend entirely on the specific organ where the deadening, i.e., the extinction of the organ sensation, took place. The dissociation of an arm appears harmless if compared with the immobilization of eyes and forehead, or even parts of the brain.

We would object less to the irresponsible brain operations and lobotomies which are performed to kill the Devil in the organism, if they served to disclose the dynamic *functions* of the brain. Such questions as, "Does the brain move? Does it contract and expand when working, just as other organs such as the heart, intestine, glands, etc., do?" are of the most importance for medical pathology and the understanding of the organismic functions. It would be highly important to invent a device which would enable the brain specialist to observe the brain in its *natural* state. Cutting out "windows" in the skull to study the brain, as was done with apes and with some human beings, won't help. The living organ does not move when a severe operation has been performed in its vicinity. This is shown by the edemas and similar dysfunctions occurring after operations. All I want to say here is this:

There is good reason to believe that *in the schizophrenic process parts of the brain, most probably the base with its nerve roots, become immobilized;* just as in chronic constipation the intestines are immobilized, or in a tumor of the stomach peristalsis ceases to function. This would appear as a new, hopeful and functional approach to the *somatic* disturbances in schizophrenia. It would require abandonment of the mechanistic view of the brain function. The brain would have to be regarded as an organ like others within the total functioning of the organism, as a special *"transmitter"* of total plasma functions, and *not as the source of motor impulses.* For if the brain is the source of impulses, then the next logical question is: *Who gives the orders to the brain?* It amounts to the assumption of an imp in the brain, if one says that the motor impulses *originate* in the gray substance.

There are many species without any brain at all, who function fully as far as living functions, including judgment, are concerned; and we know from experiment that brainless dogs continue to function, even if severely impaired by the operation.

To return to our patient:

The situation at this point was characterized by her closeness to total bodily convulsions and genital activity; but the block in her forehead and eyes constituted a major obstacle which had first to be removed before she could be permitted to develop further on her way toward natural genitality.

### 24th session:

The patient came beaming with joy. She had felt very happy and at ease. Her eyes were clear and the look was alert. The color of her face was ruddy and fresh. She had, for the first time in her life, passed through a menstrual period without psychotic reactions. She had visited many friends, among them a girl in the mental institution. Her respiration was much improved, though it was not completely without restriction.

The next step was quite clear: I had to bring her back to where she had been the previous day. She would have to "pump up" more emotion, to learn to stand it without "going off," and then to proceed further.

In the course of deep respiration, a tremor appeared over her chin and in the masseter muscles. She said: "When my emotions kick me on the one side, and society on the other side, I feel like getting down, hurting myself, becoming syphilitic or something like that . . ." Later on: "Emotions want to break out here . . ." She pointed to her stomach and *then down toward her genital. . . .* "Then I am able to commit anything . . ."

One cannot expect to have these connections presented more clearly.

### 6. THE RATIONAL FUNCTION OF THE "DEVILISH EVIL"

It is necessary to sum up again the basic functions which were found by orgonomic research in the depth of man's biophysical functioning, in order to understand fully the meaning of CHARAC-

TER STRUCTURE. In the light of orgone biophysics, this "structure" appears as the sum total of the relationship between the orgonotic energy system and the sensory-motor system which has to perceive the plasmatic currents, to execute the energy discharges and to coordinate all energy functions into an orderly, total, unitary functional system: "orgonotic system." In the schizophrenic process, the system of perception is flooded by high-pitched biophysical sensations which are not integrated into the total biosystem and, therefore, lead a *separate existence*, as it were. This constitutes the "split of personality." The biosystem has a very low tolerance for *sudden increases* of the emotional, i.e., *bioenergetic* level of functioning. Disorientation, hallucinations, speech deterioration and murderous impulses are likely to appear with a *sudden* increase in energy level if the tolerance is low. This has nothing to do with "psychology." The "psychology" of the schizophrenic is a *result* and not a cause of the process. When the perception is split off from the bio-energetic excitation, the bodily sensations are experienced as "foreign," as "evil," "devilish" influences by "supernatural powers" ("supernatural" in the sense of "beyond" one's own self). In this harrowing confusion, the biosystem develops destructive impulses to protect itself against the Devil. It is, in fact, the remainder of sane personality which does the fighting against the Devil.

Let us follow further the events in the patient:

The patient had scarcely uttered the words: "Emotions want to break through here . . . [in the genital] . . . ," when she became pale and silent; she lay there immobile, as if absent; she did not respond to questions. After a while she said in a very timid manner: "I have just said the Lord's prayer . . . The emotions are gone."

She left the session calm and slightly absent-minded. The next day I received the following letter (Italics mine.—W. R.):

March 18, 1942

So it is all emotion—*you did not know about the music that was playing Liszt's Hungarian Rhapsody*—or others—*the notes go through me*—not through you or anyone else—to tell me something—I don't usually know what—tonight it was my bigness—you couldn't understand that—nor could anyone else on earth.

There are colors and darknesses and shadows and lights—it was raining hard tonight I walked in puddles I was going to take my shoes off and walk by your house, the people stared in the train and on the street—I went in to eat on your main street and a woman was there after talking to the boy in the store about hospitals and Bellevue—they had worked there—they are made to speak then to annoy me but they smiled not with me—at me—the people in the train were having a good time—*and they wanted me out of the way*—but I stayed anyway—

I came home and found I had passed a city test I once took—so maybe I'll be a typist for the city—that I would not be able to quit easily though—

Just human and emotional?—You couldn't know—You said I didn't believe in my forces—but they believe in me—they send rain and tell me they know—I won't see you for 2 days maybe I can forget you and your work—86000 Jews were killed—slaughtered by the Nazis in Russia today—all for crucifixation of Christ—There were nails through his hands and one through his feet—I wonder if he bled much Blessed Mother forgive me—Thine is the Kingdom the Power and the Glory forever and forever Amen

You crucifier of the Blessed Sacrament—You should pay and yours after you—I am protected from mine enemies the rain marks them for having annoyed me—something will happen to you—Adler died when I told him he would—Katz of Psychiatric died also—You shall have many troubles—you may think they are the natural outgrowth of things but I will know better—

You could have been so helpful but you went your own inimitable way—the epitome of knowledge—spheres that go round and round—Help when I needed it you would not give—I am protected and sheltered and if sometimes made to suffer it is for a definite reason—The Jew in me must be made to suffer so that others can survive—

On thee, Oh Lord, our faith rests—that takes thee to eternal life

Command and I shall obey no ties can find me no powers save those can stay me from performing my predestined destiny—Please tell me oh Lord—

If your interest has waned I am willing to stop—if your Ego keeps

inflating I am also willing to stop so I must take first aid to help the
wounded humans survive—

Mummies and madmen grow dark in the sun—(after thought)

You, too—F.


I suggest that we take these things very seriously. In such
schizophrenic experiences, the world which is called THE BEYOND
in common mysticism and in true religion manifests itself before
our eyes. One must learn to read this language. What is never
admitted by homo normalis, what is lived out only clandestinely
or laughed at in a silly manner, are the severely distorted forces
of nature; exactly the same forces which imbue the great sages,
philosophers, musicians, geniuses of science, in the wide realm
*beyond* the conceptions of homo normalis and his everyday
political clamor. I venture the statement that in our mental
institutions many potentially great artists, musicians, scientists
and philosophers are rotting away their lives because homo normalis refuses to look beyond the iron curtain which he drew in
front of his real life, because he dare not look at living realities.
These great souls, broken down and wrecked as "schizophrenics,"
KNOW and PERCEIVE what no homo normalis dares to touch. Let
us not be led astray by the distortions in this knowledge. Let
us listen to what these gifted and clear-visioned human beings
have to say. We can learn a great deal from them; we can learn
to become more modest, more serious, less gaudy and cocky, and
we can start realizing a few of the claims we make in an empty
manner in our churches and in our high academic institutions. I
claim, after 30 years of thorough study of schizophrenic minds,
that they look through our hypocrisy, our cruelty and stupidity,
our fake culture, our evasiveness and our fear of the truth. *They
had the courage to approach what is commonly evaded,* and they
were wrecked because they went through the inferno without
any help on the part of our neurotic parents, our conceited
teachers, our cruel directors of educational institutions, our ignorant physicians. They hoped to emerge from the inferno into
the clear, fresh air where only great minds dwell. That they
could not make it, that they got stuck in the realm of the "Devil"

is not their fault; it is the fault of the abysmal ignorance and stupidity of our homines normales.

*Our patient had experienced her emotional storm as great music.* The ignoramus will say "that's crazy." *No, it is not crazy.* A Beethoven goes through the same kind of emotional storm when he composes a great symphony which provides a huge profit for some utterly amusical businessman. It is obvious that a Beethoven has the structure to stand the same kind of great emotional storm which causes the breakdown in the schizophrenic structure. It is equally obvious to one who works with orgonomic functions that a Beethoven, in order to keep his inner world safe, withdraws his bio-energy from his acoustic nerves, that he goes deaf in order not to have to listen to the chattering of annoying "critics" and what not; the schizophrenic differs from him in that he does not keep his genius intact and does not develop it as does a Beethoven. But he suffers from the misbehavior and misdeeds of our Babbitts no less than did Beethoven; and he withdraws into his own inner world. His misfortune is that he has only partial contact with this inner world, that he is not equipped to accept it fully and to carry it further; hence the breakdown. My work with "wayward youth" in Germany left no doubt that the best of the human crop go down to ruin not because of their "badness," but because of the inferno which homo normalis calls "civilization" and "cultural adaptation." We shall have more to say about this realm of the Devil. Homo normalis, who wants his psychiatrists and biologists to be "aloof," "unemotional," "academic," "removed," so that he can continue to plant the emotional plague into millions of newborn, healthy babies, undisturbed, hates the schizoid character for its closeness to a realm of nature which is forever closed to himself.

The evening of the same day when the emotional storm had occurred our patient became restless. She had seen her parole physician and had stood her ground well. But inside herself the storm continued. It was clear to me that, should she ever become capable of coping with her strong and rational emotions, she would be saved. If not, she would certainly go down as a catatonic in the mental institution.

## 7. ANORGONOTIC REGIONS IN THE CATATONIC STATE

*25th session:*

The patient came back in a very bad state. She had fought "a desperate battle against the 'forces'." Both her arms were bandaged with tape. A huge cross, made of tape, was fixed to her stomach from the pit down to the genital and across. She told me that the "forces" had requested an account of whether she had betrayed them; they had asked whether she was ready to sacrifice herself fully, to yield to them to the fullest extent. I asked her what she meant: "It means that I have to cut a deep cross with a knife into my body . . ." She said that she did not want to do it, that she fought a hard battle against doing it, but that she did not know how to escape from the request. She had finally arrived at the conclusion that she could try to "cheat the forces": If she placed a bandage across her belly, the forces could be made to believe—"for a short time only"—that she had fulfilled their request. She wanted me to help her. Once, she said, she was close to using a razor to cut herself.

Her speech was considerably slowed down, as if all impulses had been extinguished. She was slightly dissociated; she showed mannerisms and drivelled. Her face was pale, the skin of her forehead was immobile, her eyes were heavily veiled, the skin of her body was patchy. Something had to be done immediately if commitment to the institution was to be avoided. She was in a state similar to that of shock. I took her to the metal orgone room and examined her with the fluorescent bulb. The background of this test is the following: Orgone-charged fluorescent bulbs luminate when they are slightly rubbed on the skin. I wished to ascertain whether or not her state was due to loss of surface charge. Her legs gave the normal effect of lumination. Her hair reacted only weakly, and her forehead did not react at all. It was amazing to me to hear her telling me *beforehand* which parts of her body would and which would not give lumination. She predicted the disturbance on the basis of the feeling of deadness or aliveness which she felt in a particular spot.

I tried to charge her in the orgone accumulator. After about half an hour of irradiation, she slowly began to recover. The lumination effect became stronger where it had been weak before; she could move the skin of her forehead; the patchiness disappeared; her eyes became bright again. The disturbance had been strongest in the region of the segment corresponding to the base of her brain: eyes, eylids, lower parts of the forehead, temples. After about half an hour she felt "fuller in the head where it had been empty before." Her speech had also improved considerably.

In the end she implored me not to abandon her in her fight against the "forces" and to put her through safely. I told her that I could not promise anything, but that I would do what I could to help her. She felt rather happy again.

I had gained the firm conviction during this treatment that the *immobilization of the bio-energetic functions in the optical segment, including the brain, was the center of the acute catatonic attack*. Several other cases of latent and manifest schizophrenia with catatonic tendencies corroborated this conviction. Further investigation of this dysfunction might reveal that it is generally *specific* for the *acute* schizophrenic breakdown; it may also restrict this mechanism to certain types of schizophrenia. *Its main characteristic is a standstill of the movements and, with them, of the bio-energetic functioning of the brain, especially its frontal and basal parts.*

Orgonomy has termed the stoppage of bio-energetic functioning "anorgonia." This symptomatology was first discovered in the cancerous shrinking biopathy. But now I met it in a schizophrenic during a catatonic attack. It was correct to assume that most of the symptoms of the catatonic attack were due to a more or less complete standstill of bio-energetic functioning at the *periphery* of the organism. This standstill appeared as accompanied or even caused by a withdrawal of bio-energy to the core of the biosystem. Immobility, flexibilitas cerea, perseveration, torpidity of speech or mutism were, accordingly, to be regarded as direct expressions of the immobilization. On the other hand, such symptoms as automatic movements, mannerisms, echolalia, and particularly the sudden breakthrough of severe rage could be understood in terms of an attempt of the remainder of mobile bio-energy to break through the immobility by forceful or by automatic movements from the center outward. The relief which is usually experienced by catatonics after an attack of rage, and the following improvement in the disease picture, would corroborate our interpretation. The more complete the armoring, the deeper toward the biological core it spreads, the greater must the rage be in the outbreak. In other cases, such an outbreak would be impossible and deterioration with loss of weight and stoppage of biofunctions one by one would result. It is also to be assumed that a paranoid schizophrenic picture changes more or less suddenly into a catatonic one, if the biosystem has lost its capacity to endure strong biophysical outbursts of energy. The complete final contraction of the biosystem in such cases would be the reaction to the attempts at expansion by the remaining life impulses.

It should be especially emphasized that *the intolerance of healthy expansion on the part of the sick organism constitutes the core of the disease.*

## 8. THE FUNCTION OF SELF-DAMAGE IN SCHIZOPHRENIA

We know from therapy of mental biopathies that suicide or self-injury are brought about by unbearable bio-energetic stasis in the organism when neither work nor destructive actions nor orgastic gratification are accessible for discharge. The psychological "motives" of such actions are secondary and incidental; usually, they are merely rationalizations of the action. In the schizophrenic, and especially in the catatonic type, self-injury acquires a special function. This became clear when the attempts at self-damage in our patient revealed their motivation.

*26th session:*

I took her to the orgone room and examined her skin surface again with a gas-filled, orgone-charged bulb.* Then I asked her to show me the parts of her skin where she felt dead, and to rub

---

* *Cf.* my article, "Orgonotic Pulsation," on "lumination," 1944.

the bulb against these spots. To my great amazement she pointed to exactly the same spots where she had inflicted cuts: At the joints of her hands where she had once cut herself; at her palms, at the saddle of her nose; at the temples, and, most emphatically, at her sternum, where she had several times cut crosses into the skin. These spots did not give lumination of the orgone-charged bulb, in contradistinction to other spots. They were felt as "dead" in her self-perception, and they were uncharged, i.e., "dead," objectively.

This is a most important new piece of information on the bio-physical state in the schizophrenic psychosis. In our patient, the idea of "sacrifice" to hostile "forces" was obviously built upon the foundation of correct perception of a severe bio-energetic dys-function of her skin surface. She behaved in exactly the same way as many schizophrenics in mental institutions; they knead their skin, touch their forehead, rub their fingertips against walls, try to move their eyelids, rock their limbs, etc., in a stereotyped manner; some do that for years on end. These stereotypies and automatisms have not been understood hitherto. Now it appears as if these catatonic activities were expressions of a desperate but futile attempt to regain the feeling in the parts of the body which went dead. I would like to emphasize especially the catatonic facial grimaces. Catatonics usually have severely stiffened, mask-like faces. Grimacing seems, therefore, to be an attempt at mobil-ization of the deadened facial musculature.

Theoretically, the detachment of single parts of the body or of whole organ systems from the realm of self-perception would, according to these biophysical findings, be direct results of a deficiency in orgone charge in the respective parts or organs. The compulsion-neurotic biopath only feels a general emptiness and deadness; the schizophrenic biopath perceives the dysfunc-tion much more clearly and immediately. He can tell us exactly where the dysfunction is located, if we do not refuse to pay close attention to what he is saying, and to understand his language of emotional, i.e., *bio-energetic* expression.

We are justified in drawing the conclusion that the schizo-phrenic mind describes *objective* processes. Normal, healthy functioning of the organism expresses itself in and is governed by an even distribution of bio-energy in the biosystem. I know well that we are moving here along pathways which no one has yet studied scientifically. It is not only *new* land, but also No Man's Land, so to speak. The self-perception of well-being and happiness, of strength and security is due to the coordination into one whole of all the self-governing partial functions of the various organs of the organism. Accordingly, the feeling of dissociation, splitting, depersonalisation, etc., in the schizophrenic biosystem must be due to discoordination of the single organs and energy field systems in the body. It is as if some of the organs—I suggest especially the brain—lead *separate* existences detached from the total organism; as if there were no CONTACT and no UNITY between the bio-energetic units called "organs." The mental and the emotional confusion and disorientation is the direct result of a *sane* self-perception of this dissociation.

Our patient reacted in a quite unequivocal manner: When the "veiling" of her forehead set in, she felt at the same time *as though the convolutions of her brain were tangled up "like entangled intestines."* Well, to me such a description appears full of *rational* meaning. In spite of the routine objections of mechanistic neurology, it seems improbable that the brain should have convolutions like the intestines and that at the same time it should *not move*, like most other organs, when it performs its work of coordination and transmission of central impulses. Is it not most reasonable to assume that the brain is built up of intestine-like convolutions precisely because *it moves* in the manner of peristalsis while functioning? Some healthy individuals who are used to hard thinking relate clearly that they feel great heat in their brain and in their foreheads when they think with great effort; that they feel a "glow" and that this glow disappears when the effort is over; on the other hand, we see pale, immobilized, cold foreheads in cases of mental deficiency and pseudo-debility. If some thought is given to the question, it seems self-evident that the brain would not behave differently from other organs during strong functioning. Heat production is a well-known indication of physiological effort, in the muscles and in the emotional state of sexual excitement. Lack of heat production is readily seen in cases with low bio-energy, as in cancer biopathies, anorgonotic weaknesses, anemia, etc. There is, therefore, no reason whatsoever to assume that the brain tissue does not develop more energy, and with it, more heat and motion during hard work.

I know well enough that this assumption sounds peculiar and strange to classical pathology to which the brain is an immobile organ, in spite of the erroneous assumption that it is the brain with its thalamic and subthalamic appendices which generates all impulses of life activity. I do not agree with this theory. I believe that it is utterly wrong; that it is contradicted by obvious facts of living functioning such as the fact of *brainless* living beings and by important aspects of natural philosophy in general. The visual proof of brain motility is hard to adduce, as I said before. But there can no longer be any reasonable doubt that it is the *brain which is functionally (and not, to begin with, structurally) disturbed in schizophrenia.* Mechanical and structural changes appear later as *results* of the functional bio-energetic dysfunctions; among them, stoppage of motion and discoordination of the bio-energetic field action appear to be the most essential ones. We must admit atrophic changes of disuse in the brain tissue just as we see them in muscular atrophy. If it is true, as it seems to be, that the shape of the organs reflects the form of motion of bio-energy, then the brain with its twisted and rich gyration is an excellent example of the bio-energetic function of organic forms.

The emotional and bio-energetic dissociation in the schizophrenic leads, as we well know, sooner or later to a general decay of the organism with bad body odor, loss of weight, severe disturbances of biochemical metabolism, and sometimes also with true cancerous developments. The schizophrenic shrinks biophysically, too, because of the loss of the capacity to draw and to maintain the normal level of bio-energy.

To return again to our patient who yielded so much insight into the riddles of schizophrenia:

I treated her for several weeks with the orgone accumulator. The orgone had a strongly positive effect on her; it caused, as it does in other cases of organismic contraction, an expansion of the autonomic nervous system. Her face reddened, her eyes became clear again, her speech became faster and more co-ordinated, and she would even feel pleasure in the orgone accumulator after 15 to 30 minutes irradiation. This was a great new hope for possible biophysical treatment of incipient schizo-phrenia.

The combination of physical and psychiatric orgone therapy was very helpful. Acute withdrawal of bio-energy could be dealt with by means of the accumulator alone. Psychiatric orgone therapy helped to bring to the surface schizophrenic mechanisms from greater depth.

During the *27th session* the patient was mostly good-humored, the skin of her forehead was mobile, and her eyes very alert and clear. But her respiration was still restricted. It is possible to "pump to the surface," as it were, the remainder of pathological mechanisms. As long as it is still possible to induce anxiety by means of respiration or certain typical attitudes of the body, the biophysical structure has not really been cleaned of its dysfunc-tions. When I "pumped up" her emotions, she lost her gaiety, the "forces were near," the forehead became pale and immobile: "Something is interrupted between the skin of the forehead and the brain," she said. This, she said, was always the case when the "forces" were around; it usually disappeared with them.

During the following period (*28th to 32nd sessions*), the patient seemed very much improved. She said repeatedly: "I don't know whether I want to get well. . . ." Saying that, she meant that she did not know "what would happen to her" if she became well. On several occasions she kept imploring me: "Please, help me against the forces . . . they are not around now, but I know they will come back . . . I am so afraid of them . . . save me. . . ."

It had become unequivocally clear by now that the "forces" were her *distorted* perceptions of the plasmatic orgonotic stream-ings; that she loved them and dreaded them at the same time; that whenever the streamings became strong, she would fall into a stupor-like state. The sensing of "forces," flight into psychotic mechanisms, and immobility of the optical segment formed a single functional unit.

I could see that she fought against a mean, cruel expression in her eyes. I encouraged her to let go and to force this expression out. She succeeded with some effort, and immediately felt much better; but at the same time she also seemed to come very close to a catatonic state whenever she produced the expression of strong hate in her eyes. Once she got up, went, in a stuporous manner, to the closet, took the heater, and put it, switched on, before the door of the closet; then she built a cross from hangers on the door. She "had to soothe and appeal to the forces," she said. She also told me a little later that she "felt only parts of her brain"; other parts "were twisted," and, "therefore, she was confused."

I knew well that she would have to pass through a severe anxiety attack with possible complete relapse into catatonia when the plasmatic streamings broke through in full force. This seemed to depend entirely on whether or not she would yield to full respiration. One could see each time that she flattened her respiration when the "forces" became too strong.

During the following four weeks (in spring) she improved very much. She worked well in the office where she had taken a job; she was sociable and gay; the attacks of withdrawal became rare and were not as strong as they used to be. True, off and on she would return to her schizophrenic attitude and action. For example, she came once with her abdomen wound up in adhesive tape "in order to keep myself together. . . ." A neurotic biopathy would simply have expressed fear of bursting; our patient actually took measures against bursting in a typically psychotic way. But we both understood what was going on, why she did such things, and she knew perfectly well when she would stop doing them. I had taken great pains to tell her everything about the danger ahead, and she had understood with truly schizophrenic intelligence.

She had also learned slowly to produce the expression of murderous hate in her eyes, without becoming frightened by it. This gave her some feeling of security against her fear of committing murder; she realized that one can express murderous hatred fully, and that this did not mean that one actually had to commit murder.

I worked continuously and cautiously on the inhibition of respiration in her throat, with some success. But she never gave in fully to *emotional* respiration. She had shifted her main sensations from her chest to her abdomen; this was an indication of the shift in the perception of her orgonotic streamings toward the region of the *genitals.*

Once she tried in a playful manner to put a noose around her neck "in order to see whether she could hang herself." These actions still had the timbre of danger about them; but it was greatly reduced by the playfulness and the humor which went into them. I knew well that she was not yet beyond the possibility of actually committing suicide. Her parole physician noticed the great change, and encouraged her therapeutic effort. This psychiatrist was very helpful and kind.

It was clear that bio-energy and the sensations accompanying it were moving strongly toward the *genital* region. The preorgastic sensations were near. Therefore, the still prevailing block in her throat constituted the main therapeutic problem. I knew: If this block should fail to budge in time; *if the genital excitation should break through in great force with the block in the throat still present, then she would definitely become catatonic.* It was a race against time to remove the block in the throat, before the full development of genital excitation.

One day she gave in fully to her respiration and SHE FELT IMMEDIATELY THE IDENTITY OF ORGONOTIC STREAMINGS AND "THE FORCES." She knew it instantly and quite clearly, with no doubt left whatsoever. Her chest structure moved quite automatically. She had strong sensations of streaming in her whole body, with the exception of the genital region proper from the mons pubis downward. She asked: "Would it be possible to make the body whole without touching the soul?" This was a most peculiar question. Did the "soul" represent the genital sensation or even the genital itself? Most probably it did. We would expect this to be so when the "forces" represented the bodily streamings; when, furthermore, the peak of bodily streamings was experienced in the genital organs, as "nature has prescribed," then it was logical that also the "soul" was represented by the pre-orgastic sensations in the genitals. They had been split off from perception for such a long time that they could not be perceived other than as foreign forces and as the "soul," the most prominent part of self-perception. This was confirmed when she insisted that she "did not want to have her soul cured."

The patient was very cooperative for weeks on end. Each time when natural respiration brought forth genital excitation she objected in a psychotic manner and cramped the muscles of her thighs, the deep adductor muscles, in a way familiar in all types of cases.

### 33rd session:

The genital organs are biological tools of energy discharge and of procreation of the species. The latter function is widely known and acknowledged. Homo normalis, who is the heir of homo sapiens, who in turn is the heir of homo divinus, has, on the other hand, condemned the biophysical function of energy discharge; it returned as the DEVIL in the phantasy life of man. The biologically strong individual did not or could not sacrifice his rational judgment to the demands of ecclesiastical thinking; the great natural force came into conflict with the dependence of the individual on his kin and his society. Under these circumstances, the genital forces continue to function, but they are split off from the rest of the organism as "bad" or as "sin," and return as the DEVIL, as "forces from beyond" in the realm of schizophrenia and mysticism in general.

This fact became clear beyond any shadow of a doubt during the further progress of our patient. Since Tausk in 1919, it has been known in psychiatry that the genital apparatus constitutes the persecutor in the schizophrenic delusion. But it was not known that this had a much deeper biophysical significance; that it was the *strong sensation of living streaming* in the body, and not merely the genitals, which becomes alien and unbearable in the adolescent as well as in the psychotic. The genital organs are so predominant only because their excitation induces the strongest sensations of aliveness.

I told the patient that she had now the task of learning to *feel* her genital region just as clearly as she felt other parts of her body. She let her respiration go fully, but soon became confused and patchy in her face whenever she came close to streamings in her pelvis. I saw her cramping severely in her thighs for the first time. *The "forces" began to break through to the area where they belonged: namely, into the genital region.*

She spoke in a secretive manner, fearfully and in a hushed voice; she said that no one had understood her with regard to "these feelings." She began to describe extensively what she experienced when "it happened or began to happen in that region." The forces somehow make the *things in the room around her take on a "queer expression";* they become quite "peculiar." Not that they would change their shape; but they acquired an ALIVE EXPRESSION, the meaning of LIVING BEINGS. "Something strange emerges from them"; they "seem to want to tell me important things, as if animated." Then she became confused and anxious.

At first I could not understand why "things became alive around her" when she herself was close to becoming genitally excited. Then it became clear:

*In strong biosexual excitation, the orgone energy field of the organism expands considerably; all sensory impressions become acuter and sharper; this also happened to her; but since she did not perceive this biological process as her own, since the excitation was split off from self-perception, the* ORGONE ENERGY FIELD AROUND HER, AS EXPERIENCED IN VERY VIVID SENSE IMPRESSIONS, APPEARED AS A FOREIGN, STRANGE FORCE, WHICH ENLIVENED THE THINGS IN THE ROOM.

Accordingly, the projected psychotic persecutory sensation appears as a *true* perception of a *real* process: THE PSYCHOTIC PERCEIVES HIS OWN ORGONE ENERGY FIELD OUTSIDE HIS ORGANISM. The contents of the sensation, such as projected homosexual or destructive ideas, are secondary to the bio-energetic perception of the orgone energy field.

Let us pause for a moment and consider how safe this assumption is, apart from the clinical experience brought forth by our patient:

The orgone energy field meter, constructed in 1944,* demonstrated the existence of an orgone energy field beyond the skin surface of the organism.

An orgone-charged electroscope reacts to the energy field of the moving palm only, and not to dead wool.

The oscillograph reacts when the electrode is attached to a wet towel and when a living organism or organ such as the hand is touching the towel.

Bions which are strongly charged with orgone kill bacteria and cancer cells at a distance and attract other bodies. This capacity disappears when death occurs.

The existence of the "sixth sense," the orgonotic perception beyond the surface of the organism can, therefore, not be doubted.

I explained to the patient the function of the orgone energy field as seen in bions, blood cells and at the field meter. She understood it and paid me the compliment that I was the first person she knew who could explain to her her deep experiences in an understandable manner.

I would like to mention here briefly two cases of paranoid reaction which demonstrate the fact that persecutory sensual hallucination in certain instances follows the perception of orgone energy OUTSIDE the skin surface of the organism.

Several years ago I treated a woman who suffered from vaginal anesthesia. She was married, but had never experienced any sensations in her pelvis. After some time, the orgasm-reflex began to appear; soon it was far enough developed to reactivate the natural physiological functions in the vaginal mucous membranes and the glands. She reported that her husband seemed rather gratified by the development in their relationship. However, a few days later she brought her husband to me in despair: *he* had developed the idea that I, in a malicious way, was influencing him with electrical currents through her vagina. It was immediately evident that he had developed a paranoid persecution idea. He

---

* *Cf.* THE DISCOVERY OF THE ORGONE, vol. II, 1948.

went into an institution with the diagnosis paranoid schizophrenia.

Why did the husband break down psychotically when his wife developed strong vaginal streamings and excitation? We could not have answered this question before the organismic orgone energy functions were discovered. Now it seemed clear: His own energy system could stand the genital embrace only so long as no strong sensations occurred. When his wife began to recover, her organism quite obviously had induced currents and strong sensations in *him*. His organism reacted to this experience with a split in a paranoid fashion. I had cured his wife; therefore, I had influenced him with electricity through her vagina. He showed the typical schizophrenic eye symptoms.

This case shows that actual physiological changes take place in the organism of one mate when the genital functioning changes in the other mate. This is true for dulling of sensations as well as for increased excitation. We see it often happen in orgone therapy that a husband or a wife improves when the bio-energetic situation changes to the better in the partner who is under treatment.

A man with clear-cut psychotic mechanisms used to react with severe anxiety after turning his eyeballs upward. He felt as if he were being choked to death. One day, I let him turn his eyeballs upward again. This time the reaction was particularly strong. In the course of the anxiety attack, he stared into one corner of the room, ripped his eyelids wide open, began to scream and pointed in terror toward the corner: "Don't you feel it," he screamed, "there, it's right there, coming out of the wall, staring at me." Then, with a sudden jump, he jumped up and ran with terror *into that corner* from which he felt the stare had come. I led him into this reaction several times. It subsided gradually and finally disappeared altogether.

In this case, too, a "projection" had occurred. Bio-energetically, however, I had no reason to doubt that his orgone energy field had become excited far outside of his body and that this had made possible the psychotic reaction. To return to our patient: During the following few weeks she was happy, worked well and had no delusions; the "forces" seemed gone. But one day, when she saw her parole physician again, she told him that she did not know whether to continue the work with me; that she became confused and did not understand the mechanisms which I explained to her.

*She had turned against me in a malicious manner.* During her sessions with me she behaved in a haughty, arrogant way, as if she despised me. The treatment made her incapable of living in the real world of real human beings; she was losing the "credo" of a "beyond" which seemed so much a part of her. How would she be able to exist in this world if she were going to become genital? She knew well, she said, that people are ill; but she did not want to exchange her world for reality as it is.

She refused my suggestion that she could develop the ability to live her own life without having to escape into her schizophrenic world. To that she answered that the world as it is does not permit human beings to live the happiness of sexual union without imposing severe chains and pains. She, therefore, preferred her world of delusions where she was her own master and protected by the "forces."

Her judgment of the social situation, as far as the sex-economic way of living was concerned, seemed quite rational. Not a single one of her critical ideas could have been refuted on the basis of human welfare or social security or moral integrity. For instance: During her puberty there had been moments of great sanity and lucid judgment; she clearly longed for a boy to embrace her and to love him; but then came the thought of *where* to love him, and *what to do with her relatives* who would have hindered and plagued her had they only guessed what she was doing; she was afraid of being sent to a reform school; she had known that she would become a criminal if she were caught and taken to an institution. She had not known at that time that she would later spend many years in a mental institution. But her suffering from her bodily, frustrated excitations had become so strong that she finally welcomed the dullness of mental institutions.

Should she have yielded to her sick mother who nagged her all day long, hated her father, spoke disparagingly about him, smeared his name wherever and whenever she could, because he had withdrawn from her? Or how could she have developed her great intelligence in some field of human endeavor when she had no room of her own, when her mother opened all letters addressed to her? She had been squeezed between her overpowering bodily craving for a man and the social impossibility in her life situation of satisfying this desire. The period of this dilemma was short but agonizing. Then, for the first time, it began to happen that things around her became alive and seemed to "tell her things." First she was curious; but when they grew stronger, she became frightened and finally confused. Where did *she end* and where did the *world around her begin?* She could tell less and less. Then murderous impulses would come up and she had a hard time refraining from hurting people. Therefore the walls of the institution appeared as a refuge from great strain and persecution on the part of her own organism.

During the following weeks she was clear and cooperative; she wished that I "would free her from her experience of animated objects" which frightened her so much. She felt deadly afraid of the "other world." I asked her to describe this "other world." She drew this diagram:

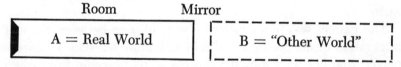

The power of the "forces" manifested itself in their ability to open world B for her when she felt anxious in world A. This "other world" was "quite real" although she knew perfectly well that it was "*not real.*"

The patient began to perceive the deadness in her throat. She understood for the first time in several months what I meant when I kept telling her that she held her respiration; that she should try to press her air out; that she should let her chest "fall" or "go down."

She felt anxious when the chest moved downward with the air passing through her glottis. When she felt a strong excitation in her lower abdomen, she said: "I am afraid of something I do not feel, but I know it is there. . . ."

The projection and mystification of the bodily streamings were the result of *lack of clear perception of an organ sensation which was nevertheless perceived.*

It is very difficult to put such biophysical functions into proper words. These functions are beyond the realm of words and ideas. It is very difficult to formulate in words an experience in which a process in the organism *is* perceived and yet is *not* perceived *as one's own.* But there can be no doubt whatsoever that this is exactly the key to the understanding of the schizophrenic split and projection of bodily sensations. Her sharp intelligence manifested itself again when she formulated quite spontaneously the difference between a hysterical and a schizophrenic experience: The first, she said, consists in an alienation of an organ from the total body experience; the latter consists in an alienation just as in hysteria *plus misinterpretation and mystification of the detached perception.*

This description is in agreement with the most skilful biopsychiatric comprehension of the process. It fits every type of mystical experience; mysticism perceives a body-own process as alien and originating "beyond" one's person, or beyond one's earth.

The patient was in a constant disequilibrium between rational integration of her feelings and schizophrenic delusion. I had expected that her schizophrenic process would develop fully when her self-perception made contact with her bodily excitation in full force. My expectation proved correct.

*34th session:*

The patient came with vivid schizophrenic delusions. Soon after the last treatment when she had made contact with her bodily streamings, a diarrhea had set in. She had had "twisted intestines . . . and something had moved downward toward her genitals." She had vomited everything she had eaten; she was bothered by severe flatulence. During the night, she had seen many peculiar forms and figures in her room with rainbows around them. It was obvious that the orgone energy had moved rapidly in her body and had brought about the excitation of her intestines. It was further obvious that she had misinterpreted most of her sensations. She complained: "I do not trust you . . . you are at one with them [with the 'forces']; they use all possible means to harm me . . . they poisoned the food so that I had to vomit . . . they made it rain to annoy me . . . they never before mingled with everyday life . . . now they do . . . that's your fault. . . ."

The idea of being poisoned may well be understood as a result of excitations which are bounced back at the upper intestines in reversed direction, i.e., in impulses to vomit. I persuaded her to yield more to the "forces." She succeeded in giving in more fully. When severe tremors in her total body set in, she went off again. I brought her back by pinching her. But her eyes remained empty and "faraway." The skin of her forehead was immobile; she trembled with severe anxiety.

This was in itself a great step forward. I had expected it. I had known that all her schizophreniic symptoms would flare up once her organ sensations developed and were perceived fully. But I did not know what the outcome would be: *complete catatonia* or *recovery?* The risk had to be taken since catatonia would have been the only outcome without therapy anyhow. I also knew that the danger of suicide was great. I assured myself of her confidence and honesty. She confided that when her hands went completely dead for a while the other day, she had had the impulse to cut them off. ". . . If only I could trust you . . ." she said repeatedly. ". . . They have got hold of me now . . . they do with me what they want . . . I cannot fight them any longer. . . ." It struck me that she had refused a cigarette I had offered her during the treatment. She was suspicious of being poisoned.

### 35th session:

The patient came in a state of complete vegetative shock. Her skin was spotty from blue to red. She trembled and her eyes were severely veiled. She could scarcely speak. At first she seemed willing to cooperate. But when convulsions occurred in her face and shoulders she suddenly jumped up, pulled a knife from behind her back and went at me. I made it a habit to be on the lookout for such things. I grabbed her hand, squeezed the knife out of her fist and told her sharply that she should lie down and

not move. She screamed: "I have to kill you . . . I have to . . .
I must. . . ."

For more than two decades I had experienced and understood
the murderous rage against me on the part of people who became
frightened to death by my scientific, factual description of the
orgonotic streamings. I had met this terror in presidential can-
didates, communist liberators, fascist mystics, well-adjusted
psychoanalysts, neurotic court psychiatrists, neurosurgeons, directors of mental institutions, hopeless cancer pathologists, schizophrenics, politicians of all kinds, scheming wives of co-workers,
etc. So I knew what I was dealing with: She was blue with rage;
she tried again and again to jump upon me, to get at my throat,
and to kick me. . . . She did it openly and frankly, while the biopathic psychoanalyst who feels threatened by my teachings goes
around sneaking and gossiping, telling people that I was in a
mental institution or that I seduced all my female patients or that
I have just been buried. I preferred the behavior of my patient
by far. After some time, she broke down in a quite unschizophrenic manner and cried bitterly like a child. She cried for a
long time, and it was emotionally complete. At intervals, she became furious, cursed her mother, her father, the world, the whole
system of education and medicine, the state hospital and the
physicians there. In the end she calmed down and explained:

After the last treatment, *spontaneous movements in her lower
abdomen had plagued her;* she had felt them fully; *her genital
had "itched" severely for the first time in her memory; she had
tried to satisfy herself, but without success.*

I had to take strong precautions against possible disaster. I
knew that in case the therapy did not succeed in making the
patient capable of tolerating and integrating her bodily sensations,
the worst could be expected to happen. I notified her relatives
to take the necessary steps to commit her to the institution. One
will ask again why I took the great risk, why I did not commit her
immediately. My answer is again: The scientific results of this
experiment were tremendous; to commit the patient would have
meant stopping the flow of scientific information; it would also
have meant extinguishing any hope of her recovery. She was on

the verge of recovery and deserved a chance to reach it. The final outcome proved this attitude correct. But at that time I did not know the final outcome.

### 36th session:

The patient came late; she had not wanted to come. "I do not like it [the situation] . . ." she said. "I felt pleasure all over my body; my body is one now, but I do not like it. . . ." She was almost completely relaxed; her respiration functioned well. "I would like to go back to my old world. . . . I loved the forces. . . . I am afraid I might want badly to sleep with a boy. . . ." (She had *never* embraced a man.)

She showed all the well-known signs of severe pre-orgastic *pleasure anxiety*. The prospect was: She would either become frightened to a sufficiently great extent to withdraw again fully and probably finally; or she would break through to full health.

### 37th session:

She came in complaining about the movements in her abdomen and in her genital region. She had no power over these movements. On the contrary, the movements had great power over her body. Before, she could do nothing to the "forces," but she could, so she said, kill me because I had brought about this situation of movements in her body. She could not live with these movements. If I were dead, then the influence I was exerting upon her would cease, and with it also the movements in her body.

Let us pause for a moment again to think over this situation: The therapeutic result was doubtful as far as restoration of complete sanity was concerned. As a clinical confirmation of the whole theory of organismic orgone biophysics the situation was invaluable, rich in further possibilities, with a broad outlook on the whole realm of human character structure. To sum it up, the following conclusions seemed safe:

1. The murderous hate I and my co-workers had met in so many people, laymen and professionals alike, was due to the provocation of spontaneous movements in the body, in bodies

which had never experienced such autonomic movements, well-known to every healthy, unarmored individual.

2. These movements, if *alienated* or *excluded* from the realm of full perception ( = self-perception) constitute the experiences of every kind of mysticism. That a psychopath like Hitler preferred to kill in Spring thus becomes easily understandable.

3. The influencing "forces" in schizophrenia are identical with the plasmatic movements in the organism.

4. Many types of crime and murder are due to such sudden changes in the structure of potential or actual murderers.

5. Chronically armored human organisms tolerate only low levels of bio-energy and the corresponding emotions. What constitutes high-pitched joie de vivre in unarmored individuals, their buoyance, their aliveness, namely, the functioning of bio-energy on a high level with a strong energy metabolism, is utterly unbearable to the armored individual. *Sudden* changes from a high to a very low energy level constitute acute depression. On the other hand, *sudden* changes from a chronically low to a very high energy level constitute dramatic and dangerous situations because of the inability to tolerate strong sensations and emotions.

It is, therefore, to be expected that biopsychiatry will sooner or later succeed in describing human structures and characteristic reactions in terms of *"bio-energetic metabolism," "emotional tolerance"* of biophysical excitation, and *"capacity for energy discharge."*

Such an *energetic* point of view would enable us to handle, finally, "human nature," not with complicated ideas and experiences, but with simple energy functions, as we are handling the rest of nature.

### 38th session:

The patient felt fairly well, was coordinated, clear. She had tried to satisfy herself; she had felt a strong throbbing in her vagina. However, she had "detached" her right arm; she could not press the hand in handshaking. I explained to her that some deep inhibition manifested itself in this detachment of her right arm, that we had to get it out of the depth. "This would be much too dangerous," she said.

We were dealing clearly with a very old and deep blocking of the motion of physical self-gratification with the right hand.

### 39th session:

I knew that I had to put her through the genital emotions as quickly and as safely as possible if a final breakdown was to be avoided. She was very mobile and clear that day. When the respiration had "pumped up" enough organismic energy, her PELVIS BEGAN TO TWITCH spontaneously. Strong streaming sensations set in and she refused to continue. She declared suddenly that she was confused (she was *not*); at the next parole meeting she would hide from the parole physician the fact that she felt much better in order to keep the door open for return to the asylum. "If I let go further it will take my brain away. . . ." She meant she would lose consciousness: ORGASM ANXIETY was coming to the foreground. At the end of the session, she made the sign of the cross in the Catholic manner.

At 11 p.m. that evening she called me on the phone to tell me that the moon "had thrown shadows on the floor of her room," and that that was the "sign to her from them," but she had been unable to call the "forces." I succeeded in quieting her down.

### 40th session:

She was very unhappy. I knew that she had been very excited sexually the night before, that she had not been able to obtain gratification, and that she had reached a most crucial point in her life. She told me that she had tried desperately to get the "forces" back, but that she had not succeeded in doing so "in spite of the contact with the moon." She was convinced that the "forces" refused her company because she was "Jewish." Furthermore, she said that she did not want to lose her world; she could not live in "this world."

It was clear what she meant by the word "Jewish." It meant to be "sexual" and "swinish" at the same time. The ambiguity of these emotional experiences derived from the fact that she wanted to feel her bodily forces, but did not want to feel or be "swinish." This was in complete agreement with the clinical experience of orgone biophysics: *The human animal longs for full feeling and realization of his biosexual emotions; at the same time he rejects them and hates them because of their perverse distortion.* "GOD" represents the former, and "DEVIL" the latter; both are fused into one painful, confusing entity. This becomes quite obvious in schizophrenics, but is also present and clearly expressed in homo normalis.

Was her refusal of the world of homo normalis justified? Of course it was. This world had ruined her natural biological structure ("GOD") and had implanted the "DEVIL"; her mother had done this to her. The schizophrenic knows the ways of homo normalis and has full insight into their disastrous results. Homo normalis, on the other hand, is a Babbitt who does not understand the schizophrenic world of *rational* judgment, nor, for that matter, his own.

It is a major objective of this case history to describe the psychotic crisis in relation to the orgonotic streamings and emotions of the biosystem. It is of the utmost importance to concentrate one's attention on this single fact, and not to be distracted by the maze of schizophrenic mechanisms and delusory ideas. We must penetrate to the common denominator which characterizes the schizophrenic breakdown, regardless of the contents of the delusions. *The center of the schizophrenic breakdown is determined by overwhelming orgonotic plasma streamings which flood a biosystem incapable of coping with the emotional storm.*

Psychiatry has understood that the psychotic system is an attempt at reconstruction of the lost EGO (= WORLD). But it could not tell why this world of the EGO breaks down. The psychotic reconstruction is a result, and not a cause of the disease. This must be kept well in mind. Also, the "narcissistic fixation in childhood" is not a cause of the breakdown but only one of the conditions under which the breakdown occurs. *The core of the problem is the biophysical split between excitation and perception and the resulting intolerance of the biosystem of strong emotions.*

## 9. CRISIS AND RECOVERY

The patient went through the following three distinct periods at the end and after the treatment: 1. Great well-being and sanity; 2. Sudden catatonic breakdown; 3. Full recovery, with freedom from psychosis for over 5 years after treatment.

### 1. *The rapid approach to health:*

The first period lasted about a month. In the beginning, she used to cry very often "Because the 'forces' do not want me any more; because I am Jewish. . . ." With the bodily sensations and the return of their perception the "forces" were gone completely.

Then she began to enjoy her newly acquired health. She used to call me up saying that she did not need the treatment that day, that she felt fine and happy, that she preferred to play tennis instead or to see a show. She worked efficiently and happily at the office.

During the treatment she breathed fully; she let her emotions develop freely, cried, laughed, talked very intelligently and without a trace of blocking or perseveration. But I did not trust the situation fully, because of my experiences with reactions to severe orgasm anxiety. I knew *she was not safe until she had yielded to her biological role as a female animal in the embrace with a man whom she could really love.*

The "forces were not around any more." No trace of any schizophrenic symptoms was to be seen on the surface. But there were many indications that there were schizophrenic functions still at work in the depth, even though without a high pitch of bioenergy.

She hesitated to acknowledge the accomplishment of orgone therapy. We know that patients who do not appreciate good results are somewhere and somehow hostile, due to a remainder of anxiety.

She said emphatically that she thanked only the great LORD for her recovery. She developed the idea that "health" meant continuous, uninterrupted happiness, without any interference of sorrow and worries. She did not accept my statement that health meant also the ability to stand the impact of unpleasant situations and worries.

She felt her genital region as belonging to her, and no longer as dead or alien; but she claimed to have no desire for the sexual union. There was no doubt whatsoever that she did not admit the problem of sexual union to full scrutiny. She was evasive and glib about the subject of a serious love life.

Then slowly the suspicious indications of oncoming disaster began to increase.

She began to call me a "faker" and a "dangerous man" who provoked "bad things" in people. She did "not want any orgastic potency," she said, although she had come to me explicitly because I had elaborated this concept of emotional health.

One day she came with a metal cross hanging from her neck; she had bought it for ten cents "in order to appease the 'forces.'" I warned her not to be too optimistic but to expect more devilish things from the depth of her emotions. She laughed at that and assured me that I was exaggerating.

She showed signs of escape from further therapy. She wanted to come only for another few sessions. She said I was not cultivated enough, not subtle enough for her. She would go to the police to accuse me of "doing bad things."

Then, one day, she did not want to cooperate at all, remained in her overcoat and left soon thereafter. She phoned that same evening, excused herself for her behavior and told me that she still needed me very badly. Then, events rapidly turned for the worse:

### 2. Sudden catatonic breakdown:

The patient came to the next session in a very bad state of health. She had had a "horrible night"; things and forms had become "alive" in the room; a shadow had appeared on the wall and had stretched out an arm to take hold of her. "I felt no anxiety, but it was a horrible experience," she said.

She felt a little better when bodily currents developed and when she permitted their perception.

But the following day she came completely confused, with

severe dissociation in speech and ideas. All things were "queer"; all actions were terribly complicated; when something went wrong she thought that the "forces" were interfering with her will. Her job at the office was a great burden, scarcely bearable. Her speech during the whole session was severely retarded and mostly unintelligible, but she tried very hard to make herself understood.

She remained in the treatment room at 7:20 p.m. to dress. One of my assistants found her at 8:50 p.m. in a cataleptic position; she could not move; she had remained there in the same position for an hour and a half. Very slowly and with great effort she told us that she had been unable to call for help. Her organism had reacted with catatonic catalepsy, that is, with a total block of motility, to the strong plasmatic currents which threatened to overcome her.

The following day the patient had recovered from her cataleptic attack, but she had developed a *delusion of grandeur* instead This new delusion had obviously the function of preventing the flow of bio-energy in her organism and the perception of nature in herself.

When during the treatment strong pre-orgastic sensations occurred, she suddenly said: "*I am too great and too good to be an animal. . . .*" A few minutes later: ". . . The 'forces' force me to cut deep into my left cheek. But I shall master myself; I am stronger than they [the 'forces']. . . ."

To the expert in orgone-biophysical functioning, this reaction was clearly the expression of a delusion of strength due to the new and gratifying experience of biophysical, vagotonic *expansion* of her plasma system. Still incapable, as she was, of accepting and enjoying the pleasure function fully, she turned against it by means of her delusion: Now she was even stronger than the "forces," i.e., still stronger than the *animal* in her. This was soon confirmed in a very drastic manner. The following day I received this letter from her:

Thursday
Added adjunct—the affective (should be effective) advocates of the lyceum in Rome. You do not see that by immortal power of Will

of survive and achieve. "My mind" is in a state of confusion about the pieces fitting in and my good boss and job. You did not fit the pieces for me no one did or does and that's why I go to psychiatrists to find out.—The water babies, the Goddess Diana, and the Dr. Doolittle stories when I was a kid. I am very very old from Buddha and Mohammed in caves and Isis on an alter of crucifixion I am always depressed by nature of myself. I must have a clear answer not by "changing my thoughts" as you said—that solves nothing—but you are very very kind my thoughts are not thoughts but impregnated knowledge given into my head. Sentences written in books that know how and why I suffer written for my eyes alone without the author's knowledge or will. Impregnated thoughts.

But the bad panic is from the terrific confusion which hurts.

Here's another message to add to your collection. It may prove someday extremely valuable—I would not have to say "I told you so."

Do you know who I am? I told you I would tell you the complete picture—and the Greeks and Romans—ancient of course—fit right into the picture. I suppose you have heard of "*Isis*"—

### I AM HER RESURRECTION

And there are those who are opposed to Foreign Forces—there are probably five all told.—The Lord on the left, the others are more or less somewhat antagonistic—It is these that sometimes bring fear because they are often against me and torture me cleverly. You see the complete reincarnation is not always present and when only part is there I am open to abuse from these other forces. I have no priestesses, etc. left—not in this world so I have to fight myself—and I am not always full of the complete super-power to do so easily—the Lord of course—is my ally. When I am complete as this evening in your home—there is Nothing I cannot do—should I so wish—coming home there was a policeman ordering someone to put the lights out in a store —for air-raid precaution—I was hoping he would say something to me or someone would—to order me to do something—Fools that people are they cannot appreciate the greatness of me—they do not see it— they only see something strange but they do not know the power.

The question of suicide is difficult because of the question of status beyond—would I go back to my original birth or forward into the future queenliness—until the question is solved I can do nothing. Death is another force, he is quite a kind, serious figure—he came years ago—but not since. The One today was the same as last week but that is Evil, I think—You see I as Isis am not fully on the same standing as the Others—principally one reason because I am pre-destined to live here on earth and carry on that life—that problem I have never been told the answer to—what the main reason behind this being on earth is—

That's enough to write
F.
Names are so meaningless
just family left-overs—not at all
real—

She had become the goddess Isis because of her strong bodily sensations; the psychotic distortion of the feeling of strength and "mission" and contact with the universe was clearly due to her inability to permit full perception of the natural orgonotic strength and to enjoy it as a living organism, whole and sane. Therefore my statement seems justified that the schizophrenic, in contradis-tinction to the neurotic, has the full power of his natural orgonotic energy function; he differs from the healthy animal, including man, in that he splits off perception from excitation and thus trans-forms his feeling of strength into delusions of grandeur, and his weak perception of faraway excitation into delusions of the "Be-yond" and persecution.

These insights seem to be of first-rate importance for the understanding of the whole realm of psychotic delusions; it does not matter whether the split is brought about by high tempera-ture, as in postpuerperal amentia, or by post-syphilitic structural lesions as in the paralytic delusion, or by a truly schizophrenic split. The essence remains the same:

Once the unitary function of the organism is split, the bio-physical processes in the organism will be perceived as a force alien to the ego, in the form of hallucinations or delusions of vari-ous kinds. The specific mechanisms which distinguish a delusion in general paresis from a delusion in puerperal fever or a delusion in dementia praecox are not important here. What is important, however, is the *basic dissociation of the perceiving apparatus from the biophysical system of excitation.*

Our patient described this pathological situation very clearly during lucid moments in that period of her breakdown:

"THE WORLD IS VERY FAR AWAY . . . AND YET VERY CLOSE . . . IT DOES NOT CONCERN ME AT ALL . . . AND YET I FEEL EVERYTHING AROUND ME IN A PAINFUL WAY. . . . When an airplane flies by, I have the clear feeling that the motor makes a louder noise in order to *annoy me*. . . . The birds are singing louder in order to give me hell. . . . That sounds silly, but I sincerely believe that they do it for that purpose. . . . The human beings look at me and observe carefully everything I am doing. . . . I can scarcely stand all the many impressions. . . . How shall I be able to perform my work? . . . I would like to go back to the hospital where I do not have to do the work and be responsible."

Later on:

"*Would you permit me to swallow this cross?* It could help me to stand all that better. When there is only *one* 'force' around me, I can stand it; but when there are many of them around, then I cannot stand it; my ability to stand it is not sufficient."

This is plain language, indeed. One has only to learn to listen to it to understand it, instead of "shocking" such broken-down people. Homo normalis shuts himself up in his room behind drawn blinds when the bright sunlight annoys him, when he cannot stand the impact of natural forces. The old gossiping spinster keeps on telling bad stories about loving couples, because her organism cannot stand the excitation which is brought about in her by the functioning of love around her. The biopathic Führer kills millions of people because he cannot stand any alive expression. The criminal kills the one who provokes in him the feelings of humanity and goodness. The schizophrenic falls apart emotionally and biophysically.

The patient fell into a stupor that same session, recovered and was taken home by one of her relatives.

The following day at 1:30 p.m. she swallowed the cross she had carried on her chest. She came to the session with great pain. She had at first only taken the cross into her mouth. Then "it went down quite by itself. . . ." It had hurt in the pharynx, but finally it had slipped through the esophagus. She had intended "to please God" by this action, and to stop people from looking at her. She had been frightened when she had swallowed the cross, but God had smiled at her. She wanted to walk on a high mountain, to stretch her arms toward heaven; then God would come close to her and would embrace her.

*Her intense desire for the genital embrace was thus disguised in the form of the psychotic delusion of being embraced by God.*

I let her eat a good deal of bread immediately. She looked at the bread and said: "Here there are eyes [the holes in the bread] looking at me. . . ."

She was taken to a private physician who Xrayed her. The cross was in her stomach. The physician knew of the orgone-therapeutic experiment and cooperated in order to help keep her out of the institution. But all efforts were in vain. In my long career as a research physician, I have seen many a human being rather die than admit the perception of his bio-energetic sensation of streaming. I have witnessed people go to war rather than risk punishment for telling the truth. Therefore, it did not surprise me to see this patient prefer to go to the mental institution than admit full genital excitation in her organism.

The cross was later eliminated naturally. But the following day I received this report from one of her relatives who was guarding her:

*Report as of May 23, 1942:*

"I first became aware of some change in her behavior when she asked her mother to leave, and said that she would prepare something to eat. I later learned that she insisted that the mother leave the house. She did set things out to eat. When I looked up next, she was standing at the sink with a glass in her hand which she was hitting up against the side of the sink. It refused to break and then she tried to hit it with a small drain shovel to no avail. I thought she would hurt herself so I approached and offered to break the glass for her. She gave me the glass which I broke. She picked up the pieces and carefully put them in the pail.

"There was no further incident during the meal. She remained in the kitchen watching me; her eyes had a strange look. After the meal, I prepared a shower for myself. Then suddenly, while under the shower, I was very much surprised to see her appear in the bathroom with a large kitchen knife in her hands. She was completely nude. This is the first time I had ever seen her nude before me.

"I asked her what she wanted the knife for. She said that she used it to open the door, to lift the latch. Then she laid the knife down upon the washstand and looked at me. I pretended to go on washing but all the time I kept watching her. She just stood there saying nothing and looking at me. I tried to make conversation with her but it was no good. All of a sudden, she jumped up on the rim of the bathtub in which I was, put her hands around my throat, and tried to push me under the water. My throat was soapy and her grip was insecure. I took hold of her wrists and forced her off the bathtub. I asked her why she did that. She said that she wanted to see me under the water. She stood looking at me for some time and then left.

"When I came out of the bathroom, she was in another room. The lights were out and she sat in the gloom. I did not go into the room but I listened as intently as I could. After some time, I heard the sound of tearing. What it was that she was tearing I could not tell, and so after it continued for some time, I went to see what she was doing. She had completely torn the pages out of the book, "The Function of the Orgasm," by Dr. Wilhelm Reich, and she was about to start on another copy of the book, when I took it from her. She now had her bathrobe on and continued to walk about in the dark.

"When I noticed her again, she had climbed upon a dresser in the hall and stood there in a catatonic condition, a cigarette dangling from her hand. After about ten minutes, during which time she stood upon the dresser immobile, I called Dr. Reich to ask him what I should do. He suggested that I take her down and bring her over to the phone to talk to him. I took her by the hand and pulled her down. She sank into my arms rather easily. But when I started to carry her over to the phone, she began to kick and insisted that I let her down. I did. She put on her bathrobe and sat down to talk to Dr. Reich on the phone. I left her alone and went into another room.

"Dr. Reich had suggested to me that I give her two sleeping pills and put her to bed. But after talking on the phone, she was much better and said that she wanted to visit some married friends of ours with whom she had an appointment. We both went to see them and spent the evening there. While she was not completely well, she was pretty clear. When we got home about 2 A.M., she took two sleeping pills and went to bed.

"She slept all through Sunday and refused to get up either to eat or for any other reason. She finally got up on Monday morning, but she didn't go to work that day."

A few hours after I received this letter, the patient phoned me. She wanted to "do something, but cannot tell me what. . . ." I knew the patient's status well enough to feel sure that she would not do anything cruel. I knew that deep-seated schizoid mechanisms had broken through and were still breaking through; that she was acting out some of them, but also that her attachment to the treatment and her confidence in me were strong enough to keep her from dangerous actions. *The element of mutual trust had great weight in our relationship.* She had promised me that she would go to the hospital if necessary; I had to trust her promise if the cure was to be achieved. One cannot bring a schizophrenic back to sanity if one does not support his sane structure and rely on it. *She knew that I trusted her, and this was the most powerful guarantee against real danger.* The further development as well as the final outcome proved this attitude to be correct.

In the afternoon of the same day her relative called up: She had undressed completely, had climbed on a high chest of drawers and remained there in the *position of a statue;* she had told her relative that she was the Goddess Isis. She had also approached her brother in a sexual manner, after she had tried to drown him in the bath tub.

One hour later her brother called up again: She was still standing there immobile; she apparently could not move. I advised her relatives to keep a cool head; I told them that she was going through a certain emotional situation, that keeping her out of the hospital, if at all possible, was essential, but that they should call the ambulance if they felt that the situation was dangerous. *They did not have to call the ambulance.*

I also told them to call me immediately at any time if there should be any change for the worse. They did not call me until the afternoon of the following day. The patient had gone to bed the previous evening greatly exhausted. Now at 4 p.m., she was still in bed and did not want to get up. Her mother tried hard to *pull* her out of bed. I told them to let the patient sleep; she was obviously exhausted and needed rest after the great strain she had lived through.

The patient slept through until the afternoon of the *third* day, and came to see me at 6 p.m. She "had been at the hospital to write herself in again, *but the hospital was closed.*" I told her that she *should* go back to the hospital if she felt the need to do so. She said that she did not know whether she ought to go back or not. She was afraid that she would deteriorate completely if she went back. I had to agree that this danger was present and that it was great.

It was perfectly clear in this session, after the great attack, that she was both *perfectly clear and very close to a complete catatonic breakdown* at the same time. I had never seen great clarity and sanity paired with a catatonic status in such a manner before. Usually a state of clarity and sanity returns *after* the patient breaks out of the catatonic stupor by way of violent rage. Here no rage was visible, but *clarity fought against immobilization*. Which function would win out in the end? I did not know; nobody could tell.

Her catatonic immobilization was very strong, making greater the contradiction in her strong urge to communicate with me, to talk to me, to tell what was going on in her. She spoke very clearly but very slowly, each word coming forth with great difficulty. Her facial expression was mask-like; she could not move her facial muscles; but *her eyes were not veiled;* on the contrary, they had the glow of great sanity and insight. Her speech, though slow, was clear and orderly, logical and to the point.

She told me in the course of about three hours that she "*had fallen into the other world completely*" the other day. The "forces" had succeeded in pulling her into this other world against her will. She had finally succeeded in coming back into *this* world. But she still felt far, far away. She had no contact with things and people at all. Everything seemed removed as if into the far distance. She felt completely indifferent as to whether it was 9 o'clock in the morning or in the evening, whether the people around her were laughing or crying, whether they liked her or not. She tried hard to come close to people and experiences, but was unable to do so.

She stared at a bright spot on the floor where light was reflected from the window. She knew it was light, but at the same time it appeared strange to her, *"foreign"* as it were, and as if it were "something alive." It seemed clear to me that *she perceived impressions clearly, but that at the same time* SHE COULD NOT MAKE CONTACT WITH HER OWN PERCEPTIONS.

The difference between her inner situation before treatment, and now, consisted in that previously the state of clarity had alternated with the state of confusion; *now she was confused but at the same time she knew perfectly well what she was confused about.* This was a great step forward toward health. These insights into the process of the cure itself are immeasurably important. They tell us not only what is going on in a catatonic stupor, but they also reveal important functions of self-perception, and of CONSCIOUSNESS itself. Every natural scientist knows how decisive these insights are for a future comprehension of the greatest riddle of all natural science, the function of SELF-PERCEPTION. And during the whole experiment I felt and acted far more as a natural scientist than as a psychiatrist. I would advise that only psychiatrists equipped with great psychiatric skill *and* thorough knowledge of the problems of the mind should attempt such ventures in exploring natural functions in man. But, on the other hand, there can be no doubt that such risky research is indispensable if mastery of a vast realm of the emotional plague is to be finally obtained by medicine.

She remembered well that she had tried to drown her brother and to turn on the gas. But she claimed that "IT wanted to do it," that she had tried to resist "IT" but did not succeed. Therefore, she wanted to go back to the hospital. It was clear that, if she managed to keep her clarity, the psychotic functions would cease. This required that she should *not* hide behind the protective walls of the hospital.

Of the rest of the period of catatonia, she remembered only the day when she had stood there as the goddess Isis; she could not remember the following two days when she lay in bed, immobilized. She had been catatonic for two days and was amnestic to it.

I let her talk as much as she wanted. She described again and again the alienation of the world in different words and pictures. In the end, I took her into the orgone accumulator. Her reactions became faster after some 20 minutes and she left in good condition. The first decisive victory over the catatonic breakdown had been won.

She came back the following day a bit slowed down again. Irradiation in the orgone accumulator removed the plasmatic contraction promptly again. This was very hopeful. It became clear *that the orgone accumulator would someday play a great role in the overcoming of catatonic states of biophysical contraction of the organism.*

I must confess that I felt greatly astonished about the results obtained with the orgone accumulator, although I was already then—some 7 years ago—well acquainted with its vagatonic effects. Nevertheless, the whole thing appeared amazing and incredible even to me. Therefore, I could well understand the reactions of distrust on the part of physicians who had never worked with orgone energy.

I informed her brother of her great improvement, but warned again against too great optimism. I also advised him to be ready at any time to commit the patient to the institution. The patient agreed to all this.

Then the following morning she met with disaster. The whole significance of the police mentality of mental institutions became apparent in a grotesque manner. *In spite of the information the officials had about the experimental therapy and the good results obtained so far, and in spite of their own approval of what was going on, they had the patient taken away the following morning at 7:30 to Bellevue Hospital by two psychiatric nurses and by force, without conferring with me or her relatives. The patient did not resist.*

This godlike omnipotence of institutional psychiatrists is the greatest obstacle to true efforts concerning rational mental hygiene. They could have and should have at least informed the relatives and me. No. They felt almighty after the worst was over, the patient having been handled skillfully and painstakingly by an experienced biopsychiatrist, by the relatives and by the patient herself; the latter behaved, in view of the situation, admirably. I sincerely hope that the mental hygiene movement will one day be able to clip the wings of the court and institutional psychiatrists, and will force them to listen and to pay attention to new and hopeful medical efforts in cases where they themselves betray nothing but utter ignorance. The whole effort of many months was in danger of breaking down because of this action on the part of officials. I did not succeed, then, in finding out how it had come about. There can be no true mental hygiene as long as such things are permitted to happen.

It is true, the patient had reacted in a dangerously psychotic manner on several occasions. It is also true, and I knew it very well, that I had taken a great risk. But we take risks every single day of our life, if in nothing else than in walking under roofs with loose bricks. Yet, we do not jail the owner of the house with loose bricks. We do not jail the parents who produce criminals *en masse*. And we do not jail the judge who sentenced an innocent man to die in the electric chair. Therefore, we cannot become excited at all over such well-controlled actions of a schizophrenic. Our patient was, on the whole, in spite of everything, much less dangerous than a single psychopathic neurosurgeon who keeps knowledge out of his mental institution, or a dictator who rules millions. Nobody asked that Hitler be jailed; yet they took away this patient who struggled so bravely for health. It is obvious that there is far more behind such institutional actions than mere safeguarding of the public.

Another fact is important here. We medical orgone therapists who work with deep human emotions know very well from experience that even the most adjusted neurotic will sound wild and insane during orgone therapy to the ear of an uninformed neurologist. Were such a neurologist to listen to a single therapeutic session of orgone therapy, he would surely run to the district attorney, as he in fact once did in New Jersey in the U. S. A.

When deep emotions, especially hatred, break through the armor, a procedure which is absolutely necessary for cure, we know that we have created an *artificial* situation involving *genuine* emotional forces. We know the emotions are *potentially* dangerous, but the process of breaking through was deliberate. Usually we have the patient well in hand, and we have prepared the emotional breakthrough for days or weeks with the greatest care. The same applies to cutting open an abdomen for an operation. Nobody will accuse the surgeon of murder. And nobody objects to the cruel method of shock "therapy" or the piercing of the thalamus with long needles or to the frantic brain operations which kill patients.

Since ignorance in emotional matters is widespread; since, furthermore, every ignoramus thinks he is an "expert" because he has emotions himself and can, therefore, judge biophysical or psychological processes, the situation in biopsychiatry is different from that in surgery.

I myself was not quite sure how much of the emotional situation in this patient was due to therapeutic procedure and how much was due to a genuine psychotic breakdown. The jailers were far removed from any such consideration. More will have to be said later about the hatred of homo normalis against the schizophrenic. It took only a few days to convince me fully that the patient had reacted psychotically *in accordance with the therapeutic situation, and not as a consequence of a psychotic breakdown.* She had taken the injustice in an *admirable* fashion. She wrote the following sane letter from the hospital to her brother, a short time after the commitment:

May 28, 1942

Thanks a lot for writing so soon—I know the manner of my leaving and the unexpectedness of it, must have been a great shock to you and Mom—I, myself, was shocked, so I can imagine how you people felt.—Anyway, the only thing I can say is that it was an unnecessary step for the hospital authorities to have taken—but since there was nothing I could do at the time to stop their taking me—I "took it" as nicely as possible.

I am a little bothered about my job.—I am wondering if it would be possible for me to take up where I left off, if I leave here soon enough. I would hate the thought of losing the excellent reference that I know they would give me—unless they are angry because I left without giving them notice.

If you get this letter in time to come out this Sunday, fine; if not, next week will do just as well. If possible, try and get Dr. Reich to come out with you—I'd like to see him.

When you write again, send me E's address—it is in my address book (which is on my table in my room). Let me know if she got in touch with you and if she was angry about my not being able to go with her on the A.Y.N. trip this Saturday.

Watch for the Red Cross first aid Certificate, I was expecting in the mail within a week or so.

Keep in touch with O. and M. and let me know as soon as she has her baby, and of course how she is feeling.

Tell Mom to send out some anklets for me. Tell her, also, not to worry—I feel fine and am hoping that it will be very soon that I leave here.—

Lots of love,<br>F.

I found out later that her commitment was due to a misapprehension on the part of the parole physician about her description of the "forces" which were coming through in orgone therapy. Her letter from the institution sounded sane and perfectly rational. Her cure had developed far enough to enable her to stand up against the impact of the cruel method of commitment. I received the following letter from the patient which shows clearly that her reactions were only the usual reactions during psychiatric orgone therapy:

June 6, 1942

I don't know what to make of things all around—my being picked up and brought back here to the Hospital was some shock—I might have thought a lot about going back—but never seriously expected them to go to the length of forcing me back—In my opinion—they have some nerve—I never did anything to give them a right to do that to me—and without warning, too—did my brother tell you?—I could have made a fuss and refused to go—but I knew they had straight jackets in the ambulance-bus with them and there were enough of them to drag me down by force—so I just gave in as graciously as I could—I fitted in here just as before—I work all around the place and help out—but I've felt "off" a couple of times—here at least it doesn't make a damn bit of difference—but I would like to go on a "bat" and let loose—the only trouble with that is that it will land me in the violent ward and I will lose all the privileges I have gotten—for being good, so well-known, and such a good worker—I don't know if it is worth it—we will see—

Anyway, Christ, etc. are sort of still around—that is in an influence sort of way—to mix things up for me—but not enough to make any difference so far—I wonder if electric shock would do any good—Incidentally, how on earth could I call you if I was here Sunday—you don't think they would let a patient make a phone call, do you —I can't even write you this letter without the doctors, nurses, attendants reading it and censoring it and probably not sending it out—so my brother is sneaking it out for me—

I think you all (doctors) stink! I don't know who's right and who's wrong—or what's the right way—or who's who—Should I tell these doctors that I intend to see you when I get out? I don't see any doctor here, anyway—only at the final staff meeting, when they decide whether to let you go home or not—

What's the matter—do you think you are too big to come out to see a patient? I asked my brother to ask you to come—but he said you couldn't—so I guess that's why—I don't know who is on my side and who isn't—

There is the constant threat of transfer to back buildings which are awful—and the noise, stink, and awfullness of the place as a whole—

Did you tell these doctors or the parole doctor about anything that happened when I was home?—Is that why I was brought back?—

If I have you to blame—I'd hate you the rest of my life—"

Then the institution began to exert its typical influence:

Sunday

I am writing this while waiting for my brother to come back. I don't know anything about anything—what's more—it isn't at all bad here—As a matter of fact—it's swell—We have parties every night—Me and some other patients who are privileged like me and some attendants——

It is all done on the sly, of course—I can't see any future life at all.

We shall see—what is more—Christ and Death, etc. come around again—bothering me—I'm "sitting on a powder keg" because I'm very suspicious of this swell time I'm having here—I suspect that Christ, etc. are piling it all on so that there can be a Big eruption to smash it all up—just to annoy me——

I'm somewhat in a fog during the day and evening—but not today—much—you know—dulled, etc. far away—

I don't even know about continuing with you after—I don't know anything—

It's all fake

Anyway—
F.

I wrote a letter to the parole physician who had misunderstood her report on her reactions in therapy. I asked him to give her a chance at recovery and to transfer her to a private institution. The physician agreed to that, but the deterioration which I had expected began to make rapid progress. I shall reproduce here the letters I received during that time. They give a rather clear picture of what happened to her; in her fight for life and recovery the patient showed great insight, expressed in a psychotic manner. If the reader takes care to study her letters thoroughly, to separate the psychotic expression from the content of her ideas, he will have to agree that these schizophrenics deteriorate not because of too little but because of too much and too clear contact with the world of armored man. It is true that the idea of Jesus appears in a typically psychotic manner in her as it does in many psychoses. But it is also true that Jesus was nailed to the cross by a pack of sick, cruel, murderous homines normales.

Thursday, November 19, 1942

It's awful and I don't know what to do. The other night I found out the why of the world and the war and almost everything. They were drinking gallons of blood in front of me. The devil is red because of that and he gets redder and redder and then the blood goes to the sun and makes it on fire. Jesus was dripping blood on the cross by drops and this was being swallowed then he was seated on the side of the devil and drinking too—the table was round oblong of flowing thick blood (no feet on it) Mother Mary was at the corner watching. She was white as a sheet—All her blood had been drained off and consumed. She saw her son drinking that and suffered. I did not want to see it or hear it or know the why of everything—that why but they force me to see and hear—Maybe because of Isis—whom they used all these thousands of years in between I don't know what to do.

F.

The other night I found out the why of the world and the war and almost everything. They were drinking gallons of blood in front of me . . .

*This statement was perfectly true, in full accordance with reality.* Hitler and other militarists were shedding millions of gallons of blood. The hook-up with the red of the sun is psychotic, of course, and yet we feel inclined to think about this connection.

I had no message from the patient for several months. Then in February 1943, I received the following letter. It was clear that she was still fighting bravely and that she tried hard to hold on to me:

Feb. 14, 1943

Things are screwy as hell—the world and all the people in it stink—Everybody is out to cut everybody else's throat—with large, butcher knives—They kill 8 million—they were the Jews and they keep us in here alive—it makes no sense—nothing does—I'm not supposed to be eating and I eat so I'm paid back with intrigue and pettiness—All around me—just to trap me in the middle of it all—I have to be 115 lbs.—For a long time now and I get close to it and then eat tons and gain it all back—the 10 disciples are still waiting to be taken out of the catacombs and I can't draw them out until I'm 115 lbs.—Now they are with the right hand side—The Lord and they help me on my promise to not eat but I do eat and, as I said before, get paid back plenty—so much that I can't always cope with it all. I don't know anybody today only about generations ago—centuries ago—eons ago—ancient sage—

Only *work* today is *right* and *real*—I love it—it never fails you—never—the work is a straight line—

You told my brother you would write—please, please do—I don't know anything and I'd like to hear about the straight corners from you—Thanks a lot—                                      F.

Great insight into the realities of our society and our ways of life, though expressed in a distorted manner, was characteristic of this letter, too, and is the way many a schizophrenic looks through us.

The patient stayed in the mental institution another few months, more than a year in all. Her brother kept me informed about her state of health. She came out of the institution severely injured emotionally, *but she had stood the ground which she had gained during only three months of orgone therapy, excellently.* She seemed less psychotic now, but she had changed her character in the direction of a compulsion neurosis. She was petty, mean, nasty toward her relatives, in short, she had become a typical homo normalis. Her greatness and the "spark" of genius were gone. The brother married a girl of another faith. Earlier, she would not have cared at all. She would have taken it philosophically. Now she objected on petty religious grounds, exactly like her mother whom before she had fully seen through and whom she imitated now. She did not work in the office any more as she had done during most critical periods of her psychotic condition. She just went around dull and without interest, clinging to her hated mother in the typical neurotic manner. The experience of her violent commitment had been too much for her. Orgone therapy was not resumed until October, 1944, a year after her release from the institution.

### 3. *Slow recovery:*

Her biophysical status on October 4, 1944, was the following:
*Respiration* was functioning well, air was passing through the glottis, only slightly restricted.

*Orgasm reflex* was functioning easily and fully.

*Vaginal self-gratification* with orgastic release was obtained at regular intervals.

*Eyes* were still slightly veiled but considerably improved.

THE SCHIZOPHRENIC SPLIT

*Total behavior* was yielding and coordinated.

*"Forces"* were "very weak" but "still around in the far distance."

*A slight pressure* in the depth between the eyes was felt occasionally.

*Skin of the face* was ruddy.

In the course of a few exploratory sessions, shock-like indications of catatonia still were discernible, but on the whole the situation seemed satisfactory. I succeeded in releasing her crying fully. Thereupon, she asked me to let her speak at length and about "something very important." She had found the origin of her idea that she was the goddess Isis:

As a child, she remembered now, she had felt that she understood the world so much better than others, especially the grown-ups. She had always felt that the human beings around her were ill in a certain way which she could not fully understand. The main thing in these experiences had been her astonishment that she was capable of knowing so much more than the others. Slowly, she had developed the feeling of standing apart from the rest of human beings, and she began to believe that she HAD KNOWLEDGE OF THOUSANDS OF YEARS. In order to explain to herself this extraordinary fact, she had to assume that such a thing was only possible if the goddess Isis had been reborn in her body. In relation to the everyday course of petty events, this idea appeared queer to her, and she had felt, therefore, still more apart. Then she had begun to feel her body very strongly concentrated in her genitals. This was contrary to everything in her environment. Slowly, she had learned that the feeling in her body could be weakened or "removed" if she forced herself to stiffen up. Then the excitations used to subside. *She had felt these excitations as overpowering and beyond her control.* Later, she had learned to master them, but she still felt them around. The return of the overpowering forces was usually announced by a strong feeling in the upper abdomen. Sometimes only this aura remained; at other times, the forces had come back in full force. Now she understood perfectly clearly that the overpowering forces of her early childhood and the later "evil forces" from "beyond" were one and the same thing.

I had the impression that, in spite of this insight, a certain amount of doubt was left in her mind as to the true meaning of the forces.

She continued to improve greatly. Her eyes became clearer, but off and on a pressure would return in her eyes. She explained eagerly: "But it [the pressure] is BEHIND the eyes, not in the eyes. . . ." I could only confirm this statement.

Four months later the patient was again overtaken by a cata-tonic attack, but she overcame it. I suggested continuous daily irradiation of the region of the sella turcica with orgone energy.

I saw the patient again in January, 1947. She read a great deal, had good appetite. She had had intercourse with great pleasure, but without final orgasm. In November of the same year she came again to ask my advice: The orgastic release during inter-course was still not functioning properly. But she worked well and felt well on the whole.

I advised her not to see any physician any more, not even me, and to try to forget the whole tragedy of her life. She begged for continuation of therapy with me, but I felt that she should be-come entirely independent and advised her to learn to stand on her own feet.

On August 4, 1948, I received the following letter:

I am writing to tell you how very much I was impressed by your book, "Listen, Little Man!" I cannot write I enjoyed the book since what you wrote about the "Little Man" is too sadly true, and I find myself fitting into those shoes.

I want you to know that the antagonism and even hatred which I showed toward you and your work during therapy, stemmed from my knowledge (at times even conscious) that I was getting too close to the break-through of my body into feeling and perhaps love. This was something I could not permit—I had severely controlled my body all my life and even consciously damned it to extinction—treating my body as dirt, hating it and neglecting and torturing myself in punish-ment for early feelings and masturbation. This same hate I had for my body was hate which I projected on to you. Forgive me for this, Doctor, this hate has done a great deal of damage to my body and mind. I would like to tell you that in spite of my "maliciousness and pettiness" your work with me did me tremendous good, I am aware of what harm I am doing to myself and others around me and why I am doing these things. Also, I find myself thinking and feeling that my body wants to be healthy and that my retreat into the "ivory tower" of mental illness only changed the color of the picture, but not the picture itself. I might make myself mentally ill to be something "special" to be certain that my body will keep far in the background, but I am gradually finding out that a healthy "active" body is more pleasure—physically and mentally.

So, I think you will see that I am getting there, however slowly, through your help. The process is slow since I still have a great number of tensions, and sometimes blocks which I can't seem to do anything about. Often my small courage fails and then the dark picture of hate, delusions, and suffering comes back but not permanently so, thanks for everything and I pray to God I have courage. F.

At the end of 1948 I heard that she was in good condition with the exception of a letter I received from her telling me how "rotten" she was "in her core" and how "unworthy to live in this beautiful world." I told her to stop worrying about it and to go on enjoying herself. She had not mentioned the "forces" any more.

A few weeks later she visited me. She seemed perfectly coordinated, her eyes sparkled with intelligence and penetrating knowing. She worked well and even studied a great deal. However, her genital love life was not in order. She had no boyfriend. She had met one whom she liked. One evening they were together alone. She knew that it would happen that night, that he would embrace her. She had brought some sleeping pills with her. She put some sleeping pills into his wine glass, and he fell asleep. I advised her to remove the last obstacle with the help of one of our psychiatric orgone therapists.

Seven years have elapsed since the end of the therapeutic experiment; a period of time long enough to make possible a sound judgment of the result obtained, but not long enough to give a final answer as to whether such patients will *stay sane*. This will depend on many conditions beyond the reach of individual orgone therapy. They are essentially of a *social nature*.

It is mainly the question whether homo normalis will change

his way of living and thinking *basically,* a question which awaits a highly uncertain answer. The elucidation of the fact that the way of life of homo normalis creates the schizophrenic breakdown in millions of healthy newborn infants will, if seriously considered and executed practically, be a part of this all-important answer. It is quite obvious that for some time already, and justly, homo normalis has come under sharp scrutiny as to the soundness and rationality of his ways of being. We can learn from such experiences in individual schizophrenics what homo normalis does to millions of newborn children. The prevention of the disease "schizophrenia" means changing radically the whole system of education of small children, and not only changing the schizophrenic. The latter will always remain an individual answer only, useless as a social endeavor.

This statement does not mean that we should stop studying the schizophrenic mind. It has much to tell us about human functioning, about the problems of perception and self-perception, about the function of consciousness which is far less understood than the unconscious. It can tell us much about how to help individual human beings who are in the beginning of a breakdown. But the main issue in this as in all other similar tasks of medicine and psychiatry will be the world of homo normalis, so long as he cherishes age-old ideas and laws which do untold harm to the biological core in every child of each new generation.

In this process of mastering the emotional plague, we shall encounter homo normalis at his worst; in the form of the righteous mystic and of the mechanistic human animal who run away from themselves for exactly the same reasons that forced our patient into the catatonic breakdown: *the horror of the plasmatic currents in an organism* which has become incapable of coping with strong bio-energetic emotions and has lost the natural function of self-regulation. All attacks upon our scientific work during the past 25 years have come from such individuals in various organizations and social bodies. Homo normalis has fought orgone biophysics for the same reason that made him burn witches by the thousands, that makes him "shock" patients by the millions: *The horror of the life forces in the human animal, which he is unable to feel in himself.* If we do not muster the courage to maintain this insight, we shall fail as psychiatrists, physicians and educators.

For the first time in the history of medicine the emotional plague, which is built and maintained on the fear of the organ sensations, has found its medical opponent. This is our great obligation: TO ENABLE THE HUMAN ANIMAL TO ACCEPT NATURE WITHIN HIMSELF, TO STOP RUNNING AWAY FROM IT AND TO ENJOY WHAT NOW HE DREADS SO MUCH.

INDEX

# INDEX

ABRAHAM, 144, 165n., 195
Abstinence rule, 131ff.
"Active" or "passive" technique, 38
Actual neurosis, 14, 128
ADLER, 158f.
Affect-block, 74f., 162, 184f., 195, 197ff.
  and vegetative streaming, 319
ALEXANDER, 41, 214, 216, 222, 300
"Algolagnia," 210
Alloplastic adaptation, 159
Ambivalence, 200, 284
"Analytic material," 7, 29, 73f.
"Analytic passivity," 5, 37
"Angstlust," 244f.
Anorgonia, 321n.
Anxiety, 213
  and bodily contact, 228
  and sexuality, 285ff.
"Arc de cercle," 365
Armor segments, 370ff.
  chest segment, 376ff.
  diaphragmatic segment, 379ff.
  ocular segment, 371
  oral segment, 372
  pelvic segment, 388f.
  and plasmatic streamings, 372f.
Autoplastic adaptation, 159

BAKER, 406n.
BEETHOVEN, 432, 462
BENEDEK, 212ff., 257
BERNFELD, 209, 296
Binding of anxiety, 164
Blank screen, 30, 139
Brain, 467f.

Bursting, 210, 333ff.

Castration anxiety, 103, 106, 110, 127, 133, 156, 334
Cathartic therapy, 10
Chaotic situation, 21, 24, 35
Character, *see also* Compulsive character, Genital character, Hysterical character, Masochistic character, Phallic-narcissistic character
Character and repression, 160f.
Character-analysis
  indications and dangers, 114ff.
  and resistance analysis, 49ff., 303f.
  and symptom analysis, 46f., 67
  typical phases, 299f.
Character armor, 44, 145ff., 341f.
  "gaps," 163
  in genital character, 164ff.
  in hysteria, 191
  layering, 314ff.
  and muscular armor, 343
  in neurotic character, 164ff.
  structure, 323
"Character attitude," 364
Character differentiation, 149ff.
Character formation
  function of, 145ff., 218
  sociological function of, xxii ff.
Character neuroses and symptom neuroses, 41ff.
Character-neurotic reaction basis, 42, 114n., 130, 148, 173ff., 178
Characterology, xix ff.

511